THE NEW MILLENNIUM: CHALLENGES AND STRATEGIES FOR A GLOBALIZING WORLD

This collection represents a significant contribution to the dialogue on the complexities of globalization and the challenges that face the international system as it enters the new millennium. The essays contribute to the understanding of the delicate balance between transnational and national issues as the world integrates on some levels while continuing to manifest disintegration on other levels. The book emphasizes the importance of an interdisciplinary perspective in understanding the dynamics underlying the process of global transformation. The essays are organized along broadly interconnected thematic lines: a global perspective, a regional view, economic and technological trends, and the individual in a globalizing world. The interdisciplinary nature of this text makes it ideal for courses which include issues of human rights, security, finance, and technology.

This book is dedicated to my mother,
Eluri Udayarathnam, a global citizen before her time whose
inspiration and encouragement has prepared me and
countless others for the globalized world of the
twenty first century.

The New Millennium:
Challenges and Strategies
for a Globalizing World

Edited by
SAI FELICIA KRISHNA-HENSEL

Ashgate

Aldershot • Burlington USA • Singapore • Sydney

JX
1931
1999
.N49
2000

Published by
Ashgate Publishing Limited
Gower House
Croft Road
Aldershot
Hampshire GU11 3HR
England

Ashgate Publishing Company
131 Main Street
Burlington
Vermont 05401
USA

Ashgate website: http://www.ashgate.com

British Library Cataloguing in Publication Data
The new millennium : challenges and strategies for a
        globalizing world. - (Global interdisciplinary studies
        series)
        1. International cooperation - Congresses
        I. Krishna-Hensel, Sai Felicia
        327.1'7

Library of Congress Control Number: 00-133618

ISBN 0 7546 1391 7

Printed and bound by Athenaeum Press, Ltd.,
Gateshead, Tyne & Wear.

Contents

v

Foreword

It is a truism that we live in a rapidly shrinking planet. Daily we hear terms such as globalization, the global economy and global competition. As each of us sits on our own little island of personal experience, these terms often become so abstract as to render them almost meaningless. We sometimes lack the vocabulary to make sense of our "shrinking world". The collection of works contained in this volume represents an important step in developing a vocabulary that deals with globalization and all that term implies. By examining the forces now shaping our world, from communications technology to regionalism to democratization, the authors help us understand how these forces are working and anticipate how they will continue to change the way we live. Solutions to problems such as human rights and poverty must be attacked at the same time as we struggle with political corruption, financing our economic activities, and ensuring national and regional security. The very complexity of these problems demands integrated, multi-level solutions, and the authors' insights light our way. I was privileged to participate in the Paris conference, and am heartened that it produced this interesting and useful vehicle for sharing that experience.

John J. Veres III
Director
Center for Business and Economic Development
Auburn University Montgomery

Introduction

This volume draws together a representative selection of contemporary research on the changes confronting the international system in the new millennium. Most of these papers were presented at the CISS/ISA Paris Conference, which was held on August 9-10, 1999. This was the first international comparative and interdisciplinary conference convened to discuss these historic issues and it provided a forum for scholars from all over the world to come together to analyze the challenges confronting the world system. An important goal of the meeting was to offer strategies, in cooperation with policy makers and practitioners, to deal with global problems. This occasion marked the beginning of a significant interdisciplinary effort towards the study of global change.

The underlying theme of this collection of essays is the complexity of the challenges faced by the international system as it enters the new millennium. The shape of the new world order is being driven by many forces unleashed through economic interdependence and global communications. The boundaries of the international system, historically, determined by national and regional politics are being redrawn today along new ethno-political lines. Ethnicity has become a major force in determining nationalism. In the changing world of globalization, it is revealing an elasticity, which enables peoples to define, select, and transmit an identity that may lead to more equitable socio-political arrangements. In many ways, it has replaced the role of political ideologies in the international system. The changing world invariably presents a number of challenges that require a coordinated effort in dealing with them. The extent and diversity of these problems requires a multidisciplinary effort for understanding the issues involved. In the analysis often lies the strategy for dealing with the issue. It is hoped that these scholarly analyses will contribute to the understanding of a complex process that has come to characterize the future of the international system. This book is distinctive in emphasizing the importance of interdisciplinary analysis and in its organization of the contributions along broadly interconected thematic lines. This is a global effort to understand globalization. It is hoped that the volume will be a significant contribution to the dialogue on globalization that is underway at this time.

The first section takes a global view of change and explores broad trends of the future. The role of globalization in determining the shape of the new international order is explored in the introductory essay. This assessment emphasizes the complexity underlying the interpretation of globalization as an engine driving change, as well as a description for the conditions brought about by change itself. The paradigm of the three faces of globalization is offered as an analytical framework for describing the different perspectives of a complex and often controversial phenomenon. In the second essay, Mehdi Mozaffari avers that globalization represents a new era in international politics as well as in the destiny of mankind. He explores the relationship between global capital and global civilization concluding with a call for a new definition of civilization. In the third chapter, James Scarritt offers a neo-Parsonian perspective for a theoretical framework that can be used in formulating strategies to deal with the multiple challenges of the new millennium. The information-energy exchange theoretical framework is presented as a means towards developing and testing theories about the interrelations between globalization, democratization, and social movements. The global perspective also involves several studies that analyze broad underlying issues in the international system of the new millennium. Liisa Laakso assesses the challenges to the international community posed by collapsed or weak states in the next chapter. Her paper considers the waning power of states in a world that is increasingly driven by market forces and economic competitiveness, aptly noting that weak states can have unwanted consequences for the international system. In the concluding essay of this section Linda Dolive examines how democracy as a form of governing provides the foundation for and sustaining of corruption. Court records, indictments, and media accounts reveal corrupt legislators and executives at the pinnacles of power in the major industrial democracies of France, Great Britain, Italy, Japan, and the United States. The paper discusses the types of, extent of, and nature of corruption among democratic regimes and assesses the conditions allowing corruption to flourish. She concludes that facilitating conditions for political corruption derive from numerous democratic characteristics and norms.

The growing significance of regional issues in a globalizing world is the focus of the next group of papers. These studies relate the lessons of regional issues to the wider arena of global politics. Guy Poitras assesses the prospects for regionalism in a globalizing world. Regionalism, hegemony, and other basic terms are defined in preparation for an examination of the turning point in the perception and role of regional groupings. North America is used as the main point of reference to identify several critical issues facing regionalism at the turn of the century. These are posed as basic questions, ranging from the very nature of regions to problems of bridging the North-South gap. The problematic future of North American regionalism will be determined by how global forces and domestic forces combine to influence policies for implementing and extending regionalism. The conclusion of this analysis is that regionalism is at a crossroads. Erhan Buyukakinci presents a compelling picture of a new and active Russian role in the redefinition of the European security environment. Since the break-up of the USSR in December 1991, Russia has sought ways to establish itself as an independent force in international relations, notably in the European security. This work aims to discuss Russia's points of view on its position in Europe and on the European security and defense identity and to observe how Moscow could reply to the initiatives taken apart from its capacity of intervention. Dimitri Christopoulos addresses the misperceptions of ethnic minorities in Greece and the divergent opinions within the Greek polity. Contemporary perceptions of minorities in Greek politics are ambivalent. He asserts that the traditional moral disapproval of cultural diversity has been followed by a newly emergent and somewhat forced tolerance towards minority rights. This situation has created an enormous confusion as far as the very concept of human rights is concerned. The paper discusses these misleading perceptions, by also elaborating another-equally possible and necessary-policy towards minorities in the country. John Doyle's paper ponders the global implications of the Northern Ireland peace agreement. He approaches the issue from the perspective of citizenship in contested states in a post- 2000 era. He argues that the Northern Ireland peace agreement of 1998 offers the prospect of fundamental change in the nature of citizenship in Northern Ireland and points towards a more equal and just society. In its division of issues of citizenship rights from the question of formal sovereignty and state allegiance it offers a challenge to the weakness of the existing literature on citizenship and equality in contested states. The success of the peace process in persuading at least some Ulster unionists to sign the agreement, despite their previous opposition to equality measures, provides an insight into perspectives on citizenship held by political actors in contested states that may prove useful for conflict resolution strategies in other contexts.

The next section examines issues in communications and economies. Nayantara Hensel's paper assesses the implications of banking regulation and reform on the financial system of the new millennium. As the new millennium approaches, the worldwide banking sector is faced with the challenges presented by globalization and the consequent shift in the balance of power in the banking system. These challenges, broadly defined, include those resulting from: 1) the wave of cross border mergers; 2) international competition; 3) the development of new financial products; 4) technological innovations, such as online banking; 5) reductions in national hegemony (e.g. with the EC); 6) national policies; and 7) fluctuations in the domestic economy (e.g. Asia). This paper examines the recent role that each of these challenges has played in the European, Asian, and American banking systems and discusses the possible future interactions of these forces as the international banking system evolves toward a new, stable equilibrium. Philip Bryson meticulously traces the origins and outcomes of the Asia crisis in a retrospective essay. He ventures beyond the usual interpretation of the Asian economic crisis as primarily a financial phenomenon and explores the fundamental issues that underpin the decline of the economic system. He demonstrates that the rapid and extreme decline of stock values and national currencies of the affected countries occurred as a result of the poor investments and economic performance of banks and firms preceding the financial crisis. This paper attributes the cause of the Asian crisis to underlying corporate governance problems and opines that they have not yet been satisfactorily resolved. The emerging role of enterprise information portals in the arena of global communications is presented by Ronald Sims, Eric Erickson, and Jeffrey Erickson. The case study focuses on their transformational role in European business practices and anticipates closely the possible outcome in other regions of the world. This paper anticipates the future of communications technology in the world of the twenty-first century. Daniel Papp and David Alberts set the stage for a new scenario on national security in the information age in the next chapter. This paper addresses the role played by advanced information and communication technologies in the national security equation of the United States. The implications for change in strategy, doctrine, tactics, and operations, are fundamentally different from traditional theories.

The increasing importance of the individual in a globalizing world as one of the principal forces impelling social and institutional reform is the focus of the final section of the volume. Marlene Wind's paper examines human rights in a post-sovereign world. She explores the relationship between legal globalization and the new human rights regime. This paper argues that sovereignty has come under increasing pressure in recent years due to increasing global emphasis on human rights in world affairs. This analysis illustrates the transformation of human society that might put the individual at the center of attention in world affairs in the new millennium by investigating recent cases. It also traces the development of the concept of sovereignty and human rights in different historical époques. The paper concludes with a critical examination of the question as to whether human rights can be generalized and promoted as a universal value across cultural differences. Rekha Datta's study of child labor in India takes takes the view that this is a widespread situation. The study strongly emphasizes that child labor is a global problem that goes beyond an economic issue to the fundamental rights of children in the free world. This paper takes an interdisciplinary approach to child labor as a human rights issue transcending its regional base and argues for the need for an integrated approach towards eradicating the problem. Elaine Levine focuses on the human rights problems spawned by the ongoing economic crisis in Mexico and the interaction with changing conditions in the US labor market in her study of the transference of poverty in Mexico to poverty in the United States. The channeling of large numbers of newly arriving Mexican immigrants into low paying jobs that are generally rejected by most sectors of the US born population has profound social and economic implications. The combined effects of adverse circumstances in the labor market and in the school system, as well recent cuts in government social spending have made it even more difficult for recent Mexican immigrants and their children, than it was for other groups who arrived prior to 1980, to experience any significant upward socioeconomic mobility.

The papers depict the diversity of issues that confront scholars at the threshold of a new century. The views represented are those of the individual contributors who are entirely responsible for the contents of their papers. I am grateful to the contributors for their untiring efforts and enthusiasm in meeting the publication schedule. This cooperative endeavor has resulted in the presentation of these important perspectives in a timely manner. Many individuals provided support and encouragement in the course of the production process. I am especially grateful to Kirstin

Howgate at Ashgate Publishing, Roger Hung at CBED, and my family for their patience and help during the production of this book.

Part I
The Global View

1 Globalization and the International System

SAI FELICIA KRISHNA-HENSEL

The transition into a new millennium is an opportune time for assessing the changing international system. It provides a convenient benchmark for studying systemic transformation. The international system that was marked by a polarization between East and West, communism and capitalism, development and underdevelopment has in recent years seen the familiar bipolar world being replaced by a seemingly unpredictable international system dominated by the one remaining superpower. The twentieth century has been a century of truly global occurrences. For the first time, in human history, there is an awareness of the sweeping reach of wars, environmental change, and social movements. Over the last century events and trends have set in motion a process that has led to the metamorphosis of the international system from a disparate collection of societies and geographical entities into a more interdependent and somewhat integrated whole. The extent of this integration is yet to be understood fully, but it is quite evident that the forces driving the transfiguration of the international system today stem from a variety of sources including, economic imperatives and rapid advances in communications technology. Developments in communications have contributed to an increase in public information and often served to familiarize societies with each other. The spread of ideologies has also fueled the process of change and led to the modification and conversion of traditional political and social systems. Thus, the forces of change, which are often driven by material considerations, also represent visionary aspirations that lead to a general reassessment of man and his environment. This alteration in peoples' perception of themselves and the universe they inhabit is an important, though often overlooked element of the transformation process. Throughout history, territorial expansion and communications have been accompanied by profound changes in perceptions of self and community.

3

The voyages of discovery of the sixteenth and seventeenth centuries not only led to a tangible changeover in the socio-economic-political character of the states of Europe, the discovery of the "New World" led to a transformation in the mind set of the peoples at the time. The "New World" came to represent new opportunities and new beginnings. Today, globalization offers similar transfiguration in material terms as well as in peoples attitudes towards themselves, others, and the planet that we inhabit.

The Context: Beginnings

The protean world today is a product of a process known simply as "globalization". Scholarly opinion is divided on the origins of globalization. Historical scholars have suggested that globalization pre-dates the twentieth century, while others see it as a purely contemporary phenomenon. This dilemma is best explored by reference to historical developments, as well as classical theories of social change.

Some of the seeds of globalization were present in the writings of classical theorists who sought to understand a changing world. The concept of interconnectedness that is characteristic of globalization owes much to the classical theories of social change that sought to describe society in organic terms.[1] The functionalist perspective with its organic approach towards social analysis accentuated the interrelatedness of social phenomena. Similarly the rationalization/modernization perspective predicted the inevitability of commonalties over differentiation in societies.

The idea of moral individualism began to emerge in discourses in the 17th and 18th centuries and represented a new way of conceiving the importance of the individual in society. Durkheim also noted the increasing individualism that was beginning to characterize Western civilization. He interpreted individualism as a moral doctrine and social philosophy that exalted individuals and made them the primary objects of moral regard. Durkheim further elaborated on the relationship between the rise of industrial society and individualism. The centrality of the individual in the modern world was presaged in these thoughts. In the contemporary world, the moral dignity of the individual has acquired great import and it is increasingly being secured through legal institutions.[2]

To Max Weber, the progress of modern science and technology was inextricably linked with the rationalization process which made it possible to achieve goals most efficiently. Bureaucratic organization was the structure through which this could be achieved, but it was also an institution that possessed the unfortunate potential of diminishing the importance of the individual in the scheme of things.[3]

Malcolm Waters posits that globalization in some measure or another has always been present, but that it was non-linear until the middle of the past millennium (Waters,1995) This proposition raises the interesting issue of awareness and recognition. To many scholars, the recognition of the phenomenon, its definition, and its analysis establishes the process beyond any question.

Globalization may be seen as a "floodlight" illuminating the state of the changing international system, and we have yet to understand how, where, why, and how much positive systemic change can be atttributed to globalization, and how much to other equally important factors. Improvements in material conditions, such as health and education lead to greater expectations and hope for a better and just life amongst groups and individuals. This has always been true throughout history. Social, political, and religious revolutions often emanate from a righteous desire for a more perfect social order. Dissasisfaction with existing conditions, as well as a vision of greater perfection underlie such social upheavals. Inevitably, the improvement in the lives of some may lead to a diminishment in the lives of those who had been benefiting from the status quo.

It is possible to characterize globalization as a facilitator of rapid change, as well as the condition resulting from change. There is little doubt that the term can be and is being used to describe a process, as well as to describe a condition. While there is no consensus on a common interpretation of the nature of globalization or on its influence on the international system, there is an acknowledgement that globalization has many faces. The process is both creating and destroying boundaries, systems, cultures, and institutions. Assessments of its effects vary between an optimistic view of global influence to a negative interpretation of its effects on the world system. The optimists see globalization as a channel of prosperity and of enlightened values, such as democracy and human rights from west to east, while simultaneously providing an outlet for skills and labor from east to west. The more critical interpretations of the effects of globalization tend to stress the erosion of cultural identity and values, the rise of supranational authority destroying national sovereignty and identity, the transfer of destructive knowledge and technology, and economic competition that places the labor force of western nations at a disadvantage. To this polarization of perspectives, can be added a third reality, that the world has indeed shrunk and there are issues that result from this compression that have to be approached from a cooperative position. This third reality may prove to be the area of real understanding of the global transformation that is in progress, and the most difficult area in which to achieve a consensus amongst states on common strategies to be pursued. This is also the area with the greatest promise for a new way of managing the globalizing world.

The Three Faces of Globalization

This paper suggests that there are three faces of globalization, the enabler of positive change, the destroyer of traditional boundaries and cultures, and the preserver of the planet, the facilitator of concerted policies and actions in a globalized environment. All three are requisite for the understanding of the international system in the new millennium. This multifaceted approach is suggestive of the triple attributes of the Creator (Brahma), the Destroyer (Shiva), and the Preserver (Vishnu) that are embodied in the religious pantheons of South Asia (Basham, 1992: 312-313). The model incorporating the tridimensionality of globalization would serve as a reference for examining some of the key issues, such as sovereignty, human rights, global values, and technologies.

Hope and Disillusionment: Two Faces of Globalization

For many, idealism underscores globalization. There is a sense that national interests are generally narrow and will eventually be replaced by a morally and legally superior transnational or international set of imperatives. There is a corollary belief that law, international covenants, and contractual agreements will provide for a stable international system. Finally, the hope that the imperfections of the present system will be replaced by an overarching humanitarian set of values underscores the promise of a globalized world. On a theoretical level this is an admirable perspective, however, it does not accurately reflect the realities of the world today. Arguably, there has been progress towards a kinder, gentler world, and there is greater awareness of injustice, but there is yet no effective way of perpetuating that humanitarianism (Krauthammer, 1999).

If we agree that a globalized world is an interdependent world then we need to ask what this means for the component elements of this world. Global interdependence is seen by many as a path towards integration of the international system. Both communications technology and economic interdependence, focus on the effect of globalization as an integrative force. Many also assume that integration will inevitably result in the elimination of inequality. The assumption that globalization is integrating the world, albeit against its will, is to overlook the fragmentation that it is producing simultaneously. An assessment of the impact of globalization reveals little progress in reducing economic disparity between the regions and states of the world. On the political level there is no evidence of universal commitment by the members of the international system to the development of more equitable and inclusive institutions and structures. On the religious front there is no dramatic increase in levels of tolerance between the adherents of diverse belief systems. Thus, it would seem that some of the expected outcomes of an integrated world have not lived up to their promise. An explanation for this might lie in the perception that globalization is a phenomenon originating in the west, spreading western culture, ideas, values and patterns of governance across societies. In fact, the growth of religious fundamentalism, especially amongst non-western cultures has shown a sharp rise in recent years. It is ironic that much of this is a reaction to the very forces of globalization that seek to emphasize secularization. This is implicit if, as some commentators have suggested, we trace the origins of global integration to the influence of American political and economic ideals on the international system in the post World War II period (Beinart, 1997). The rise of terrorism, ethnic conflict, religious fundamentalism, and other forms of protest can then be interpreted as reactions against the spread of western dominance. Peoples' sense of moral inferiority and superiority may provide an explanation for this reaction. If there is a feeling that somehow economic superiority is intertwined with moral superiority, then it poses problems and is not likely to be well received. The perception that economic development comes neatly bundled with western culture, values, and religion prevents its universal acceptance. This leads to an important question whether, given the interconnectedness of social/economic/political/religious phenomena, it is realistic to separate the strands out so that developing societies can select economic principles without adopting the political institutions and moral values of the west that steer the current phase of globalization.

Sovereignty

The speed of globalization has accelerated changes that were already present. Sovereignty is a case in point. The erosion of sovereignty as an exclusive and absolute principle is not new. The abrading of sovereignty was foreshadowed in the formation of international organizations, such as the United Nations which professed recognition of the autonomy of states, while simultaneously assuming the right and responsibility of intervention on behalf of the international community. Traditional analysis of the international system has looked at sovereignty as the domain of the state, on the assumption that the modern state system was countenanced and acknowledged throughout the world. This overlooks the problems arising from the delineation of international borders in many parts of the third world in the post-colonial and post-war period. These borders were often drawn with little understanding of pre-existing ethnic and tribal territoriality. Linguistic, religious, and ethnic factors were sometimes, misrepresented, over or underemphasized, and underrated in the pursuit of the establishment of a modern nation state. When we look at the range of ethnic conflict, tribal and community loyalties, however, as well as, the continuing influence of religious groupings within secular states, it is difficult not to conclude that there was a measure of arbitrariness that accompanied state creation at this time.

It is also important to consider that the ability of governments to effectively exercise power within nation-states is greatly diminished by the free flow of information and goods across their borders that results in greater exchange of ideas and influences between peoples (Held, 1991:207-9). The arguments in favor of the decline of the effectiveness of nation-states in the face of globalization, generally emphasize a polarity of world government versus state governance. The balance between global responsibility and state sovereignty is delicate and a modus vivendi has yet to be universally agreed upon.

Intervention

International intervention challenges and complicates assumptions of sovereignty, testing the boundaries of state and regional rights. Intervention takes many forms, disaster aid and assistance, military intervention, hostage negotiations, political negotiations, refugee relief, economic assistance, and international crime prevention. Intervening entities can be nations, regional bodies, and international organizations and institutions. In some instances, intervention is welcomed, especially when the recipient nation seeks aid. In other instances, it is seen as an infringement of sovereignty (McMahon, 1996). The dilemma that confronts the international system in the new century is the adoption of intervention standards that are widely acceptable. Attitudes toward intervention are based on and reflect political concerns, as well as moral and ethical concerns. Arguably, assistance is a benign form of intervention, or is it? It is entirely possible that recipients of assistance may actually resent such help as extremely intrusive. This is likely to be the case when aid is accompanied by restrictions and requirements whether they be of a financial, humanitarian, or military nature. The complexity of the issues involved are only beginning to be understood, as we begin to see that there are many ways of interpreting an intervention. The issue of sovereignty continues to be a challenge for the globalizing world.

Finally, there is the perceived threat to state sovereignty by multi-national corporations. The economic benefits of corporate enterprises are particularly relevant for the developing world. National goals are bound to economic growth, promoted by investment and trade relations with international companies. The power of multinationals is indisputable and it has raised very legitimate concerns about the rights and responsibilities of companies within the nations where they operate. The implications are serious for human rights, as well as for democracy and corruption in emerging economies. Global corporations are increasingly coming under pressure to intervene when human rights issues, such as child labor and exploitation of low wage labor are involved in their overseas operations. Neither the host nation nor the companies are comfortable with such pressures, the countries view this as intervention designed to deprive them of economic growth opportunities, while the corporations see this as an additional layer of responsibility.

National Identity and Global Community

One of the arguments against globalization is that it erodes national culture and identity. National identities are often intertwined with national norms The national identities that compose the societies of modern states have evolved from traditional tribal/ethnic/regional identities that have been incorporated into multicultural nation states. The nation state has always struggled with promoting an overarching national patriotism over the more natural loyalty to tribe, religion, and ethnic group. The success of this effort has varied depending on the region and the political leadership of the moment. Yugoslavia was deemed to be a successful multinational state during the Tito period. With the departure of the strong hand, the traditional loyalties, rivalries and hostilities were harnessed to achieve political goals even if it meant fragmentation of the region and its economic and political institutions. As traditional and emerging cultural identities increasingly dominate the political spectrum it is pertinent to enquire into the feasibility of a global community.

Nations have increasingly heterogenous populations, and the idea of cultural diversity and tolerance is advocated strenuously in the face of recurring incidents of ethnic, religious, and tribal conflict. Most national governments make some allowance for the presence of cultural and religious diversity in their populace, but insist on unity in political values and institutions. As fragmentation occurs amongst multicultural nation-states, it is tempting to consider what place if any supra-nationalism will have in the international system. The struggle to establish broad national loyalties accompanied by a sense of cultural identity remains one of the challenges of the modern state. The prognosis for success in this area appears to be very dubious. Thus, to speak of an international community is not a reality but a hope and an admirable goal. E.H.Carr has pointed out that there is a legitimate distinction to be made between believing that there is, inherently present, a concord of interests amongst states, and making the achievement of such a concord, the objective of political action (E.H. Carr, 1964).

Human Rights and Economic Interdependence

Human rights has received increased emphasis in the twentieth century, although as we have seen it has its roots in the regard for individualism reflected in the discourse of classical theorists of change. The primacy of human rights issues has effectively given the global community a raison d'etre to hold nation states accountable for policies and actions towards their populations. In addition, as we have noted, the concern with human rights has followed multinational corporations in their dealings with third world states. Economic globalization, as we have seen, promotes economic ties, but also unwittingly perhaps acquires responsibility for improving workers conditions and restrains exploitation. It is no longer deemed sufficient to create opportunities for workers in developing nations, it is equally important to ensure humane labor conditions. Enlightened profit making is replacing simple commercial benefits. International corporations thus take over responsibilities that have traditionally been exercised by national governments.

Such responsibilities are also assumed by international organizations which become the enforcing agencies of global concerns. For example, international economic agencies, such as the World Bank and the IMF link aid with socio-economic-political progress. Thus, nations that do not meet global standards in these areas are penalized for more than economic mismanagement.

Therefore, from the optimistic perspective, economic globalization can be seen as creating opportunities for poor nations to share in the global largesse, while simultaneously ensuring that workers rights are not neglected. On the other hand, the negative face of globalization reveals a different image. The workers in industrial nations find themselves uncompetitive, underbid by cheaper overseas labor. The benefits of globalization for some, represent the seeds of insecurity for others. It is such concerns that were reflected in the WTO meeting protests in Seattle in December, 1999.

Modernization, Global Values and Norms

Integration into the global community comes with a price tag, the adoption of global norms. The values of internationalism, legalism, and humanitarianism are representative of a global value system.[4] This global trend comes up against the reality of strong regional and cultural values. There is a growing body of evidence to suggest that global political values are being promoted over state and regional values. Can a globalized world have an acceptable set of collective values and can these coexist with national and cultural value systems? The question that needs to be answered is when do global norms become more significant than national norms. It is a question that has no easy answers. Global values and norms do intrude on regional and national values. They represent themselves as superior or more enlightened, more concerned with the rights of individuals and minority groups. They are supportive of the aspirations of breakaway ethnic and political minorities, and thus may be seen as undermining national sovereignty. Is this the most realistic prognosis for the future international system? These are the questions that face the community of global scholars. Somewhere, underlying all of this is that most important of issues, the morality and value judgments that are represented in this relationship between the global and the national.

Where do the values and norms of the global community originate? What are these norms? The argument that global humanitarian values are rooted primarily in western experience is controversial, as we have noted, but not necessarily untrue. Global values are a product principally of the modern international system. The emphasis on democratic principles, concern with human rights, and the idea of collective responsibility for human actions has been articulated and implemented aggressively during the modern era. Many of these ideas have been present in non-western societies and predate the modern period, however, they have come to characterize the efforts and goals of the contemporary international system. Much of this can be attributed to broader communication between peoples and societies.

The assumption that globalization and modernization are closely interlinked and even synonymous merits consideration. The relationship between the two is complex. It is the ease and the scale of global relations that can be attributed to the technological and economic imperatives of modernization.

Global Technologies

Globalization, is highly dependent on "transfers" of ideas, culture, products, services, images, information, and people. Media and communications, are playing an ever more significant role in determining peoples attitudes, expectations, and behavior. The process began earlier in the century with the dramatic disclosure of human rights abuses in World War II, when information about the Holocaust became public knowledge. Policy imperatives took shape as news about atrocities was communicated to a global audience. The influential role played by information cannot be overstated. Perhaps equally important was the manner in which this information was presented. Here again, the written word was often enhanced by dramatic newsreel footage. Technology was playing an important role in shaping public perception and having an impact on policy.

Without the technological breakthroughs international communication may have taken longer or been substantially different in its outcome. It is tempting to speculate on an international system which no longer possesses the range of communication that presently exists. The printed word is designed for those who are literate in the language. Notwithstanding the dominance of English as a global language, there are millions of non-English speaking people who are excluded from the western press. Video and T.V. are media conduits which reach across the boundaries of literacy and language competence. If ideology was dependent on the written treatise, and promoted by politicians, the ideas of the twenty-first century will be visual and promoted by the camera journalist. This brings up the issue of media influence on socio-economic change, as well as on policy making. To the dictum "the pen is mightier than the sword" may be added a codicil, "the picture is worth a thousand words". Images determine concern, images interpret and misinterpret, emphasize and de-emphasize, portray bias and fairness, images empower the powerless, and influence the decision maker. Without the modern image, globalization loses its reach, societies change in slower and different ways, and the international system may develop in wholly undetermined directions.

Technology, today, is also playing a significant role in determining the outcome of the political process. Candidates for office, political parties, legislative measures, all of these are presented in a crisp soundbyte for the busy modern person. There is often no reflection on these impressions and the world places greater responsibility in the hands of the journalist. What is unclear is whether there is any reciprocal influence on the media itself. In other words, how is information selected for dispersal? Is the technology itself influenced by anything besides possibly economic considerations? The role played by consumers of information and technology in the selection of that information and the medium through which it is dispersed is not clearly understood as yet.

There is a general assumption that technology is politically and morally neutral and, therefore, likely to be eagerly embraced. Yet, technology cannot be entirely disassociated from the value system of its producers. It serves as a conveyor of these values through the communications network. In the hands of those who master the technology, but do not subscribe to the values of its producers, it is likely to be misused. This is exemplified in instances of terrorists use of easily available information on nuclear technology, bomb making, bacteriological samples, and also when hackers penetrate the security of computer systems. Values and technology are balanced in a delicate equation.

If, we can agree that technological determinism is at the heart of globalization, then the next logical question is how widespread is its influence? Is it possible that societies which have limited or no access to advanced technology, such as, phones, computers, airplanes, are less likely to feel the effects of change? There is a case to be made that "consumerism", also an outgrowth of globalization brings people into contact with the expectations and enhancements characteristic of the wealthiest states. Does political change come from something as simple as material needs, self awareness, and dawning recognition of people power? Some would argue that this is so. The case for integrating China into the global economic community certainly assumes that happy Chinese consumers make good democratic citizens. The hope is that consumerism empowers and a people empowered gradually become democratized. Democratized peoples demand more justice and equality and are in a position to make their views heard. Poor populations have no leverage on political and economic institutions. Consumers can boycott products and be demanding. The winds of change arrive with the packages and material goods of international trade. There is seemingly an assurance that globalization will promote democracy more effectively that government efforts (Beinart, 1997).

Global Realities: The Third Face

A Globalizing World: The Case for Cooperation

Massive population transfers in the wake of regional conflict and war, the ease of the spread of disease, and environmental pollution, are not wholly dependent on, nor do they totally arise from interdependence and communications. They are often the product of local conditions, but they have a global influence. It is in the study of the changes that are launched by such events that we see how necessary it is to have a global base of policy and action. This is where the complexity of a shrinking world becomes clearer as we move aside the optimism of global education, the spread of enlightened political ideals, and the economic transformation of poor nations to focus on the issues of environmental pollution, disease, and new global threats.

The Global Environment

It is beyond the scope of this paper to delineate the enormous problems associated with environmental degradation and global climate change. It is important, to acknowledge that these are threats that know no boundaries and are beyond the scope of individual states' capacities to develop effective strategies. Environmental summits have been convened in recognition of the need for concerted action and policy. Some agreements have been reached, but there is still a wide gap in the perception of and response to common threats.

Disease, Health, and Global Threats

The transplanting of microbes and vectors into new geographic locations provides opportunities for infecting new and vulnerable populations. The process of disease transfer, resulting from the association between diverse elements like animals, plants, people etc changes has been on the increase with improved communications (Anne E. Platt, 1996: 122). Closely related to infections of human populations, is the growing threat of bio invasions when organisms are transferred from their native environments into areas where they can prove to be extremely destructive to the local economy. When exotic organisms establish themselves in new habitats they kill people, plants, birds, and fish. This was sadly demonstrated by the impact of the Columbian expeditions of the sixteenth century on the populations of the New World.

Global health and disease is an area where information and intervention play an important role. Acquired Immune Deficiency syndrome (AIDS) is commonly acknowledged to be a global health problem (World Resources, 1992:84). Ignorance, poverty, and lack of coordinated health policies are a potent contributors to the unchecked spread of this disease. In addition, many vector-borne diseases, such as malaria are spreading beyond their traditional confines due to the increased opportunities for organisms to be transported across regions. Similarly, increases in cholera, diarrhea, and other water and food borne diseases are also occurring at increased levels. Local immunization programs are often insufficient and ineffective, requiring intervention by international teams. Similarly, in the area of children's health, an international committment to immunization programs represents a policy of promoting public health as a preventive measure against future disease. The role played by international agencies, such as WHO, UNICEF, and UNDP in transcending national and regional barriers and achieving results is substantial.

The imperatives of global health suggest that countries would do well to move toward reliance on an international response in these matters. This becomes even more essential when we consider the possibilities of biological and chemical warfare in addition to the ongoing concerns of the natural spread of diseases in an increasingly interconnected world.

Security and Global Communications

The far reaching consequences of new threats suggest the need for an integrated response. As noted above, scenarios involving biological warfare, terrorism and threats of a similar nature will require global action. To this progression of events must be added the latest national security threat- internet subversion. The implications of this new kind of terrorism are very serious, impacting on individual privacy, as well as institutional security. Defense, finance, trade, health, and a host of domains can be seriously compromised by lone individuals who may be impossible to trace. This is a threat situation that has no precedence in human history and it is likely to be one of the single most destructive elements of a globalizing world.

National security acquires new dimensions when enemies are not other nations, but individuals, often within one's own society. Further, the motivations are less clear, not being connected with political power or national interests, or ideologies, but a mere fascination with technology's possibilities. Curiosity may be a factor, expanding the reaches of one's technological skills might be another, and quite as likely, it culminates in the thrill of achievement and powerfulness. This can at best be seen as an assertion of personal power, linking somewhat indirectly to the whole issue of the rise of the individual in society.

The borderless world of the new millennium needs new organizational structures, new value systems, and new security responses. The present institutions and policies designed to deal with groups and nation states are not adequate to meet the kinds of challenges that can be posed by individuals in society. This David and Goliath scenario is a new one for most analysts of the international system, and exposes the vulnerabilty of a globalizing world, distracting from its potential.

Conclusion

It is possible to see the process of globalization or "transnationalization" as a two part process, which involves compression on a large scale and transformation on a regional or local scale. Compression emphasizes the unity that may lead to what many feel are common values, ideas, tastes, culture, etc. This is the first face of globalization. Transformation on the other hand is the unpredictable, where challenges nationalisms and cultural identities may be strengthened or undermined in reaction to the sweeping winds of global unification. In this unpredictability and disruption we see the second face of globalization. Globalization has weakened traditionally restrictive geographical and cultural boundaries, making it ever more difficult to contain problems. With the growing deficiency of territoriality as an organizing principle, new relationships between peoples will emerge, leading to new social and cultural groupings (Waters, 1995). The third face of globalization appears at this stage, presaging the cooperative strategies that are needed for the challenges of the globalizing world. Globalization may be likened to the skin of an orange, that outwardly integrates. Within lie the internal contents, the individual segments and hard seeds, On the surface globalization unites, obscuring the separation within. As long as the outer surface unifies, the distinctions within can co-exist harmoniusly.

Notes

[1] Auguste Comte's Law of Three States posited a correlation between the maturing mentality of humankind and socio-political organization. Thus, the positive stage characterized by industrial development envisaged a social unit which consisted of the entire human race, a 'global community' if you will (Martineau,1896). This is further reinforced by Comte's conviction that society can only be studied on an organic scale providing the whole view

rather than the view of parts (Martineau, 1896). This functional view of society as an organic whole, diminished the importance of the individual as the unit of study. Nevertheless, this does point to an increasing interest in an element of what we may characterize today as a 'global' perspective.

[2] Durkheim's differentiation of the principles of 'mechanical' and 'organic' solidarity presaged the debate over minimization of individual differences in the interests of the common good, as contrasted with the fragmentation of the common interests that accompanies the differentiation within organic solidarity. Of importance to his attempts at reaching a broad understanding of society, the interconnectedness of social phenomena, Durkheim owes much to the influence of Montesquieu and Comte.

[3] Max Weber's view about the inescapable rationalization of the world has obvious implications for the synthesizing power of bureaucratic coordination. The organizational principle embodied in bureaucracies is the hallmark of modern societies. The rational mode is at once efficient and depersonalizing, an argument that may be applied by critics of globalization today.

[4] Charles Krauthammer describes internationalism, legalism, and humanitarianism, as the three pillars supporting a liberal American foreign policy that seeks to bring about a gentler international system. He is struck by the confidence placed in the supremacy of international moral, legal, and ethical institutions over national ones. Similarly he finds the belief in laws, treaties, and binding international contracts as guarantors of a stable world to be contrary to reality. He notes that a pro-active humanitarianism to ensure the eradication of exploitation and injustice to be hopelessly optimistic.

References

Basham, A.L. (1992), *The Wonder that was India*. Calcutta: Rupa and Company.
Beinart, Peter (1997, October 20), "An Illusion For Our Time: The False Promise of Globalization". *The New Republic*.
Carr, E.H. (1964), *The Twenty Years Crisis:1919-1939*. New York: Harper and Row.
Deutsch, K. (1953), *Nationalism and Social Communication*. Cambridge, Mass: MIT Press.
Drake, J. A. et al. (eds) (1989), *Biological Invasions: A Global Perspective*. Chichester, U.K.: John Wiley and Sons.
Dunning, J. (ed.) (1993) *Multinational Enterprises in a Global Economy*. Workingham, Addison-Wesley.
Durkheim, Emile (1965), *Elementary Forms of the Religious Life*. New York: Free Press.
Eriksen, T. Hylland (1993), *Ethnicity and Nationalism: Anthropological Perspectives*. London: Pluto Press.
Falk, Richard (1995), "Towards Obsolescence: Sovereignty in the Era of Globalization". *Harvard International Review*, Summer 1995.
Featherstone, M. (ed) (1990), *Global Culture*. London: Sage.
Garrett, Laurie (1994), *The Coming Plague: Newly Emerging Diseases in a World Out of Balance*. New York: Farrar, Strauss, Giroux.
Garret, W. and R. Robertson (eds) (1991), *Religion and the Global Order*. New York: Paragon.
Gellner, E. (1994), *Nations and Nationalism*. Ithaca: Cornell University Press.
Giddens, A. (1991), *Modernity and Self-Identity*. Cambridge: Polity.
Held, D. (ed.) (1991), *Political Theory Today*. Cambridge: Polity.

Huntington, S. (1991), *The Third Wave*. Norman: Oklahoma University Press.

Kedourie, Elie (1966), *Nationalism*. London: Hutchinson.

Kidd, Colin (1999) *British Identities Before Nationaliasm: Ethnicity and Nationhood in the Atlantic World, 1600-1800*. Cambridge: Cambridge University Press.

Klein, Lawrence R. and Fu-Chen Lo (eds) (1995), *Modelling Global Change*. Tokyo: United Nations University Press.

Krauthammer, Charles (1999, March 15), "A World Imagined: The Flawed Premises of Liberal Foreign Policy". *The New Republic*.

Krishna-Hensel, Sai Felicia (1999), "Population and Urbanization in the Twenty-First Century: India's Megacities" in B.Baudot and W.Moomaw (eds), *People and Their Planet: Searching for Balance*, St. Martin's Press, New York.

Martineau, Harriet (1896), *The Positive Philosophy of Auguste Comte*, London: Bell.

Mc Knight, Bill N. (ed) (1993), *Biological Pollution: The Control and Impact of Invasive Exotic Species*. Indianapolis: Indiana Academy of Science.

McMahon, Jeff (1996), Intervention and Collective Self-determination, *Ethics and International Affairs*, vol.10, pp. 1-24.

Morse, Stephen S. (1990), "Regulating Viral Traffic", *Issues in Science and Technology*, Fall, 1990.

Morse, Stephen S. (ed) (1993), *Emerging Viruses*. New York: Oxford University Press.

Platt, Anne E. (1996), "Confronting Infectious Diseases", *State of the World, 1996: A World Watch Institute Report on Progress Toward a Sustainable Society*. New York: W.W.Norton & Company.

Pollis, Adamantia (1982), "Liberal, Socialist, and Third World Perspectives of Human Rights" in Pollis and Schwab (eds) *Toward a Human Rights Framework*. New York: Praeger.

Smith, Anthony D. (1991), *National Identity*. Reno: University of Nevada Press.

Spruyt, Hendrik (1995), "Decline Reconsidered: The Complex Nature of Modern Sovereignty", *Harvard International Review*, Summer 1995.

Stallings, Barbara (ed.) (1995), *Global Change, Regional Response: The New International Context of Development*. New York: Cambridge University Press.

Swatos, W. (ed) (1989), *Religious Politics in Global Perspective*. New York: Greenwood Press.

Wallerstein, Immanuel (1980), *The Modern World System II: Mercantilism and the Consolidation of the European World Economy, 1600-1750*. New York: Academic Press.

Wallerstein, Immanuel (1989), *The Modern World System III: The Second Era of Great Expansion in the Capitalist World Economy,1730-1840s*. San Diego: Academic Press.

Waters, Malcolm (1995), *Globalization*. London and New York: Routledge.

Weber, Max (1927), *General Economic History*. New Brunswick, N.J.: Transaction Books.

Weber, Max (1958), *The Protestant Ethic and the Spirit of Capitalism*. New York: Charles Scribners Sons.

Weber, Max (1978), *Economy and Society*. 2 volumes. Berkeley: University of California Press.

World Resource: A Guide to the Global Environment, 1994-95. A Report by the World Resources Institute in Collaboration with the United Nations Environment Programme and the United Nations Development Programme, New York: Oxford University Press.

Wright, Robert (2000, January 17), "Continental Drift: World Government is Coming. Deal With It", *The New Republic*.

2 Mega Civilization: Global Capital and the New Standard of Civilization

MEHDI MOZAFFARI

In the history of humanity, each epoch has its own designation, characterizing the main trends of that particular period: The 'iron age', the 'middle age', the 'atomic age'. At the edge of the 21st century, the world is experiencing the 'global age' or the 'age of globality'. Globalization is the designation of our epoch which depending upon the observer's preferences is understood and interpreted differently. For some, globalization is a *process* which "denotes movements in both *intensity* and *extent* of international interactions" (Clark 1997:1). Or as "intensification of worldwide social relations which link distinct localities in such a way that local happenings are shaped by events occurring miles away and vice versa" (Giddens 1990:64). For Giddens, globalization is also 'high modernity', because "modernity is inherently globalising.... modernity is inherently future-oriented, such that the 'future' has the status of counterfactual modeling" (p. 177). From this perspective, globalization is certainly interpreted as a process, but one which distances itself from the traditional structures and habits ultimately building the features of future. For others, globalization is considered as a *value*; which puts an end to one history and marks the beginning of another; a peaceful Kantian democratic world (Fukuyama 1992). For others, globalization is an *anti-value*; because of its uneven impact on and its destructive aspects for the undeveloped or semi-mature economies phenomena. Then there are those for whom globalization is an *ideology*. From this perspective, there is no alternative to globalization which justifies "the need for repressive police and military forces to prevent destabilization of the world economy by outbursts of protest from the disadvantaged outsiders" (Cox 1996:23). Conversely, but in the same spirit, globalization means "the universality of rule by the proletariat which does not define itself nationalistically" (Galloway 1999:4). Despite their different orientations, all these definitions converge in two points. First, there is a general consensus that globalization is an undeniable fact and a reality of our epoch. Though the consensus as to the causes and origins of globalization is lacking. Second, globalization whatever its origins "compress[es] the time and space aspects of social relations:" (Mittelman 1996:3, Robertson 1996:8). Therefore, the two notions of *time* and *space* are essential to understand the concept of globalization.

Parallel to increasing globalization, is the fact that since the fall of the Berlin wall closely followed by the end of the bipolar system, the normative and ethical dimensions of international relations have become critically important. Questions related to human rights, democratization and respect for the environment, humanitarian intervention and the sanctioning of crimes against humanity have come to dominate debates among scholars of international politics and international public opinion, as well as decision-makers' policies. The question is how to understand, in theoretical terms, the essence of the above-mentioned transformation in international politics. Shall we again try to find an appropriate answer in Neorealism; the dominant school? Neorealism which during the cold war was "a problem solving form of knowledge applicable to superpower rivalry...explaining the world and proposing action" no longer has this monopoly (Cox 1998:1-2). As a theoretical approach it is inadequate to explain how a transformation at unit level - the disintegration of the USSR - led to the change of the international system; and it is unable to explain why the rupture of a bipolar system led to the rise of normative and ethical concerns. Kenneth Waltz denies the importance of cultural, ideological or religious factors in the behaviour and policy of the states (Waltz 1979:80). But the end of the cold war, caused by the disintegration of a unit and the sharp enhancement of cultural and civilian dimensions in international relations contradict Waltzian assumptions. In fact, the revival of the normative school is due to the quality of attributes of the late bipolar system. The struggle between the USA and the USSR was not merely a nuclear or strategic struggle. It was, at the same time, a struggle between two diametrically opposed philosophies of life, between two antagonistic ideologies and between two different civilizations at large. (See Figure 1.)

If, as claimed by Neorealists, during the cold war the bipolar system had been a purely a-cultural rivalry between two superpowers, one may legitimately ask why the end of the bipolarity led to the emergence of a world in which liberalism and capitalism (under various forms) became dominant? The Neorealist school has no answer to this question.

Figure 1 The status of world civilizations before 1990

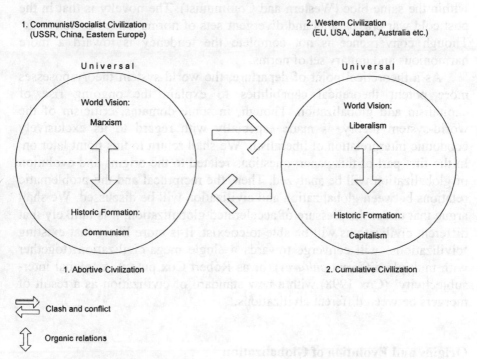

One might argue that the rise of new normative and ethical dimensions in international politics, and its central place in the western states' policy the post cold war era's move towards democratization, human rights, free market encouragement and a struggle against racial, ethnic and religious discrimination, and humanitarian intervention are not contradictory to the national interests of western powers. On the contrary, these issues reinforce the power position of the West world-wide. Therefore, putting an emphasis on new normative and ethical dimensions is simply carrying out *realpolitik* through other means. This is probably Neo-realists' best argument. In fact, it reaffirms our core argument that with the beginning of the current era, the frontier between *power politic* and *normative politic* tends to diminish. Should states and other international actors arrive at the conclusion that their interests are best served by respecting human rights and other components of the new standard of civilization which facilitate their gaining prestige, credibility and power, it implies that military capabilities are not values in itself; they are of course necessary elements as usual, but far from being sufficient. Precisely because the new set of norms limits the use of force, unless it is ordered, recommended or justified by the new and accepted norms. This situation is new. Before the end of the cold war, the world witnessed 1) the existence of parallel and divergent sets of norms, 2)

an instrumental use of norms, and 3) a gap between norms and politics even within the same bloc (Western and Communist). The novelty is that in the post cold war era, parallel and divergent sets of norms tended to converge. Though convergence is not complete the tendency is toward a more harmonious and unitary set of norms.

As a theoretical point of departure, the world-system theory posesses more potent theoretical capabilities to explain the ongoing rise of capitalism and globalization. Though, in some domains, criticism of the world-system theory, is made especially with regard to its exclusively economic interpretation of liberalism. We shall return to this point later on. In the first part of this paper, questions related to the origins and evolution of globalization will be analyzed. Then, the reciprocal and the problematic relations between globalization and civilization will be discussed. We shall argue that under the pressure of accelerated globalization, it is unlikely that different civilizations will be able to coexist. It is more likely that existing 'civilizations' will converge towards a single mega-civilization (together with multiple different *cultures*), or as Robert Cox puts it, a 'global inter-subjectivity' (Cox 1998) with a new standard of civilization as a result of mergers between different civilizations.

Origins and Evolution of Globalization

Globalization in our understanding is not equivalent, identical or reducible to *internationalism*, or the *intensification of interdependence*, though these are part of it. Globalization goes beyond these concepts. It implies not only the relations between states and international as well as transnational organizations, but it also embraces relations between citizens world-wide; influencing their identity, their language, their culture. Globalization, in this sense and as a reality of our time, has its own history. However, there is no consensus about the genealogy and chronological origin of globalization. When did Globalization emerge, when did it become a reality, and, from which epoch can we talk about the existence of globalization? To these questions, three types of answers are identifiable. First, there is the thesis of many anthropologists who believe that the inceptions of globalization cannot be dated, rather it is related to the history of humankind. It started the very moment that the first human community was established. So, nothing is new; we have always been living in a global world. In direct opposition to this thesis, is the theory that globalization represents something absolutely new as a direct consequence of the end the cold war and the collapse of the only potent challenging power (the USSR). Fukuyam probably best represents this group.

Between these two lines of thinking, is a third which rejects the assumption that globalization is an anodyne phenomenon which existed from the beginning of our history, while at the same time not accepting that globalization can be reduced to the decade, following the end of the cold war. For Ian Clark, real globalization together with fragmentation starts with World War I, when the "war integrated some colonial economies more deeply into the international economy, fostered the enunciation of universalist (if antagonistic) ideologies in the shape of Lenninism and Wilsonianism" (Clark 1997:7). World War II "was without question, a *world* war that has impact on human lives, economic system, political philosophies.....and served as a catalyst for the globalizing of political ideas, none more so than the concept of human rights" (Clark 1997:199). Without contesting Clark's argument that the two world wars and their respective aftermath contributed enormously to the accelerating of the globalization process, we believe that there is evidence to attest that the origin of globalization goes back several centuries, to the time of the rise of capitalism. To illustrate this idea, we find it fruitful to borrow Fernand Braudel's concept of 'historical time'. For Braudel, different aspects of human and social life have different tempos. Accordingly, a history of mentalities moves at a different pace than a history of the material life with which it interacts. Braudel believes that there are three levels of time. The level of *immediacy* (l'histoire événmentielle), consisting of events which can be recorded but which are not self-explanatory. To be explained, they must be put within their context in time and space. The second level is called *conjonctures*, an intermediate time frame necessary to explain the 'immediacy'. The *conjonctures* in turn are explicable within the framework of the *longue durée*, a 'historical structure created by collective human activity over periods of time which comes to be regarded in common sense as the natural order of things' (Cox's translation, 1998:27, Braudel 1979: chapter 1). To apply the Braudelian model of time to globalization requires some modifications. That which refes to *longue durée*, will be conceptualised as *structural*. That which refers to *conjunctures*, will be denoted *technological*, and finally we shall paraphrase *immediacy* as *civilizational*. It is in this spirit that - within the given space - we shall go through the study of these three cumulative phases/waves of globalization. Since structural and technological origins are intertwined, they will be discussed in the same rubric.

International Economy, World Economy and Global Economy

The structural transformation of the world took place in Europe during the sixteenth century. It is continuing its course in our days and will do so for the foreseeable future. It is a *longue durée* phenomenon par excellence called *capitalism*. Capitalism here is defined as a 'historical capitalism', which is quite different from all previous historical social systems. What distinguishes historical capitalism is that "in this historical system, capital came to be used (invested) in a very special way. It came to be used with the primary objective or intent of self-expansion" (Wallerstein 1995:13-14). Another difference resides in the non-availability of one or more elements of the process - the accumulated stock in money, the labour to be utilized by the producer, the network of distributors, the consumers. More specifically, in the pre-capitalist formation:

> One or more elements were missing because, in previous historical social systems, one or more of these elements was no 'commodified' or was insufficiently 'commodified' What this means is that the process was not considered one that could or should be transacted through a 'market'. Historical capitalism involved therefore the widespread commodification of processes-not merely exchange processes, but production processes-that had previously been conducted other than via a 'market' (Wallerstein 1995:15).

To Marx, capitalism is a system of *commodity* production. "In the capitalist system producers do not simply produce for their own needs, or for needs of individuals with whom they are in personal contact; capitalism involves a nation-wide, and often an international, exchange market" (Giddens 1971/1990:46). In Marx's own words, "capitalism withdraws from the spheres with low rates of profit and invades others which yield a higher profit" (quoted by Giddens 1971/1990:51).

Following the path of expansion of capitalism, the treaties of Westphalia (in 1648) and subsequently the rise of nation states, are interpreted by world-system theorists as a necessary, even inevitable consequence of historical capitalism in expansion. It is explained by the fact that the capitalist world-system from being among many worlds is becoming the historical social system of the entire world needed to construct "territorial organizations capable to regulating social and economic life and of monopolizing means of coercion and violence" (Arrighi 1997:5-6). On the other hand, the concentration of capital in the core zone created both the fiscal base and the political motivation for creating relatively strong state-machineries, the many capacities of which ensured that the state machineries of peripheral zones became or remained relatively weaker (Wallerstein 1995:32). In short, national states are a differentiated form of capitalist power. It must be stressed that the capitalist system based on the Westphalian national state, which led to the *international* economy is distinct from *world* economy. While the former was predominantly about movements in trade, investments, and payments crossing national frontiers that were regulated by states and by international organizations created by states, the latter, in contrast, "was the sphere in which production and finance were being organized in cross-border networks that could very largely escape national and international regulatory powers" (Cox 1996:22). In other words, the 'international economy' was based on *territoriality*, while the 'world economy' is at work in a *de-territorialized* universe (Hassner 1993:53). The distinction between the two stages of evolution of capitalism is crucial to grasp the real sense of globalization. Globalization is not about intensification of the classic international economy; because the global market is not the sum of national markets. The whole is more than the sum of its parts. Globalization is about the expansion of the world economy which became a reality during the nineteenth century. In its elementary form, globalization is what Lenin called *imperialism* which "emerged as the development and direct continuation of the fundamental characteristics of capitalism in general" (Lenin: *Imperialism, the higher stage of capitalism*, chapter VII). Lenin was far from being the only thinker who was preoccupied by the idea of the expansion of capitalism. Before and after him, a range of specialists, thinkers and theorists focused their study (some of them their entire life) on this topic. To give an idea of the importance Marxist authors attached to capitalism, nothing is perhaps more revealing than the title of Marx's own axial work: *Das Kapital* and not *Das Beruf*! In a sense, one could argue that Marxism (and with it Communism) was not an alternative to capitalism; actually it was a *reaction* to it. As a matter of fact, this reaction is apparent already in their *Manifesto* calling and preaching for the 'unification of proletarians' *against* the 'unified front of capitalists'. Marx himself and Marxist theorists of the 19th century and the beginning of the 20th century did in general correctly predict the development and expansionist tendencies of capitalism. What they failed to predict was the extraordinary capacity of capitalism to overcome its contradictions...so far. Rudolf Hilferding is among the authors (i.e. Bukharin, Luxembourg) who in his major work *Finance Capital* (1910), explained the new mechanism of expansion of capitalist economy and its evolution from international economy to world economy. To Hilferding:

> Finance capital marks the unification of capital. The previously distinct spheres of industrial capital, commercial capital and bank capital are henceforth under the control of high finance, in which the magnates of industry and the banks are closely associated. This association, which is founded on the suppression of competition between capitalists by great

monopolistic combines, has, of course, the effect of changing the relations between the capitalist class and the state (*Finance Capital*: 40 in Brewer 1980:85-6).

The further expansion of capitalism during the 20th century confirmed Hilferding's prediction. Capitalism continued its way towards more expansion, it became a world-economy by ignoring national borders and by making the states the agents of globalization from which they (at least states in the high developed capitalist economy) drew substantial benefice. The empirical work is also beginning to 'confirm the expectation that highly mobile capital may place limits on the ability of governments to choose not only an autonomous monetary policy but an expansionary fiscal policy as well' (Simmons 1999: 64).

In the above discussion, it has been demonstrated that capitalism evolved from an 'international economy' to a 'world economy'. Its evolution however did not stop there; by the extraordinary progress and vast innovation in the domains of technology, communication networks and the electronic industry, capitalism became progressively a *global economy*. A 'global economy' is "an economy with the capacity to work as a *unit* in *real time* on *planetary scale*" (italics added) - (Castells 1996:92). In this definition, all three elements of globalization are present in a unified form. 'Unit', means a comprehensive system with its internal logic and its own dynamics. 'Time' is real and synchronic. 'Space' is planetary and no longer limited to national, regional or even cultural borders. In such a system, capital is managed around the clock in globally integrated financial markets working in real time. The labor markets are not yet global; thus the arrow goes in direction of globality. In a world becoming more and more mobile, the labor follows production and services which in turn follow cheaper wages and favorable taxation. Of course, it does not imply that protectionism is history or that every company sell world wide. It merely implies that trades, productions and transactions in the core (the USA, the European Union and Japan) of the system are becoming predominantly global, giving birth to what Susan Strange called a non-territorial 'business civilization' (Strange 1990). In her view, the key aspect of globalization involves neither trade nor investment: It is the adoption of common practices and standards. (Strange 1996). In many respects, the rise of a global economy drastically transformed the face of the global world. It stimulated the homogenisation and standardization of products which in turn produced a 'global life style'. It also established a framework and a guideline for good conduct in international trade (6.6 trillion US dollars in 1997). The general and multilateral rules on trade are now considerably reinforced by the World Trade Organization (WTO). Among these rules are: Reciprocity, non-discrimination, decreasing tariffs (not increasing), consulting and dispute resolution etc. The third and perhaps most significant consequence of global economy is the time conditioned gap between finance and production. Money is fungible and extremely mobile. New technologies allow billion dollars-worth of transactions to take place in seconds in the electronic circuit around the globe. Capital flows become global and are operating in *synchronic* dimensions. The development of production takes place in a *diachronic* dimension. As a result of this gap, global finance has come to dominate production (Cox 1998:28, Castells 1996:93). Consequently, changes in the mobility of capital will inevitably influence the development of the nation state, by the fact that while capital flows globally, the nation state is fixed. In this situation, "the different states compete to attract and immobilize the flow of capital. The relation of particular national states to global capital is mediated through the competitive process of attraction-and-immobilization" (Holloway 1996:130). The problem with global finance is that it is not bound to any global regulatory institution. Disconnected from economic realities, global finance is left to the un-controlled financial market mechanism, which only takes care of individual interests; causes turbulence (e.g. financial crisis in Asia and Latin America in 1998) and misery for millions of people. The laissez-faire orientation of the market has taken refuge in the lame conviction that, in due course, the invisible hand associated with economic growth would overcome economic hardship, a view completely lacking in empirical support (Falk:1999:423). George Soros (who is an 'insider' of the global finance and a beneficiary of the lack of regulations in this domain) thinks that the present international economic system is highly unstable, and that it has within it the makings of another catastrophe like 1929. Furthermore, in his new book, he criticizes the current situation in the financial market, because "instead of acting like a pendulum, financial markets have recently acted more like wrecking balls knocking over one economy after another" (Soros 1998: xvi). Other commentators like Paul Hirst who are skeptical about the ungovernability of financial markets admits however to the urgency and necessity of its regulation by "extending public governance at both national and inter-national levels, with the aim of combining growth with fairness within and between nations" (Hirst 1997:425). The lack of rules and principles for a sector on which the future of humanity may depend justifies the necessity of common civilization.

In this part, we have demonstrated that globalization is a new phenomenon distinct from classic interdependence. It has also been demonstrated that the capitalist system evolved from an international economy to a world economy and subsequently to a global economy - one of the major characteristics of contemporary globalization.

Global Civilization

The substantial transformations in the structure of the international system during the last decade combined with a deeper globalization in the economic sphere, and in particular the technological revolution in communication networks have affected mind, identity and values at the individual level as well as in the quality of international society. Therefore, the intensive and worldwide debate on civilization(s), is in itself symptomatic of the new era in international politics, revealing at the same time the existence of different approaches to civilization as a new paradigm in a world moving toward globalization. There are essentially four major tendencies: 1) Civilizations as a matter of future clash and conflicts, therefore the wise policy is to preserve the 'uniqueness' of Western civilization. This is Samuel Huntington's thesis (Huntington 1996). The same argument is used by certain fundamentalists who reject any dialogue with other civilizations and believe in the absolute superiority of their own civilization (Khomeini 1971). 2) Opposite to this approach is a multitude of scholars and politicians who argue in favor of the absence of clash and the existence of patterns of dialogue and cooperation between different civilizations with the purpose of reaching the universal society and human governance (Morin 1987, 1993 and 1997, Braudel 1993, Toynbee 1956 and 1995, Fukuyama 1992, Donnelly 1989 and 1998, Falk 1995 and 1999). 3) The third group is those who believe in both globalization and fragmentation. From their point of view, the world undergoes a deep process of globalization, one McWorld tied together by technology, ecology, communications, and commerce. At the same time the world is threatened by retribalization, a kind of lebanonization of national states in which culture is pitted against culture, people against people, tribe against tribe - a Jihad (Barber 1992/1996, Clark, 1997). 4) The fourth and last group embraces those who believe in peaceful coexistence of different civilizations but not in universal civilization (Ames 1997). This tendency is generally defended by representatives of illiberal or authoritarian regimes (e.g. Khatami 1997, Mahathir bin Mohammad of Malaysia 1997). Our theoretical approach to the problematic of 'civilization and globalization' is inspired by the above-mentioned approach (2). Globalization has a very destructive aspect: It generates anonymity, reduces individual cultures to a common denominator and standardizes identities. However, it is also a unique opportunity to promote communication and understanding between people of various cultures and encourage their mixing (Morin 1996). From this perspective, there is no clash between civilizations, by the simple fact that since the information technology revolution and the restructuring of capitalism have induced the networking society (Castells 1997), the very existence of *different and multiple* civilizations is questionable. The idea of the existence of different and multiple civilizations side by side, and/or against each other belongs to the pre-technological revolution period where, in absence of the modern and sophisticated world-wide communication and information networks, the contact between different civilizations occurred sporadically and by war and voyages. In the age of new technology, the character of *interaction* is substantially changed by the process of '*internetting*'. The 'internetting' here is a metaphor indicating the vast and sophisticated web of communications' networks which permanently and instantaneously connects individuals and groups to each other (including TV). It is noticeable that for the first time in history, the formation of super-text and meta-language integrate into the same system the *written, oral,* and *audio-visual* means of human communication. In this way, much actions/-interactions occur via the net; creating at the same time an almost common terminology and rules which must be respected for the purpose of the continuation of the new system (the web). The new common terminology and common rules will progressively create a new culture (the 'web culture') which is shared by individuals and groups belonging to different conven-tional cultures! Those who in our days constitute the 'virtual communities'.

Globalization is uneven. Its impact on the center of the world (Western countries) is deeper and more visible than in other parts of the world. The process is identical, however, and the differences concern only the degree and intensity of its implication. Benjamin Barber identified two diametri-cally opposite trends: One towards McWorld (essentially in the 'center') with uniform fast food, fast music, fast computers: MTV, Macintosh, and McDonald's. The other one characterized by Jihad, a total fragmentation and disintegration which roughly speaking is the dominant trend in the 'rest' of the world. This picture, in the way that Barber describes it, does not correspond to the real picture of the present world. It is an over-simplification of the situation with a strong dose of exaggeration about a new global totalitarianism. One could validly argue that the search for individual, local and national identity is not necessarily contradictory to globalization. On the contrary, the different identity claims (i.e. local, regional, religious and cultural) must be seen precisely as a means of regulation aiming to keep globalization within acceptable limits for various human communities; and also as an effort against subjugation and anonymity. In Giddens' words it is true that globalization 'pulls away' from the nation-state, but at the same time globalization also 'pushes down' - "it creates new demands and also new possibilities for regenerating local identities. The recent upsurge of Scottish nationalism in the UK shouldn't be seen as an isolated example. It is a response to the same structural process at work elsewhere" (Giddens 1999:31-32).

What is the impact of globalization on the deterioration and improvement of values? We argue that no fundamental human value has deteriorated in the process of globalization. On the contrary, globalization has stimulated people's attention to their *own* identity. The Basques are becoming more Basque, the Scots more Scottish and the people of Jutland more 'J'. At the same time, all together, these people are becoming more European and more planetary, taking positions on questions such as child labor in India, air pollution in the Ukraine, assassination of women and children in Algeria, and violation of human rights every where. It is within the same spirit that Giddens talks about the increasing interconnection between the two extremes of extensionality and intensity: Globalizing influences on the one hand and personal dispositions on the other. The more tradition loses its hold, and the more daily life is reconstituted in terms of the dialectical interplay of the local and the global, the more individuals are forced to negotiate lifestyle choices among a diversity of options. Reflexively organized life-planning becomes a central feature of the structuring of self-identity (Giddens 1991). Parallel to this, the system of local and parochial identity and loyalty is replaced by the system of multi-identity and multi-loyalty as mentioned above. Consequently, Barber's 'lebanonization' must be understood rather as a process of mutual recognition of each others' identities and loyalties than as a process of complete fragmentation, denying each others' identities. As a matter of fact, Lebanon is now going through such a re-construction.

We also argue that globalization has made democracy the dominant discourse. The world has never been as *democratic* as it is today. Beginning with (Western) Europe which is now fully democratic compared with the situation 25 years ago. (Eastern) Europe is also becoming democratic, but needs improvements. Also Latin America, large parts of Asia, Africa and even the Middle East. Except for some regimes like Saudi Arabia and some extremist groups (world-wide) who reject the concept of democracy, nobody opposes this. The concept of 'civil society' has reached even a country like Iran. Continuing my argumentation, I emphasize that what is true for democracy as a current dominant trend is also valid for human rights which is becoming a global issue. In fact, the global character of human rights has reached such magnitude that the *universal* character of human rights is now directly challenging the validity of some anti-universalistic theses like 'Asian values', 'Islamic values' and 'Christian ethnicity'. The defenders of these parochial values - especially among the representatives of the illiberal regimes - intend to go back to the period when there were no standards of civilization and no norms concerning genuine human rights.

What makes the difference between before and after globalization, before and after the fall of the Berlin wall is that a new civilization which could be a common place for humanity is emerging in place of a variety of multiple civilizations. For the task of clarification, we have to distinguish between two types of civilizations. Civilization with a capital (C), and civilization with (c). The first category refers to different Civilizations which we defined elsewhere (Mozaffari 1998:31). Following our definition, a Civilization is 'a junction between a *world vision* and a *historical formation*' (italics added). This definition is very close to Cox's new definition, when he describes Civilization as "corresponding between material conditions of existence and inter-subjective meanings" (1998:8). It is interesting that both definitions are formulated at the same time (for the same workshop) but completely independent of each other. By 'world vision', we mean 'a set of cultural systems, an ideology or a religion'. By 'historical formation', we mean a 'coherent political, military and economic system'. So, when a specific world vision and a specific historical formation merge, the result of this fusion is called 'Civilization'. Each Civilization possesses its own standard. The standard of Chinese Civilization is different from the standard of Islamic Civilization. As the standard of European Civilization is different from the standard of Indian Civilization etc. In other words, the standard of each Civilization represents the identity card and the DNA of the same Civilization. Furthermore, the standard of Civilization is the criteria which determines who is 'barbarian' and who is 'civilized'. 'Barbarians' in one Civilization could be considered 'civilized' in another one, and vice versa. The standard of Civilization constitutes 'civilization' (see Figure 2).

There is a direct correspondence between the real power of a Civilization and the extension of its standard. When one Civilization becomes stronger than another, its standard will prevail as the dominant standard. The dominant standard is often imposed on others (i.e. 'capitulation', 'unequal treaties'), and can also be 'interiorized' and voluntarily accepted (conversion to a religion, adherence to democracy, etc.). Rejecting

Figure 2 A world with multiple civilizations

C = Civilizations

C = Standard of civilization

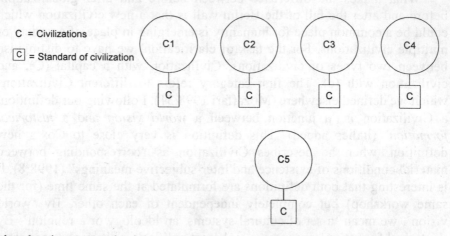

the dominant standard or opposing it is punishable. The punishment can take different forms: *Jihad* against the non-Muslims, economic sanctions against Iraq, permanent criticism against human rights conditions in China. Weak Civilizations produce only weak standards. 'Weak' in terms of the degree and the scope of applicability and acceptance. The standard of a declined Civilization can not survive after its extinction. The above assumptions leads us to question about the nature of the emerging Civilization. As it has been argued, a 'historical formation' and a 'world vision' constitute the two indissociable pillars of a Civilization. We know that there are convincing facts that the 'historical capitalist system' stands as an indisputable dominant historical formation of our time. It is a fact that after the collapse of the Communist Soviet, there is no other potent economic system which could be able to represent itself as a new historical formation. Saying that capitalism represents the dominant formation does not necessarily imply that there is only one capitalist model. Capitalism takes different colors, different intonations and different forms. Capitalism can be 'hard' and 'ultra' of which Thatcherism and Reaganism stand as examples. It can also be 'soft' and 'social' as expressed through the social democratic conception of capitalism. A range of other forms of capitalism, e.g. Russian capitalism, Asiatic capitalism, Chinese capitalism, Petro-capitalism, etc. are capitalist in so far as they function according to certain general laws: Laws of supply and demand, laws of profit and investment, respect for private property and free circulation of capital. Differences are in degree and orientation (social or hyper-liberal) rather than in their substance. Therefore, it is a matter of fact that for the first time in history, a specific historical formation became a global historical formation.

Consequently, because of the absence of another historical formation, except for capitalism, we cannot say that today a non-capitalist civilization exists. Hypothetically, the rise of a new civilization is not excluded; but the coming civilization cannot escape from the imperative of capitalism (e.g. a Green capitalist civilization vs. a hyper-liberal civilization).

By the establishment of a civilization, the existence of a historical formation is necessary, thus not sufficient. It needs a second pillar; a world vision. What is the world vision of contemporary civilization? We argue that the increasingly dominant world vision originated in Europe and expanded to the American continent to become 'Western' and is progressively on the way to becoming 'global'. In reality, the European civilization is the youngest among civilizations. It has only a few centuries - most likely only five centuries - of experience. This civilization arose on the ruin of Greek and Roman civilizations. It was profoundly inspired and extensively enriched by multiple sources, the Mediterranean and Middle Eastern cultures in particular. In this respect, a number of elements enables European civilization to become global and thus unique. Let us enumerate a few. Basically, many other civilizations arose to accomplish a pre-established project. Often, such projects had some kind of a religious substance (Confucianism, Judaism, Islam, etc.). European civilization is among the rare civilizations which emerged without a pre-constructed project or any 'principe fondateur original', as expressed by Edgar Morin (1987:33). Europe did not proclaim to be the 'promised land', and Europeans did not consider themselves as the 'chosen people'. Before the emergence of Europe, the continent was beset by turbulence. It became a civilization by accident not following a predestined plan as a result of a 'big bang'. Surprisingly, Europe did not invent a new religion similar to the great religions. From a non-European culture she borrowed Christianity and refined and adjusted it for her own purpose. Today, Europe and Christianity are perceived almost as identical, but originally Europe is a non-religious civilization. Precisely, the non-religiosity of Europe qualified her to be inclusive and not exclusive. Without such a characteristic, Europe could hardly produce the Universal Declaration of the Right of Man and Citizen (1789). It seems obvious that the opportunities of a non-religious civilization to embrace several religions and a variety of different ideas and ideologies are greater than of one which is absorbed by a single religion or a single ideology. Instead of religion, Europe invented *dialogy* which is distinct from the Greek *dialectic*. While the latter is deterministic (thesis, anti-thesis and synthesis), the former is based on dialogue, compromise and uncertainty; A free and qualified, say Habermassian dialogue (the difference between dialectic and dialogy provides us with an explanation for the failure of Marxism as an ideology. Marxism based on dialectic is rather a Greek theoretical construction than a European one). Precisely, dialogy combined with the lay spirit led Europeans to *humanism* to which we might add other European concepts such as: *liberty* and *rights*. Questioning the identity of Europe, Fernand Braudel answers as follows:

> Imagine that it might be possible to assemble the sum total of our knowledge of European history....and to record it...in a electronic memory. Imagine that the computer was then asked to indicate the one problem which recurred most frequently, in time and space, throughout the lengthy history. Without a doubt, that problem is liberty, or rather liberties. The word liberty is the operative word (Braudel 1993:315).

Prior to Braudel, François Guizot (1787-1874) arrived at the same conclusion. Guizot argued that

> while in other civilizations the domination of a single form and a single idea has been the cause of tyranny, in modern Europe, the diversity of elements, which constitute the social order, the impossibility under which they have been placed of excluding each other, have given birth to the freedom which prevails in the present Europe (Guizot 1846/1997:31).

The European world vision is constituted essentially of the above-mentioned elements. In order to give these elements a common designation, we need an adequate concept which is not without epistemological difficulty. At a first glance, *liberalism* should be a qualified candidate. However it is a problem that this etiquette is charged with a number of ideological prejudices. Liberalism is sometimes considered identical to capitalism, especially by world-system theorists. On the other side, liberalism is seen as an ideology based exclusively on primacy of individual versus social. What we mean by liberalism here is rather a philosophical doctrine whose basic principle and ethos is full of respect for human liberty, human dignity and human rights. Perhaps, this political philosophy could be best entitled by a neologism: *Social-liberalism*. A world vision based on such basic principle is also able to promote democracy, to protect minorities and to regulate the excess of capitalism. The above-mentioned world vision is most visible through its emanated standard of civilization. As it has been noted, each civilization needs to

Figure 3 Global civilization

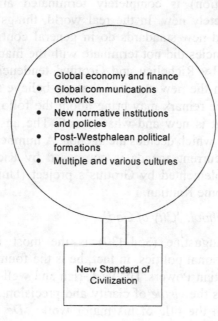

- Global economy and finance
- Global communications networks
- New normative institutions and policies
- Post-Westphalean political formations
- Multiple and various cultures

New Standard of Civilization

establish and proclaim its standard of civilization. As for Europe, this standard was designated to regulate inter-European relations and relations between Europeans and non-Europeans. No standard is static and eternal, it evolves as long as the Civilization to which it belongs remains dynamic.

We argue that today's standard of civilization originates from the newest and youngest civilization which is European and Western. All other standards become either obsolete, absorbed by the new standard, or are completely marginalized. (See Figure 3.) We shall briefly analyze the main trends in the evolution of the current standard of international civilization.

Standard of Civilization: God's Rights, State's Rights and Human Rights

Contemporary world dominating Standard of Civilization (SC) has a long history. The purpose of this study is not to go through the whole history of SC. Within the space given, we intend to present the most significant phases and momentum in the evolution of SC. The best way is probably to identify some major periods to illustrate the main trends of SC's development. In this connection, we believe that three periods or three schools have an axial importance; the Augustinian period, the period inaugurated by the tandem Richelieu/Grotius, and the Kantian period. The beginning of each period does not imply that the previous period (within the same civilization) is completely terminated and, that the arising standard is completely new. In the real world, things go differently. The fact is that old and new standards do in general continue to coexist. The Augustinian tendencies did not terminate with the inauguration of the new waves dominated by Richelieu and Grotius' tendencies, and, today both theses coexist with the new standard that we believe to be predominantly Kantian. The above remark may bring about the following question: How then to know what is new and what is not? The answer is that the new standard is the one which decides the agenda. A number of facts in our time confirm that the current agenda is composed by Richelieu's concept of *raison d'état* supplemented by Grotius's project (United Nations) and is proceeding to become Kantian.

The Augustinan School: 'City of God'

Saint Aurelius Augustine (354-430) is the most influential Christian theorist of international politics. In fact, he is the founder of the normative code for the Christian Powers. His vast, rich and well-argumented work in this field possesses the *virtue* of clarity and precision. These equalities are obvious already in the title of his major work: '*De Civitate Dei Contra Paganos*/ The City of God Against the Pagans'. Augustine's concept is highly purposive targeting two defined goals: Establishing the reign of God on the earth and combating the Pagans. Despite the fact that the City of God is in reality Rome, and that the Pagans are in reality the Barbarians, long after his death, Augustine's ideas on war and peace and on an ideal international order took an absolutely broader scope inspiring the later conceptual and political development of the notion of just war, which imply the justification of the use of violence by Christian Powers in the name of charity and to defend the right belief. The traces of Augustine's school are clearly visible even in the 16th and 17th centuries when modern states were in the process of articulation. The normative code of *the republica Christiana* was extensively discussed and analyzed even reformulated by writers like Vitoria, Suárez, Gentili and even Grotius, who were all the precursors of natural law but strong believers in the Christian foundation of international politics. It means that until the signature of the treaties of Westphalia in 1648, the existing standard of civilization was theocratic, religious and Christian. At that time, there were other civilizations than the European one, each of them having their own standard. Among civilizations like the Chinese, Inca, Maya, Indian, all subjugated to Europe, only the Islamic civilization was present in Europe. The Muslim Ottoman empire was at the same time a major European power. Therefore, much theoretical works were consecrated to the regulation of Muslim-Christian relations. Since the Muslim and Christian standards (on Islamic standard, see Khadduri 1966) were substantially and purposively different from each other, the supremacy of one could only be decided by the demonstration of power. In the power struggle which went on for two to three centuries, the European standard finally prevailed. And so the European Christian powers imposed (at least partially) their own laws and judiciary on the European Ottoman empire (i.e. 'capitulation'). Similarly, the first European 'humanitarian' interventions took place to save Christian lives inside Muslim countries. In our days, the Augustinian approach is not completely over. Within European/-Western civilization, there are tendencies and forces which still believe in a Christian civilization excluding every other. In this respect, the attitude adopted by the German Christian-Democrats under Chancellor Helmut Kohl is an indication. The public discourse and tentative delivered and employed by the Vatican to the revival of a 'Christian Europe' after the collapse of Communism constitute yet another indication of the survival of Augustianism.

The Westphalian School: State's Rights

As previously mentioned, world-system theorists claimed that the rise of national states was a necessary condition for the expansion of capitalism. One could challenge this assumption by arguing that the real cause and purpose of Westphalia reside elsewhere. Capitalism as a system has enough potential to survive and function with or without national states. The current situation, that we are witnessing at the end of the 20th century, attest to the fact that while capitalism is rising in an unprecedented pace and intensity, the Westphalian state form is declining. One must remember, the circumstances which led to the signing of the treaties of Westphalia on 24 October 1648. These treaties were signed to put an end to the *religious* Thirty-Year-War in Europe. With the signing of the treaties of Westphalia on October 24, 1648, relations between states entered into an era of secularization. Consequently, the rules of the game transformed. Thus, religion was no longer a source of conflict (nor cooperation) among states; i.e. henceforth, states did not resort to war for religious reasons. Ironically, the basic idea of 'international' secularization came from Cardinal de Richelieu (1585-1642) a religious official personality who operationalized the concept of *raison d'état* (previously invented by Giovanni Botero in *Della Regione di Stato*, see Staatsräson 1975: chapter 1) which was in clear opposition to every other '*raisons*'; the Catholic church first of all. Henceforth, the '*stato*' can have, and has its own independent and self-sufficient reason. Richelieu's concept was a revolutionary one; because it transformed the '*stato*' from the position of *word* to position of *concept*;

and similarly from being an *act* (passif and dependant) to *action* (actif and independant). By doing this, *"raison d'état* replaced religion as the determining principle of alliance between European princes" (Watson 1992:191). Richelieu is also the originator of another concept which is one of the pillars of today's Neorealism; the *balance of power* (in his word *équilibre*) initiated with the purpose of a French anti-hegemonical alliance against the Habsburgs. Stephen D. Krasner sharply rejects the crucial importance that scholars generally attribute to the Westphalian settlement. He claims that "Westphalia was not a beginning or an end. Sovereign practices had existed hundreds of years before 1648 and medieval practices continued for hundreds of years after" (Krasner 1993:264). Pursuing his crusade against what he calls the 'conventional view', he opposes to the idea that the peace of Westphalia marks a turning point in history (ibid:235). Perhaps Krasner's critique resulted from his textual lecture of treaties and his closed approach to the date of 24 October 1648. Indeed, if one proceed to read these treaties, paragraph by paragraph, 'nation-state' or 'national interests' are not explicitly mentioned. What is true and important is to be found somewhere else: In the spirit of the Westphalia Treaties, and not necessarily in their literal stipulation. Their crucial importance must be found. The day of 25 October 1648 probably looked very much like the day of 23 October, that is not the point. The point is that Westphalia was perceived by European rulers as a *rupture;* the beginning of a new epoch. Consequently, they acted in accordance with the new rules of the game. The Westphalian settlement legitimized a Commonwealth of sovereign states, established a hierarchy of constituted states and secularized the relations between different European entities. In Hedley Bull's words "the starting point of international relations is the existence of *states*" (Bull 1985:8). But, "the kingdoms and principalities of Western Christendom in the Middle Ages were not states: They did not possess internal sovereignty because they were not supreme over authorities within their territory and population; and at the same time they did not possess external sovereignty since they were not independent of the Pope or, in some cases, the Holy Roman Emperor." (Ibid: 9). All these things did not happen in one day, but the motto and the direction went toward the creation of 'nation state', as the new actor of international politics. Furthermore, in a sense, Westphalia was the prolongation and one of the consequences of Renaissance and modernism which started in the Middle Ages and resulted in *separation* (i.e. State and Church) and *individualization.* In other words, the secularization of interstate relations was accomplished and reinforced by the internal secularization within the Western states. The separation of church and state, the emergence of modernity and scientism, the triumph of nihilism and the "death of God".

Once the idea of *states* and *nations* (State-Nation) had settled, philosophers and jurists tried to formulate a new corpus of laws in order to regulate relations between states. It is true that at the beginning, some of them, e.g. Suárez and Gentili were inspired by Christian values, but gradually, lay values became more and more relevant to this purpose; dominating finally the normative sphere of international law - especially after the French revolution in 1789. In this respect, Vattel's *The Law of Nations* and Abbe de Malby's *Droit public de l'Europe* can be mentioned among many others. Yet, Grotius (1583-1645) stands as being the one who "by insisting that natural law was the principal source of the law of nations, and that this law would remain valid even if God did not exist, implied that international society might ultimately dispense with Christian foundations. It is true that the search for principles on which Catholic and protestant states might find a basis for coexistence led necessarily in the direction of secular principles" (Bull 1985:28-29).

The Grotian school introduced a new path in the field of international political theory as well. In early modern Europe, apart from the Augustinian school and papal ambitions which became marginalized after all, two other schools stand: The Westphalian, which is the central purpose of this rubric, based on sovereignty of states and princes, and, the Kantian which will be discussed in the following. Against these two doctrines:

> Grotius advanced the third position, that states and the rulers of states in their dealings with one another were bounded by rules and together formed a society. On the one hand princes and peoples had indeed become independent of one another and of the central authorities and were sovereign. But on the other hand they were not in a state of nature, but part of the great society of all mankind (Bull 1992:72).

As we know, it was from the Grotian project that, many centuries later, sprang the League of Nations and the United Nations.

The study of both *political* evolutions in Western societies from the Westphalian epoch until our days, parallel to its *normative* evolution, show that there is a logic and a natural development where both evolutions accompanied each other. We are not pretending that everything in this respect is perfect; and that painting a sublime picture of the West is alien to our discernment. The West is responsible for colonialism and illegitimate actions around the world (colonial wars, Holocaust, the Vietnam war, etc.). However, this has nothing to do with the harmonious and endogenous 'civilized' evolution of the West. The answer to Western cruelties must be found elsewhere. The reality is that the internal secularization within Western societies, naturally and logically, led to international secularization. Undoubtedly, there is an inherent logic between Locke, Rousseau, Voltaire, Kant and Grotius´ writings and the *Universal Declaration of*

Human Rights of 1948 as well as every other Declaration (e.g. the Vienna Declaration of 1995) following this one. The cumulative political and ideational evolution is significantly missing in other civilizations and cultures. The secularization of international relations did not prevent inter-European wars nor did it reduce their scope. European powers, constituted in nation-states, continue to conduct war among themselves, however it is no longer for the glory of God or even for the sake of the promotion of lay values and ideals, but for reasons of state i.e. *national interests* and *national security*. The Napoleonic Wars were intended to defend and spread the achievements of the 1789 Revolution, i.e. the *Declaration of Rights of Man and Citizen* and the application of the lay trinity; *liberté, égalité* and *fraternité*. This was the *ideational* purpose of Bonaparte. Most likely, he had a set of *intentional* purposes which was the inspiration of a world empire under French leadership.

Between the two World Wars, the *ideology* became the dominant factor in world conflicts and cooperation. Four types of idelogies occupied the western scene: Nazism, Fascism, Marxism-Leninism and Liberalism. While the two first were defeated by the two latter, the two victorious camps (Liberalism and Leninism) started a *tous azimuts* struggle which went on until the fall of the Berlin wall in 1989. It is common knowledge that the ideological struggle was not religious but secular.

After the disintegration of the Soviet-Russian empire and with this the end of the ideological era, some scholars tend to argue for the 'end of history' while others predict the upcoming of clashes between Civilizations. Clashes of Civilization is a new concept based on the assumption that the core of future conflicts and struggles will no longer be between 'nation states' nor on 'national interests' or national security, but that the world will be witnessing a confrontation between *Civilizations;* three of which are predicted to play a major role in the future: Western civilization on the one side and Islamic and Confucianist (together) on the other.

The Kantian School: Human Rights

The 'Kantian School' is considered here as a metaphor for an accumulation of ideas beginning with the perpetual and democratic peace - republicanism - and ending with human rights, cosmopolitanism and universalism. We argue that after the end of the cold war, parallel to and because of the accelerating process of globalization, the world system is moving towards a new phase which is shaped mostly by the Kantian project. This transformation is not yet completed, the transition is continuing. However, a considerable number of concordant facts which confirm the direction of the movement do exist. The first indicator is translated by the visible pressure against the Westphalian model and with it, the pressure against the classical concept of sovereignty of states. The pressure is overwhelming and is exercised simultaneously at the system level (globalization), at the actor's level (citizen and non-governmental organizations: Green Peace, Amnesty etc.); and at the level of UN in the form of humanitarian intervention. Following the most recent development in the domain of humanitarian intervention, some states do intervene militarily on the territory of other states without the consent of the latter and without a mandate from the UN's Security Council (e.g. NATO's intervention of March-April 1999 in ex-Yugoslavia). Georg Sørensen argues that sovereignty is constituted of two elements: Constitutive and regulative. He believes that the "constitutive core of sovereignty: Constitutional independence possessed by states which have territory, people, and government remains stable" (Sørensen 1998:8). What is changing is the regulative element consisting of the question: "how do states go about dealing with each other in war and peace, how do they get to be members of the society of states..." (p. 9). We believe that Sørensen is right on this point; thus the Kosovo war (subsequent to Sørensen's article) demonstrates that under certain circumstances even the constitutive component of states' sovereignty could be subject to imposed restrictions by an exogenous intrusion, in the name of humanitarian intervention. In general, such restrictions are limited in time and space. The 'safe heaven' and 'non-fly-zone' in north and south Iraq respectively since 1991, and UN's 'mandatory' administration of the Kosovo province since 1999, are among the examples of restricted constitutive elements of sovereignty of the target states. These geographically limited restrictions will ease once international society's requirements - expressed explicitly by the UN Security Council – are met. In the same spirit, the Kantian idea of republicanism increasingly attracts the attention of scholars and citizens in general. One scholar describing this new trend states that "in republican terms, society is neither an artifice of relations among self-regarding agents nor a jointly negotiated device to advance their several interests...In the world of states, independence is provisional and limited; sovereignty must be divisible, or there can be none." (Onuf 1998:5). The second indicator is visible in the extension of democratization world-wide. This topic is already discussed and needs no further discussion. However, since the Kantian perpetual, democratic peace is conditioned by democratization, we shall conclude that the extensive democratization will ultimately lead to a more peaceful world. Furthermore, the past few years´ extension of democracy suggests the possibility that a new epoch is at hand. This has forced us to reconsider the concept of sovereignty. "No longer does it suffice to say that states' governments individually or collectively engage in acts of 'inadmissible intervention, and that these acts are directed against the governments of other states" (ibid:140). The fourth indicator, of course, is the promotion of human rights in a world scale with many ramifications among which the most recent and equally most interesting development took place in the domain of sanctioning crimes against humanity. The 'Pinochet affair' illustrates that the change is not limited to specific spheres; it touches even the normative framework of *diplomatic* immunity which so far has been among the most stable and less flexible set of rules. General Pinochet, late president of Chile and senator for lifetime was arrested in London for 'the crimes he had committed while he was in power'. He was denied diplomatic immunity by Britain's highest court (Court's judgment of 28 October 1998 and of 24 March 1999). Prior to this event, the *International Criminal Court* was established in Rome on 17 July 1998. This Court has the power to exercise its jurisdiction over persons for the most serious crimes of international concern (article 1). It is true that the case of Pinochet is not yet settled definitively (April 1999), nor is the ratification of the Statute of Court completed (especially because of USA's reluctance). Nevertheless, these events indicate that a new epoch in international politics is on its way.

The above-mentioned indicators and many other factors (e.g. ecology, gender, prohibition of torture) attest that the change of the international system is not limited to a merely quantitative transformation resumed by the move from a bipolar to a (perhaps) unipolar system. In fact, the change is also qualitative and value oriented. In another form, "concern for a common 'standard of civilization' raises the possibility of a contemporary cosmopolitan culture" (Gong 1984:92). A such culture and the new values discussed in the above are the pillars of the new standard of Civilization.

Conclusion

It was argued that with globalization a new era is initiated in international politics and in the life and destiny of humanity at large. In this connection, it has been demonstrated that the most significant consequences of globalization are illustrated by: 1) The 'global economy' especially in its financial dimension which we called 'global capital' and; by 2) the emergence of a global civilization. We analyzed both and came to the conclusion that despite the fact that - in different degrees and different ways - both originate from the same source, each of them is obeying its own internal logic and following its own dynamic. While the logic of the global capital is characterized essentially by the individualistic and corporate profit and self interest, global civilization is designed to provide a good life for humanity. The contradiction between these two avenues is not yet resolved. And presumably, it will take a long time until a possible solution will be found. However, in so far as both are evolving, it seems plausible that they meet each other somewhere on the route. World-system theorists predict a catastrophic scenario due to the ultimate contradictions within the capitalist system. The 'Kantians' are more optimistic, believing in the positive effects of democratization which shall ultimately succeed in regulating the existing unregulated global capital. For the task of explaining the global economy, we found the world-system theory sufficiently fruitful; however one-sided and deterministic. Therefore, we used it as a 'theory' and not as an 'ideology'. In order to explain the global civilization, we propose a new definition for civilization: Inspired by Fernand Braudel's notion of time, we introduced some corrections for the sake of fitting it into our purpose. We believe that the distinction between 'Civilization' and 'civilization' is important to understand the evolution of civilizations, and not least to test the vitality of a civilization. Finally, we arrived at the conclusion that in a globalizing world and in the absence of any other civilization which might correspond to the proposed definition, talking about *different* civilizations is a discourse belonging to the pre-globalization era.

References

Ames, Roger T. (1997), 'Continuing the Conversation on Chinese Human Rights', in *Ethics and International Affairs*, vol. 11, pp. 177-204.

Arrighi, Giovanni (1997), 'Globalization, State Sovereignty, and "Endless" Accumulation of Capital', Fernand Braudel Center.

Barber, Benjamin (1996), *Jihad vs. McWorld: How the Planet Is Both Falling Apart and Coming Together - And What This Means for Democracy*, USA, Ballantine Books.

Braudel, Fernand (1993), *A History of Civilizations*, New York, Penguin Books.

Braudel, Fernand (1979), *Civilization matérielle, économie et capitalisme Xème-XVIIIème siècles: Le Temps du Monde*, Paris, Armand Colin.

Brewer, Anthony (1980), *Marxist theories of imperialism*, London, Routledge & Kegan Paul.

Bull, Hedley (1985), *The Anarchical Society*, London, Macmillan.

Bull, Hedley (1992), 'The importance of Grotius in the Study of International Relations', in H. Bull, Benedict Kingsbury (eds), *Hugo Grotius and international relations*, Oxford, Oxford University Press.

Castells, Manuel (1996), *The Rise of the Network Society*, Oxford, Blackwell.

Castells, Manuel (1997), *End of Millennium*, Oxford, Blackwell.

Clark, Ian (1997), *Globalization and Fragmentation*, Oxford, Oxford University Press.

Cox, Robert W. (1996), 'A Perspective on Globalization', in James H. Mittelman (ed.), *Globalization: Critical Reflections*, Boulder, Lynne Reinner.

Cox, Robert W. (1998), 'Civilization and the 21st Century: Some Theoretical Considerations', Paper prepared for the Third Pan-European International Relations Conference, Vienna, September 16-19.

Donnelly, Jack (1989), *Universal Human Rights in Theory & Practice*, Ithaca, Cornell University Press.

Donnelly, Jack (1998), 'Human rights. A new standard of civilization?', in *International Affairs*, vol. 74, no. 1 January.

Falk, Richard (1995), 'On Human Governance: Toward a New Global Politics', Cambridge, Polity Press.

Falk, Richard (1999), 'The Pursuit of International Justice: Present Dilemma and An Imagine Future', in *Journal of International Affairs*, vol. 52, no. 2 Spring, pp. 409-441.

Fukuyama, Francis (1992), *The End of History and the Last Man*, London, Hamish Hamilton.

Galloway, Jonathan F. (1999), 'Is It The Global Economy, Stupid?', paper presented at the 40th Convention of International Studies Association, Washington DC, February 16-20.

Giddens, Anthony (1971/1990), *Capitalism and modern social theory*, Cambridge, Cambridge University Press.

Giddens, Anthony (1990), *The Consequences of Modernity*, Cambridge, Polity Press.

Giddens, Anthony (1991), *Modernity and Self-identity: Self and Society in the late Modern Age*, Cambridge, Polity Press.

Giddens, Anthony (1999), *The Third Way*, Cambridge, Polity Press.

Gong, Gerrit W. (1984), *The Standard of "Civilization" in International Society*, New York, Oxford University Press.

Guizot, François (1846/1997), *The History of Civilization in Europe* (translated by William Hazlitt), London, Penguin Classics.

Halliday, Fred (1995), *Islam and the Myth of Confrontation*, London, I.B. Tauris.

Hassner, Pierre (1993), 'Beyond Nationalism and Internationalism', *Survival*, 35 (2).

Hirst, Paul (1997),'The global economy: myths and realities' in *International Affairs*, 73, 3, pp. 409-425.

Holloway, John (1996), 'Global Capital and the National State' in Werner Bonefeld and John Holloway (eds), *Global capital, National State and the Politics of Money*, London, Macmillan.

Huntington, Samuel P. (1996), *The Clash of Civilizations and the Remaking of World Order*, New York, Simon & Schuster.

Khadduri, Majid (1966), *The Islamic Law of Nations: Shaybani's Siyar*, Baltimore.

Khatami, Mohammad (1997), *Bim-e Mowj* (Fear of the Wave), Tehran, Simây-e Javân.

Khatami, Mohammad (1995), *Az 'Donyây-e Shahr' Tâ 'Shar-e Donyâ'* (From 'World City' to 'City World'), Tehran, Ney.

Khomeini, Ruhollah (1971), *Hukumat-e Eslâmi* (Islamic Governance), Najaf, Nehzat-e Eslâmi.

Khomeini, Ruhollah (1989), *Vasiyyat Nâmeh-e Siyâsi* (Political Testament), Tehran.

Krasner, Stephen D. (1993), 'Westphalia and All That', in Judith Goldstein and Robert O. Keohane (eds), *Ideas and Foreign Policy*, Ithaca, Cornell University Press pp. 235-264.

Mahathir bin Mohammad (Prime Minister of Malaysia) (1997), *Declaration* (annual meeting of Association of the South East Asian Nations, 28 July).

Morin, Edgar (1987), *Penser l'Europe*, Paris, Gallimard.

Morin, Edgar (1993), *Terre-Patrie*, Paris, Seuil.

Morin, Edgar and Samir Naïr (1997), *Une Politique de Civilization*, Paris, Arléa.

Mozaffari, Mehdi (1998), 'Can A Declined Civilization Be Reconstructed? Islamic *civilization* or *civilized* Islam?', in *International Relations* (UK), vol XIV, no. 3, December.

Onuf, Nicholas G. (1998), *The Republican Legacy in International Thought*, Cambridge, Cambridge University Press.

Saint Augustine (1966), *The City of God Against the Pagans*, London, William Heinemann Ltd, 6 vols.

Simmons, Beth A. (1999), 'The Internationalization of Capital', in Herbert Kitschelt (et al. ed.), *Continuity and Change in Contemporary Capitalism*, Cambridge, Cambidge University Press.

Soros, George (1998), *The Crisis of Global Capitalism*, New York, Public Affairs.

Sørensen, Georg (1998), 'Sovereignty: Change and Continuity in a Fundamental Institution', Aarhus, Department of Political Science.

Strange, Susan (1990), 'The name of the game' in Nicholas Rizopoulos (ed.), *Sea changes: American Foreign Policy in World Transformed*, New York, Council of Foreign Relations.

Strange, Susan (1996), *The retreat of the state: the diffusion of power in the world economy*, Cambridge, Cambridge University Press.

Toynbee, Arnold J. (1948), *Civilization on Trial*, New York, Oxford University Press.

Wallerstein, Immanuel (1996), *Historical Capitalism with Capitalist Civilization*, London, Verso.

Wallerstein, Immanuel (1997), 'Liberalism and Democracy: Frères Ennemis?', Rijksuniversiteit Leiden.

Waltz, Kenneth N. (1979), *Theory of International Politics*, Reading, Massachusetts, Addison-Wesley.

Watson, Adam (1992), *The Evolution of International Society*, London, Routledge.

3 Globalization, Democratization and Social Movements: A Neo-Parsonian Perspective

JAMES R. SCARRITT

As we approach the new millennium, scholars and citizens are thinking more seriously than ever about strategies for dealing with the challenges of the globalizing world, as indicated by the title of this book. Prominent among these challenges are controlling corporate globalization without severely reducing productivity; sustaining and consolidating newly established, fragile democracies; and facilitating attainment of the goals of the many non-governmental organizations and social movements that have recently arisen in response to or as parts of globalization and democratization, while managing the conflicts that they have generated. The purpose of this paper is to present a theoretical framework that can be used to develop and test hypotheses about the interrelations among these phenomena in a manner that will lead to the formulation of strategies to deal with the multiple challenges of globalization in the new millennium. The paper is a "think piece" that attempts to begin the ambitious task of addressing some of the major issues of the new millennium in a new and different way, a task that the author plans to continue in later publications. In this "first cut," hypotheses, examples and citations are drawn disproportionally from Africa, the area of my empirical research; later publications will attempt to expand the application of the framework more systematically to a global scope.

Theoretical Framework

For a long time I have applied an evolving theoretical framework, based on my interpretation of the later work of Talcott Parsons, to various cases of African political and socioeconomic change (Scarritt, 1971, 1972a, 1972b,

47

1976, 1979, 1980, 1985, 1986, 1996). In this framework the capitalist world-economy, international political forces, and the cultural, stratification, political, and economic subsystems of societies interact in terms of both facilitative energy and regulative information. Within the global system and societies, the economy is the most energy intensive subsystem, and culture is the most information intensive, while politics and stratification are in between, combining energy and information more evenly. But the continuous interaction between information and energy occurs in all subsystems of the global system and societies and in the specific structures within them (analyzed in terms of four structural levels: values, norms or rules, collectivities, and roles), and provides the dynamic force that constantly changes some of these structures while maintaining others. The mutual interdependence of energy and information can be understood through an analogy with a home heating system in which the thermostat provides the information and the furnace provides the energy; neither can keep the home at a given temperature without the other. Information without energy lacks effectiveness, while energy without information lacks direction. Thus the maintenance or change in global, societal and communal structures requires a variety of information-energy exchanges. Contrary to mainstream criticisms of the Parsonian framework (summarized in Robertson and Turner, 1991, pp. 8-11 and largely refuted in subsequent chapters of that volume), I contend that this approach is not too abstract for application to the real world, conservative, value-deterministic, or biased in favor of societal integration and against global economic power. Instead, the framework conceives of the globalizing world and the many types of smaller units of which it is comprised as constantly changing in response to multiple and complex information-energy exchanges in which causality flows in both directions. Alexander (1983), who is not uncritical, emphasizes multidimensionality as the most important characteristic of Parsons' theorizing.

Although specific institutions--sets of rules (information) for the behavior of collectivities and occupants of roles within them (energy) in specific structural contexts--were always part of my framework, they have become more important in it in the course of my collaboration with Shaheen Mozaffar (Scarritt and Mozaffar, 1990, 1995, 1999; Mozaffar and Scarritt, 1999). Thus the current version of my theoretical framework is in the tradition of socially embedded institutionalism, which argues that institutional variables are necessary but not sufficient in social explanation because their nature, stability and consequences are to a significant degree dependent on more macro level social variables (Koelble, 1995, p. 232) as well as on the degree to which individual behavior is congruent with institutional rules. Institutions are not always the purposeful creations of individuals, as conventionalists assume (Grafstein, 1992), but there is a significant element of conscious design in them, and thus participants in them are capable of positive or negative learning with regard to the attainment of goals (Bermeo, 1992). Designed institutions will be reinterpreted as they operate in a given social structure as explained below, but even so, institutional creation-stabilization (institutionalization) and change are often less difficult than substantial economic development and almost always less difficult than fundamental social transformation. Previous "new institutionalist" theorizing has included a wide range of institutional variables, and social embeddedness has been conceived in equally diverse ways (Immergut, 1998; Knight, 1992; North, 1990; Thelen and Steinmo, 1992), but the concept of information-energy exchange has not been employed. These exchanges occur within stable institutions, by definition in relatively stable forms, and within weak, partially formed institutions in various degrees of instability; they also occur in various forms in institution-social context relationships.

The most general assumptions about change that emerge from this framework are the principles of inertia and increased indeterminate conflict: forces pushing for change must overcome the natural tendency for social structures and institutions to remain the same, and the attempt to do so will increase conflict in which the outcome is indeterminate in the medium as well as the short run because the complex system of multiple relevant information-energy exchanges takes time to establish a clear and stable direction of change. Examples of the actualization of these assumptions will be given in subsequent sections of this chapter. The sources of change may be internal or external to societies or both at the same time; external sources include the global system, regional organizations, and other societies. For example, democratization in Africa, both in the 1960s and the 1990s, has involved significant external diffusion, although internal forces have been more important in the latter period. (I argue below that internal forces must be predominant in democratic consolidation.) Students of diffusion have long recognized that this process involves adaptation of diffused structures to the receiving societies, often involving substantial reinterpretation of these structures, so that the interaction between information and energy within and among subsystems of societies and the institutions of which they are composed, as well as in their relations with the global system, will determine the fate of diffused institutions. This is a third (slightly less) general assumption emerging from the framework, and examples of its actualization will also be given below.

In this framework democracy is a set of characteristics that may be present in varying degrees in global, societal and community political subsystems, and thus it involves the relatively even balance between energy and information that characterizes politics. Globalization, NGOs (community-based, national or international) and social movements (ethnopolitical, specific interest or identity, or class-based) involve the interaction among several subsystems (stratification, economy, politics and culture) and structural levels, and thus contain varying energy and information balances: globalization, most NGOs, and class-based movements are more energy intensive, while ethnopolitical and other identity movements, some NGOs, and some specific interest movements are more information intensive. The utility for causal analysis of these ways of defining these central concepts will now be discussed, starting with globalization because it is the broadest but least clearly defined of these concepts, potentially encompassing all of the others. The causal roles of each of these phenomena in the interactions among them will be discussed in subsequent sections. The conclusion will brief discuss the implications of these possible combinations of causal relationships for developing a strategy to deal with the challenges of the new millennium.

Globalization, according to Randall and Theobald (1988, pp. 235-42), has three central dimensions: economic, cultural, and political. The economic dimension is often viewed as having causal primacy (Baker, Epstein and Pollin, 1998; Hoogvelt, 1997; Mittelman, 1996, p. 3). It involves "the organization of production and consumption of goods and services at the global level ... achieved mainly through transnational corporations" (Randall and Theobald, 1998, p. 235), and it "...is a market induced, not a policy-led process" (Mittelman, 1996, p. 3). The globalization of finance capital is often considered to be the most advanced aspect of the economic dimension (Hoogvelt, 1997), but there is a lively debate about how far various dimensions of globalization have advanced (reviewed in Hirst and Thompson, 1996). The cultural dimension has been, by and large, the result of "developments in communication and information technology" (Randall and Theobald, 1998, p. 237). It reinforces the economic dimension through creating a consumer culture, but also creates "access to a range of social and cultural experiences with which the individual or group may never have the opportunity to engage" (Held, 1995, p. 123) and may broaden global dialogue (Bhagwati, 1997, p. 278). Finally, the political dimension includes global awareness and networking around issues, "a proliferation of international or governing regulatory organizations and of international regimes," and "a trend toward the globalization of social classes and social movements" (Randall and

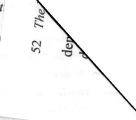
Theobald, 1998, pp. 239-40). These dimensions and their do not comprise a single smooth or cumulative process, b dialectical relationships with one another in which universa trigger particularistic responses and *vice versa*. This u conception weakens but does not eliminate the causal economic dimension.

According to this definition, which will be employed here in a slightly modified form, globalization involves a much wider variety of information-energy exchanges than democratization does: the energy of the economic dimension is provided primarily by capitalist transnational corporations and competition among them, and is guided by capitalist values and norms; but this energy comes up against, in varying degrees, alternative energy from national governments, ethnopolitical, local community, specific interest and identity, or class-based social movements, guided by a variety of alternative values and norms. These information-energy exchanges cross over the boundaries of all four subsystems of the global system and societies. Democratization and various types of social movements are omitted from the definition of globalization used here, so that their empirical relationships with it can be examined.

The definition of democracy employed in this framework is purely procedural but not minimalist. Democracy is "a configuration of ... rules which specify that: (a) access to public offices in which government power is vested must be determined by *contestation* at regular intervals, (b) the outcome of this contestation (who will occupy public offices and the policies they will formulate and implement) must be determined by the free broad-based *participation* of all eligible citizens and some form of majority rule, (c) *civil and political liberties* of citizens must be guaranteed against government infringement to ensure that they can freely join and establish civic associations and political groups, express and debate a diversity of ideas and issues, and choose public officials" (Scarritt and Mozaffar, 1995, pp. 192-3). These rules must apply at both the national and local, grass-roots levels and in the linkages between them (Randall and Scarritt, 1996, p. 21; Diamond, 1999, pp. 121-49; Crook and Manor, 1995; Rondinelli, 1981; Smith, 1979, 1996; Vengroff and Umeh, 1997). Diamond (1999, pp. 10-12) calls this liberal democracy. It is my belief that democratic procedures are necessary but not sufficient to bring about policies promoting greater equality, domestically and internationally, but of course this belief is not part of the definition of democracy employed here. It does justify the utility of a more than minimalist procedural definition, however. More than minimal democratic procedures--specifically contestation over policy outcomes as well as public offices, and local as well as national

..ocratic procedures--are necessary for greater equality. Since .emocracy is not sufficient to produce this outcome, equality or policies promoting it cannot be included in the definition of democracy, and democracy is entirely within the political subsystem of the global system, societies, and local communities. Democratic political institutions, like all institutions, involve information-energy exchanges. Democratic values and norms provide information that guides democratic institutional practices, while the latter provide the energy necessary to sustain the former.

Transitions from authoritarianism to democracy generally create unconsolidated democracies (Sandbrook, 1996), which tend to have high levels of conflict because significant actors' commitments to democracy are widely known to be contingent on their preferred outcomes, leading to mutual distrust and fear that loss of power will be permanent. In a number of countries, transitions are recent and have not taken place in the type of socioeconomic setting generally thought to favor democracy, and emerging political institutions frequently manifest instability in various forms. These transitions are being sustained in varying degrees by the operation of new democratic institutions; elections vary in the degree to which they are free and fair, political rights vary in the degree to which they are protected, etc. Although there are a number of definitions of democratic consolidation, most of them are similar in many respects. A synthetic and useful definition derived from the literature (Bratton and van de Walle, 1997, p. 235; Diamond, 1999, pp. 65-72; Gunther, Diamandouros and Puhle, 1995, pp. 3, 9; Higley and Gunther, 1992, pp. 3-8; Linz and Stepan, 1996, pp. 5-6; Linz, Stepan, and Gunther, 1995, pp. 78-9, 83-4; Przeworski, 1991, p. 26; Przeworski *et. al.,* 1995, pp. 107-9; Shin, 1994, pp. 144-6; Valenzuela, 1992, pp. 58-70; Whitehead, 1989, p. 79) is relatively high institutionalization of democracy (all significant actors accept the legitimacy of the various democratic rules of the game, act in accordance with them, and expect to continue doing so), and the absence of anti-democratic institutions. Consolidation is an ideal type, but the potential for consolidation is a variable, although this distinction is ignored by critics of the concept of consolidation such as O'Donnell (1996). Democratic consolidation is usually followed by democratic persistence, although it may also be followed by de-consolidation (Gunther, Diamandouros and Puhle, 1995, pp. xiii, 3, 413; Przeworski *et al.,* 1995, p. 11; Schmitter 1995b, p. 15).

The third focus of this analysis is on NGOs and social movements rather than on the broader concept of civil society (which can be defined in a variety of ways; see White, 1996) because the former are the components of civil society that are most explicitly oriented toward change and thus most active and effective in relations with globalization and democratization. There is no satisfactory term that includes these two components but excludes less change oriented components; thus the separate terms NGOs and social movements are employed, even though they are seen as generally acting in very similar ways in the relationships that are discussed below.

As Fisher (1998, p. 5) indicates, "The term NGO has many different meanings." Unlike many analysts, she focuses on member-serving grass roots organizations (GROs) based in local communities and nationally or regionally based grass roots support organizations (GRSOs) in developing countries, as well as on the formal and informal networks of non-governmental organizations in which they participate. She (1998, p. 5) points out that there are "probably over 200,000 ... locally based membership organizations that work to develop their own communities" in the developing world. They are linked together by formal organizational umbrella networks, "social movements that are not formally organized," or a combination of the two (80-8). These GROs and GRSOs are in turn supported by international NGOs (INGOs), based primarily in the developed world, although such support can contain elements of domination. NGOs of the same or closely related types have begun to cooperate with one another internationally, forming transnational advocacy networks (Keck and Sikkink in Meyer and Tarrow, 1998, pp. 217-28). The autonomy of domestic NGOs in developing countries from states and INGOs, as well as the autonomy of GROs from GRSOs, is crucial to the ability of all of these types of NGOs to have significant effects on globalization and democratization through the creation or reinterpretation of information and the generation of organizational energy.

The concept of social movements is employed in my framework to bring together ethnopolitical movements, "new" specific interest or identity movements, and "old" class-based movements, as they are defined in the emerging synthesis within political process theory, the predominant theoretical approach in the current literature (McAdam, McCarthy, and Zald, 1996; McAdam, Tarrow, and Tilly, 1997; Sommer, 1998; Tarrow, 1994). In spite of their different social bases and political strategies and tactics, all of these are social movements as defined by Meyer and Tarrow (1998, p. 4): "collective challenges to existing arrangements of power and distribution by people with common purposes and solidarity in sustained interaction with elites, opponents and authorities." They mobilize energy through varying combinations of organizations and both formal and informal networks in response to political opportunities (conflicts or changes within political institutions), and they utilize information in the form of new or existing "cultural frames" to attract followers and advocate political and social change. Successful movements create new political opportunities. This entire process clearly involves complex energy-information exchanges. Social movements vary significantly, both among states and within a given state, in the extent to which they are institutionalized and the extent to which they cooperate with the state.

More or less peaceful and institutionalized competition among ethnopolitical movements--which have a base in ethnic identity but are, like all social movements, constantly molded by political interaction with one another and the state--has been pervasive in post-independence Africa south of the Sahara and common in other parts of the developing world, and violent ethnopolitical conflict, although less frequent in most areas, has had devastating consequences for many of the participants. The Minorities at Risk project (Gurr, 1993; Gurr *et al.*, 1993) designates several types of ethnopolitical groups that generate movements through political action: the most important are communal contenders who compete, within shifting multiethnic coalitions, for political power and economic gain within accepted state boundaries, and ethnonationalists who want autonomy or changed boundaries. The latter are much more likely to be involved in violent conflict (for Africa, see Scarritt and McMillan, 1995) because demands for autonomy or independence are often a last resort strategy for relieving repression (Mozaffar and Scarritt, 1999). In some countries one-party or military regimes reduced at least the primarily peaceful protest associated with communal contention, while these types of regimes almost always exacerbated violent ethnonationalist rebellion. As discussed below, ethnopolitics can be viewed as an independent causal force, as a tactical tool employed in pursuit of class interests or political power, or as some combination of these two positions (Bates, 1983; Dornbos, 1991; Kasfir, 1979; Saul, 1979, pp. 391-420). As indicated above, ethnicity is information intensive, consisting of identities formed by one's own group and outsiders. Ethnopolitics is less so, not only because of its substantial political component, but also because ethnopolitical groups react to their position in the stratification system--whether privileged or disprivileged--and one aspect of this position is economic.

Among the many types of specific interest or identity movements, environmental, labor and anti-poverty, women's, population, human rights, and democracy movements are especially relevant to globalization and democratization. These movements are found in most developing countries, but their strength varies significantly among regions and among countries within each region. Generally speaking, they are weakest in Africa, but their strength there has varied over time as well as among countries. Different types of movements within developing countries have begun to cooperate with one another around issues of globalization and democratization, although the extent of such cooperation also varies significantly among countries.

Globalization as Cause

Globalization is more often discussed as a cause than an effect. As indicated above, the economic energy of multinational corporations pursuing maximum profit and deriving legitimacy from capitalist values and norms is said to be effectively incorporating national economies into its web of interactions: financial flows, investment, trade, migration, and Structural Adjustment Programs. It is asserted that any resistance that national governments (democratic or authoritarian), NGOs, and social movements may attempt is being easily overcome, and these counter-institutions are gradually being weakened to the point of insignificance, although states may persist as agents of globalization (Ake, 1997; Held, 1991; Held and McGrew, 1993; Mittelman, 1996, pp. 2-6, 205-13, 229-37; Veseth, 1998). In the process this energy is creating, or at least strengthening the hegemony of, a global free market and a consumerist, mass media-based culture that legitimizes this system of economic interactions and isolates individuals from one another (Sklair, 1991, p. 41; Ake, 1997, p. 289; Kiley and Marfleet, 1998, pp. 3-5, 14). Ethnopolitical identities and movements, it is said, will eventually be weakened, if not completely undermined, by this overwhelming economic energy, even though it is recognized that they--along with other interest/identity and class-based social movements and GROs--are in some cases being strengthened in the short run due to globalization's weakening of the state, but also as centers of "futile" resistance to globalization.

Formal democracy, it is said, is being promoted by this globalizing economic energy and globalized media information (Randall and Theobald, 1998, pp. 242-45; Mittelman, 1996, pp. 8-9, 213-17; Diamond, 1999, pp. 49-60) for a number of reasons, but primarily because it is seen by the top executives of multinational corporations and political leaders interested in promoting corporate interests as the type of regime that is historically most compatible with capitalism and most able to assure legitimacy for global capitalist activities, especially during economic downturns. Formal democracy is also fully consolidated in countries in which most multinational corporations have their headquarters. But beyond adherence to democratic rules defined in minimalist ways, the substance of full democracy is not required for economic globalization, and is actively resisted when it interferes with corporate activities, other aspects of globalization, and the increasing inequalities that they generate (Robinson, 1996, pp. 13-72; Schwartzman, 1998, pp. 175-79).

A positive causal connection that is often alleged to exist between globalization and democratization is through the intervening variable of economic growth. A large body of literature finds a positive relationship between economic wealth (*per capita* income) and democracy, although the exact nature of this relationship is in some dispute (Londregan and Poole, 1996; Moore, 1996). Burkhart and Lewis-Beck (1994) find an essentially monotonic relationship. Lipset *et al.* (1993) find an N-shaped relationship. Muller (1997) finds an inverted U-shaped relationship, which he says is because inequality--which is negatively related to democracy--is at its peak in middle levels of *per capita* income. Przeworski and Limongi (1997), who analyze data on 135 countries between 1950 and 1990, find that democratization can occur at any level of *per capita* income but that its chances of survival increase substantially at higher levels. In the contemporary globalizing world, it is argued, economic growth--and especially a level of *per capita* income that is sufficiently high to sustain democracy--can only be achieved by accepting the prescriptions of economic globalization. It is usually admitted that these may have short-term negative effects on the poor and vulnerable in developing countries, but--it is believed--these effects can be effectively countered by safety net policies, and in the long-run economic globalization and Structural Adjustment Programs will be good for everyone (Bhagwati, 1997). This is the best strategy for economic development because globalization has made any alternative unrealistic.

Although many elements of both of these conflicting portrayals of the effects of globalization have considerable explanatory power, a more complete explanation of relationships among globalization, democratization, NGOs, and ethnopolitical, class and interest/identity movements would need to incorporate a number of additional information-energy exchanges. While the state socialist ideological alternative to free market economics and the autonomist ideological alternative to economic globalization have lost much of their former appeal to national governments and class-based movements, many countries (in contrast to certain groups within them) and hundreds of millions of people suffer from the effects of corporate globalization and feel that the globalized corporate media reject their values and norms, provoking the particularist responses from NGOs and social movements that Randall and Theobald discuss (see also Ake, 1997). Most of these responses are "non-ideological" in the sense of not being connected to a coherent set of ideas that claims to offer a comprehensive solution to global challenges, but all of them connect energy and information in clearly discernable ways that challenge the values and institutions of corporate globalization. This information is spread much more broadly and quickly thanks to the facilitation of "bottom up" as well as corporate communications by the information technology revolution that is part of globalization (Guigni, McAdam, and Tilly, 1998, pp. 235-7; Meyer and Tarrow, 1998, p. 5). It is certainly the case that the power of these challenges from national governments, interest and identity movements, and GROs is substantially decreased in some ways by the weakness of the connections among them, but it is also the case that their power is increased in other ways by this characteristic. Corporate economic globalization is far more vulnerable to a series of particularist attacks from a number of directions than it is to a coordinated assault based on a single energy-information source.

Taken together, these sources can even challenge global corporate capital's claim to provide the only path to economic growth, as will be discussed in the following sections. This is due in part to what Diamond (1999, p. 93), borrowing from Miles Kahler, calls the "orthodox paradox," the need to have a strong state to successfully implement market economic policies. Thus there are limits to the weakening of national governments by economic globalization, and weakening can be accompanied by some strengthening of states, or at least of nationalism, which is probably the strongest form of anti-globalizing information (Randall and Theobald, 1998, pp. 262-4; Held, 1991, p. 158; Veseth, 1998, pp. 35-9). Political globalization has even more ambiguous effects on national governments (Hirst and Thompson, 1995, pp. 422-37). International regulatory organizations are often viewed as reducing the power of national governments and weakening their democratic accountability, but they may also provide information and/or energy that helps strengthen national governments. Global networking around issues and the globalization of social movements can be facilitated by the multiplicity of governmental levels (Hipsher in Meyer and Tarrow, 1998, p. 155), and may challenge corporate economic globalization more than they challenge national governments.

Democratization as Cause

Although democracy can exist at global, national, and local levels, democratization has occurred and been analyzed primarily at the national level, and a recent analysis of democratic transitions in Africa suggests--correctly I believe--that their domestic political causes are more important than domestic economic or international causes, including globalization (Bratton and van de Walle, 1997). Since economic globalization has not made national governments insignificant, whether or not they are democratic will have significant consequences. Democracy, especially consolidated democracy that is present at the local and global levels as well as the national level, can have significant effects on globalization, NGOS, and various types of social movements (Sakamoto, 1994, pp. 1-5). In this section, I first examine the hypothesis that a country's past history of democracy is a major cause of democratic transition and consolidation, which emphasizes democracy as a causal force. I then turn to the analysis of the consequences of democratization for globalization, NGOs, and social movements.

The diffusion of democracy to Africa in the terminal colonial period was partial and reinterpretation was extensive (Scarritt, 1972b). Reinterpretation occurred through a variety of information-energy exchanges between weak democratic institutions and their societal environment of economic underdevelopment, inequality, and ethnopolitcial cleavages that were sometimes intense. These exchanges intensified a colonially created political culture that was and still is primarily neo-patrimonial and clientilistic, but also contains alternative democratic, egalitarian values and norms in most African countries. There is a significant element of diffusion in the current wave of democratization, and significant reinterpretation has already taken place. African economies have not experienced much economic growth or inequality reduction since independence and most will probably not experience such changes in the near future, while underlying ethnopolitical and other social cleavages have essentially remained constant and are also unlikely to change dramatically. Thus, if the probability of democratic sustainability and consolidation at the dawn of the new millennium is greater that in the 1960s--or in what Young (1996, pp. 55-7) calls the weak second wave of democratization at the end of the 1970s--when democracy was sustained for only a short time and consolidation did not occur, it is primarily because of the additional experience of democracy--usually limited democracy--in some countries in the intervening years. Political energy and various types of information can substitute to some degree for the economic energy that is not provided because of the absence of growth, and together can provide the organizational and material resources (energy), modification of behavior (energy and information) and legitimacy (information) that is needed to produce democratic consolidation (Scarritt,

1986; Scarritt and Mozaffar, 1990). The stronger and more democratic the institutions, the more likely it is that transitions can be sustained and democracy can be consolidated in the presence of economic decline and/or intense cleavages (Bienen and Herbst, 1996; Ottaway, 1997). Modified versions of this argument apply to other developing areas.

In my framework the *strength of, democracy within, and interaction among* political and social institutions is of primary importance for predicting the sustainability of democratic transitions and potential for democratic consolidation in a country. The institutions that are crucial for sustainability and consolidation because they most effectively combine the necessary energy and information are constitutional design, electoral systems and the vote-seat disproportionality that they produce, multipartyism, party strength and internal competitiveness, associational scope and strength, decentralization, and civil and political rights. This list of institutions is an attempt to include the crucial ones without increasing the number to the point at which parsimony is totally sacrificed. The significance of each of the three variables listed above within each of these institutions or among them for sustainability and consolidation potential is discussed in extensive literature that cannot be cited here. Constitutional design and electoral system are usually determined in the transition process and tend to remain stable for a period of years until they are explicitly amended, while the other institutions change more frequently and in smaller increments (are closer to continuous variables). All of these institutional variables have histories going back at least to independence, and their past values on the three variables affect their current values (Karl, 1990). The military, at least in Africa, must be removed from politics for a successful transition to democracy to take place, and it will therefore have no role in sustaining transition or affecting the potential for consolidation. Military intervention is democratic breakdown.

Reinterpretation of democracy is inevitable, but the stronger, more democratic, and more positively interrelated the crucial institutions, the less likely it is that reinterpretation influenced by neo-patrimonial political culture, class action by the wealthy, and underdevelopment will prevent democratic consolidation, although these social structural forces may delay consolidation and make it difficult even with optimal institutional development (Clapham and Wiseman, 1995). This hypothesis is in accordance with the general assumptions of my framework that are discussed above: overcoming inertia, medium-run conflict, and reinterpretation. The greater the party strength and internal competitiveness, decentralization, associational scope and strength, and civil/political rights and the longer the history of moderate multipartyism in the pre-transition period (all aggregations of yearly values), the more likely democratic transition is to be fully sustained through several elections and to lead to consolidation. The combination of relatively high levels of most or all of these variables will lead to a very high probability of sustainability and consolidation. High levels of some variables can compensate partially but not completely for low levels of others. More specifically, party strength and internal competitiveness can compensate most extensively for weaknesses in other variables, while change in constitutional design and electoral system, the level of associational scope and strength and the extent of decentralization can compensate to a lesser degree for weaknesses in other variables.

Institutional learning occurs over time (Bermeo, 1992; Przeworski *et al.*, 1996), often quickly in response to crises, affecting the consolidation process in various ways, both positive and negative. More specifically, positive learning is most likely to occur within a given constitutional design and electoral system when associations are widespread and strong, parties are strong and internally competitive, multipartyism is stable at an intermediate level, and decentralization is extensive. If consolidation is not advancing, positive learning will increase the chances for changes in the constitutional design and electoral system that will facilitate consolidation by increasing the levels of other institutional variables or reducing the impact of their low levels. Diamond (1999, pp. 192-217) finds that institutional strength and performance are the strongest predictors of democratic legitimacy, and points out (198-9) that "... habituation reshapes political norms and values to democratic institutions..." The extent of actualized (in contrast to legally guaranteed) civil and political rights is dependent on other institutional variables, but because it often involves governments' accepting democratic norms by not repressing their opponents for criticisms and hostile (but legal) actions, is an important indicator of consolidation potential (Kaballo, 1995 agrees). My framework does not assume that some countries will consolidate, but neither does it assume the opposite.

Given the predominance of internal political institutional factors in explaining democratic sustainability and consolidation, it is not surprising that the economic (growth and equality), political (almost by definition), conflict resolution, and cultural performance of consolidated democracies is superior to that of authoritarian regimes on most counts, although considerable uncertainty exists about the comparative performance of unconsolidated democracies and authoritarian regimes because of differences in definitions of concepts, methodologies, time periods, and data sources utilized in various studies (Burkhart, 1997; Diamond, 1999, pp. 77-93; Knack and Keefer, 1997; Lindenberg and Devarajan, 1993; Przeworski and Limongi, 1993; Remmer, 1996). Thus consolidating democracy is very likely to improve many aspects of performance, which in turn will support further consolidation, facilitation of social movement goals, resolution of ethnopolitical and other movement-generated conflicts, and resistance to those aspects of corporate globalization that are opposed by the elites and people of a country. Facilitation of social movements has been so extensive that some scholars refer to consolidated democracies as "social movement societies" (Meyer and Tarrow, 1998). As indicated above, consolidating national democracy involves a number of related and mutually reinforcing energy-information exchanges within the political subsystems of societies. A number of authors (Diamond, 1999, pp. 117-60; Fisher, 1998, pp. 135-57) emphasize the importance of consolidating democracy at the community level for increasing citizen participation and power and maximizing the impact of democracy on globalization, ethnopolitics and other social movements. This process involves a different, although overlapping set of energy-information exchanges, which are likely to involve overcoming the resistance of local elites in many communities.

The evidence on unconsolidated democracy's effects on government performance in general, and on responses to globalization, NGOs and social movements specifically, is very incomplete and inconclusive, but there is important evidence from the areas on which this chapter focuses that its effects are positive. First, analyses based on data from the Minorities at Risk project, both global (Gurr, 1993) and African (Scarritt and McMillan, 1995), suggest that higher levels of democracy, even if unconsolidated and involving restricted competition (such as internally competitive African one-party states), lead to peaceful ethnopolitical protest rather than violent ethnopolitical rebellion. Preliminary analysis of a recently created data set on all contemporary ethnopolitical groups in the forty-eight countries of sub-Saharan Africa (Scarritt and Mozaffar, 1999) points in the same direction. Democracy gives ethnopolitical movements more freedom to act, but also creates greater realization that they do not have to engage in the last-resort strategy of violent rebellion. Nonviolent communal contention within multiethnic coalitions, emerging out of a relatively democratic past, can facilitate democratic sustainability and consolidation, although more fully competitive elections may stimulate greater ethnopolitical conflict even in such relatively favorable circumstances. The strength of parties and related institutions will be crucial in determining the likelihood of each of these outcomes. Second, Fisher (1998) presents many examples of NGOs working effectively in new and unconsolidated democracies because national and local governments perceive that they are helpful in improving the state's legitimacy, stability, and political and economic performance.

NGOs and Social Movements as Causes

As we have seen, both globalization and democratization affect the degree and form of NGO activity and social movement mobilization; these forms of mobilization also have independent causal effects, however, they can reinterpret globalization as well as democracy. Although I omit social movements from my definition of globalization in order to investigate empirical relationships between the former and the latter, movements are included in Randall and Theobald's definition, giving globalization its dialectical nature. While I emphasize the strong political component in ethnopolitics, there is also an ethnic component, although it is not primordial or unchanging. The interaction between the two components is strongly affected by the history of an ethnopolitical group's organization and mobilization activities as well as by the type of regime in the country in which it is located (Gurr, 1993; Scarritt and McMillan, 1995). The same dual causal logic applies to class-based and specific interest or identity-based social movements; they are all anchored in both the political and (at least) one other societal subsystem and are involved in continuously changing information-energy exchanges among these subsystems. Although class is anchored in "objective" positions in the economic subsystem, class identities, as well as ethnopolitical and most other identities, are quite flexible. For example, they can change as NGOs and movements develop strategies for maximizing their gains and minimizing their losses from corporate economic globalization and democratization.

Ethnopolitical, class, and specific interest/identity movements, especially in combination with community-based GROs and supportive GRSOs, can be crucial in both the transition and consolidation stages of democratization if they are autonomous, well-organized and democratic, form broad coalitions (Sandoval in Guigni, McAdam and Tilly, 1998, pp. 194, 198; Melucci and Lyyra in *ibid.* p. 224), and engage in non-violent protest and the specific democracy-supporting activities discussed by Diamond (1999, pp. 239-50), which include monitoring, stimulating participation, civic education, and leadership selection and training. Protest, which is not emphasized by Diamond and other conventional democratization theorists because it does not indicate the moderation in the expression of demands or the strong institutionalization that they value highly (Diamond, 1999, pp. 228-31), is vitally important in providing both information about popular dissatisfaction with policies in an open and forceful way, and mobilizing energy to change these policies. Social movement mobilization has been shown to be especially effective in democratic transitions, but some authors suggest that movement demobilization tends to occur after such events as "normal" democratic institutions come into operation (Hipsher in Mayer and Tarrow, 1998, p. 154; Hipsher in Guigni, McAdam and Tilly, 1998, pp. 150-5). The latter suggests (p. 150) that movement demobilization after transitions is caused by a more favorable but not entirely favorable configuration of power, the adoption of moderate orientations by both elites and movement leaders, and the strength and density of party-movement ties, all of which limit further political opportunities for movements, weaken their organizations, modify their framing, and thus increase the perceived costs of continued mobilization. I would add the absence of support from NGOs and undemocratic organizational features of political parties to this list of obstacles that need to be overcome if social movements and NGOs are to work effectively for consolidation in the post-transition period.

GROs are especially crucial in bottom-up democratization (Fisher, 1998, pp. 15, 107), which we have seen is an essential component of consolidating deep democracy, but GRO networks and GRSOs can be important in consolidating democracy at the national level. Democracy dominated by elites is not really democracy, and NGOs and movements deepen mass participation by involving large numbers of people in contexts that are meaningful to them. The combination of ethnopolitical, class, community, and specific interest/ideology mobilization involves the largest number of people by operating in a wide variety of contexts. Fisher (1998, pp. 109-31) discusses ways in which autonomous, well-organized and democratic NGOs that are in effective networks can combine advocacy and cooperation with governments to promote democratic consolidation. Diamond (1999, pp. 228-33, 245) and Tilly (1993-94, pp. 21-2) recognize that a pluralism of democratically organized NGOs and movements deepens democracy.

All social movements do not facilitate democratic consolidation. Various types of movements, but especially ethnopolitical ones, and some NGOs can inhibit consolidation by directly opposing it, making demands that unconsolidated democracies truly cannot meet, or engaging in extensive violence (Tilly, 1993-94, pp. 19-22). I believe, as indicated above, that these are likely to be last-resort strategies for NGOs and movements, even in the uncertainty generated by unconsolidated democracies, adopted when leaders perceive them to be the only viable ones.

It is in conjunction with democratic consolidation and their activities in support of it that this combination of NGOs and movements has been most effective in resisting corporate economic globalization, although they can also resist it directly apart from democratization. For example, Mittleman (1998, pp. 861-6) describes "core strategies" of resistance to corporate globalization in the area of environmental destruction that are similar to those just discussed for democratic consolidation. As indicated above, corporate globalizers support formal democracy, as the political regime under which they believe that they can most effectively pursue their goals, and this belief is probably correct if other things are equal. More importantly, mobilization by NGOs and movements means that other things are not equal. Effective mobilization and protest by large numbers of people in a variety of contexts that are meaningful to them more than cancels out the advantages of democracy for corporate globalizers with regard to both the provision of different information and the accumulation of economic and political energy. Such mobilization will be very likely to increase short and medium-term conflict, but the more democracy is consolidated the more likely it is that conflict will be kept from becoming violent or destabilizing.

Using Multiple Information-Energy Exchanges to Develop a Strategy for Meeting the Challenges of the New Millennium

The implication of the preceding analysis is that *strategies for dealing with the challenges of the globalizing world in the new millennium must be developed through information-energy exchanges among large numbers of people acting within GROs, various types of social movements, democratic governments, and corporations*. Thus these strategies cannot come primarily from scholarly analyses. What this analysis has attempted to do is to portray the complexity of the relevant information-energy exchanges and point out some of the directions that they might take that would provide mutually reinforcing steps toward possible solutions. In concentrating on these possible positive interactions and arguing that commonly discussed obstacles can be overcome, this chapter may appear overly optimistic. There is certainly no guarantee that these obstacles will be overcome, and my framework emphasizes that increased short to medium-term conflict will almost certainly result from the pursuit of a coherent strategy. But it also emphasizes that if those favoring such a strategy can muster sufficient information *and* energy, they can overcome the inertia and active resistance that they encounter and manage the conflict associated with their efforts.

References

Ake, C. (1997), 'Dangerous Liaisons: The Interface of Globalization and Democracy', in A. Hadenius (ed), *Democracy's Victory and Crisis*, Cambridge University Press, New York, pp. 282-96.

Alexander, J. C. (1983), *Theoretical Logic in Sociology, Volume Four, The Modern Reconstruction of Classical Thought: Talcott Parsons*, University of California Press, Berkeley.

Baker, D., Epstein, G. and Pollin, R. (eds) (1998), *Globalization and Progressive Economic Policy*, Cambridge University Press, Cambridge.

Bates, R. H. (1983), 'Modernization, Ethnic Competition and the Rationale of Politics in Contemporary Africa', in D. Rothchild and V. Olorunsola (eds), *State Versus Ethnic Claims: African Policy Dilemmas*, Westview Press, Boulder, CO.

Bermeo, N. (1992), 'Democracy and the Lessons of Dictatorship', *Comparative Politics*, vol. 24, pp. 273-91.

Bhagwati, J. (1997), 'Globalization, Sovereignty, and Democracy', in A. Hadenius (ed), *Democracy's Victory and Crisis*, Cambridge University Press, New York, pp. 263-81.

Bienen, H. and Herbst, J. (1996), 'The Relationship Between Political and Economic Reform in Africa', *Comparative Politics*, vol. 29, pp. 23-42.

Bratton, M. and van de Walle, N. (1997), *Democratic Experiments in Africa: Regime Transitions in Comparative Perspective*, Cambridge University Press, Cambridge.

Burkhart, R. E. (1997), 'Comparative Democracy and Income Distribution: Shape and Direction of the Causal Arrow', *Journal of Politics*, vol. 59, pp. 148-64.

Burkhart, R. E. and Lewis-Beck, M. S. (1994), 'Comparative Democracy: The Economic Development Thesis', *American Political Science Review*, vol. 88, pp. 903-10.

Clapham, C. and Wiseman, J. A. (1995), 'Conclusion: Assessing the Prospects for the Consolidation of Democracy in Africa', in J. A. Wiseman (ed), *Democracy and Political Change in Sub-Saharan Africa*, Routledge, New York, pp. 220-32.

Crook, R. C. and J. Manor (1995), 'Democratic Decentralisation and Institutional Performance: Four Asian and African Experiences Compared', *Journal of Commonwealth and Comparative Politics*, vol. 33, pp. 309-34.

Diamond, L. (1999), *Developing Democracy: Toward Consolidation*, Johns Hopkins University Press, Baltimore and London.

Dornbos, M. (1991), 'Linking the Future to the Past: Ethnicity and Pluralism', *Review of African Political Economy*, no. 52, pp. 53-65.

Fisher, J. (1998), *Nongovernments: NGOs and the Political Development of the Third World*, Kumarian Press, West Hartford, CT.

Gasiorowski, M. J. (1995), 'Economic Crisis and Political Regime Change: An Event History Analysis', *American Political Science Review*, vol. 89, and pp. 882-97.

Grafstein, R. (1992), *Institutional Realism: Social and Political Constraints on Rational Actors*, Yale University Press, New Haven, CT.

Guigni, M. G., McAdam, D. and Tilly, C. (eds) (1998), *From Contention to Democracy*, Rowman & Littlefield, Lanham, MD.

Gunther, R. P., Diamandouros, N. and Puhle, H. -J. (eds) (1995), *The Politics of Democratic Consolidation: Southern Europe in Comparative Perspective*, Johns Hopkins University Press, Baltimore and London.

Gurr, T. R. (1993), 'Why Minorities Rebel: A Global Analysis of Communal Mobilization and Conflict Since 1945', *International Political Science Review*, vol. 14, pp. 161-201.

Gurr, T. R. *et. al.* (1993), *Minorities at Risk: A Global View of Ethnopolitical Conflicts*, U.S. Institute of Peace Press, Washington, DC.

Held, D. (1995), *Democracy and the Global Order*, Polity Press, Cambridge.

Held, D. (1991), 'Democracy, the Nation-State and the Global System', *Economy and Society*, vol. 20, pp. 138-72.

Held, D. and McGrew, A. (1993), 'Globalization and the Liberal Democratic State', *Government and Opposition*, vol. 28, pp. 261-85.

Higley, J. and Gunther, R. (eds) (1992), *Elites and Democratic Consolidation in Latin America and Southern Europe*, Cambridge University Press, Cambridge.

Hirst, P. and Thompson, G. (1996), *Globalization in Question*, Polity Press, Cambridge.

Hirst, P. and Thompson, G. (1995), 'Globalization and the Future of the Nation State', *Economy and Society*, vol.24, pp. 408-22.

Hoogvelt, A. (1997), *Globalization and the Postcolonial World: The New Political Economy of Development*, Johns Hopkins University Press, and Baltimore.

Immergut, E. M. (1998), 'The Theoretical Core of the New Institutionalism', *Politics and Society*, vol. 26, pp. 5-34.

Kaballo, S. (1995), 'Human Rights and Democratization in Africa', *Political Studies*, vol. 43, Special Issue, pp. 189-203.

Karl, T. L. (1990), 'Dilemmas of Democratization in Latin America', *Comparative Politics*, vol. 23, pp. 1-21.

Kasfir, N. (1979), 'Explaining Ethnic Political Participation', *World Politics*, vol. 31, pp. 365-88.

Kiley, R. and Marfleet, P. (eds) (1998), *Globalization and the Third World*, Routledge, London.

Knack, S. and Keefer, P. (1997), 'Does Inequality Harm Growth Only in Democracies? A Replication and Extension', *American Journal of Political Science*, vol. 41, pp. 323-32.

Knight, J. (1992), *Institutions and Social Conflict*, Cambridge University Press, Cambridge.

Koelble, T. A. (1995), 'The New Institutionalism in Political Science and Sociology', *Comparative Politics*, vol. 27, pp. 231-43.

Lindenberg, M. and Devarajan, S. (1993), 'Prescribing Strong Economic Medicine: Revising the Myths about Structural Adjustment, Democracy, Economic Performance in Developing Countries', *Comparative Politics*, vol. 25, pp. 169-82.

Linz, J. J., and Stepan, A. (1996), 'Toward Consolidated Democracies', *Journal of Democracy*, vol. 7, no.2, pp. 14-33.

Linz, J. J., Stepan, A. and Gunther, R. (1995), 'Democratic Transition and Consolidation in Southern Europe, with Reflections on Latin America and Eastern Europe', in R. Gunther, N. Diamandouros and H. -J. Puhle (eds), *The Politics of Democratic Consolidation*, Johns Hopkins University Press, Baltimore and London, pp. 77-123.

Lipset, S. M., Seong, K. -R. and Torres, J.C. (1993), 'A Comparative Analysis of the Social Requisites of Democracy', *International Social Science Journal*, vol. 136, pp. 155-75.

Londregan, J. B. and Poole, K. T. (1996), 'Does High Income Promote Democracy?' *World Politics*, vol. 49, pp. 1-30.

McAdam, D., McCarthy, J. D. and Zald, M. N. (eds) (1996), *Comparative Perspectives on Social Movements: Political Opportunities, Mobilizing Structures, and Cultural Framings*, Cambridge University Press, Cambridge.

McAdam, D., Tarrow, S. and Tilly, C. (1997), 'Toward an Integrated Perspective on Social Movements and Revolution', in M. I. Lichbach and A. S. Zuckerman (eds), *Comparative Politics: Rationality, Culture and Structure*, Cambridge University Press, Cambridge, pp. 142-73.

Meyer, D. S. and Tarrow, S. (eds) (1998), *The Social Movement Society: Contentious Politics for a New Century*, Rowman & Littlefield, Lanham, MD.

Mittelman, J. H. (1998), 'Globalization and Environmental Resistance Politics', *Third World Quarterly*, vol. 19, pp. 847-72.

Mittelman, J. H. (1996), *Globalization: Critical Reflections*, Lynne Rienner, Boulder, CO.

Moore, M. (1996), 'Is Democracy Rooted in Material Prosperity?' in R. Luckham and G. White (eds), *Democratization in the South: The Jagged Wave*, Manchester University Press, Manchester, pp. 37-68.

Mozaffar, S. and Scarritt, J. R. (1999), 'Multiple and Changing Identities: Why Territorial Autonomy Is not a Viable Option for Managing Ethnic Conflict in African Plural Societies', *Nationalism and Ethnic Politics*, vol. 25.

Muller, E. (1997), 'Economic Determinants of Democracy', in M. I. Midlarsky (ed), *Inequality, Democracy, and Economic Development*, Cambridge University Press, Cambridge, pp. 131-49.

North, D. C. (1990), *Institutions, Institutional Change and Economic Performance*, Cambridge University Press, New York.

O'Donnell, G. (1996), 'Illusions about Consolidation', *Journal of Democracy*, vol. 7, no. 2, pp. 34-51.

O'Donnell, G. (1994), 'Delegative Democracy', *Journal of Democracy*, vol. 5, no. 1, pp. 55-69.

Ottaway, M. (1997), 'From Political Opening to Democratization?', in M. Ottaway (ed), *Democracy in Africa*, Lynne Rienner, Boulder, CO, pp. 1-14.

Przeworski, A. (1991), *Democracy and the Market: Political and Economic Reforms in Eastern Europe and Latin America*, Cambridge University Press, Cambridge.

Przeworski, A. and Limongi, F. (1997), 'Modernization: Theories and Facts.', *World Politics*, vol. 49, pp. 155-83.

Przeworski, A. and Limongi, F. (1993), 'Political Regimes and Economic Growth', *Journal of Economic Perspectives*, vol. 7, pp. 51-69.

Przeworski, A. *et al.* (1996), 'What Makes Democracies Endure?', *Journal of Democracy*, vol. 7, no. 1, pp. 39-55.

Przeworski, A. *et al.* (1995), *Sustainable Democracy*, Cambridge University Press, Cambridge.

Randall, V. and Scarritt, J. R. (1996), 'Cautionary Notes on Democratisation: Lessons from India and Zambia', *Journal of Commonwealth and Comparative Politics*, vol. 34, pp. 19-45.

Randall, V. and Theobald, R. (1998), *Political Change and Underdevelopment: A Critical Introduction to Third World Politics, 2nd. ed.*, Duke University Press, Durham, NC.

Remmer, K. L. (1996), 'The Sustainability of Political Democracy: Lessons from South America', *Comparative Political Studies*, vol. 29, pp. 611-34.

Remmer, K. L. (1995), 'Theoretical Perspectives on Democratization', *Comparative Politics*, vol. 28, pp. 103-22.

Robertson, R. (1992), *Globalization: Social Theory and Global Culture*, Sage, London.

Robertson, R. and Turner, B. S. (1991), *Talcott Parsons: Theorist of Modernity*, Sage, London.

Robinson, W.I. (1996), *Promoting Polyarchy: Globalization, US Intervention, and Hegemony*, Cambridge University Press, Cambridge.

Rondinelli, D. A. (1981), 'Government Decentralization in Comparative Perspective: Theory and Practice in Developing Countries', *International Review of Administrative Sciences*, vol. 47, pp. 133-45.

Sakamoto, Y. (ed) (1994), *Global Transformation: Challenges to the State System*, United Nations University Press, Tokyo.

Sandbrook, R. (1996), 'Transitions without Consolidation: Democratization in Six African Cases', *Third World Quarterly*, vol. 17, pp. 69-87.

Saul, J. S. (1979), *The State and Revolution in Eastern Africa*, Monthly Review Press, New York.

Scarritt, J. R. (1996), 'Measuring Political Change: The Quantity and Effectiveness of Electoral and Party Participation in the Zambian One-Party State 1973-1985', *British Journal of Political Science*, vol. 26, pp. 283-97.

Scarritt, J. R. (1994), 'Nonviolent versus Violent Ethnic Political Action in Africa', in P. Wehr, H. Burgess and G. Burgess (eds), *Justice Without Violence*, Lynne Rienner, Boulder, CO, pp. 165-89.

Scarritt, J. R. (1986), 'The Explanation of African Politics and Society: Toward a Synthesis of Approaches', *Journal of African Studies*, vol. 13, pp. 18-25.

Scarritt, J. R. (1985), 'Control and Facilitation: Toward a Synthesis of Approaches to the Meaning of Development and the Explanation of Development Strategies in Africa', *Politeia*, vol. 4, no. 2, pp. 2-23.

Scarritt, J. R. (1980), *Analyzing Political Change in Africa*, Westview Press, Boulder, CO.

Scarritt, J. R. (1979), 'The Decline of Political Legitimacy in Zambia: An Explanation Based on Incomplete Data', *African Studies Review*, vol. 22, pp. 13-38.

Scarritt, J. R. (1976), 'Importancia de las estrategias de ordenacion y ritmo para lograr el cambia: lost Estados africanos de hablo inglesa', *Revista Mexicana de Sociologia*, vol. 38, pp. 559-78.

Scarritt, J. R. (1972a), 'Culture Change Theory and the Study of African Political Change: Problems of Relevance and Research Design', *The African Review*, vol. 2, pp. 553-71.

Scarritt, J. R. (1972b), *Political Development and Culture Change Theory: A Propositional Synthesis with Application to Africa*, Sage Professional Papers in Comparative Politics, III, No. 01-029, Beverly Hills and London.

Scarritt, J. R. (1971), 'Elite Values, Ideology and Power in Post-Independence Zambia', *African Studies Review*, vol. 14, pp. 31-54.

Scarritt, J. R. and McMillan, S. (1995), 'Protest and Rebellion in Africa: Explaining Conflicts Between Ethnic Minorities and the State in the 1980s', *Comparative Political Studies*, vol. 28, pp. 323-49.

Scarritt, J. R. and Mozaffar, S. (1999), 'The Specification of Ethnic Cleavages and Ethnopolitical Groups for the Analysis of Democratic Competition in Contemporary Africa', *Nationalism and Ethnic Politics*, vol. 5, pp. 82-117.

Scarritt, J. R. and Mozaffar, S. (1995), 'Toward Sustainable Democracy in Africa: Can U.S. Policy Make a Difference?', in W. Crotty (ed), *Post-Cold War Policy: the International Context*, Nelson-Hall, Chicago, pp. 190-210.

Scarritt, J. R. and Mozaffar, S. (1990), 'Change and Continuity in the British Colonial State in Africa: Integrating Theoretical Perspectives', in E. S. Greenberg and T. F. Mayer (eds), *Changes in the State*, Sage, Newbury Park, CA, pp. 149-66.

Schmitter, P. C. (1995), 'Transitology: The Science or the Art of Democratization?' in J. S. Tulchin with B. Romero (eds), *The Consolidation of Democracy in Latin America*, Lynne Rienner, Boulder, CO, pp. 11-41.

Schwartzmann, K. C. (1998), 'Globalization and Democracy', *Annual Review of Sociology*, vol. 24, pp. 159-81.

Shin, D. C. (1994), 'On the Third Wave of Democratization: A Synthesis and Evaluation of Recent Theory and Research', *World Politics*, vol. 47, pp. 135-70.

Sklair, L. (1991), *Sociology of the Global System*, Prentice-Hall, London.

Smith, B.C. (1996), 'Sustainable Local Democracy', *Public Administration and Development*, vol. 16, pp. 163-78.

Smith, B. C. (1979) 'The Measurement of Decentralisation', *International Review of Administrative Science*, vol. 45, pp. 214-22.

Sommer, H. (1998), Non-*Violent Direct Action, The Cycle of Protest, and the Demise of Apartheid, 1970-1994*, Ph.D. Dissertation, University of Colorado at Boulder.

Tarrow, S. (1994), *Power in Movement: Social Movements, Collective Action and Politics*, Cambridge University Press, Cambridge.

Thelen, K. and Steinmo, S. (1992), 'Historical Institutionalism in Comparative Politics', in S. Steinmo, K. Thelen and F. Longstreth (eds), *Structuring Politics*, Cambridge University Press, New York, pp. 1-32.

Tilly, C. (1993), 'Social Movements as Historically Specific Clusters of Political Performances', *Berkeley Journal of Sociology*, vol. 38, pp. 1-30.

Valenzuela, J. S. (1992), 'Democratic Consolidation in Post-Transitional Settings: Notion, Process, and Facilitating Conditions', in S. Mainwaring, G. O'Donnell and J. S. Valenzuela (eds), *Issues in Democratic Consolidation: The New South American Democracies in Comparative Perspective*, University of Notre Dame Press, Notre Dame, IN, pp. 57-104.

Vengroff, R. and Umeh, O. J. (1997), 'A Comparative Approach to the Assessment of Decentralization Policy in Developing Countries', in D. W. Brinkerhoff (ed), *Policy Analysis Concepts and Methods*, JAI Press, Greenwich, CT, pp. 141-58.

Veseth, M. (1998), *Selling Globalization: The Myth of the Global Economy*, Lynne Rienner, Boulder, CO.

White, G. (1996), 'Civil Society, Democratization and Development', in R. Luckham and G. White (eds), *Democratization in the South: The Jagged Wave*, Manchester University Press, Manchester, pp. 178-219.

Whitehead, L. (1989), 'The Consolidation of Fragile Democracies: A Discussion with Illustrations', in R. Pastor (ed), *Democracy in the Americas: Stopping the Pendulum*, Holmes & Meier, New York, pp. 76-95.

Young, C. (1996), 'Africa: An Interim Balance Sheet', *Journal of Democracy*, vol. 7, no. 3, pp. 53-68.

4 State Collapse and International Community

LIISA LAAKSO

Introduction

Much has been written about factors contributing to the strength of a state. In the literature these factors are ranging from military power and the size of the economy to the ability of the government to make an economic intervention in order to create room for public welfare policy. Although economic development and industrialisation are not equal with state strength, most observes seem to assume that very weak states are found in the third world (see Migdal, 1988). In its extreme it is possible to speak about collapsed states (Zartman, 1995). These situations can be related to civil wars or a continuous abuse of government power. It seems to be so that in countries lacking viable public institutions and regulations, economic and political actors rely on private survival strategies and security. Competition between these actors easily turns into a war-like-situation and central authority, if it exists, becomes predatory in nature. Thus politicised ethnicity, armed insurgencies, human rights violations, refugees and economic decline are indicators of state collapse.

For the international community the collapsed and very weak states pose major challenges. To put it simply the international community cannot interact with central government where it does not exist any more (Young 1999, 24). In this article I will outline the international background of state collapse in the third world, its implications especially with regard to humanitarian emergencies and the new international regime of political conditionality and co-operation with non-state actors as responses to the situation. As a special case I will discuss political conditionality and co-operation with collapsed states under the Lomé convention, which is an intergovernmental agreement between the European Union and African, Caribbean and Pacific countries.

71

End of the Cold War and State Collapse

End of the cold war made the vulnerability of many states in the third world more obvious than before. Although the weakness of many states was acknowledged earlier, the international system was able to sustain a facade of their sovereignty by assuring political, military, economic and development support through diverse channels. When the cold war was over, these states had very little to rely on. As noted by Marina Ottaway 'in the three preceding decades, the survival of existing states, no matter how weak or bankrupt, could be taken for granted; but today, the list of states that have either collapsed or could easily do so is growing' (Ottaway, 1999: 315). In this way state collapse is related to the legacy of the cold war.

For example the African states were important recipients of strategically motivated aid from the both blocks of the cold war during the 1970s and 1980s. The then most notable recipients of military support - Angola, Chad, Ethiopia, Liberia, Mozambique, Somalia, Sudan, Democratic Republic of Congo (DRC, the former Zaire) - form a group of very weak or collapsed states today (Clapham, 1996: 156, 159).

Besides also a new regime type has emerged as a result of weakening of many states. While ending ethnic conflicts with negotiated settlement has proved to be difficult (see Licklider, 1995), this new regime type originates in military victories of ethnic guerrilla movements. Such regimes can be found in the Democratic Republic of Congo, Rwanda, Ethiopia, Uganda and Chad (Young, 1999: 35). In contrast to the cold war era, the international community has tolerated these violent take-overs. Immediately after the military victory the international community has given important signals of support to the new regime hoping that they would be more democratic and less corrupted than the regime it replaced. However, in a context of a weak state, military victory has often led to exclusionary politics. Thus it is not surprising that these new regimes themselves are facing new ethnic or regionally based insurgencies.

State Collapse and Humanitarian Emergencies

The social and humanitarian consequences of state collapse can be drastic. The post-cold war era has also been an era of humanitarian emergencies. Raimo Väyrynen has defined humanitarian emergency as a 'profound social crisis in which a large number of people die and suffer from war, disease, hunger, and displacement owing to man-made and natural disasters, while others may benefit from it'. By utilising international statistical data he singled out 25 such humanitarian crises in 1993–95 (Väyrynen, 1996: 19). Half of them were 'complex humanitarian crises' where violence and poverty reinforced each other, and ten of these complex cases were located in Africa. These crises often result from deliberate use of coercion by the powerful groups seeking material and political gains and are characterised by economic and political 'order' in which private gains of the elites can be so high that they have no real incentives to peaceful resolution. Therefore it might well be that only external intervention can alter the crisis.

And indeed, the end of the cold war raised expectations that the ideological division of the world and self-interested involvement of superpowers would be replaced by new global thinking enabling humanitarian intervention. The 1992 United Nations Security Council sponsored military action in Somalia illustrates both the new expectations and the disillusionment. From the beginning the United States dominated the operation, whose purpose was to guarantee the delivery of humanitarian relief aid to an estimated 1.5 million people threatened with starvation. But as Peter Schraeder has noted, President Bush's decision to send over 20,000 combat troops to Somalia – as such the largest American direct military undertaking in Africa so far – stemmed from presidential politics rather than careful planning and realistic assessment of the situation (Schraeder, 1994: 12–25). More than anything else, it was Bush's interest to be remembered as a 'decisive leader' when the media delivered reports on starving children and raised public awareness of the situation in Somalia, which explains the hastily prepared operation.

Almost immediately after their landing, the American forces became involved in the clan-fighting in the country: first by defending themselves, then by efforts to isolate General Mohamed Farah Aidid's forces and finally even by attacks against that faction of the war. Less than a year after the sending of the troops, killings of American soldiers in Mogadishu raised a firestorm of criticism in the United States and led President Clinton to withdraw all American soldiers. The long-term implications of the whole Somalia experience became evident half a year later, when Clinton introduced a new United States policy toward any United Nations Security Council sponsored military operations. According to the new principles, the support of the United States for any such operations in cases of a threat to international security and urgent need for relief aid after widespread violence and interruption of democracy or a gross violation of human rights depends on 1) clear objectives, 2) the availability of sufficient money and troops, 3) a mandate appropriate to the mission, 4) a realistic exit strategy and 5) consent of the parties before the force is deployed. This is a far cry from and new kind of multilateral responsibility (Schraeder, 1995: 59).

In many respects the case of Somalia revealed a lot of the actual process that can determine the character of international actions with regard to a collapsed state and humanitarian emergency. First of all it showed that the media played an important role in the agenda setting. The Somalia case also showed that when a national (rather than international or regional) actor takes the decisive action, public awareness could become an issue of domestic politics of that actor – this time in the United States.

In the case of Rwanda, the Clinton administration not only refused to provide troops requested by Secretary-General Boutros-Ghali, but also instructed administration spokespersons to avoid labelling the conflict as genocide apparently in order to keep down the public awareness of the distress in Rwanda but also to avoid the international legal obligation to intervene in case of genocide (Jehl, 1994). The plain reality seems to be that without the support of the United States, the United Nations reactions to humanitarian emergencies have become cautious if not indifferent. The lack of sufficient resources and political will have undermined United Nations' efforts also in other conflicts. It has even been suggested that the United Nations has been motivated rather by avoidance of potential failures than concern about the suffering of the victims of humanitarian emergencies (see Barnett, 1996).

Political Conditionality

At the same time the international community has intensified the co-ordination of strategies to dealing with countries that belong to the group of weak or collapsed countries. The challenge to avoid humanitarian emergencies concerns nothing less than designing a legitimate state power in the context of serious fears about survival on the part of some groups. The emerging regime of political conditionality since the end of 1980s is a response to the increased international awareness of this challenge.

Initially political conditioning of aid according to the performance (not only need) of the recipient countries evolved from what has become to be known as 'the first generation conditionality', i.e. economic conditionality introduced by the International Monetary Fund (IMF) and joined by the World Bank (see Stokke, 1995: 7).

Among the donors conditionality is not a new invention, but has been part and parcel of development co-operation from the very beginning. Political considerations played a prominent role during the cold war. Then conditionality was often based on ideological divisions in the line of superpower confrontation. However, the competitiveness neutralised the real effectiveness of conditionality even in this limited sense and the blocks ended up supporting authoritarian regimes, which only 'ideological' reputation was that they were not supported by the other block. In any case in the form of independent action, political conditionality is not very effective, therefore the need to co-ordinate the action of different donors.

As far as their bilateral aid relationships are concerned, donors have their own strategies, interests and priorities, which cannot be controlled by others. But in multilateral settings like in the EU, for instance, different member states have to participate in the negotiation of the regime, which then at least in principle can bind their behaviour even in bilateral co-operation.

Political conditionality can legitimate development co-operation in terms of donors' priorities and extend their control over the recipient state even so that the notion of recolonisation is not far from reality (see Baylies, 1995). However, whether it is based on negative or positive sanctioning, it is hardly a tool that could solve the problems of the international co-operation with collapsed states. The most radical consequence of political conditionality is, of course, that government-to-government development co-operation with certain countries can come to an end.

But while it might be difficult to influence the policies of a state that for most of the citizens is 'criminal' or 'irrelevant' (see Widner, 1995), it is not possible to cut all the relationships with such states. The economies of such countries are part of the globalized world in many ways. Refugees and illegal trade are just examples of the negative effects for the regional and international systems. The populations living in these countries need humanitarian aid and more general development aid. Thus a decision not to co-operate with such countries is hardly a possible alternative. There is an obvious dilemma between the need of aid and responsible and effective use of this aid.

The Lomé Convention

It is useful to look at the issue of international co-operation with weak or collapsed states at a practical level. In this respect the Lomé Convention, which is a comprehensive trade and development co-operation agreement between the EU and 71 African, Caribbean and Pacific (ACP) countries, provides a good example.[1] The Convention was preceded by the Yaoundé Conventions (signed in 1963 and 1969) that regulated the relationship between the European Communities and mainly Francophone newly independent countries. The first Lomé Convention (1975-80) extended the special relationship to former British colonies. It introduced the concept of 'partnership' but not the idea of policy dialogue or political conditionality.

In practice conditionality and the question of the relationship between human rights and development co-operation was, for the first time, raised in 1976 because of the human rights violations in Uganda under the regime of Idi Amin. The Community suspended official aid channelled through the National Indicative Program (NIP) in Uganda until the end of Amin's regime, but continued humanitarian aid, such as food aid. These punitive measures went formally against the Lomé I. Thus the Commission proposed to codify the punitive measures in the Lomé II (in force 1980-1985). But this proposition was opposed by some EU member states, and the ACP countries emphasised strict separation between economic development and political considerations (see Diop 1994). Therefore, the Lomé II did not contain any political provisions either.

However, since mid 1980s the introduction of human rights in the agreements between the EU and third countries has gradually changed the content of EU's co-operation with the ACP countries. Human rights were first included as a fundamental objective of the EU in the preamble of the Single European Act in 1986 and then in the Maastricht Treaty, which stipulates the inclusion of a human rights clause to all treaties between the EU and a third country. '[T]he general objective of developing and consolidating democracy', 'the rule of law', and 'respecting human rights and fundamental freedoms' are mentioned in the Maastricht Treaty as objectives that the Community should take account in all its policies affecting developing countries (Articles 130u, 130v). (Laakso and Lehtinen 1998.)

It was for the first time in the Lomé III (1985-90) that the positive approach with regard to human rights was codified. In Article 4 and Annex 1 the attachment of both parties to human dignity and to economic, social and cultural rights is announced, but without any consideration of sanctions in the case of violations. This political dimension was further strengthened in Lomé IV (in force in 1990-) and Lomé IV bis revised in Mauritius in 1995. According to Article 5, the EU may establish financial means to promote an active human rights policy. It also provides a clause of non-execution of agreement in the case of human rights violations. Still a positive approach without any clear provision for sanctions is favoured.

Article 5 defined the principles of Lomé co-operation by announcing the relationship between human-centred development, the promotion of fundamental rights and the participation of civil society in the context of decentralised co-operation. Concepts of 'democracy' and 'the rule of law' were introduced along with 'human rights'. The respect of these fundamental principles was said to constitute the basis for EU-ACP relationship. It also stipulated that 'good governance' has to be taken into consideration along with these fundamental principles. In the case of violation, the EU could examine appropriate measures, which, however, were not specified. These political considerations were further developed in the Resolution of the Council on human rights, democracy and development in 1991. It stressed the importance of human rights, democracy, good governance and limitation of military spending. Again priority was given to a positive approach, based on an open and constructive dialogue.

Yet, despite the lack of a legal basis, there were several cases of suspension during the early 1990s. Cases of suspension include the Sudan in 1990, Equatorial Guinea, Togo, Zaire and Malawi in 1992, Gambia and Rwanda in 1994, Haiti between 1991 and 1994, and Nigeria in 1995 (European Commission, 1997). These suspensions have mainly concerned technical and financial co-operation (NIP), while trade arrangements, humanitarian assistance and the support for NGOs continued.

Finally the Lomé IV bis (1995-) instituted the formal basis for political dialogue in development co-operation. Article 366a sets for the first time a legal framework for political conditionality, i.e. the suspension of co-operation in the case of violations. If there are violations EU should start consultations and dialogue with the contracting party and together analyse the situation and its remedying. According to article 366a suspension of aid is possible only if these consultations fail. So far this introduction of negative measures has not yet led to the establishment of an effective operational framework.

In 1996, the suspension of aid to Nigeria after a military coup in the country followed formally the procedure of consultations. In this case the suspension was implemented very quickly, as it was by coincidence possible to get the parties together for formal consultations due to other meetings that had been scheduled earlier. In the case of Togo, the co-operation had already been suspended since 1992, and the success of the electoral process in June 1998 was set as a condition for the reprogramming of new funds. This condition was largely undermined by serious electoral irregularities. The current consultation process that was initiated in July 1998 under article 366a has been slow and has focused on the modalities to re-launch the democratic process.

In the current convention, there are no mechanisms or evaluation criteria for the reprogramming of suspended co-operation. Besides the government-to-government structure of the Lomé framework has led to difficult situations, like in the case of Nigeria, where the European Union had to negotiate with the military regime in order to get a permission to allocate the frozen aid to the NGOs in the country. There are no rules on the transfer of allocated funds to other purposes in the case of suspension. The suspensions in Nigeria were decided by a common position of the Council under article J.2 that is a binding document for all member states. Simultaneously the decision of the European Parliament to establish a special budget line on 'Human rights in Nigeria', targeted to the NGO co-operation, has multiplied initiatives outside the traditional government-to-government framework.

In general, the Lomé Convention is recognising the importance of non-state actors. Most importantly according to the annex LXXX of the Convention both the EU and ACP governments should provide information for civil society actors in the implementation of development co-operation programmes. In the process of negotiating the future of the Lomé Convention civil society actors have been more involved than ever before. According to the negotiating mandate of the European Commission the 'partnership' in the new convention should be extended to a wide range non-governmental actors.

This is yet a far cry from formal and legal basis for such a co-operation. Although there has been national platforms for dialogue between non-governmental actors in almost every ACP country, only in few cases have these mechanisms been developed into permanent bodies. In general the civil society actors are criticising the Lomé process for lack of access to adequate information of the Convention. A special problem in countries, which have experienced major political and economic changes, is that civil society organisations are still weak and thus face constant problems of representation (Graumans, 1999).

Co-operation with Collapsed States[2]

It is not surprising that the Lomé Convention, which is an intergovernmental agreement, does not have an answer to the question how to deal with countries lacking a legitimate central state and representative government. This, however, does not mean that there were no experiences of co-operation with such states under the Convention. The most notable case is Somalia, which has been a partner country of the EU since the Yaoundé Conventions. After the collapse of its central government in 1991, Somalia became the first country where the European Development Fund (EDF) allocated under Lomé for NIP, has been used in the absence of central government. The EU has been the major provider of development aid to Somalia since 1991.

Until the fall of Siad Barre's government the European Union attempted to support several development programmes in Somalia but constantly faced difficulties in spending the allocated funds. In January 1991 the EU closed its office in Mogadishu and from 1991 to 1993 the aid was almost exclusively humanitarian aid and emergency food aid. But already in 1992 the European Parliament was looking for ways to use the unspent funds allocated to the government of Somalia under Lomé Conventions. Finally the Commission itself took the role of the National Authorising Officer (NAO) in Somalia. European Union aid under the EDF needs to go through NAO, which represents the recipient government. Thus the Commission technically replaced the government authority and EDF funds could be used in the absence of a government. The actual work focused on rehabilitation and was carried on in areas where there was functioning local government.

While this kind of co-operation required that the European Union develop direct links with authorities that had local or regional legitimacy, the EU, as the most important donor to Somalia, also assumed a leading role in the co-ordination of international aid, because the national authorities were not able to co-ordinate the international aid. In other words the European Union developed relationships to public sector authorities both beyond and below the non-existent national government, at local and international level. In 1993 Somalia Aid Co-ordinating Body (SACB) was established. Between 1993 and 1997 the EU acted through its Special Envoy as a spokesperson for the international community - even so that some Somalis considered the Special Envoy as an 'honorary representative of Somalia' (Visman, 1999, 9).

Important forum of managing the co-operation has also been the Intergovernmental Authority on Development (IGAD), a regional body whose members are Eritrea, Ethiopia, Djibouti, Kenya, Somalia, Sudan and Uganda. IGAD's mandate was extended in 1996 to encompass conflict prevention, management and resolution. The EU is a member of the Intergovernmental Authority on Development's Partner's Forum (IPF), which has established a subcommittee on Somalia in 1998. It includes representatives from IGAD, the Organisation of African Unity (OAU), UN, League of Arab states, Italy, Egypt, Yemen, the United States and the European Union.

Somalia has not been able to ratify Lomé IV, because it has no government. However according to a special article (364A) Somalia can accede to Lomé IV when it has an internationally recognised government. However, no new EDF funds can be released to Somalia before it has a government. So far the co-operation has been based on funds that were saved before 1991. Besides the fact that Somalia does not have a government means that it is not represented in the current negotiations and nobody addresses its special problems.

Liberia is the other example of a country where the EU has adopted the role of the National Authorising Officer. In 1990 EU had to close its offices in Monrovia and most of the EU projects were soon stopped.[3] The government of Liberia which in practice represented only a faction of the previous government of Samuel Doe, did not oppose EU's proposal to take the authority of NAO as this was seen a temporary arrangement. Official recipient of the aid according to the arrangement was the 'people of Liberia' instead the state (Brusset, 1999).

Angola is the third example of a conflict-ridden country, but in contrast to Somalia and Liberia, Angola has had an internationally recognised central government. Yet a large part of the country has not been under its control. Angola has suffered from internal conflict since its independence in 1975. It signed the Lomé convention in 1985, but the conflict situation in the country has prevented it from defining and implementing a clear development policy. It is not surprising that the main emphasis of EU's development co-operation has been on the humanitarian assistance. As a matter of fact Angola has a record of being one of the most poorly performing recipients of development aid: the government simply has not been capable to use the funds allocated to development projects.

In spite of Angola's poor performance, after the signature of the Lusaka Protocol in November 1994, which marked until then the most promising peace process in Angola, the EU substantially increased its aid to the country. It became one of the major recipients of EU aid. The intention of course was to support the peace process. The bulk of this aid constituted from humanitarian aid, food aid and rehabilitation projects. In it's the humanitarian co-operation the EU worked mainly through international NGOs. When the situation in the country deteriorated again in 1997, this aid has continued, but most of the development projects have been postponed or are proceeding with a very low space (Sanches, 1999).

A very different example from the recipient countries with prolonged conflict situations like Somalia, Liberia and Angola, is Haiti. However, also there the EU has faced the problem of interacting with a collapsed state. Haiti, where the income level is one of the lowest in the world, is a country with enormous development needs but poor capacity to absorb international aid effectively. Its difficult steps towards democratisation have been regarded as something that should be rewarded by the EU.

Haiti was integrated to the Lomé Convention in 1989, but before the actual aid programme had hardly been launched, the EU suspended its aid due to the military coup in 1990 overthrowing the new democratically elected government of Jean Bertrand Aristide.[4] But the return of Aristide to power in October 1994 brought also EU aid back to the country.

In this situation the EU released funds through the European Community Humanitarian Office (ECHO) in order to ensure a quick disbursing of aid as the normal programming of aid through the EDF and NIP would have required more time. As noted by Koulaïmah-Gabriel, this decision can be criticised, because it is very clear that the humanitarian needs were no less acute during the military rule than they were after the return of Aristide. Thus the sudden use of these funds went against the principle that all ECHO funds are politically neutral. Simultaneously however, ECHO was the only flexible instrument that the EU was able to use in order to give a quick political signal to the country.

Thus ECHO's work in Haiti cannot be characterised as emergency work. Yet the sudden disbursement of humanitarian aid was realised through international NGOs that had to design quickly quite expensive projects for the EU funding, which of course raises questions of sustainability of such development co-operation. These kinds of projects usually do not contribute to the ability of the public sector to take them over after the aid is finished. But although ECHO was not an appropriate instrument to tackle with the economic and structural causes behind the development problems in Haiti, there were ways in which the emergency funds actually were used to address more structural problems like water supply. In those projects attention was also paid to the sustainability of the work with local NGOs (Koulaïmah-Gabriel 1999).

A particular character of delivering development aid through ECHO is that the aid can be managed through the EU, which then can fund NGO projects. The second state of EU co-operation in Haiti, however, was to start co-operation under the EDF, which requires the management of the beneficiary government. As a matter of fact 20% of the new agreed EDF was to go to budgetary support, while infrastructure, agriculture and governance were other major areas of co-operation. In June 1997, however, the situation became particularly complicated. Because of the alleged irregularities during the April 1997 elections, the government of the Prime Minister Rosny Smarts resigned. After that the country was governed without a government and state budget, endangering the use of EDF.

The EU has tried to be flexible for instance in cases where it has not been possible to pass necessary legislation at the Parliament for the management of EDF (like in the case of setting a maintenance fund for roads). In the absence of the government the president has appointed by degree a NAO. This has made it possible to continue disbursing funds under EDF. It is yet not clear what is the accountability of the NAO in Haiti and how it is ensured that the development programmes funded by the EU do fit into the national development policy.

In summary one can conclude that the EU has responded to the collapse of the central government by *ad hoc* manners through different mechanisms. The most important of them is to allocate funds throng humanitarian assistance and to work through NGOs. In the absence of a legitimate government EU has absorbed the role of the NAO by itself or in the case of Haiti accepted a NAO nominated by the president. In the case of Somalia there has been a conscious attempt to build regional government, which at least potentially could also provide a channel to manage development co-operation in a country without central government.

The danger, however, is that for the EU the most important thing appears to be the ability to disburse funds allocated to a particular country, not to ensure that the development impact of these funds is optimal. Flexibility then can mean innovative means looking for ways to allocate funds, instead of building the capacity of the local administration to take responsibility of the development projects. In this respect even the support given to NGOs runs a risk of exacerbating the relative weakness of the state. For instance in Haiti the NGOs seem to have much more expertise and technical knowledge on many development issues than the government has. A clear indicator of this is that NGOs are the most important source of employment for many professionals (Koulaïmah-Gabriel 1999). Channelling the aid through NGOs can contribute to the rolling back of the public sector and with it the local public accountability of the development work even though much of this work can never become economically sustainable but requires public funds, so far coming from the donors' budgets.

Concluding Notes

Collapsed states and weak states that have a risk to collapse are a dynamic part of the post cold war international system. This is not so much because of any 'new international order', but because of the fact that the superpower rivalry sustained weak states, which are now perhaps for the first time really facing the difficult task of nation-building and state-building. In a globalized world this task is very much an international task, too. Political conditionality in international development cooperation is just one example of the instruments foreign countries and multilateral organisations have used when trying to strength the states in the third world and to prevent state collapse there.

However, as the case of the EU's development co-operation under the Lomé Convention shows, political conditionality is an instrument that is very difficult to codify and needs to be based on country specific considerations. Even more importantly political conditionality cannot answer the difficult question between needs and performance. Those who are performing well are seldom those whose needs are greatest.

By the same token the international community has had to develop strategies to co-operate with collapsed states. The fact that in many countries like in Somalia, the state collapse is not a temporary situation, means that *ad hoc* measures are not enough. The interests of the Somali people needs to be brought to the international agenda, while long-term strategies to support state-building should also be kept in mind. The question of legitimate public authorities in such countries is a complicated issue. Yet it should be solved in order to enhance sustainable development and to prevent 'neocolonisation' which is an obvious danger if the local ownership of the development policy is not ensured and the donor agencies have to assume the role of the local state.

Notes

[1] Its overall importance is enhanced by the fact that the European Union is the second largest multilateral donor after the World Bank, and the Lomé Convention is the most important arrangement of development aid relations for it. The combined bilateral and multilateral aid of the 15 member states constitute more than half of the total financial aid flows from DAC countries to developing countries. Most of the official development aid of the EU is allocated under the Convention (see Laakso and Lehtinen, 1998).

[2] The studies referred to in this chapter were presented at a seminar on "Aid Selectivity and Performance Criteria in an ACP-EU partnership" organised by ECDPM and ECPR in Kampala, Uganda, 22 - 24 February 1999.

[3] Like Somalia Liberia was one of the first signatories of the Lomé Convention.

[4] It needs to be noted that otherwise the EU played a low profile in its support to the democratic forces, and very much left the initiative to the United States.

References

Barnett, Michael N. (1996), 'The Politics of Indifference at the United Nations and Genocide in Rwanda and Bosnia' in Thomas Cushman and Stjepan G. Meštrovi (eds.) *This Time We Knew It. Western Responses to Genocide in Bosnia*, New York University press, New York, pp. 128–62.

Baylies, Carolyn (1995), 'Political Conditionality and Democratisation' in *Review of African Political Economy*, No. 65, pp. 321–37.

Brusset, Emery (1999), 'EU Cooperation with Politically Fragile Countries: Experiences form Liberia', Channel Research Ltd., Mimeo.

Clapham, Christopher (1996), *Africa and International System: The Politics of State Survival*, Cambridge University Press, New York.

Diop, Abdoulaye (1994), *Droits de l'homme, democratie et politique de cooperation au developpement de l'Union Europeenne*, rapport de stage, Institut international d'administration publique, Paris.

European Commission (1997), 'Guidelines for the negotiation of a new co-operation agreements with the African, Caribbean and Pacific (ACP) countries', Communication to the Council and the European Parliament.

Graumans, Anne (1999), 'Draft of the Desk Study on Experiences of Dialogue in the EU-ACP Partnership', mimeo, Association INZET, Amsterdam.

Jehl, Douglas (1994), 'Officials Told to Avoid Calling Rwanda Killings "Genocide"', *New York Times*, June 10, 1994: A8.

Koulaïmah-Gabriel, Andrea (1999), "EU Cooperation with Haiti: a test case for aid selectivity with weak states", ECDPM, February 1999, Mimeo.

Laakso, Liisa and Lehtinen, Terhi (1998), 'Emerging Regime of Political Conditionality, The Case of the Lomé Convention', Paper presented at the Third Pan-European International Relations Conference and Joint Meeting with ISA, Vienna, 16-19 September, 1998.

L' Impact de la construction européenne sur la Convention de Lomé IV-Conséquences Du Traité de Maastricht (1994), Bureau d'information européenne S.P.R.I.

Licklider, Roy (1995), 'The Consequences of Negotiated Settlements in Civil wars, 1945 – 1993', *American Political Science Review*, Vol. 89 No. 3, pp. 681–690.

Migdal, Joel S. (1988), *Strong Societies and Weak States: State-Society Relations and State Capabilities in the Third World*, Princeton University Press, Princeton.

Ottaway, Marina (1999), 'Ethnic Politics in Africa: Change and Continuity' in Joseph, Richard (ed.) *State, Conflict, and Democracy in Africa*, Lynne Rienner, Boulder, 299–317.

Resolution of the Council and the Member States Meeting in the Council on Human Rights, Democracy and Development (1991), adopted on 28 November 1991, Brussels.

Sanches, Adérito Alain (1999), 'EU Cooperation with Politically Fragile Countries: Lessons form Angola', mimeo.

Schraeder, Peter (1995), 'The Clinton Administration's Africa Policies - Some Comments on Continuity and Change at Mid-Term', in Centre d'Etude d'Afrique Noire, ed. *L'Afrique politique 1995: Le Meilleur, le Pire et l'Incertain*, Karthala, Paris, pp. 47–72.

Schraeder, Peter (1994), *and United States Foreign Policy toward Africa: Incrementalism, Crisis and Change*, Cambridge University Press, Cambridge.

Stokke, Olav ed. (1995), *Aid and Political Conditionality*, Frank Cass, London.

Visman, Emma (1999), 'Cooperation with Politically Fragile Countries: Lessons from EU Support to Somalia', Safeworld, London, Mimeo.

Widner, Jennifer (1995), 'States and Statelessness in Late Twentieth-Century Africa,' *Daedalus*, Vol. 124, No. 3, pp 129–154.

Väyryncn, Raimo (1996), 'The Age of Humanitarian Crises', *The United Nations University/ World Institute of Development Economics Research, Research for Action*, No. 25, WIDER, Helsinki.

Young, Crawford (1999), 'The Third Wave of Democratization in Africa: Ambiguities and Contradictions' in Joseph, Richard (ed.) *State, Conflict, and Democracy in Africa*, Lynne Rienner, Boulder, pp. 15–38.

Zartman, William ed. (1995), *Collapsed States: The Disintegration and Restoration of Legitimate Authority*, Lynne Rienner, and Boulder.

5 Political Corruption: Its Democratic Precursors and Sustainers

LINDA L. DOLIVE

In the year preceding the new millennium, each month brought forth revelations of corruption at the highest levels of political power. Indonesia, South Africa, Brazil, and Russia figured prominently among transitional countries whose political leaders seem to regard public office as an "official permit for illegal activities" (Buckley, 1999). Indeed, in Brazil as in many other countries, part of the attraction of elected office is that legislators are protected from prosecution for corruption. The removal of immunity requires at least a majority vote by their legislative colleagues. On the last day of 1999, President Boris Yeltsin of Russia resigned. The first act of his handpicked successor was the issuing of a decree to prevent prosecution of Mr. Yeltsin and his family from any future charges of corruption or abuse of office. As a major source of external and vital funds for the often-corrupt transitional states, the World Bank has adopted an international strategy to treat corruption as a symptom of underlying illnesses of these states. This strategy holds out the possibility then of curing the patient through treating its weak areas (Schmemann, 1999).

Yet, if corruption is a symptom of a sick state, the world's leading democracies need urgent treatment too. As the new millennium began, under investigations for corruption were long lines of democratically elected politicians previously thought untainted. The architect of German unification and former sixteen-year Chancellor, Helmut Kohl, admitted accepting massive illegal campaign contributions for his party, the Christian Democratic Union. The current CDU party leader, Wolfgang Schaeuble, also admitted to accepting illegal funds. The party's parliamentary chief financial officer, Wolfgang Huellen, committed suicide. His suicide note cited fear of a financial audit.

Since the German parliamentary inquiry has revealed a major contributor of illegal funds was the French company, Elf Aquitaine, French prosecutors are not investigating the allegation that the late fourteen year French President Francois Mitterrand requested Elf to illegally contribute to Chancellor Kohl's electoral campaign. President Mitterrand rejuvenated the French Socialist Party in the 1970s partially through his denouncing "the money that corrupts, the money that buys people off, that crushes, that kills" as a description of the opposition ruling party then in power (Europe's Rotten Heart, 2000, p. 23). Once in political office, many of Mr. Mitterrand's own ministers engaged in corruption. The Socialists' return to parliamentary power in 1997 continued the cycle of corruption its predecessor, the Gaullists had committed in the early to mid-1990s. Finance Minister Strauss-Kahn resigned last fall under charges of fraud and forgery.

France and Germany's neighbor, Belgium, likewise, manifests corruption among its top leaders. The 1999 national election saw the ouster of a government tainted by many corruption scandals ranging from police mishandling of murder cases to distribution of unsafe foods. Twelve of its leaders, including the deputy Prime Minister and the former NATO secretary-general are on trial for allegations of bribery.

Belgium also figures prominently in investigations of corruption in the last year of the old millennium because Brussels is the headquarters of the European Commission. Rampant corruption in the European Union led in 1999 to the resignation of all fifteen Commissioners en masse. The Commission's personnel policies encouraged financial impropriety to such an extent that an editorial in The Economist advised the Commissioners this common sense dictum, "If you must give jobs to your relations, make sure they do not steal anything" (Europe's Neilogistical Reforms, 2000). Also in 1999, the Commission's own anti-fraud unit reported the European Union lost a billion dollars during the year through crime and corruption centered on smuggling operations.

In the fall of 1999 the European Parliament approved Romano Prodi as the new "clean" President of the Commission along with new Commissioners to signify a clean break with the past. Mr. Prodi, the former Italian Prime Minister, is under investigation in Italy for corruption during his tenure as head of the state holding company IRI. His partisan supporters in Italy allege the charges are an attempt to distract attention from " more serious" allegations of corruption by Silvio Berlusconi who was Mr. Prodi's predecessor as Prime Minister. Mr. Berlusconi, the current leader of the parliamentary opposition, is in January 2000 in his third trial on charges of false accounting and tax fraud. Previously he was found guilty in two different trials for bribery and false accounting. His prison sentences have been suspended or are under appeal. Mr. Berlusconi's personal attorney who was the Defense Minister in his cabinet is also under indictment for bribing judges to give favorable verdicts in Mr. Berlusconi's earlier trials.

Western Europe is not unique in exhibiting a pattern of corruption within democratic regimes. In Israel many leaders presently are either under investigation or have been convicted of corruption. The charges range from bribery to misuse of public funds to illegal campaign contributions. The leaders include the incumbent Prime Minister Barak, former Prime Minister Netanyahu, the current President Weizman, and the former Justice and Interior Ministers.

These continuing investigations in Israel, France, and Italy demonstrate that corrupt activities are not the monopoly of one side of the political spectrum. Cabinet ministers and party leaders of both the right and left abuse public office. Opponents share a culture of corruption when holding the power of state.

In the international system of the new millennium, political corruption is a global concern. Both domestic publics and world leaders have condemned its harmful effects on the polity and the economy. Major global actors such as the International Monetary Fund and the World Bank argue that corruption negatively impacts governmental effectiveness and economic growth (Little and Posado-Carbo, 1996; Hessel and Murphy, 1999). Scholars, likewise, enumerate negative aspects of corruption (Nelken and Levi, 1996; Kaufmann, 1997). These views contrast with earlier functional approaches toward corruption where corruption was seen as beneficial to developing states and transitional societies such as in integrating new groups into the political system and in stimulating economic development (Heidenheimer, 1970; Huntington, 1968; Scott, 1972).

Although studies show a similarity of the types of corrupt behaviors whether in transitional, developing states or stable, democratic states ("Where does corruption flourish," 1999), the extent of as well as the insidious effects of corruption are especially pronounced today in the post-communist and developing states. Plundering of these states by their leaders for private gain is common practice. For example, under the Nigerian presidency of Sani Abacha, the world's 11th-largest oil exporter country imported fuel to the profit of its corrupt leaders (A global war, 1999). Former Russian Prime Minister Chernomyrdin is alleged to have $5 billion skimmed from gas and oil deals (Myers, 1996). The Swedish economist Aslund estimates at least 70% of the Russian bureaucrats in charge of privatizing oil resources take bribes (Schmemann, 1999).

State assets have become the spoils in many transitional states, which often lack institutionalization, have inadequate legal systems, and manifest no legacy of a civic culture or civil society. Accordingly, many of the explanations for along with proposed solutions to corruption in these countries stress their transitional status; e.g. with the institutionalization of a democratic regime, a supportive legal environment, a conducive political culture, and a capitalist economy producing growth, corruption will decline. Such advice is misplaced. Abundantly demonstrated in the experiences of the industrialized, democratic states is that political corruption is not an aberrant condition.

How democracy as a form of governing provides the foundation for and sustaining of corruption is the focus of this paper. This focus departs from the customary study of corruption in two ways. In established democracies, corrupt behaviors have commonly been viewed as deviations from the norm. Yet as Scott (1972, p. viii) pointed out corruption is "a regular, repetitive, integral part" of the operation of political systems.

Most studies also look to indigenous factors in individual countries (Johansen, 1990); however, contextual analyses falter in comparative perspective. Oft-discussed explanatory variables for corruption in democracies include size of the public sector, the amount of government involvement in the economy, and the kinds of party and electoral systems. Yet both Italy and Japan with different size public sectors experience wide-scale corruption. The welfare state is more pervasive in Great Britain than in the United States, and yet the United States with "less state" is also perceived as less clean. The Italian and Japanese systems for years were widely known to be systemically corrupt and yet the political class endured. This paper will discuss corruption as a dominant norm facilitated by democratic "rules of the game." It will illustrate that political corruption occurs at the pinnacles of power in France, Germany, Great Britain, Italy, Japan, and the United States.

Democracy is defined in its representational form of regular and free elections. Most scholars expound on additional characteristics such as limited governmental powers and civil liberties of its citizens which are denoted by the term, liberal democracy (Diamond, 1997). The countries cited in this paper would meet the electoral and liberal criteria of democracy as well as the economic supporting conditions of affluence (Przeworski et al, 1997). Corruption is defined in its general form to be use of public office for private gain. Other authors have elaborated upon the term "private gain" to encompass remuneration in economic, social, political, or ideological terms (DeLeon, 1993) including partisan and patronage purposes (Galeotti and Merlo, 1994; Stigler, 1972). These definitions allow that there are different degrees, kinds, and levels of democracy and of political corruption.

Corruption thus involves the misappropriation of the powers of public office and cooperative behavior. There must be both a corrupter and a corrupted for corruption to occur. Public officials and private agents interact. Modern economies are based on public-private relationships. Politicians obtain campaign funds and businessmen obtain access to special governmental privileges (Dolive and Potter, 2000). Given the primacy of business in capitalist economies and the primacy of elected officials in democratic polities, a mutually beneficial environment for corruption exists. This supportive environment for connections between politicians and business provides a social legitimacy (Calavita et al, 1997). Corruption becomes a driving force of politics (Dolive, 1999).

In the United States, this supporting condition is often referred to as "legalized bribery," whereas other countries like Italy and Japan make such actions "illegal" but do not enforce the laws. As will be discussed later, the most often given refrain in those instances where formal prosecution of corruption is pursued is that the corrupt practices are done by "everybody" and have been the practice for years. When major political and business leaders "have something" on each other and each benefits as long as the nature of their relationship is kept secret, cooperation and predictable behavior perpetuate a corrupt system. If exposed, corrupter and corrupted both point to the system as the culprit and themselves as the victims.

Nonetheless, court records, indictments, and media accounts do reveal a plethora of corrupt top executives and legislators in the industrialized, democratic states. U.S. Vice-President Spiro Agnew resigned his office in 1973 because of corruption as did later in 1989, the Speaker of the U.S. House of Representatives Jim Wright. In France in 1996 alone under investigation were eight former ministers, two former party leaders, dozens of parliamentary deputies and local mayors, and heads of some of the largest companies ("Who's next," 1996). Earlier in 1993 a Prime Minister under suspicion of corruption committed suicide, and this year in 1999 former Prime Minister Alain Juppe, currently mayor of Bordeaux and a parliamentary deputy, and Roland Dumas, the head of the Constitutional Court and a former foreign minister, were under investigation for corruption. In Great Britain corruption scandals in the last decade occasioned the resignations of cabinet ministers and new proscriptions against paid advocacy by members of parliament. These regulations resulted in a drop from 240 to 80 paid consultancies among members of the House of Commons (Carney, 1999).

Italy, however, leads western democracies in the extent of publicized instances of corruption. Stemming from the "Clean Hands" judicial investigations begun in 1992 were 6,059 officials under investigation by 1994 (Jamieson, 1996) which eventually encompassed five former Prime Ministers and one-third of the members of parliament. Japan, on the other hand, demonstrates that corrupt elected officials are not confined to western democracies. Prime Ministers and party leaders have resigned in the 1990s. One-half of the members of the Diet also admitted to accepting secret donations (Wilkinson, 1993).

A common area of collusion is campaign financing. Politicians obtain campaign funds and businessmen obtain access to special governmental privileges (Dolive, 1998; Potter, 1998). Currently, former German Chancellor Kohl and his party, the CDU, is the center of attention. More information and allegations about the ever-widening circle of corrupt officials become public each week as the inquiries unfold. In Germany, as elsewhere, politicians obtain money to finance ever more expensive electoral campaigns from people who want their interests implemented in public policies. The French oil company Elf wished to buy the former East German oil refinery Leuna. The arms dealer Karl Heinz Schreiber wanted German tanks allowed to be exported to Saudi Arabia.

The activities and incentives for corruption remain similar across countries; the campaign finance laws vary as to the illegality of the activities. Mr. Kohl violated campaign finance laws he enacted as Chancellor. A January 2000 U.S. Supreme Court opinion on campaign contributions points out the danger to democracy from politicians compliant with the wishes of large contributors. Dissenting justices counter that campaign contributions are political speech. Debates over laws to deter corruption endemic in campaign financing continue while incumbent office holders are reticent to cut off the largesse of major contributors.

In the 1980s in the United States in the two years prior to the bailout of savings and loan institutions by the American taxpayer, political action committees representing savings and loans interests increased their contributions by 42% to Congressional campaigns for a total of $12 million in the decade (Calavita et al, 1997). These figures do not include the substantial honoraria for speeches by key House and Senate members. In fact, the House and Senate Banking committees whose members were major beneficiaries of the contributions were referred to as the "cash and carry" committees. The savings and loan sector reaped a many fold return on their investments in elected officials: the estimated cost to taxpayers not including interest payments on government bonds is $150 to $175 billion.

If interest on the bonds is added, the cost approaches $500 billion (ibid.). The new transitional states follow this trend as they engage in electoral politics. For instance, Mikhail Kodorkovsy, one of the seven Russian bankers who financed President Yeltsin's successful 1996 campaign said, "Politics is the most profitable business in Russia today" ("The endless winter," 1997, p. 113).

Another common area of collusion is kickbacks for government contracts or favorable regulations. Russia is often described as a Wild West free-for-all where state assets are the spoils to be gained by the new industrialists and politicians working together ("Boost for reform," 1997). In this regard, the "New Russians," the conspicuous consumption new class created by rampant often corrupt opportunities offered through the privatization of state enterprises resemble the American "robber-barons" of the late 19th and early 20th century (Kranz, 1995). As many studies have demonstrated, political leverage has been very important in creating great personal fortunes in the U.S. (DeLong, 1998). Echoing his late 20th century compatriots, railroad magnate Collis Huntington wrote in 1877:

> If you have to pay money [to a politician] to have the right thing done, it is only just and fair to do it.... If a [politician] has the power to do great evil and won't do right unless he is bribed to do it, I think... it is a man's duty to go up and bribe...
>
> DeLong, 1998, p. 9.

The return on bribing as an investment can be seen in the U.S. government's provision of $24 million in financing and 9 million acres of land; and some claim that Huntington and his partner Leland Stanford built their railroad without putting up any of their own money. Indeed, subsidies to build western railroads "transferred" $100 million of the public's money to the politically well connected (DeLong, 1998). Other industrialists of this time period also reaped the benefits of corrupted politics; for instance Senator Aldrich of Rhode Island was called the "Senator from Standard Oil." Massachusetts congressman Oakes Ames admitted in order to keep political support and subsidies, he distributed construction company stock to fellow legislators and future President Garfield, the Vice President, the Vice President elect, and relatives of President Grant among others (DeLong, 1998).

In the 1990s, the chief executive of FIAT, Italy's largest company, explained how his company won public contracts in Italy by paying bribes to elected politicians through secret bank accounts in Luxembourg and the Bahamas (McCarthy, 1993). Enso Papi, a manager of a FIAT company, testified that he was given, "a notebook recording the various 'obligations' and the dates they should be paid...Illegality was so regularized that I didn't feel I was committing a criminal act" (della Porta and Vannucci, 1999, p. 197). Earlier in the United States, court proceedings revealed that the Gulf Oil Corporation had for 15 years regularly laundered money through its subsidiaries in the Bahamas and distributed over $5 million of the cleaned money to politicians (Ermann and Lundman, 1996).

Likewise in Japan, a basic feature of politics has been illegal connections between politicians and business.   The Sagawa Kyubin Delivery Company, for instance, made payoffs worth hundreds of millions of dollars to influential members of most political parties.   The Recruit Cosmos Co. bribed politicians with unlisted stock shortly before public issuance.   Businessmen uniformly said bribery was necessary for new entrepreneurs to obtain access to special economic and political privileges (Nester, 1990). The earlier 1950s kickback scandal revealed that all major shipbuilding companies paid large bribes to politicians to obtain favorable legislation (Johnson, 1997).

So routine are kickbacks that specific percentages of contracts may be expected. Della Porta and Vannucci (1999) cite standardized kickbacks of 10% in some U.S. local governments; a "fair price" in France of the same bribe percentage for awarding of public contracts; and a fixed percentage of contract value in Belgium.   In Italy, the Minister of Public Works was charged in the Clean Hands investigations of taking bribes from businesses at the set rate of 2.5% of the value of the awarded contract while the Minister of Health was charged with receiving a 5% return (McCarthy, 1997).   Italian businessmen confirmed bribe percentages varied by the nature of the sector: "5% on building contracts, 10% on cleaning services, and 15% on maintenance and refurbishment (della Porta, 1999, p. 254).

In Japan construction firms paid key politicians bribes of 3-5% of project bids (Wilkinson, 1993).   So embedded in the system were the bribery expectations that when the political incumbents changed, the newly elected incumbent was often as in Italy told by his predecessor who to solicit and what amount of pay-off to expect or as in Japan met by business supplicants tendering the obligatory envelope of cash they had been accustomed to paying to the prior political incumbent (della Porta, 1995; Hellman, 1993; McCarthy, 1997; Potter, 1995). Thus the system continued irrespective of which political parties won elections; the dominant parties coopted the opposition parties by sharing the rewards of office (Dolive and Potter, 1999).

Public attitudes about corruption demonstrate its detrimental effects on the polity. Across cultures, corruption is condemned and the values of honesty and integrity of governors are heralded. For instance, in non-western societies with a gift-giving tradition, bribery is differentiated in that gift giving was not committed in secrecy nor seen as a violation of duty (Carney, 1999). In post-communist Russia, 88% said "connections" and 76% said "dishonesty" are the essential tools for getting ahead (Hessel and Murphy, 1999). Survey research in the long-established democracies also reveals skeptical and distrusting publics.

For instance, in Great Britain 73% of the respondents in a Gallup poll of the 1990s said the ruling party is disreputable and 52% of the respondents in a MORI poll said that their MPs put their own interest first (Mortimore, 1995). Similarly, 48% of the French in a 1992 poll said they would have a better opinion of the ruling party if it took "a tougher attitude toward scandals" (Fay, 1995, p. 670). Two 1994 polls reported that 70% said "corruption was rife among members of parliament and entrepreneurs" (Ruggiero, 1996, p. 129), and 71% thought members of parliament were the most corrupt element in public life (Jamieson, 1996). The Italians are dissatisfied with the functioning of their democracy, don't trust parliament, dislike politicians, and believe legislators quickly lost contact with their voters (della Porta and Vannucci, 1997; Wilson, 1994). Japanese citizens view politics as dirty and dishonest and feel their elected officials are distant, arrogant and likely to break the law (Martin and Stronach, 1992; Richardson, 1974).

Most revealing perhaps are time series analyses showing growing political alienation and distrust by public in the Anglo-American democracies. In Great Britain, 64% of the 1994 electorate said, "Most MPs make a lot of money by using public office improperly" (compared to 46% of those polled in 1985). Fifty-nine percent of the 1994 respondents disagreed with the statement, "Most MPs have a high personal moral code (up from 35% in 1984). Eighty-seven percent in 1994 agreed, "Most MPs will tell lies if they feel the truth will hurt them politically" (compared to 79% in 1985). Seventy-seven percent agreed in 1994 that "Most MPs care more about specific interest than they care about people like you" (compared to 67% in 1984) (Transparency, 1998).

Putnam (1997) discusses the psychological disengagement from politics and government in the United States over the last thirty years, which has paralleled the physical disengagement of non-voting. He notes Americans have become much less trusting between 1966 and 1992 as reflected in long-term data series. In response to the question, "How much do you trust the government in Washington to do what is right - all of the time, most of the time, some of the time, or almost never?" Seventy-five percent in 1992 (up from 30% in 1966) chose one of the two least trusting responses. Similarly, the number of Americans more alienated politically has doubled (over 60% in 1992 as compared to less than 30% in 1966) as demonstrated in their responses to five questions:

> The people running the country do not really care what happens to you.
> Most people with power try to take advantage of people like yourself.
> You are left out of things going on around you.
> What you think does not count very much anymore.
> The rich get richer and the poor get poorer.

Putnam, 1997, p.36.

Against the above described backdrop of voter apathy and cynicism, the U.S. November 2000 elections are expected to exemplify the high cost of getting elected and the overriding role of special interest contributions. The successful candidates may be elected by less than one-fourth of eligible voters in the most expensive Presidential and Congressional campaign in history with an estimated cost of $1 billion (McFeatters, 1999).

Corruption creates a circle of mistrust which simultaneously is a precondition and a result (della Porta and Vannucci, 1997). Publics who condemn political corruption also rationalize and tolerate it. For example, one Italian reformer before the 1994 parliamentary elections said, "People are so shocked by the criminality of their rulers in the past they say not it can't be true. It has to be an exaggeration" (Freemantle, 1995, p. 237). Other constituents are aware of the benefits spread to them through corrupt officials. For example, the Japanese construction industries are not only national but also local, and local firms benefit from the parliamentary pork barrel.

Most importantly in their actions and particularly as voters, citizens tolerate corruption. Corrupt leaders may be continuously reelected to office. Japan and Italy demonstrate two of the most notorious instances of voters supporting corrupt leaders. The former Japanese Prime Minister, Tanaka Kakuei, was convicted of accepting more than $1 million in bribes in the Lockheed scandal and subsequently reelected to parliament by the largest margin in his career. Increased governmental allocations to his electoral district were a staple. Tanaka enriched not only himself but used his ill-gotten personal wealth often to buy political support. His "discerning eyes saw above all that money was indeed the mother's milk of politics and that whoever controlled the largest amount of it in the political system, controlled the system" (Johnson, 1995, p. 193).

In Italy, although indicted on numerous corruption charges, former Prime Minister Silvio Berlusconi was not only reelected to parliament but became the principal opposition leader. Indeed, corrupt politicians are often harder to dislodge from office because they can reinvest their payoffs to buy support. Another Italian politician said, "The race for power is a race for money" (della Porta, 1999, p. 263). Former U.S. Supreme Court Justice Louis Brandeis, writing in 1913, understood the reason why corrupt politicians remain in power, "They control the people through the people's own money" (DeLong, 1998, p. 11).

Leaders' responses to corruption also contribute to its pervasiveness. They deny accountability, threaten the exposers, blame the system and/or their opponents, evade sanctions, and play the victim (Dolive, 1998). Indicted Japanese and Italian politicians publicly stated that they did not feel being clean was an expectation for public office holders.

Former Italian Prime Minister Bettino Craxi was very candid both in speeches to the parliament and in court. He asserted since everybody had known what had been going for years, that the corruption charges against him were a political assault. "Parties have relied on, and continue to rely on, the use of funds that come in irregular or illegal forms" (Burnett and Mantovani, 1998, p. 87). "I never denied the reality, never minimized it, never underestimated the moral, political and institutional significance of the issues that have burst into the open.... the illegality that's been there for a long time, maybe from time immemorial" (ibid., p. 111). He continued in his parliamentary speech to point out that the Parliament had regularly as required by law approved transparently phony party budgets and that this system had been "accepted by consensus and shared by all" (ibid., p. 112). Mr. Craxi subsequently threatened the judiciary while remaining a fugitive in Tunisia.

Former Italian Prime Minister Berlusconi used his access to television to criticize judges as assassins and publicly swore "on the heads of my five children" that he had never corrupted anyone (Frei, 1996, p. 272), but then in the same statement admitted illegal payment had been made, but excused himself as a victim of a corrupt system. Other Italian compatriots echoed this theme upon their arrest for corruption, "I do not consider myself a criminal. Indeed, I consider myself personally honest, nevertheless, I admit I formed part of a dishonest system" (Little and Posado-Carbo, 1996, p. 6).

Leaders perpetuate a corrupt system in another way as well. Turnover in elected office has occurred in all the countries, yet the old habits of previous corrupt office holders often endure. Last year, the Japanese "reformer" Arai Shoki committed suicide to avoid being arrested for accepting an illegal donation. The Italian Berlusconi, who first obtained office in 1994 as the "new face" of an untainted politician was subsequently revealed to not only have been a prime beneficiary of that old corrupt system but also to use the powers of his top political office to personally benefit himself.

In Great Britain and France, respectively, the governments of Tony Blair and Jacques Chirac won elections partially based on their charges of sleaze and scandals against their opponents, the long-ruling Conservatives and Socialists. The new occupants soon also faced allegations of corruption. Three French ministers resigned because of accusations. Investigations still continue on others. British Prime Minister Blair quickly came under suspicion for changing public policy on tobacco advertising in return for a one million pound contribution to his Labour Party.

Democracy as a form of government, in and of itself, does not stem corruption. Its value neutral institutions depend upon the consciousness of its leaders and public to provide the values. When societal norms excuse and expect corruption, a self-perpetuating circle ensues. Furthermore, the most common form of corruption, bribery, is by nature a secret, mutually beneficial arrangement in which the participants share an interest to not expose their complicity. The individual actors, whether corrupted or corruptor, focus on short-term gains rather than long term consequences for society.

So too do the publics. Although, as illustrated through the survey data above, politicians as a group may be distrusted and voters alienated from major institutions, a different picture arises when constituents talk about their own legislators. Even when concerned about corruption, voters also have other concerns as well, which may take priority. For instance, voters may condemn dishonesty and yet support dishonest politicians if they feel other issues are more important, such as economic well being. American voters revealed in exit interview polls of the last presidential election their perception that the incumbent was dishonest but received their vote anyway.

On the other hand, there are a number of characteristics of democratic systems, which provide facilitating conditions for corruption to flourish. The qualities of success for a corrupt politician are the same qualities possessed by a non-corrupt politician: each needs the ability to create connections, establish ties of trust, encourage the exchange of favors, build reciprocal obligations, and foster loyalty (della Porta and Vannucci, 1999). That public officials can often benefit personally from their public decision turns politics into a business (della Porta, 1996) -- a situation reinforced with the decline of ideological politics. In the words of Francis Fukuyama: "All the big issues that used to divide the left and right -- the cold war, inflation, crime, welfare -- have just collapsed as partisan issues" (Bronner, 1999, p. 1). His argument that liberal democracy and a market-oriented economy are ascendant in the world today is echoed by numerous other scholars in edited collections by Diamond et al (1997) and Hadenius (1997).

The expense of getting elected creates incentives for politicians to bestow favors on selected private groups in return for the financial contributions necessary to win. The social legitimacy of business in a capitalist economy translates into political capital not possessed by other groups. Contributions from Lockheed, Gulf Oil, and FIAT are viewed very differently than would be contributions from groups with perceived lesser social legitimacy or economic utility. The symbiotic relationship between politics and business often results in condoned and fostered corruption by both the political and economic elites. Lawmakers become the beneficiaries of breaking the law (Dolive and Potter, 2000), and the politically well connected transfer the people's wealth to their own pockets.

Corruption in democratic systems, in sum, is not an exception to the norms and rules, but rather is conditioned and sustained by those norms and rules. The comparative study of corruption as it affects the quality of democracy becomes more fruitful when corruption is not viewed as a deviant condition in democracies. Just as scholars for many years have compared democracies in terms of party systems, distribution of governmental powers, and political culture, so too can corruption be studied as a political phenomenon.

The types of, extent of, and nature of corruption among democratic regimes can be assessed against differing institutional, social, economic, and political characteristics. The brief survey of corruption in the countries discussed in this paper suggests a number of questions to comparatively explore: At what level does corruption undermine elite or system legitimacy? Under what conditions does corruption become a politically salient issue? What is the interaction of electorates and leaders? In the words of Linz (1997), do undesirable leaders corrupt the electorate or do voters condone actions detrimental to democratic quality? Johnston (1997) posits that it is imbalances in political forces that account for the differences in corruption syndromes in democracies. To what degree can the imbalances be adjusted? How do political structures affect the incidence and type of corruption? And finally there are numerous relationships to explore of the costs of corruption.

References

'Boost for reform' (1997, September 27), *The Economist,* pp. 55-56.

Bronner, E. (1999, July 11), 'Left and Right Are Crossing Paths', *The New York Times, Section* 4, pp. 1 and 5.

Buckley, S. (1999, October 24), ' Brazilians Tire of Lawmakers as Lawbreakers,' *The Washington Post,* p. A31.

Burnett, S. and Mantovani, L. (1998), *The Italian Guillotine: Operation Clean Hands and the Overthrow of Italy's First Republic,* Rowman & Littlefield, Lanham, MD.

Calavita, K., Pontell, H. and Tillman, R. (1997), *Big Money Crime,* University of California Press, Berkeley.

Carney, G. (1999), *Conflict of Interest: Legislators, Ministers and Public Officials.* TIWorkingPaper.[Online]. Available: http://www.transparency.de/documents/work-papers/carney/index.html

della Porta, D. (1996), ' Actors in Corruption: Business Politicians in Italy', *International Social Science Journal,* vol. 48, pp.349-364.

della Porta, D. (1995), 'Political Parties and Corruption: Reflections on the Italian Case', *Modern Italy,* vol. 1, no.1, pp.97-114.

della Porta, D. and Vannucci, A. (1999), *Corrupt Exchanges: Actors, Resources, and Mechanisms of Political Corruption,* Aldine de Gruyter, New York.

della Porta, D. and Vannucci, A. (1997), 'The "Perverse Effects" of Political Corruption', *Political Studies,* vol. 45, pp.516-538.

DeLeon, P. (1993), *Thinking about Political Corruption,* M.E. Sharpe, Armonk, NY.

DeLong, J.B. (1998), *Robber Barons.* Pp. 1-22. [Online]. Available: http://econ161.berkeley.edu/Econ_Articles/carnegie/DeLong_Moscow_ paper2.html

Diamond, L. (1997), 'Promoting Democracy in the 1990s: Actors, Instruments, and Issues', in A. Hadenius (ed.), *Democracy's Victory and Crisis,* Cambridge University Press, Cambridge, pp. 311-370.

Diamond, L., Plattner, M., Chu, Y. and Tien, H. (eds) (1997), *Consolidating the Third Wave Democracies,* The Johns Hopkins Press, Baltimore.

Dolive, L. (1999), "When Criminals Rule: Corruption and Politics." Paper presented at the American Society of Criminology Annual Meeting, November 17-20, Toronto.

Dolive, L. (1998a), 'Politicians as Criminals: Public Sector Corruption in Europe', *Security Journal,* vol. 11, pp. 219-223.

Dolive, L. (1998b), "Corrupt Politicians and State Organized Crime". Paper presented at the World Conference: Modern Criminal Investigation, Organized Crime and Human Rights, September 21-25, Sun City, South Africa.

Dolive, L. (1997), " Political Corruption: European Variants." Paper presented at the American Society of Criminology Annual Meeting, November 19-22, San Diego.

Dolive, L. and Potter, D. (2000), 'Electoral Corruption in Italy and Japan', in D. Rounds (ed.) *International Criminal Justice: Issues in Global Perspective,* Allyn & Bacon Needham Heights, MA., pp. 241-257.

Dolive, L. and Potter, D. (1999), "Political Corruption in Parliamentary Democracies: A Comparison of Italy and Japan." Paper presented at the International Studies Association Annual Meeting, February 16-20, Washington, D.C.

'The Endless Winter of Russian Reform' (1997, July 12), *The Economist,* pp. 3-18.

Ermann, M.D. and Lundman, R. (1996),' Corporate and Government Deviance: Origins, Patterns, & Reactions', in M.D. Ermann & R. Lundman (eds), *Corporate and Government Deviance,* Oxford University Press, New York, pp. 3-44.

'Europe's Neilogistical Reforms' (2000, January 22-28), *The Economist.* [Online].

Available:http://www.economist.com/editorial/freeforall/current/eu9348.html
'Europe's Rotten Heart' (2000, January 15), *The London Times*, p. 23.
Fay, C. (1995, October), 'Political Sleaze in France: Forms and Issues', *Parliamentary Affairs*, vol. 48, pp. 663-76.
Freemantle, B. (1995), *The Octopus: Europe in the Grip of Organized Crime*, Orion, London.
Frei, M. (1996), *Italy the Unfinished Revolution*, Sinclair-Stevenson, London.
Galeotti, G. and Merlo, A. (1994), 'Political Collusion and Corruption in a Representative Democracy', *Public Finance*, vol. 49, pp. 232-243.
'A Global War against Bribery' (1999, January 16-22), *The Economist*, pp. 1-7. [Online]. Available: http://www.economist.com/editorial/freeforall/current/sf1211.html
Hadenius, A. (ed.) (1997), *Democracy's Victory and Crisis*, Cambridge University Press, Cambridge.
Heidenheimer, A.J. (1970), *Political Corruption*, Holt, Rinehart and Winston, New York.
Hellman, S. (1993), 'Politics Almost as Usual: The Formation of the Amato Government,' in G. Pasquino and P. McCarthy (eds), *The end of post-war politics in Italy: The landmark 1992 elections*, Westview Press, Boulder, pp. 141-159.
Hessel, M. and Murphy, K. (1999), *Stealing the State, and Everything Else: A Survey of Corruption in the Postcommunist World*, TI Working Paper, and pp. 1-12. [Online] Available:http://www.transparency.de/documents/work-papers/hessel/index.html
Huntington, S.P. (1968), *Political Order in Changing Societies*, Yale University Press, New Haven.
Jamieson, A. (1996, March), 'Political Corruption in Western Europe' *Conflict Studies*, pp. 1-21.
Johnson, C. (1995), *Japan: Who Governs?* Norton, New York.
Johnston, M. (1997), 'Public Officials, Private Interests, and Sustainable Democracy: When Politics and Corruption Meet', in K.Elliott (ed) *Corruption and the Global Economy*, Institute for International Economics, Washington, DC, pp. 61-82.
Kaufmann, D. (1997), 'Corruption: The Facts', Foreign Policy, vol. 2, pp 114-131.
Kranz, P. (1995, August 14), 'Organized Crime Is Shooting Its Way into Big Business', The *ChicagoTribune*.pp.1-3.[Online].Available:http//www.nd.edu/~astrouni/zhiwriter/spool/121html
Linz, J. (1997), 'Some Thoughts on the Victory and Future of Democracy in A. Hadenius (ed), *Democracy's Victory and Crisis*, Cambridge University Press, Cambridge, pp. 404-426.
Little, W. and Posado-Carbo E. (1996), ' Introduction', in Little and Posada-Carbo (eds) *Political Corruption in Europe & Latin America*, St.Martin's Press, New York, pp. 1-17.
Martin, C. and Stronach, B. (1992), *Politics East and West*, M.E. Sharpe, Armonk, NY.
McCarthy, P. (1997), *The Crisis of the Italian State: From the Origins of the Cold War to the Fall of Berlusconi and Beyond*, St. Martin's Press, New York.
McCarthy, P. (1993), ' Conclusion: Inching Towards a New Regime', in G. Pasquino and P. McCarthy (eds), *The End of Post-war Politics in Italy: The Landmark 1992 Elections*, Westview Press, Boulder, pp. 160-175.
McFeatters, A. (1999, July 11), '2000 Election Campaign to Cost $1 Billion', *Pittsburgh Post-Gazette*, p. A-11.
Myers, L. (1996, May), Russian Mob's Influence Growing, House Panel Told. *Chicago Tribune*,pp.1-2[Online].Available:http://www.nd.edu~astrouni/zhiwriter/spool/96050313.html
Nelken, D. and Levi, M. (1996, March), 'The Corruption of Politics and the Politics of

Corruption: An Overview', *Journal of Law and Society*, vol. 20. No.1, pp. 1-17.

Nester, W. (1990, April), ' Japan's Recruit Scandal: Government and Business for Sale' *Third World Quarterly*, vol. 12, pp.91-109.

Potter, D. (2000, forthcoming), 'Do Rules Foster State Crime? A Case Study of Political Corruption in Japan', in J. Ross (ed), *State Crime: A Comparison of Six Industrialized Countries*, Criminal Justice Press, Monsey, NY.

Potter, D. (1995), Author's interview with Kondo Makoto, Gifu University, June 23.

Przeworski, A. and Limongi, F. (1997), 'Democracy and Development', in A. Hadenius (ed.) *Democracy's Victory & Crisis*, Cambridge University Press, Cambridge, pp. 163-194.

Putnam, R. (1997), 'Democracy in America at Century's End', in A. Hadenius (ed.) *Democracy's Victory & Crisis*, Cambridge University Press, Cambridge, p. 27.

Richardson, B. (1974), *The Political Culture of Japan,* University of California Press, Berkeley.

Ruggiero, V. (1996, March), 'France: Corruption as Resentment', *Journal of Law and Society,* vol. 23, no. 1, pp. 113-131.

Schmemann, S. (1999), 'What Makes Nations Turn Corrupt?' *The New York Times* pp. A15 and A17.

Scott, J.C. (1972), Comparative Political Corruption, Prentice-Hall, Englewood Cliffs.

Stigler, G.J. (1972), 'Economic Competition and Political Competition', *Public Choice,* vol. 13, pp. 91-106.

Transparency. (1998), *Public Opinion Polls - Great Britain.* Sourcebook. [Online] Available: http://www.transparency.de/sourcebook/PartC/cVa2.html

'Where does corruption flourish', (1999), *The TI Source Book*, pp. 1-9. [Online]. Available http//www.transparency.de/documents/source-book/a/Chapter_2/index.html

'Who's Next' (1996, July 13), *The Economist,* vol. 340, pp. 48-50.

Wilkinson, J. (1993), 'Lords of corruption', *AMPO*, vol. 24, pp. 4-6.

Wilson, F. (1994), *European Politics Today: The Democratic Tradition*, Prentice-Hall, Englewood Cliffs.

Part II
The Regional View

6 Confronting the Millennium: The Prospects for Regionalism

GUY POITRAS

Introduction

The robustness of regions and regionalism in the world political economy at the beginning of the twenty first century raises an obvious question: what does this new century hold in store for regions, regionalism, and states in a highly competitive world economy?

The challenges of the twenty first century are, at least early on, the legacies of the twentieth century. What challenged or excited the world and its states toward the end of the twentieth century is still around at the beginning of the twenty first century. States are smack in the middle of these formidable challenges. They are, in some cases, the prime movers behind the challenges the world as a whole faces. But they are also under the gun as well. Challenges of the twenty first century may pressure states to respond in ways that may redefine what it means to be a state in a globalized and regionalized economy.

While this remains a world of states, it is not just a world of independent states trying to go it alone. The twenty first century will in all likelihood intensify trends that make the state a crucible for long term transformations of the world system. Telecommunications, globalized production chains, cross-national currency transfers, nonstate actors (such as firms and environmentalists), and ethnonationalist forces put pressure on the state from above and from below. As states share the global stage, they confront challenges and ponder opportunities. On the one hand, states are impelled to defend their interests against threats if not always against adversaries. These may be economic as well as strategic. On the other, they are tempted to link up in new and imaginative ways to share the gains and burdens of cross border cooperation. States must make their way in the twenty first century and to do so means that they must somehow chart a course between trends toward fragmentation and toward integration.

While economic and technological forces drive states closer together, gaps in wealth, power, and ethnicity raise the ante for conflict and contentiousness.

Regionalism is a response to many of these challenges. However, it is not a panacea for the state; rather, it is a strategy. Regionalism does not provide all the answers. Indeed, as we argue here, this strategy may lead to a set of rather obdurate predicaments. Regionalism may be a response to global challenges but it is still only one arrow in the quiver. States hope to use regionalism to make their way in an evolving world political economy.

States are not the only ones with a stake in regionalism. For one thing, the peoples of a region are affected to one degree or another. Businesses are the first to feel the impact, especially those involved in foreign trade and investment. But corporate actors hire workers and sell to consumers. They too have a stake in the course of regionalism. Just as war is too important to be left to the generals, regionalism is too important to be left to corporate CEOs. Sooner or later, regionalism ripples throughout the states that use it.

We return to our central issue: What are the prospects for regionalism in the twenty first century? Some terms must be defined before we seek to answer this question. Regionalism, regionalization, interdependence, hegemony, and integration are fundamental.

By **regionalism** is meant the efforts of states, usually in close proximity, to cooperate, coordinate, and even harmonize on matters of economic policy such as trade and investment. Examples are the European Union (EU) and its monetary union under Maastricht in particular. Other examples are NAFTA (the United States, Canada, and Mexico) and MERCOSUR (Brazil, Argentina, Uruguay, and Paraguay). **Regionalization** is slightly different. It is often linked to regionalism. However, it is a process of structural change. In this sense, it is not unlike its close relative, globalization. Economic, technological, and political links between neighbors become intensified and may occur with or without state efforts. Regionalization is therefore the growing **interdependence** of many actors within a geographic area.

In some regions, **hegemony** can be critical. It refers here to the preponderance of power held by one state over several others to the extent that the asymmetry of power is so great that the hegemony is able to dominate relations --and to set the rules of exchange-- among the states. For example, the United States enjoyed global predominance for two or three decades after World War II and retains it in North America to this day. **Integration** is a comprehensive process of creating deep and wide connections between many actors, including states, across borders. Levels of integration may be relatively low, such as free trade agreements, or they may be relatively high, such as a common market or economic union. North America is a region with relatively low integration; the EU is relatively high and MERCOSUR (at least in terms of aspirations) is somewhere in the middle.

Questions and Challenges

The prospects for regionalism in Europe, the Asia Pacific, and North America confront six basic questions. We will address these questions with respect to North America, although they are important for the Asia Pacific and for Europe as well. In Europe, regionalism is quite advanced and highly institutionalized. In the Asia Pacific, it is loosely organized. North America is somewhere in between these two poles of regionalism. Still, the six critical questions about the prospects for regionalism can be usefully directed at all three.

The six critical questions are: Is a region really a region or, if not, will it become one? Is the region a hegemony or is it a partnership? Will the states of the region fall by the wayside under the spell of regionalized interdependence? Will domestic resistance within states to regionalism affect its future development? Will regionalism stay put or will it change and expand? Will regionalism be able to bridge the North-South gap?

In the twenty first century, regionalism in North America must confront these questions. If North America as a region is to endure or prosper, then it will have to contend with powerful forces in the global political economy and within its own region. Launching a regional integration agreement (or RIA), as hard as that may be, is still easier than sustaining one. The regional and global inducements for North American regionalism also carry with them the constraints on its potential to survive beyond the fifteen-year transition period of the NAFTA.

Impressive forces influence the future of North America as a region. Cultural identity, nationalism, protectionism, value divergence, policy dissimilarities, coalition politics, and the North-South divide were not strong enough to deny a first step toward regionalism. But they remain consequential for the future of North America as a region. Regionalization of interdependence, asymmetric power relations, and transnational ties among neighbors has also contributed to the North American experiment. So too did the timely convergence over economic policy within all three states. Broadly shared features in politics, history, and culture laid the cornerstone for building a North American edifice. To some extent then, the future of North America as a region is a variation on a familiar theme about how states, firms, and peoples in Europe, Asia, and the world relate to one another.

For all regions in the world, unity always contends with diversity. Fragmentation and integration coexist. In Europe, the Single European Act and the Maastricht agreement symbolize one trend; different levels of participation among the members and the widening to the east signal another. Monetary union suggests a tilt toward unity. Still, Europe's members react differently to these tendencies. The sluggish growth of the core states contrasts with the faster growth of the periphery. In the late 1990s, France and Germany were "growing apart". Diversity in economic performance began to affect the relationship.[1] Asia is not very different in this respect. Asian views of the state and capitalism provide a loose sense of commonality but the region is more geographic than economic. Diversity and fragmentation blended uneasily with unity and integration during the economic crisis of the late 1990s.

As for North America, diversity and unity are powerful trends affecting the region's future. Fragmenting and integrative trends coexist. With a stronger sense of regionalism than Asia, North America found a rudimentary basis upon which to build a regional venture. Some unity and modest integration allowed North America to make some gains on regionalism. But fragmentation is resilient. Politics, distribution of gains, and the North-South question in North America are potent sources of fragmentation. Bringing countries closer together offers both gains and vulnerabilities. This lesson was delivered with full force in 1998. Brazil, Indonesia, and Russia experienced default, inflation, devaluation and other economically disturbing trends. In Asia, the free movement of capital, long championed by U.S. and other policy makers, fostered vulnerabilities with very severe, short-term consequences.[2]

Does North America Exist?

The brief answer is yes; in other words, North America is a region. But the real issue is more interesting. What does it mean to claim that North America is a region? That becomes a more challenging issue.

The North American states are legally committed to each other through a regional integration agreement. They are also connected to each other in ways that they are not so connected with other countries or regions. They treat each other differently and do things with each other differently than they do with those outside North America. In other words, they are regionalist by treaty and regionalized in reality.

Must there be something more for North America as a region to exist? Some would argue yes, that there must be something more than this, at least if the North American Three are to live with and benefit from their closer ties. In other words, while North America need not become like Europe, it has to become something more than it is now. That means that its members must up the ante on regionalism; they must be willing to do more than they have done so far and perhaps they must do more --perhaps even far more-- than they originally intended in 1994.

The United States, Canada, and Mexico have made prudent, moderate commitments to North America. Their view of North America is therefore limited. The region is part of strategy rather than a goal of each state. Coming more closely together is meant to help them individually as states. It was not intended to create something in and of itself, a purpose beyond the national interests of each. As such, there are no official regional standards but regionalization may in fact homogenize standards over time. There are no supranational institutions worthy of the name, although some NAFTA panels for solving disputes may suggest the beginnings of something like this. The intent was modest and therefore the coherence of the region is also modest. Of course, what is intended and what is eventually done is not always the same. For example, public debate in Canada and Mexico during the late 1990s considered the possibility that the U.S. dollar become the currency for Canada and Mexico.

Disavowing lofty ambitions about a highly integrated region is politically comprehensible. Not dealing with the problems that makes a more robust regionalism necessary is not. Ultimately, what matters is how one views the concept of region in terms of North America's own realities. North America is not and perhaps does not aspire to become a highly integrated region of similar states and economic systems but it is also true that it has only recently attempted to coordinate and manage more tightly its intra-regional relations on trade, investment, and other issues.

The twenty first century may bear witness to the emergence of a coherent, more highly integrated North America. If this does happen, NAFTA will be seen with hindsight as a vital initial step in that direction. However, it cannot serve as a charter or constitution for North America. There is more to a region than a common understanding about economic exchange. Judging North America entirely by such official regionalism is entirely too myopic. Informal, private, cultural, and economic links among the North American Three may be even more important in strengthening the ties within the North American region.

Hegemony or Partnership?

Whose North America is it? If North America is an U.S. preserve and protectorate, then the region is a hegemonic or pyramidal invention. The other view is that it is a more complex, evolving relationship between three unequal states. This is the view of the region as an emerging partnership, or the North American triangle.

The first view of whose North America is it stresses power and structure. With the Cold War over, the United States is the last superpower. The world still relies upon U.S. power perhaps far more than it should (Kupchan, 1998: 40). In this view, hegemonic decline is hyperbole. At the regional level, the United States is the core of a "natural unipolarity". North America is really an American enterprise (Clarkson, 1998: 14). Canada and Mexico are at the periphery of this unipolar system.

The second view begs to differ somewhat from the first. Asymmetry is mostly benign rather than coercive. A consensual bargain between the core and periphery blends power asymmetry and consensus (Kupchan, 1998: 42-43). Structure points to hegemony; interests point to consensus. Power is not exercised unilaterally or arbitrarily because the core and the periphery live in the same neighborhood. Moderation, self-constraint, and self-binding actions dilute the harsher possibilities of a relentless, domineering core (Ikenberry, 1998/1999: 45). Partnership can grow at the expense of paternalism in such a region.

At the dawn of the twenty first century, North America is situated somewhere between simple hegemony and complex partnership. But what will the future bring? If North America is to become a full fledged region, it must gradually move away from hegemonic paternalism and move closer to an equal partnership. North America's structure will never be egalitarian but this does not prohibit cooperation and negotiation. In fact, it requires just that. If one state breaks apart, it will affect the others. If another is unable to move out of poverty and underdevelopment, its plight may have durable impact on the others. If the core is overbearing, it may make solutions all but impossible. It may also lead the states to look elsewhere. After all, North America is unlikely to put all its eggs in its own basket.

The Fate of the State

We are told that the state is in retreat (Strange, 1996). Even so, it is not vanquished, at least not yet. The irony of North America is that the state is being used to create a region that makes less use of the state. If regionalism succeeds, the state will become less vital to the region. This can happen in several ways. First, regionalism allows for a state role, but regionalism will become less important if the North American Three flourish in a globalized economy. Why use the state to guarantee regional privileges if the more important source of growth and prosperity comes from outside North America? Second, North America is being regionalized. States are the midwives of regionalized interdependence as they are of globalization but it also is a powerful challenger to state rules and standards. Third, the trend in North America is to marginalize states. The irony of NAFTA is that states used their rule-making authority to make states less important compared to markets. After NAFTA's transition period, the state should recede from a dominant role in the economic relations among its members. However, it will enforce rules about outside trade and investment. That, at least, is the theory behind it.

To some extent, the future is already here. All three states are lessening national governmental control over their own economies and polities. Canada is already highly decentralized; Mexico, although the most centralized in North America appears to be going in the same direction. The United States is somewhere in the middle. North America does not seem to be looking for active, aggressive states searching for answers to regional or national problems. If that is what will happen in the future, the state in North America will continue to slide toward a supportive rather than a more central role in the political economy of the region.

What must be acknowledged, however, is that regionalism requires states. The state in North America is not descending a slippery slope into oblivion. A regional integration agreement like NAFTA is state-created. It is meant to regulate and disadvantage non-members in their economic ties with the members of the agreement. Politics and protectionism are part of such regional options. But such arrangements may also lean toward markets as well; they can also increase efficiency, competition and liberalization (Frankel, 1997: 207). Subsidies, tariffs and non-tariff barriers, investment codes, and other traditional types of state intervention in the economy will gradually erode.

The state will keep its hand in. For one thing, the alternatives to modest state action are far from ideal. Supranational institutions governing a host of economic policies are not the North American answer at this point. Markets and regionalization may take up some of the slack in a liberal continent, but North American states remain steadfast about their basic prerogatives. Social and political problems may challenge the state to protect some domestic groups from regionalization and globalization.

As far as the state is concerned, one can still distinguish between retreat and defeat.

The future of the state may be murky but it also is unimaginable that the state in North America will have no important or secondary role in the region. Indeed, North America as a region requires it to some extent. What has yet to be made clear is just what role the state will play in a state-sponsored regionalism based upon markets and liberalism.

Resisting Regionalism

Will domestic opposition derail regionalism in North America? The nationalist groups opposed to liberal regionalism lost the battle in the early 1990s when NAFTA was approved. Even so, they are far from defeated. On the other hand, the liberal coalitions backing free trade in the late 1980s and early 1990s were less secure at the turn of the century than they once were. Resisting North American regionalism is about who wins what and how much. It is the classic struggle over the distribution of gains.

Regionalism is impossible without state support. In the early 1990s, free trade coalitions gained the upper hand in all three states. This was indeed a breakthrough for regionalism. The Bush/Clinton support for NAFTA was critical to its eventual adoption of implementing legislation in 1993, despite ferocious opposition in the Congress. The support in Mexico for NAFTA rested upon a lack of viable alternatives to NAFTA and the political resources of a popular, semi-authoritarian regime. In Canada, the government took a leap of faith for free trade (Clarkson, 1998: 19). Popular support in Canada for free trade remained equivocal.

The advance of the neoliberal agenda and regionalism in North America slowed perceptibly in the late 1990s. A number of factors were responsible for this shift in momentum. For one thing, international economic conditions had changed. The "threat" of aggressively exporting economies in the Asian Pacific lessened considerably when several economies, including that of Japan, sank into a deep recession for most of the 1990s. Financial weakness in Asia did not awaken the same sense of urgency in North American regionalism, as did financial prowess. For another, the economic boom in North America relieved some pressure to pursue a regionalist option quite so ardently. Fueled by the U.S. economic resurgence, North America gradually pulled out of its economic lethargy of the late 1980s and early 1990s. Prosperity for many and stagnation for some has not translated into stronger support for the regional agenda on free trade. Canada's slow recovery from recession also had an impact. As for Mexico, the Mexican economy went on a roller coaster ride in the 1990s. Neoliberal leaders in favor of free trade were discredited for their management of the economy. Growing unemployment and poverty badly shook the widespread confidence and faith in Mexico's neoliberal project.

At the dawn of the century, domestic coalitions favoring free trade and liberal policies were weakened. Less formidable than they were in the early 1990s, they still have strong supporters in financial, corporate, and government circles. The United States is once again a major battleground. Nationalists, populists, unions, environmentalists, and cultural defenders have been able to deny further inroads for North American regionalism or for its extension throughout the hemisphere. The nationalist-statist coalitions are skeptical of regional cooperation because it siphons off economic help for some groups and curbs redistributive policies (Solingen, 1998: 40-41). There is probably no more important forum for the struggle over free trade than the U.S. Congress. Without a ruling free trade coalition in Congress, North American regionalism will stand still. The failure to get fast track authorization in 1997 reflected severe divisions between Congressional Democrats and the White House.[3] This problem for free trade is not so much a resurgence of protectionism as it is a lack of consensus about trade-related issues that blocks a free trade agenda from gaining momentum in the Congress (Destler, 1998: 139). The stress and strains of neoliberal regionalism and globalization are also rippling more widely throughout the societies and politics of many countries (Rodrik, 1997: 4).

Standing Pat or Moving South?

Where should North America go from here? This is another issue facing the North American Three at the dawn of the century. North America can stay where it is but it also must be a part of broader changes in the Americas. The future of regionalism may not be solely North American or even South American. It could also be hemispheric. This Pan American vision of regionalism goes back almost two centuries. It has regained momentum at the beginning of the twenty first century.

Standing pat in North America is the odds on favorite. Since 1994, when NAFTA came into effect, the momentum to push North American regionalism in new directions or to build on what was done earlier has largely been lost for the time being. The North American triumvirate is unable or unwilling to move toward either a wider regional group based on NAFTA or toward a more deeply integrated one involving the original three members.   What is more, one should not expect that the immediate future will offer up a dramatic breakthrough in North American regionalism.

A shift toward a deepened regional experiment in North America would be a bold step in regional statecraft.   Certainly, it would fire up considerable interest and controversy within all three countries.   Dramatic policy initiatives to make North America more integrated are not in the cards at this juncture.   What is more likely is less dramatic.   Integration by stealth or in other words by regionalized interdependence would be more likely.   Free trade and liberal integration schemes are politically charged in all three countries.   Domestic coalitions would have to be more widely supported than they are now to gain a major momentum for a deepened North America. Therefore, North America as a genuine community is mostly a deferred dream.   Plural identities and regionalized interdependence are more likely.

If becoming more like the EU is politically impossible in North America, then what can be said about moving toward a widened region with new members from elsewhere in the Americas? Going hemispheric is possible.   It is even more likely than deepening early in the twenty first century.   Still, there is more than one way to do this.   Including new members in NAFTA would mean allowing the rest of the Americas to join. Potential new members from South America, such as Chile, could turn North America away from itself and make it a more inclusive region.   But this has not happened.   Expanding NAFTA to the south has gone nowhere so far.   The political will in North America, especially in the United States, is clearly a major factor in the failure to widen NAFTA.

Something else could happen.   Bypassing NAFTA as the regional architecture for the entire hemisphere does not rule out a North American role in the hemisphere. If NAFTA is not widened, for domestic and regional reasons, then North America can still stake out a place for itself in a regionalism for North and South.   In this sense, the strategy could be that the ideas of North American regionalism rather than the actual structure of it might be pursued more broadly.   NAFTA will continue to exist, but North America will not put all of its eggs in that basket.

Since 1994, the same year as NAFTA came into effect, the Americas, North and South, have been moving slowly toward hemispheric regionalism.   The Miami Summit of 1994 and the Santiago Summit a few years later put most of the hemisphere on track toward a free trade area of the Americas (FTAA).   By 2005, the hemispheric states seek to create a free trade agreement including North America, South America, and most of the rest of hemisphere (except Cuba) (Feinberg, 1997: 151-160). In these ongoing negotiations, North American states put forth their ideas about trade and trade related issues. North America, as a regional pole within the Americas, may use its own regionalism as a limited model or template for hemispheric integration.

If it does in fact happen, a FTAA may not look quite like NAFTA. Negotiations over an FTAA will have to reconcile North America's way of pursuing regionalism with that of South America. Convergence is possible over some issues such as domestic liberalization, state subsidies, intellectual property rights, and other issues. But it is by no means certain that NAFTA's views on labor and the environment will be acceptable to MERCOSUR countries such as Brazil. The face of North American regionalism may be different from what that of the FTAA.

Getting the entire hemisphere on the same wavelength may be more difficult than it was for getting the North American Three to agree among themselves on NAFTA. For one thing, North America is a special place in which the United States claims a unique role. South America is more inclined to go its own way on some issues. The process of working toward a FTAA provides few clear answers so far. It is difficult to say what the FTAA will become. So far, NAFTA countries have not taken stands on the FTAA based on their bloc affiliation (Morton, 1999: 271). Still, North American states will no doubt be important to any genuinely hemispheric FTAA. To what extent any final agreement will be an amalgam of preferences from throughout the hemisphere or to what extent North American, especially U.S., preferences will hold sway over the final agreement is only for time to tell. The United States holds a lot of cards but it does not hold all of them.

North American leaders may find it difficult to exert influence on the negotiations for the FTAA. For one thing, South American regionalism has a life of its own. While it is drawn to the idea of an FTAA, the leadership from the South on this issue is unwilling to subscribe to a FTAA under any conditions. For another, the United States is a great power even in the hemisphere but it is domestically at odds over how to pursue free trade agreements. The U.S. Congress, Democratic Party resistance, and problematic leadership from the White House could cast a shadow over U.S. leadership on the FTAA. While pushing for North American views in the FTAA is more likely than widening NAFTA to the south, one should not take it for granted that the FTAA, if and when it does become a reality, is just what North America would have wanted.

That leaves the status quo. Just trying to make the original NAFTA work is at least practical if not particularly exciting. The United States, Canada, and Mexico apparently regard a little integration as a good thing.

Despite the issues it begs and the omissions it sidesteps, NAFTA does as much or as little as the three states can agree on at this point. The current North American style of regionalism is circumspect. It calls for lower level integration, minimal regional institutionalization, limited compromises with sovereignty, and a preservation of national prerogatives above all else. Even if this means limiting the economic benefits to one and all, it may be politically unsustainable to transform NAFTA into anything more than a limited venture.

North and South in North America

Will the North and South be able to build bridges and mutually prosper in North America? Building bridges means drawing closer together. It involves greater interdependence between North and South and between firms, groups, peoples, and states as their destinies become entwined. It means intensifying links and connections across borders.

There is nothing quick or easy about North-South integration, and some even doubt that it can happen at all. For some, integration of the rich and poor can do something for both. Relying on different advantages and endowments, the rich and the poor can mutually gain (Weintraub, 1995). "All boats rise together" is the liberal refrain. For others, the differences between the North and South are reason for doubt (Grunwald, 1995: 71). Rather than growing convergences in incomes and wages, only the wealthy in the developed countries may reap major benefits. Relative gains will be hard to even out.

It is too soon to tell what North America can teach us about North and South integration. Mexico's membership as a Southern country in an exclusive club of the North is the key. If large segments of Mexicans do not gain or if some gain far more in relative terms than others, then North-South integration may be hard to justify. The same can be said for the more vulnerable groups such as semi-skilled workers in the North. A very demanding test of North-South integration is that everyone gains something and no one gain an inordinately large amount compared to others.

In one sense, North-South integration has already succeeded. When it joined NAFTA, Mexico agreed to think and act like a member of the North. Mexico is willing to live with North American, especially U.S., rules of the game. North-South integration locked in Mexico's economic reforms. Mexico has moved ahead to the extent that it acts more like the North than it once did.

Mexico's integration with the United States and Canada is limited. The regionalism of North America does not demand a great deal of anyone. The RIAs of North America are free trade agreements, but little more than that. They are not highly integrated schemes requiring monetary and economic union. But integration can come from doing things together without official pacts devised by national governments. North America is being regionalized through greater connections between non-state actors. The real test of building North-South bridges may come through these informal but omnipresent activities.

What has happened so far? More time is needed to draw conclusions about North-South integration in North America. The picture so far is mixed and it may remain so for quite a while. Mexico did register absolute gains in trade volume, investment, and growth not long after the NAFTA came into effect. Some have become well off and were able to pad their already substantial assets.

Relative gains are very uneven. Of course, not every thing, good or bad, can be laid at the doorstep of North American regionalism. Each of the states remains responsible for their own economic policies. Still, the benefits of liberalism and regionalism in Mexico are decidedly mixed. The promises of such initiatives in the late 1990s were unfulfilled for many Mexicans (Pastor and Wise, 1997). This may change with time, of course, if initial pains lead to later gains. For the time being, the gaps between North and South may even be widening.

Appraising North South regional integration comes ultimately down to outcomes. Certainly, there are absolute gains, despite the 1995 downturn in the Mexican economy. But trade policy may have only marginally affected economic performance one way or the other. If North and South are to benefit, then a wide array of people and businesses north and south of the Rio Grande must enjoy relative gains as well. Aggregate gains or gains for large business are not enough to claim success for this daring experiment.

For now, it is impossible to say whether North America will successfully narrow the gap between North and South. However, if NAFTA compiles a modest record of success, it will be tempting to tout it as a model for other regional integration arrangements involving the global North and South. If the record is far less comforting or even mixed, then NAFTA and North America will have far less credibility for effectively integrating North and South.

Prospects in the New Millennium

More than most states, the United States, Canada and Mexico share a future and a region. And like most states, the North American Three have their own reasons for coming closer together to face the present and the future. Of all the factors that persuaded if not actually compelled them to come together in some fashion, the most important is the changing global political economy and their national capabilities to reap the rewards and meet the challenges it offers. Huddling together affords each of them in their own way some comfort and advantages. But none of the three are willing to forsake their own traditions, distinctiveness, and prerogatives to make North American regionalism their essential and overriding goal.

North America will hold to the idea of the state but it will set constraints on how it will guide the future of North America and its peoples. Bringing North America closer together is a limited responsibility of the nation-state in the region but the state is to do this by stepping away from an active role. Neither will the states of North America eagerly surrender what power they still have to a supraregional state. Nibbled at from below and resistant to pooling sovereignty from above, the North American states will have a constricted but still vital role in shaping the region in the twenty first century.

This century could become the century of regionalism and cooperation in North America in a way that the last century was not. Even so, the future remains formidable. The region faces issues about power and interests, asymmetry and partnership, fragmentation and integration, states and markets, regionalization and globalization. The future of North America is therefore up for grabs. Neither a goal nor a cure, regionalism does nevertheless have the potential to affect the collective well being of its members. And it consequently has the potential to influence the destinies of the region, its states, and its peoples, not to mention the world as a whole.

Notes

[1] The French economy outperformed the German economy in the late 1990s, 'Growing Apart,' *The Economist*, vol. 351, no. 8121, May 1999, pp. 48-49.

[2] Volatility in currency flows has been linked by some to the rather rapid, and even forced, pace of liberalization in these economies, N.D.Kristoff with D.E. Sanger, 'How U.S. Wooed Asia to Let Cash Flow In," *New York Times,* February 16, 1999, pp. A1, A10.

[3] President Clinton's alliance with Republicans on free trade clearly irked House Democrats who withheld the votes necessary to gain fast track approval in November, 1997, James A.

Barnes and Richard E. Cohen, 'Divided Democrats,' *National Journal*, vol. 29, no. 46, November 15, 1999, pp. 2304-2307.

References

Barnes, J.A. and R.E. Cohen (1997), 'Divided Democrats,' *National Journal*, vol. 29, no. 46 (November 15), pp. 2304-2307.

Clarkson, S. (1998), *Fearful Asymmetries: The Challenge of Analyzing Continental Systems in a Globalizing World*, Canadian-American Public Policy Occasional Paper No. 35, September, Orono, Maine.

Destler, I. M. (1998), 'Congress and Free Trade', in R.A. Pastor and R. Fernandez de Castro (eds.), *The Controversial Pivot: The U.S. Congress and North America*, The Brookings Institution, Washington, D.C., pp. 121-146.

Feinberg, R.E. (1997), *Summitry in the Americas: A Progress Report.* Institute for International Economics, Washington, D.C.

Frankel, J. A. (1997), Regional *Trading Blocs in the World Economic System.* Institute for International Economics, Washington. D.C.

'Growing Apart' (1999), *The Economist*, vol. 351, no. 8121 (May 29), pp. 48-49.

Grunwald, J. (1995), 'Expanding the NAFTA? From Early Pan American to Hemispheric Regional Integration', in R.S. Belous and J. Lemco (eds), *NAFTA as a Model of Development: The Benefits and Costs of Merging High- and Low-Wage Areas*, State University of New York Press, Albany, pp. 59-76.

Ikenberry, G J. (1998/1999), 'Institutions, Strategic Restraint, and the Persistence of the American Postwar Order', *International Security*, vol. 23, no. 3, pp. 43-78.

Kristoff, N. D. with D. E. Sanger (1999), 'How U.S. Wooed Asia to Let Cash Flow In', *New York Times*, February 16, pp. A1, A10.

Kupchan, C. A (1998), 'After Pax Americana: Benign Power, Regional Integration, and the Sources of a Stable Multipolarity', *International Security*, vol. 23, no. 2, pp. 40-79.

Morton, C. (1999), 'Progress toward Free Trade in the Western Hemisphere since 1994', in Richard E. Feinberg and Robin L. Rosenberg (eds.), *Civil Society and the Summit of the Americas: The 1998 Santiago Summit*, North-South Press Center, University of Miami, Coral Gables, pp. 249-311.

Pastor, M. and C. Wise (1997), 'State Policy, Distribution, and Neoliberal Reform in Mexico', *Journal of Latin American Studies*, vol. 29, no. 2, pp. 419-456.

Rodrik, D. (1997), *Has Globalization Gone Too Far?* Institute for International Economics, Washington, D.C.

Solingen, E. (1998), *Regional Orders at Century's Dawn: Global and Domestic Influences on Grand Strategy*, Princeton University Press, Princeton.

Strange, S. (1996), *The Retreat of the State: The Diffusion of Power in the World Economy*, Cambridge University Press, Cambridge.

Weintraub, S. (1995), 'The North American Free Trade Agreement and Developing Countries', in R.S. Belous and Jonathan Lemco (eds.), *NAFTA as a Model of Development: The Benefits and Costs of Merging High- and low-Wage Areas*, State University of New York Press, Albany, pp. 77-84.

7 The Role of Russia in the Redefinition of European Security

ERHAN BÜYÜKAKINCI

Introduction

Since the break-up of the USSR at the end of 1991, the Russian Federation has sought ways to establish itself as an independent force in international relations. As the core entity of the former Soviet Union, Russia inherited the formal Soviet positions in international relations; however, this fact did not directly give Russia the status and influence of the former USSR. So, it has tried to carve out a new role in international relations. During the past eight years, Russia's search for a definitive role in world politics has taken on a zigzag course, looking for permanent friends in a changing world of alliances. At present, Russia's status in international relations is still unresolved. The Russian Federation is neither a superpower like the USSR, nor a minor, easily dismissed power.

This work aims to discuss Russia's points of view on its own position in Europe and on the European security identity. In fact, there are two arenas in which this process is defined: first, Russia plays an active part in this development as a major actor with the American support in a global context. Secondly, at regional level, Russia is not directly included in the negotiation process relating the Western Europe. In this context, we aim rather to study the relations between Russia and the international institutions which have influence on European security. At the same time, Russian political groups' reactions vis-à-vis the developments in Europe and the priorities of the Russian foreign policy makers on the new process should be considered as intervening factors in this study.

Security Studies and Foreign Policy Analysis

The study of the foreign policy variables defined with J.N. Rosenau's famous pre-theories is mainly discussed and developed by the behaviorist works in the theories of international relations. According to behaviorist thinkers, the "security" concept could be defined from the point of view of the impact of the (external) environment on the internal variables of the foreign policy-making process of any state. The behaviorist approach did not carry out any significative study on the security interests of the states, however wanted to realize the empiric studies of interstate conflicts and disputes by using quantitative methods in the field of War Studies. Thus, the parameters consist of the "concrete" behaviors of the states. "Threat sources" which form the basis of security concept and military strategies are generally studied outside the scope of foreign policy-making process, because these subjects directly concern the military means of international politics. However, it is not possible to exclude the points of view of the states on their security concerns and their decision making process from the independent variables in the foreign policy analysis.

On the other hand, we want to discuss this following question by opening a brief parenthesis. From a general sense, it is possible to observe, in the methodology of international relations based on analytic approach with description (dependent variables) and explanation (independent variables), that the "security" concept is concretized with the decisions and behaviors of the actors and that these actors (i.e. the Nation-States for the realist approach) direct their decisions toward the existing system as dependent variables, by developing and carrying out such policies concerning their security concerns, strategies of alliance. So, the security studies are rather descriptive works, because the approaches on defence strategies, military policies and armed actions occurred in such circumstances are decisions, behaviors, and so outcomes. To quest the causality of these outcomes, the starting point is the "national interest", as suppose the realist authors. Meanwhile, we have no intention to repeat the conceptual discussion between realists and behaviorists, but the security concerns which find their origin in the question of "survival", form always the first topics in the negotiations between political actors in world politics.

The actors in world politics tend to formulate common policies based on some concepts in institutional structures, by perceiving their inability to ensure their own security by themselves. While the circumstances change, these concepts and strategies should be revised and new structures and mechanisms emerge in accordance with the new realities. Thus, it indicates, at the same time, the change of regimes and balance of power in the international system.

A New System, Old and New Institutions

In our times, attempts on security and defence policies in world politics are possible, not by the decisions taken by the single states by themselves, but by the institutionalized structures at international level. The systemic duality of the bipolar period lit its place to a pluralist regime; the increase of the number of actors led the disappearance of the logic of monolithic threat and put in agenda the diversification of threat sources. During the transition period, the redefinition of the role of some institutions in accordance with new circumstances was considered as a search for a new identity and the idea of creating new other institutions in world politics was not admitted by major powers which did not want to provoke a radical change in the existing system. To explain this reserve, it is possible to underline that the struggles of interest among states which are members in the same organizations are very clearly exposed for a long period in the history and that these institutions attained some degree of maturity from the structural and functional points of view. Because, if there exist a new process of restructuring, the clearance of the differences of approaches within the institutions and the consolidation of their policies and missions would necessitate again a long term, so the major powers opt for giving new functions and casting for a new identity to the old institutions during the transition periods. This change of identity could be found consistent to Krasner's theory of international regimes (Krasner, 1983). Whereas the harmony based on the equilibrium between the interests of all participating actors in regime, is not negatively affected, the regime can survive with conceptual changes. In fact, functionalism becomes more important.

The end of the Cold War was an end of a system based on bipolar order and some institutions, specially some of the security and defence organizations which have guaranteed the equilibrium in the old system were dissolved and abandoned their place to the new quests for partnership and alliances. At the same time, other institutions in search of new identities and missions were obliged to carry out structural changes. The reformulation of the "threat" concept in accordance with interstate and transnational elements in the post-Cold War era led the major states and the organizations able to use force at international level to quest their existence. On the other hand, military missions were diversified in their contents and goals for the consolidation of the peace in the new order and the stabilization of all the operating factors. The development of the concepts such as conflict prevention and crisis management for the disputes in regional and global politics would show which actors will be more efficient in these operations.

The Characteristics of the Russian Foreign Policy in Transition

Why are we looking first at the foreign policy variables of Russia before studying its points of view on European security? It is possible to explain this from various points of view. First, Russia is living a multi-dimensional process of transition and shows some signs of sensitivity and vulnerability towards the external environment and domestic evolution. Furthermore, Russia's new decision-making mechanism does not manage neither to formulate policies in continuation with those of its Soviet predecessor, nor to develop a relative stability during its transition process. At the same time, a vulnerable Russia has no other alternatives outside the Western support and should pursue a pragmatic policy in accordance with international circumstances to become again a world power.

The process of transition since 1989 necessitated the restructuring of the former Communist states with the rules of liberal democracy and free market economy. In this process, these states adopted special programs based on several models and wanted to reduce the risks of social tensions. Some of them were ready to these structural changes. However, it was easy to predict that this process would be long and hard in a country such as Russia, because the post-Communist transition occurs on many plans in Russia and the leaders in power did not have constant preferences among the policies to adopt. Just after the declaration of independence, the priority was given to economic policies, while the cooperation with the West was crucial to support these programs. But the political transition which began before the dissolution of the Duma at the end of 1993 showed that this transformation would provoke many problems in Russia. Even if the political regime had begun its consolidation with the adoption of a new Constitution and free elections in 1993, it is not possible to talk about a political stability in this country (Kulikov, 1997). On the other hand, the degenerate structures of the old system, such as corruption, are also present in the new regime; the presence of Russian-speaking communities beyond the Russian borders, the emergence of new interest groups which took advantage of the economic disorder and the differences of regional development increased the Russian leaders' sensitivity and the vulnerability of the Russian state at international level.

While the unstable structure of governmental variables negatively affects the implementation of economic reforms, it is possible to observe their impact on the foreign policy decisions. Because the policy-makers in the decision process want both to conserve the domestic balance in order to prevent social crises and to develop Russian interests at international level. So, it is possible to ask this question: do the interests of the Russian state consist of re-obtaining its old status of world power or does the Russian government try to get over this transitional process with less loses? Even if there are some advantages for Moscow, such as the status of nuclear State, the privileged seat in the UN Security Council, Russia has already admitted its dependence on the Western aid during this transition process. But this dependence and the risk of injury of the national interests provoke a wide fear in Russia's body politic.

The issues of Russia's predicament and the appropriate foreign policy paradigm to actualize its goals and ambitions remained inadvertently tied to the definitions of the different Russian groups. By 1992, three major clusters of opinion emerged in the Russian body politic: liberal-atlanticist, statist-eurasianist and conservative (communist-nationalist). Each had its own distinct definition of Russia's national identity (Sakwa, 1996; Prizel, 1998).

The liberal Atlanticist school, consisting mainly of the remnants of the broad coalition that propelled Yeltsin to power, has not deviated from its original approach to Russia's place in the international system. According to this school, Russia will become a normal and democratic country only when it abandons all pretensions. (Hunter, 1994, p. 148) Russia's hope for salvation lies in rapid integration with the "West". Thus, the West, primarily the United States, comprises the most important circle with the countries adjacent to the former Soviet Union taking second priority and the CIS, although pivotal for Russia both in cultural and economic terms, the least significant in Russia's quest to become a "normal" country.

Some liberal thinkers asserted that the only way for Russia to ensure that it is not separated from Europe is to support the admission of the Central European countries into NATO, since such membership would stabilize them politically and reduce their fear and hostility vis-à-vis Russia. On the other hand, the speed of Russia's normalization of the relations with other CIS states would be directly proportional to Russia's integration to the West.

The supremacy of liberal conception as the shaping force of Russia's foreign policy turned out to be short lived. Several of the basic assumptions of the liberal paradigm failed to materialize. The Western aid turned out to be far smaller than the liberals assumed. The collapse of the liberal paradigm, paralleling Russia's domestic politics, saw a migration of many of its original adherents to the centrist and even the nationalist camps.

As the break-up of the USSR caused many liberals to move to the right on domestic issues, an analogous shift has occurred within the foreign policy-makers, leading to the emergence of centrist-Eurasianist and conservative camps. The fundamental approach of the centrists is that Russia's economic, cultural, and political links to the first circle are such that it will have to remain the pillar of political and economic stability across the post-Soviet area. While most centrists concede the irreversibility of the disintegration of the USSR, most consider that Russia's predominant weight within the CIS and the presence of Russian-speaking populations in the Near Abroad are the legitimate tools of the Russian policy.

The statists are determined to integrate Russia into the core of the international system. In particular, the CIS must proceed with deeper economic and eventually political integration, with Russia asserting itself as *primus inter pares* within the Commonwealth (Dawisha-Parrott, 1995, pp. 200-201). They reason that Russia's security problems are exclusively confined to the Eurasian geography; so, they argue that it is vital for Russia to develop intimate relations with the major powers in Europe.

In his review on Russia's changing foreign policy rhetoric, Kortunov observed a certain intellectual migration within the Russian body politic. "The liberals became pragmatists (centrists) and the pragmatists became nationalists" (Prizel, p. 255). The conservative group includes members ranging from monarchists, the Russian Orthodox Church to extreme nationalists, to hardline communists. Despite their differences, these factions share a basic consensus about Russia's place within the international system and the interpretation of the Russian history.

Whereas both the Westernizers and the centrists see the ultimate goal of the Russian foreign policy as its integration into the world economy and international system, the nationalist camp aims to recreate a supranational Russian state. While there are Communists who believe in the reincarnation of the USSR and nationalists who believe in the birth of a Russian unitary state modelled on the tsarist empire, most nationalists and communists assume a more flexible position. Among the nationalists, there is a strong body of opinion that accepts Solzhenitsyn's notion of a Russian state built around the core of East Slavdom and Orthodoxy (Prizel, p. 258).

The best illustration of the Russian conservatives' views toward the West, especially the USA, was encapsulated by their attitude toward NATO. Although the liberals see NATO and the American global presence as vital elements contributing to Russia's national security, and although the centrists' main concern is the possible exclusion of Russia from NATO rather than objections to the organization as such, Russian nationalists see any NATO effort to expand its contacts with Russia and the former states of the Warsaw Pact as a sinister plan aimed at the further disintegration of Russia. To some conservatives, NATO has become an American instrument for fomenting crises and violence in order to provide a pretext for the US to bolster its global hegemony.

Despite the differences between these approaches, there appear to be a few central points of agreement in defining the course of the Russian foreign policy. Russia was intent on becoming a full partner in international relations from the very first days of 1992 and wanted to be viewed as a major power, not a "superpower", in its interaction with the major global powers. Secondly, Russia was keenly aware of the need to maintain its ties with the republics of the FSU and other near neighbors in Eastern Europe which were closely linked with the *ancien régime* (Shearman, 1995, p. 53).

The Evolution of the Russian Foreign Policy Rhetoric

In 1992, Russia appeared to be pursuing a liberal, pro-Western foreign policy, with high expectations of forging a new partnership with the West. To some Russians, the new foreign policy initially pursued by the Yeltsin government appeared to be subservience to the West. The opponents of the atlanticist foreign policy argued that Russia was subordinating its national interests to those of the West. A backlash against the atlanticist policy grew, as alternative approaches to Russian foreign policy were suggested from various quarters. Within two years, the statist approach appeared to be gaining strength, as a compromise between the liberals and the more radical nationalists.

In response to domestic pressures, Yeltsin replaced Kozyrev with a foreign policy figure of greater stature within the country in 1996. Primakov's nomination can be seen as a victory for those who favored a more assertive foreign policy over those who sought a more conciliatory and pro-Western foreign policy. Primakov maintained that the future relationship with the West would depend on whether the West could see Russia as an equal power. He often underlined that he wanted a good relationship with the Western powers, especially the US, but always in the context of advancing Russian national interests.[1] Under his direction in Foreign and Prime Ministry, Russia has appeared to have a more assertive and successful foreign policy. Although Primakov favored a strong relationship with the West, he is also known to want to pursue a multifaceted foreign policy in which Russia seeks influence and a strong role in other parts of the world, often in conflict with the Western interests and preferences. His successors, Stepashin and Putin have aimed at the continuity of statist policies; in particular, Putin seems to look for the reinforcement of Russia's position in the world affairs, although the Chechen war becomes more complicated issue.

The Russian foreign policy has sought to have concrete recognition from the strongest economic powers in the world, the Group of 7 (G7), of its own status and role. Russia was invited to G7 meetings, because the United States insisted that Russia should attend as an observer. After several meetings, the G7 has become the Group of 8. On the other hand,

Russia was invited to join the Paris Club, the major of creditor nations, with debtors primarily in the Third World. Cooperation for eight years has included significant aid from the IMF and the G7 states, but not as much Russia sought or needed.

The relationship with the West has not lived up to expectations of achieving partnership; instead, there is some dependency on the West which, from time to time, rescued the Russian government from crisis. Russia's neighbors are weaker than Russia. To the degree, that Russia has to assist or help them, Russia itself may be further weakened (Büyükakinci, 1998). Russia's limited resources mean that it cannot always exert as much influence as desired wish in the neighboring states, yet it remains significantly intervened with them economically and militarily.

The Russian foreign policy seeks to identify an independent path, involving the cooperation with the West and the continuation of its influence in the FSU area. Its intention of defining and implementing an assertive foreign policy is clouded by the persistent economic and financial crises; it cannot be independent of the Western powers so long as it is under the shadow of economic crises. It will need the G8 to bail it out of severe crises, as occurred in the summer of 1998.

After eight years, there is an emerging pattern to Russian foreign policy, but there are still unresolved issues. The gravitation toward and away from the West, and the involvement in or occasional indifference to the FSU states suggest a country in search of a direction.

Is it Possible to Expect a "Belligerent" Foreign Policy from Russia in the Phase of Transition?

In our century, the belligerent tendencies of democratizing states have received a special attention, given that so many countries are now living democratic transitions. As Mansfield and Snyder have argued, "Countries do not become democracies overnight. More typically, they go through a rocky transitional period, where democratic control over foreign policy is partial, where mass politics mixes in a volatile way with authoritarian elite politic... In this transitional phase of democratization, countries become more aggressive and war-prone, ... and they do fight war with democratic states" (Mansfield-Snyder, 1996, p. 301).

In a State with new and weak democratic institutions, "there is no reason to expect that mass politics will produce the same impact on foreign policy as it does in mature democracies" (Mansfield-Snyder, p. 318). On the contrary, Mansfield and Snyder suggest the opposite, a more belligerent foreign policy. It is possible to observe a belligerent policy provoked by the presence of weak institutions, but a second critical variable should be considered: the belligerent preferences of social groups that stand to lose in the process of democratization or in a regime transformation. In all changes of regime, the incumbent groups from the *ancien régime* forfeit some degree of power and wealth, while new groups gain new rights and privileges. When the groups from the *ancien régime* are threatened, they may seek to maintain or regain power through extraordinary means, including war (McFaul, 1998, p. 9).

Regarding contemporary Russia, Mansfield and Snyder note that "foreign policy is likewise providing the glue for an emerging red-brown coalition of nationalists and neo-communists" (Mansfield-Snyder, p. 329). More generally, regime changes creates an uncertain political context in which "bad leaders" can come to the fore, and bad leaders "are usually the catalysts that turn potentially volatile situations into open warfare" (Brown, 1996, p. 571).

From this point of view, it is possible to suggest that the democratization in Russia is prone to produce international conflict, given that many destabilizing factors are present. First, Russia's protracted and confrontational transition from authoritarian rule has produced weak democratic institutions. Second, Russia's regime change has created many losers who could try to gain from provoking domestic conflict or international war as a means of recapturing their previously held power and wealth. Third, Russia's regime change has created a political space for the new belligerent ideologies, ranging from imperialists to Nazi followers (Umland, 1997)

Russia's protracted transition to democracy has not produced the belligerent foreign policies presaged by Mansfield and Snyder. While fragile democratic institutions have offered a permissive context for elites to dominate the foreign policy process within Russia, so far liberal groups with an interest in peace, especially new economic elites created through Russia's transition to a market economy, have prevailed over illiberal groups more prone to war.[2]

Russia's volatile and incomplete transition to democracy has created the contextual factors and political groups that have produced belligerent foreign policies in other countries undergoing regime change. In Russia, these factors contributed to the war in Chechnya. Until the Russian political system develops the array of liberal institutions and norms that constrain leaders more completely from fighting wars, several changes in the status quo could precipitate increased domestic conflict or a more aggressive foreign policy in the short and medium term.

The New Role of NATO in the Post-Cold War Period

The structural features of international politics that constrained and directed security policies and practices between 1947 and 1991 have, for the most part, vanished. Most of the institutions associated with the Cold War remain in place, but they are now casting about for new ontologies of their own policies. Is NATO to be a security "blanket", on standby against the eventuality of a newly aggressive and imperial Russia? Is it to become a security regime, encompassing all of Europe, as well as North America and the ex-Soviet republics? Or can it function as a security maker, intervening in ethnic and other conflicts that appear to threaten European stability?

In the post-Cold War era, NATO has confronted the challenge of remaining relevant in a transformed European security environment devoid of the threat of an all-out attack on Western Europe from the East. Indeed, NATO's primary task during the 1990s has been adapting its own political and military infrastructure to new threats while simultaneously responding to the demands of former Warsaw Pact members for inclusion in NATO processes in order to meet their own transformed security needs.

In fact, NATO is transforming from a military alliance into a security regime. Krasner has described an international regime as "a set of rules, norms, and procedures around which the expectations of actors converge in a certain issue area" (Krasner, 1983). States participate in security regimes so that common expectations about international behavior can be fostered and implemented. For NATO in the post-Cold War era, the principle of the security regime is the "collective management" of security interests. Presumably this would include the traditional core mission of collective defence, but could also include other principles such as regional instability beyond the zone of peace, proliferation of nuclear weapons, terrorism, humanitarian actions, and peacekeeping (Larrabee, 1997).

NATO is shifting toward becoming a security regime that provides the institutions and cooperation necessary to address the evolving threats to security that have emerged in the post-Cold War era.[3] The latest actions taken with regard to the Kosovo question illustrate this evolution well. Consensus was reached early around the principle that an enforced peace on warring parties in an intra-state conflict outside NATO's zone of security was in the interests of the Alliance. NATO's earlier change in institutional procedures to allow for the deployment of resources for "out-of-area" operations and the expansion of regime rules to include a broadened view of member obligations to include stepping up to contain instability in the Balkans, support this view.

The current issue in the European security is to define the security interests of all democratic and democratizing states of the Euro-Atlantic region and determine how best to collectively address common threats to security and to manage the new threats beyond NATO's borders. NATO must decide which institutional mechanisms to adapt and choose whether further enlargement or a continually enhanced partnership process will achieve the objectives of the democratic and democratizing states of the region.

According to some analysts, alliances can hardly survive without a sufficient threat, however, eight years after the end of the Cold War, NATO shows no signs of demise. The core of NATO during the Cold War, nuclear deterrence and collective defence enshrined in Article V of the Washington Treaty, is getting less important. Simultaneously, the definition of the NATO area, as indicated in Article VI, is losing relevance with the NATO-led operations in Bosnia and Kosovo.

A single, overriding threat originating from a monolithic source has been replaced by a multitude of different threats, including the resurgence of centuries-old ethnic conflicts that were covered up by the Cold War. The new missions of NATO will form the cornerstone of the new system of international security dealing with a much wider array of threats than was the case during the Cold War. The Gulf War and conflicts in Bosnia and Kosovo suggest that future wars involving NATO allies will concern resources in the Third World and ethnic upheavals. The real issue for NATO's future is not territorial defence, but rather its structural transformation into a crisis management alliance.

NATO's Transformation and the European Security and Defence Identity

Trends in European security are towards collective security, the concept of internal management of disputes rather than organizing against an external challenge as in collective defence. However, rather than building a collective security architecture from an institution designed for that, such as the OSCE, the US has persuaded its allies to use NATO as the basis of this new comprehensive European security architecture.

NATO wants to keep its collective defence commitments which have their roots in the Cold War; so does the Western European Union (WEU).[4] But both NATO and WEU have created instruments for crisis management and peace-keeping.[5] Complementary to its external adaptation, NATO began an internal transformation which, when complete, will make the Alliance more flexible, efficient, and European in character. Between 1991-1996, the trend was towards the creation of a European Security and Defence Identity that would be independent of NATO and serve the purposes of European integration. Beginning with the French-German Corps and the WEU, various attempts to create an operational military structure outside NATO fell short. Strong US resistance to ESDI combined with reticence among some key European countries to prevent the ESDI from emerging outside the NATO context.

An ESDI that was independent from NATO, while politically popular for some European leaders pushing for deep integration after the Maastricht Summit of the EU in 1992,[6] was never really a practical option. In particular, the WEU was a security institution without military infrastructure. Without training and military exercises, the WEU had no capability to project power or promote stability in the event of a crisis.

The Maastricht Treaty refers to the Western European Union as an integral part of the development of the European Union and requests the WEU to elaborate and implement decisions and actions of the European Union which have defence implications. In the "Petersberg Declaration" of June 1992, WEU members pledged their support for conflict prevention and peacekeeping efforts in cooperation with the then CSCE and with the United Nations Security Council.[7] At the ministerial meeting in November 1992 in Rome, WEU members agreed to enlarge the organization and invited Greece to become the tenth member.[8] And in May 1994, the WEU Council of Ministers issued the "Kirchberg Declaration", according the nine Central and Eastern European members of the Forum of Consultation the status of "associate partners".[9]

At the Brussels Summit in January 1994, NATO heads of state and government welcomed the entry into force of the Maastricht Treaty and the launching of the EU, as a means of strengthening the European pillar of the Alliance and allowing it to make a more coherent contribution to the security of all the Allies. In their declaration, they also welcomed the close and growing cooperation between NATO and the WEU, achieved on the basis of agreed principles of "complementarity" and "transparency". In this context, as part of the process of further expanding cooperation with the WEU as well as developing and adapting NATO's structures and procedures to new tasks, the heads of state and government endorsed the concept of *Combined Joint Task Forces* (CJTF).

On the other hand, the Treaty of Amsterdam of the EU of June 1997 included the Petersberg Tasks.[10] It simply states that "the WEU is an integral part of the development of the EU [...]; the EU shall [...] foster closer institutional relations with the WEU with a view to the possibility of integration of the WEU into the EU...".

The end result was an arrangement between NATO and WEU that the ESDI would be developed within NATO. A primary lesson of the Cold War era was that new challenges required early, efficient, and rapid responses to crisis. The failure of international institutions to deal adequately with the early years of the Balkan crisis prompted the US to formulate a proposal to realign NATO. Recognizing that the security of its members meant going beyond Article V missions and that there might be occasions when the US might not necessarily participate in operations, the US proposed a reorganization of NATO command structures based on CJTF which would permit the creation of an ESDI that was separable, but not separate from NATO (Barry, 1996, p. 84).

It has been essential that the ESDI grows within NATO given the weak performance of Europe without the American support in the early years of the Balkan crisis. On the other hand, the economic situation in some European states has played a key role in their opting for an ESDI within NATO.

Approved at the NATO's 50th Anniversary Summit at Washington, the Alliance's Strategic Concept, which is agreed conceptual basis for the military forces of all the members, facilitates complementarity between the Alliance and the emerging defence component of the European political unification process. Member countries have reaffirmed their intention to preserve their existing operational coherence since their security depends on it. However, they have welcomed the prospect of a gradual reinforcement of the role of the WEU, both as the defence component of the process of European unification and as a means of strengthening the European pillar of the Alliance.

The Interests of NATO in the Eastern Europe and Eurasia

The development of a process for enlarging NATO and the creation of a program to facilitate cooperative military relations within NATO were both responses to the dramatically changed security environment in post-Cold War Europe. The 1991 Rome Summit announced NATO's first steps toward adapting to its new security context. Two significant measures adopted in Rome included a new Strategic Concept for the Alliance[11] and the first attempt to institutionalize NATO's expansion effort to the East.

The attempt to redefine and to adapt NATO to the post-Cold War circumstances was reflected in the creation of the North Atlantic Cooperation Council (NACC) in 1991. Its purpose was to open up greater consultation and cooperation between the members of NATO and the former members of the Warsaw Pact in a wide-range of areas including civil-military relations, military doctrines, defence conversion and conceptual approaches to arms control.

A similar attempt to embrace the former Warsaw Pact states has been taken by the WEU. In May 1994, nine countries of Eastern Europe accepted an invitation from the WEU Council of Ministers to become "associate partners" of this organization. This arrangement was designed to encourage the gradual integration of the Eastern European nations into the common European political, economic and defence structures.

The NACC has an ambitious agenda including consultations open to democratic states from Central and Eastern Europe on defence planning, principles and key aspects of strategy. Most importantly, the NACC played a fundamental role in studying the operational guidelines for peace-keeping among NACC countries thereby bringing together the ideas and expertise from NATO and non-NATO countries.

To accommodate the shortcomings of the NACC, NATO created the PfP at the Brussels Summit in January 1994. The PfP includes 44 partnerships as well as opening up a PfP Planning and Review Process (PARP) to those countries which chose to integrate closely with NATO planning where they can exchange data on their defence plans and budgets, and identify areas in which they agree to work towards improving interoperability between their military forces and those of NATO in the fields of humanitarian operations (Moltke, 1994).

Russia agreed to adhere to the PfP in 1994, after obtaining the recognition of some advantageous status as a nuclear power and a permanent member of the Security Council. The individual program of bilateral cooperation with Russia was signed only on May 31, 1995.

The real impetus in PfP in the military operations dimension of the process has been partner cooperation in NATO's Implementation Force (IFOR) and now Stabilization Force (SFOR) missions in Bosnia.[12] It was clear that with IFOR an operational role for PfP had outstripped the alliance mechanisms in place to accommodate such missions. With the Russian participation in IFOR, the opportunity to learn more about NATO and to see its transparent nature helped to alleviate Moscow's fears about the organization.

At the June 1997 meeting in Sintra, NATO's defence and foreign ministers agreed on a new set of initiatives to further strengthen PfP as an enduring element of the European security architecture. At the same time, the foreign ministers decided to replace the old NACC by the Euro-Atlantic Partnership Council (EAPC). The EAPC, composed of 44 countries (16 members of NATO and 28 partners), should ensure the permanent contacts with the political committee of NATO. Its working program takes into consideration the main clauses of the Founding Act between NATO and Russia, as well as the Charter on the special partnership between the Alliance and Ukraine, signed at Madrid on July 9, 1997.

With the creation of the EAPC, NATO carries forward its transformation on the basis of a broad, cooperative approach to security. The EAPC is thus the logical political complement to a stronger, more operational PfP. This potential was partially realized with respect to the current crisis in Kosovo. On the other hand, the Combined Joint Task Forces (CJTF) are designed to include the participation of non-NATO countries. The CJTF concept would also facilitate the use of NATO's collective assets by the WEU, as well as provide a mechanism for involving non-NATO PfP partners in NATO-led operations.

The NATO Enlargement and the New Strategic Concept

At the Madrid Summit in July 1997, NATO invited three countries, Poland, Czech Republic, and Hungary, to begin accession talks on joining the Alliance and this process was completed in April 1999. As part of the enlargement process, NATO has sought to demonstrate that its intentions were not hostile towards Russia and that there was a new organization which has evolved beyond its traditional Cold War functions.

The NATO enlargement has begun a process fundamentally transforming this organization from an institution based on well-managed military principles of collective defence into an undefined collective security architecture for European security. The selection of three former Warsaw Pact states for the first round of enlargement was evidence of the significant progress made in the post-Communist sector of Europe. Romania, Slovenia, and the Baltic States each took heart in the fact, too, that they were specifically mentioned in the summit *communiqué* as eventual members of the alliance.[13]

NATO's policy-makers argue that changes that have occurred within NATO are not due to enlargement, but due to the changing nature of the threat; and that much of NATO's adaptations can be traced to its implementation of the 1991 Strategic Concept. An updated Strategic Concept is introduced at the Washington Summit in 1999, involving a wider security role for NATO by specifying new threats. Most of the new challenges will not be threats to NATO territory requiring an Article V response. They will not only be military, but also economic, political, societal and environmental concerns. And they will also be global, regional and local simultaneously. As in Bosnia, these coalitions will include NATO members as well as non-members (Gartner, 1998).

It was clear that NATO was sincere in its efforts to work with new democracies and to promote stability in Central and Eastern Europe. However, despite much initial enthusiasm for Russia's joining the PfP,

Moscow subsequently failed to make use of the opportunities provided by the program. At the same time, Russia began to implement a consistent and organized opposition to NATO enlargement.

The Russian centrists' opposition to the expansion of NATO can be explained by their belief that such an expansion would deepen Russia's sense of isolation and betrayal by the West. Russian centrists continue to advocate the creation of a collective security body under the aegis of either the OSCE, or the UN, a structure in which Russia will be able to fully participate (Arbatov). Therefore, when the Western allies offered Central and Eastern European countries, and the successor states of the former Soviet Union an affiliation with NATO under the rubric of Partnership for Peace in 1994, most centrists argued that Russia should accept the offer or risk isolating itself further and losing all possibility of affecting the debate within NATO.

Despite his statements that Russia will not tolerate the expansion of NATO to its borders and the threats that a "Cold Peace" will succeed the "Cold War" in the European arena, Yeltsin has not at any time closed the door to a strong Russian link to the West. Recognizing that Russia might not be able to abort the expansion of NATO, Yeltsin noted that he is confident that the USA and Russia will be able to reach an agreement on the outstanding issues affecting NATO. Ensuring that NATO enlargement does not increase security and stability for some who join, will fall on two primary elements of the new NATO: the enhanced Partnership for Peace and the newly created the Euro-Atlantic Partnership Council (EAPC).

There are several costs and risks to Russia in the context of the eastward expansion of NATO. First, the approach of powerful military groupings to Russia's very borders would make it necessary for Russia to consider all its security and defence concepts, to carry out structural re-organization of the armed forces, to redeploy troops. Second, carrying out these measures will naturally strain the military budget. Third, all these changes will threaten the military reforms presently under way. Fourth, the Russian society may perceive this expansion as a direct threat.

It was supposed that the PfP program could help close the gap between the security concerns of Russia, those of Central and Eastern European countries and the West. However, it did not satisfy Moscow which hoped for some special status with NATO; this goal was opposed by both the Western governments and Central and Eastern European countries. The Russian military pressured the government not to sign PfP, partly because they feared that any reinforcement of the links with NATO might lead to a democratization of the army and to increase the civilian control over it. But the fear of Russia being isolated proved decisive in government circles, and Russia officially joined PfP on June 22, 1994.

From 1992-99, NATO was energetic in its discussion of peace-keeping but reluctant to move from theory to practice in the Balkans. With the Bosnia peace accords, NATO proved its value as an adapted institution for addressing challenges to post-Cold War European security. Specially, NATO had shown the value of multinational military planning for what became the Bosnia Peace Implementation Forces (IFOR). IFOR was especially important to the new NATO in that over a dozen PfP states, including Russia, were integrated into the command structure.[14]

Some specialists recognize that Russia is still often perceived in Central and Eastern Europe as a potential threat. Even if Moscow reduced its armed forces all the way down to 1.5 million soldiers, it would still be the largest army in Europe. On the other hand, there is a great uncertainty about Russia's political future; Moscow's military intervention in Chechnya has aggravated their fears (Smoke, 1996, pp. 270-271).

The NATO-Russia Founding Act: Relations between an Institution and a State

The NATO-Russia relationship embodied in the Founding Act requires detailed attention. The most positive experience gained via NATO's partnership with Russia has been its experience in IFOR and SFOR where US and Russian forces serve together under a NATO command in most dangerous parts of Bosnia. However, the NATO-Russia relationship is not built upon this model. Rather, it is built upon a top-down concept stressing that Russia has a "voice, but not a veto" over NATO activities.

On 27 May 1997, the leaders of the sixteen NATO members and the Russian president signed in Paris the Founding Act on Mutual Relations, Cooperation and Security between the Russian Federation and the NATO - NATO Russia-Founding Act. The idea of an agreement with Russia resulted from the realization that the planned enlargement of NATO would be extremely burdened if Russia were to be permanently excluded. The presidential election campaign in 1996 and the leadership weaknesses in the Kremlin had substantially contributed towards occasionally intensifying Russian criticism of enlargement plans to the point of sinister threats of war. This could only be countered by giving Russia an appropriate place in the European security environment.

In the preamble of the Founding Act, Russia and NATO declare that they shall no longer consider each other as adversary. A free and undivided Europe as well as a stable and enduring partnership are specified as common goals. NATO states that it shall adapt its strategic concept to the new security environment in Europe. Russia, for its part, declares that it is willing to continue the building of a democratic society and to further reduce its conventional and nuclear forces. The first section of the Act includes commitments to norms of international behaviour as reflected in the UN Charter and the OSCE documents. Both sides commit themselves to strengthening the OSCE with the aim of creating a common area of security and stability in Europe.

The second section creates a new forum: the NATO - Russia Permanent Joint Council (PJC). This is the venue for consultations, cooperation, and consensus building between the Alliance and Russia. The section III details a broad range of topics on which NATO and Russia can consult and perhaps cooperate, including preventing and settling conflicts, peace-keeping, proliferation of weapons of mass destruction, and exchanging information on security and defence policies and forces. The section IV covers military issues. NATO and Russia commit themselves to pursuing promptly the work relating to the adaptation of the treaty governing conventional forces in Europe (CFE).[15] Finally, Section IV provides mechanisms to foster closer military-to-military cooperation between NATO and Russia, including by creating military liaison missions on both sides. It does not provide NATO or Russia at any stage with a right of veto over the actions of the other.

The first effects of this exertion of Russian influence could materialize when the decision taken in Madrid to invite a first group of candidates from Central Europe to membership negotiations is due for ratification in individual NATO member states. In subsequent steps towards enlargement with respect to the Baltic states, Russia's open opposition can be expected (Haglund, 1999, p. 12). Viewed from this angle, the Founding Act has been characterized by tremendous political volatility since NATO expressly agreed at the Madrid summit to discuss the membership of other countries from Eastern and Central Europe.

Furthermore, it should not be forgotten that the exertion of influence on the basis of the Founding Act not only moved in one direction. Through the NATO-Russia Council, the Alliance was not only exposing itself to Russian influence, but, vice versa, was also able to exert an influence on the Russian negotiating partner. In particular, the NATO-Russia Founding Act is a document of transition, whose significance will result from the relationship between NATO members and from further developments in Moscow. The document has helped pave the way for the accession of Poland, Hungary and the Czech Republic to the Alliance (Kamp, 1997).

The NATO-Russia Founding Act is the expression of an enduring commitment, undertaken at the highest political level, to build together a lasting and inclusive peace in the Euro-Atlantic area. It creates the framework for a new security partnership, as one step among the others which are being taken to build a stable, peaceful and undivided Europe. It allows the Alliance and Russia to forge a closer relationship, in the interests, not only of NATO and Russia, but also of all other states in the Euro-Atlantic area.

Russia's Prospects in Redefining its Security Interests

In practice, the West is trying both to expand and to maintain a cooperative dialogue with Russia. It is pursuing the difficult goal of trying to persuade Russia that NATO's enlargement strategy follows the utopian "logic of community" rather than the realist "logic of anarchy". Through negotiating a strategic partnership between NATO and Russia, the aim has been to try and demonstrate that NATO's expansion to the East is not the threatening act of an alliance in a balance-of-power system, but the stabilizing action of a gradually developing security community, based on cooperative security ideas, attempting to extend its boundaries to embrace the former adversaries (Hunter, 1995).

Moscow continues to assert a status of global power and always considers Europe as one of the priority objects of its privileged relations with the United States, the sole superpower in world politics. For the Kremlin, the expansion of NATO can only devote the influence of the United States on Europe and support their project to draw aside definitively Russia from the process of the definition of European security identity.

These reflexes also have contributed to discredit the alternative suggested by Moscow to the enlargement of NATO: the transformation of the OSCE into a central element of the future architecture of European security. Under these conditions, Moscow has to accept openly the initiatives of the OSCE in the post-Soviet area.

There exists a unanimity among Russian political parties, both radical and moderate, that the NATO's expansion is unnecessary and provocative. Reflecting this, Moscow had asked instead that the OSCE be strengthened and endowed with the capability to make it into an effective pan-European security organization. It is possible that Moscow will seek to empty NATO of its contents in order to transform it into an organization of security like the OSCE. The USA rejected Russia's proposals to expand the OSCE as the main institution guaranteeing security in Europe (Hanson, 1998).

It is significant that the positions against the NATO's expansion were shared not only by the "falcons", but also by considerable reformers of the therapy of shock. The foreign policy makers have also developed a discourse of opposition against the membership of the Central European countries to NATO. However, it is possible to argue that this rhetoric was due rather to the domestic circumstances, since this opposition was put into agenda especially before the presidential elections of 1996 (Averre, 1998).

According to the new "Concept of the national security of the Federation of Russia" approved by Yeltsin on 17 December 1997, "the prospect for the expansion of NATO to East and its transformation into a military and political dominant force in Europe create the threat of a new division of the continent, particularly dangerous because of the maintenance of mobile troops, nuclear weapons, and in the absence of effective multilateral mechanisms of peace-keeping in Europe" (Roubinski, p. 549). "The prospect for the expansion of NATO to the East is unacceptable for Russia, because it constitutes a threat for its national security" underlines the new Concept. The Russian tactics are simple: to prevent the rise of the communist-nationalists in the political life because of the continuity of economic crises.

Could the CIS be an Answer to the Expansion of NATO?

"Russian proposals for European security are concerned not only with finding alternatives to the enlargement of NATO to the East, but also with securing Russia's position as a leader within the former Soviet Union. This is especially evident when it comes to problems of peace-keeping and peace-making in Eurasia" (Jonson, 1998, p. 104).

Since the first days of the independence of Russia, the CIS has been a central focus of Russian foreign policy. Early in its new existence, Russia made a point of the fact that it was invoking a "Monroe Doctrine" to apply to the former Soviet republics (Sakwa, 1996). During this period, many agreements and treaties have been signed, and organizations created to cement relations among the CIS states.

To understand the reason why Russia insists on asking for the recognition of the CIS as a security organization such as NATO, we should have a look on the restructuring of this institution from this point of view. At this point, it will be possible to perceive if the CIS is an artificial institution founded to promote the Russian interests or if this is an organization to prevent the creation of ethnic conflicts and regional disputes in the post-Soviet area.

The first steps on the creation of a collective security system within the CIS were made just after the CIS was formed. In early 1992, within the framework of agreements on friendship and mutual assistance, Russia, Kazakhstan and Uzbekistan prepared the Draft Treaty on CS. Then, Armenia, Kyrgyzstan and Tajikistan agreed to sign a multilateral treaty on collective security. On 15 May 1992, in Tashkent, six states of the CIS signed the Treaty on Collective Security (TCS). The signing of this treaty has become a starting point for the development of collective security system within the CIS. Another three states, Azerbaijan, Belarus and Georgia, came to a conclusion that it was appropriate to set up defensive alliance within the CIS. Having changed their previous attitude, the leadership of those countries decided that it is better to join the Treaty.

The participating states in the TCS agreed that "the participating states will conduct consultations with each other on all important issues of international security touching upon their interests and will coordinate their positions regarding those issues". A key provision of the Treaty is that the participating states agree to view aggression against one of them as aggression "against all participating states of the present Treaty". In accordance with the TCS, the participating states pledge "in case an act of aggression is committed against any of the participating states, all other participating states will render the necessary assistance to it and will also provide support with the available means in terms of exercising the rights for collective defence in compliance with Article 51 of the UN Charter".[16]

An important issue, concerning the use of the armed forces of the participating states, should be pointed out. The TCS signatories regard the use of the armed forces outside the territory of the participating states as admissible, specifying that such a use "may be conducted exclusively in the interests of the international security in strict compliance with the UN Charter and the legislation of other participating states of the present Treaty" (Art. 6).

The real status of bilateral relations of certain participating states of the Treaty (i.e. Armenia-Azerbaijan) and the measures taken by these countries against each other, draws the question whether the following obligation is universal or not : "participating states will not join any military alliances or take part in any grouping of states, as well as in the activities aimed against another participating state" (Art.1). This obligation observed in general in the relationship with the third countries, as well as the obligation "not to sign international agreements, discordant with the present Treaty" (Art. 8), suggest that the main purpose of these obligations is to restrain the signatory states from participating in other regional alliances or coalitions associated with resolving security issues.

It is only mentioned in the Declaration of Participating States in TCS, adopted by the Council of Collective Security at the Almaty session on 10 February 1995, that the participating states "view the NATO Partnership for Peace program as a real alternative to mechanical expansion of NATO". They feel that its practical implementation "should be oriented on forming a universal all European structure of military-political cooperation that would strengthen the foundation of the OSCE".

The Concept of "Collective Security" of the TCS participating states was also adopted at the Almaty session. The Concept is the aggregate view of the TCS participating states on preventing and eliminating threats to peace, collective defence from aggression, providing for their sovereignty and territorial integrity. At the same time, a plan of gradual development of the military security system on the basis of TCS was developed in 1995 in the Headquarters of the Allied Forces.

Peacekeeping, aimed at settling and preventing conflicts in the CIS States primarily through peaceful political and diplomatic means, is an inherent component of effort to provide stability in the CIS territory. In 1992, just after the CIS came into being, the issue of localization of ethnic conflicts in the post-Soviet area was most urgent; such conflicts were in existence in High-Karabakh, South Ossetia, Transdniester, Tajikistan, Abkhazia, North Ossetia and Ingushetia.

The first item of the CIS agenda to resolve crisis situations in the conflict areas was conduct of peace-enforcement and peace-keeping operations, with the use of the armed forces of the CIS. The first step in this direction was the signing in March 1992 in K'yiv an agreement regarding "Groups of Military Observers and Allied Peace-keeping Forces in the CIS".[17] This agreement had a nature of an umbrella agreement. In connection with it, in May 1992, in Tashkent, a series of documents were signed, defining the composition of these groups, technical support, legal status of the personnel, and funding. The agreement was signed by all CIS representatives, however Azerbaijan and Ukraine signed it with provisos.

The Charter of the CIS reflects striving of all the CIS states towards peaceful settlement of all conflicts and joint contributions to the pace-making activity in the CIS territory. Another important document of the CIS, the Concept of Collective Security contains a provision that the Council of CSS of the TCS "may set up collective forces for peace-keeping operations conducted in accordance with a decision of the UN Security Council and OSCE". In January 1996, the CIS participating states adopted the Concept of Conflict Prevention and Settlement of Conflicts in the CIS territory. According to this document, "peace-keeping and stability are inherent to the CIS, providing economic, social-political development of both, each participating state and the Commonwealth as a whole". According to the Concept, conflict prevention and settlement activity comprises three directions: conflict prevention measures, settlement of the armed forces and post-conflict peace building.

Generally, peace-making within the CIS plays an important role in its activity. However, there are different reasons to peacekeeping ineffectiveness: lack of experience, complexity of conflicts with the involvement of interests of many parties and confronting political groups, economic crisis and interstate political struggle within the CIS states.

Russia plays a unique role. In fact, it turned out to be the sole CIS state interested in organizing and conducting peace-making operations within the CIS and capable to do so. It acts as a mediator at the negotiations, as a party providing implementation of cease-fire agreements, contributes forces and resources and provides the budget for peace-making and peace-keeping operations. On the other hand, the CIS provides a regional forum to discuss and adopt political statements. Practical measures for conflict settlement are taken by Russia, with little support of the CIS countries (Kubicek, 1999). It is very important to note that the UN and the OSCE are not prepared for full-term involvement in conflict settlement in the CIS. The fact that all conflicts are in the areas, traditionally considered to be Russia's zone of influence, and in some cases, where the interests of a Russian-speaking population are directly involved, constitute a unique problem.

Despite persistent efforts of Russia, the TCS is likely to have the fate of dozens of other documents signed by the CIS leaders, that remain as declarations of good intentions. The attempts to create a regional collective security system, having military-political goals associated with the preservation of a single area of defence as allied armed forces, were not successful. One of the reasons is that the new independent states interpret Russia's attempts to more clearly define the formation of a security structure within the CIS with a certain deal of distrust.

Although certain elements that could constitute a security system, have been set up, the system, as a whole, is not clearly seen yet. This situation is not likely to change in the near future if the possibility is excluded that future NATO enlargement will force Russia, Belarus (Alexandrova-Timmerman, 1998),[18] and some other CIS countries, to take reciprocal measures, in terms of strengthening the foundation of a collective security system within the CIS.

Conclusion

What is concerned for Russia, it is a long quest of identity, an old theme of the Russian literature. It is also, for the same reason, the future of its relations with Europe, which have been confused throughout its history. From geographical and historical points of view, Russia will not lose its double membership to Europe and to Asia.

That is really true that Russia is living in a different world far from the ours, that this country is no longer in peace, like many other European countries. First, Russia is not in peace with itself, as the Chechen war, the political corruption and the social problems have shown. In the interior of the Russian Federation, multiple problems are in suspense, as in North Caucasus, Tatarstan or Daghestan. More generally, the struggles against anarchistic elements and organized crime only gives limited results. The question on a "Russian threat" finds its origin in the actual weakness of democratizing state, but this threat seems to be more important than the Soviet period. Because nobody is able to control all the intervening factors in such as a country in a structural transition and to anticipate the prospects of the Russian foreign policy behaviors. Russia has immense frontiers in a changing world and unstable geography. When it is known that half of its borders have a solid legal basis, it will be so easy to perceive the sense of insecurity. These changes deeply touch the Russian pride, but also its identity. But they do not really disturb the Russians when they wonder about their security in the next century. The eventuality of a dispute with the West appears practically nil to them.

In conclusion, we could meditate on the famous phrase: "the victory is more pleasant than the defeat, but it so hard poses problems". Russia is an essential partner for Europe, but remains largely unforeseeable. It would be necessary to reinforce the partnership and to decrease the unforeseen. All the possibilities of consultation, cooperation and common actions must thus be exploited, because it is essential to develop more functional and operational relations with Russia. But it is also necessary to multiply the mechanisms of transparency and to establish reciprocal confidence between the parties. Cooperation and transparency undoubtedly answer well to the ambiguities of the time.

Notes

[1] When appointed Foreign Minister, Primakov identified four foreign policy objectives: the creation of the best external conditions conducive to strengthening the territorial integrity of the state; the strengthening of the centripetal tendencies in the territory of the FSU; the stabilization of the international situation at the regional level; the development of fruitful international relations that will prevent the new tensions. L. Cooper, *Russia and the World*, N.Y., St. Martin's Press, 1999, pp. 136-137.

[2] Regarding Russia's relations both with the West and with the states in the CIS, the combination of weak democratic institutions and Yeltsin's political success have allowed a small, well-organized coalition of economic interest groups to occupy a central role in the making of Russian foreign policy. The combination of super-presidentialism, a fragmented party system, and impotent countervailing forces representing pluralist interest means that these economic lobbies can dominate the policy-making in Russia, including foreign policy. T. Aydin and O. Bekar, *Türkiye'nin Orta ve Uzun Vadeli Ekonomik Cikarları acisindan Türk-Rus İliskileri,* Istanbul, TESEV Yay., 1997.

[3] NATO provides a good example for the transformation process from the old Cold War arrangement to the new post-Cold War system. The main purpose of the Alliance "had changed from one of preventing war to actively shaping peace" and NATO "was now about much more than just collective defence." From the speech given by Javier Solana, Secretary-General of NATO, at the Russian Council on Foreign and Security Policy, 20 March 1996.

[4] The WEU has its origins in the Brussels Treaty of Economic, Social and Cultural Collaboration and Collective Self-Defence of 1948, signed by Belgium, France, Luxembourg, the Netherlands, and the United Kingdom. The Treaty was the first formal step undertaken by the European powers towards the establishment of the North Atlantic Alliance. Following the signature of the North Atlantic Treaty in 1949, the exercise of the military responsibilities of the Brussels Treaty Organization, or Western Union, was transferred to the North Atlantic Alliance, in 1951. Under the Paris Agreements of 1954, the Federal Republic of Germany and Italy acceded to the Brussels Treaty and the organization was renamed the Western European Union. The WEU was reactivated in 1984 with a view to developing a common European defence identity through cooperation among its members in the security field.

[5] NATO and WEU share the same bifurcation; in their treaties (Article V), they present the collective defence concept. On the other hand, the crisis management (non-Article V) seems to be their new mission, as indicated in the Amsterdam Treaty with the inclusion of the Petersberg Tasks and as discussed in the new NATO with the PfP and EAPC.

[6] In December 1991 in Maastricht, the heads of state and government of the European Community countries adopted a Treaty on Political Union, and a Treaty on Economic and Monetary Union, which together form the Treaty on European Union (EU), commonly known as the Maastricht Treaty. The EU is composed of three "pillars". The first, known as the Community pillar, is based upon the Treaties of Paris and Rome, as modified by the 1986 Single European Act. The second pillar is that of the Common Foreign and Security Policy which is in the process of being developed. The third pillar relates to cooperation in the spheres of civil and criminal law and home affairs.

[7] As part of the efforts to strengthen WEU's operational role, a Planning Cell was set up. WEU members declared that they were prepared to make available military units from the whole spectrum of their conventional armed forces for military tasks conducted under the authority of the WEU. It was also agreed that military units of WEU member states could be employed for humanitarian and rescue tasks; peacekeeping tasks; and tasks of combat forces in crisis management, including peace-making.

[8] Greece became full member in the WEU in March 1995. Iceland, Norway and Turkey, as member countries of NATO, were granted associate member status; Denmark and Ireland, members of the European Union, became observers. With their accession to the European Union on 1 January 1995, and following completion of parliamentary procedures, Austria, Finland and Sweden also become WEU observers in 1995.

[9] The Kirchberg meeting established four levels of membership and association within the WEU: Members, Associate Members, Observers and Associate Partners.

[10] It states that "the [European] Union can avail itself of the WEU to elaborate and implement decisions of the EU on the tasks referred to ..." These are humanitarian and rescue tasks, peace-keeping tasks and combat forces tasks in crisis management, including peace-making. In fact, the Treaty of Amsterdam did not merge the WEU and the EU.

[11] The 1991 Strategic Concept reaffirmed NATO's commitment to its fundamental principle of collective defence, while recognizing security risks of a broader nature to include proliferation of weapons of mass destruction, terrorism, and regional crises. Specifically, the Concept called for the restructuring and reduction of military capabilities in order to

move away from an emphasis on massive mobilization so that crisis management and peacekeeping roles could be fulfilled.

[12] Fifteen partner nations contributed nearly 5,200 personnel to the total IFOR contingent of 51,300 troops. IFOR represented the evolution of PfP from training and exercises in the fields of peacekeeping and humanitarian operations to joint implementation of a NATO support operation. The timing of IFOR has led many analysts to the conclusion that the IFOR deployment was "a means of saving NATO rather than saving Bosnia". The experience in Bosnia, where 16 NATO countries are cooperating in the NATO-led peacekeeping force SFOR having no less than 20 non-NATO countries, is a model for the future.

[13] The Baltic states understand that their fate is tied to Russia's comfort with their eventual accession. The Baltics are encouraged that Russia has at least swallowed the first three new invitees and is beginning to play its role in the Alliance spelled out in the 1997 Founding Act. Russia's participation in the Permanent Joint Council may soften the distance between the poles.

[14] The close and effective cooperation between Russia and NATO in the implementation of the military aspects of the 1995 Peace Agreement on Bosnia-Herzegovina has added a new dimension to the evolving security partnership. The participation of Russian troops along with contingents of Allied and other partner nations reflects a shared political responsibility.

[15] The two parties agreed on working together in Vienna on the adaptation of the Treaty of CFE, as well as on a model of common security for Europe of 21st century.

[16] There is a major difference between the Treaty and the UN Charter concerning the decision on the use of the armed forces. Unlike the UN Charter, specifying that a decision on collective use of the armed forces is made by the Council of the Heads of the CIS member States, the Treaty says that "a decision on the use of the armed forces to repel aggression [...] is made by the heads of participating states" (Art. 6).

[17] In accordance with this agreement, Groups of Military Observers and Allied Peace-keeping Forces were supposed to become a CIS practical tool for "rendering one another, on the basis of mutual consent, assistance in settling and preventing conflicts on the interstate, religious and political foundation in the territory of any CIS nation-state" (Art. 1 of the Agreement).

[18] At this point, it should be added the negotiations of integration between Russia and Belarus. In April 1996, two countries signed the Treaty of Russian-Belarussian Community which prepared the institutional basis of an eventual union at political level.

References

Alexandrova, O. and Timmermann, H. (1998), "Russia-Biélorussie-CEI", *Politique Etrangere*, 1/98, pp. 93-108.

Arbatov, A. (1994), "Russian Foreign Policy Priorities after the 1990s", in T.P. Johnson and S.E. Miller (eds.), *Russian Security after the Cold War: Seven Views from Moscow*, London, Brassey's.

Averre, D. (1998), "NATO Expansion and Russian national interests", *European Security*, Vol. 7, no.1, Spring 1998 pp. 10-54.

Aydin, T. and Bekar, O. (1997), *Türkiye'nin Orta ve Uzun Vadeli Ekonomik Cikarları acisindan Türk-Rus İliskileri*, Istanbul, TESEV Yay.

Barry, C. (1996), "NATO's Combined Joint Task Forces in Theory and Practice", Survival, Vol. 38, No. 1, Spring 1996.

Brown, M. (1996), "The Causes and Regional Dimensions of internal conflict", in M. Brown, *The International Dimensions of Internal Conflict*, Cambridge, MIT Press.

Büyükakinci, E. (1998), "Komünizm sonrası gecisin iktisadi boyutu: Eski SSCB cumhuriyetlerinin iktisadi bağimsızlık yönündeki ilk adımları (1992-1995)", *Sosyal Bilimler Dergisi*, Istanbul University Publications, July 1998.

Cooper, L. (1999), *Russia and the World*, N.Y., St. Martin's Press.

Dawisha, K. and Parrott, B. (1995), *Russia and New States of Eurasia*, N.Y., Cambridge University Press.

Gartner, H. (1998), "European Security, NATO and the Transatlantic Link: Crisis Management", *European Security*, Vol. 7, no. 3, Autumn 1998, pp. 1-13.

Haglund, D. (1999), "NATO's Expansion and European Security: after Washington Summit", *European Security*, Vol. 8, no. 1, Spring 1999.

Hanson, M. (1998), "Russia and NATO Expansion", *European Security*, Vol. 7, no.2, Summer 1998, pp. 13-29.

Hunter, R.E. (1995), "Enlargement: Part of a Strategy for Projecting Stability into Central Europe", *NATO Review*, No. 43, May 1995.

Hunter, S.T. (1994), *The Transcaucasus in Transition: Nation Building and Conflict*, Washington D.C., CSIS.

Jonson, L. (1998), "Russia and European Security: Old Wine in new bottles ?", in W.E. Ferry and R.E. Kanet (eds.), *Post-Communist States in World Community*, N.Y., St. Martin's Press.

Kamp, K.H. (1997), "The NATO-Russia Founding Act: Trojan Horse or Milestone of Reconciliation?", *Aussenpolitik - German Foreign Affairs Review*, Vol. 48, no. 4.

Krasner, S. (1983), *International Regimes*, Ithaca, Cornell University Press.

Kubicek, P. (1999), "The End of the Line for the CIS", Problems of Post-Communism, March-April 1999, Vol. 46, no. 2, pp. 15-25.

Kulıkov, A.S. (1997), "Russian Policy in the sphere of national security", *European Security*, Vol. 6, no. 3, Autumn 1997, pp. 10-54.

Larrabee, F.S. (1997), *NATO Enlargement and the Post-Madrid Agenda*, Santa Monica (CA), RAND.

Mansfield, E.D. and Snyder, J. (1996), "Democratization and the Danger of War", in M. Brown, S. Lynn-Jones, and S. Miller (eds.), *Debating the Democratic Peace*, Cambridge, MIT Press.

McFaul, M. (1998), "A Precarious Peace : Domestic Politics in the Making of Russian Foreign Policy", *International Security*, Vol. 22, No. 3, Winter 1997/98.

Moltke, G. von (1994), "Building a Partnership for Peace", NATO Review, No. 42, June 1994.

Prizel, I. (1998), *National Identity and Foreign Policy*, Cambridge, Cambridge University.

Roubinski, Y. (1998), "La Russie et l'OTAN : une nouvelle étape ?", *Politique étrangere*, 4/97, Winter 1997-98.

Sakwa, R. (1996), *Russian Politics and Society*, London, Routledge.

Shearman, P. (1995), *Russian Foreign Policy since 1990*, San Francisco, Westview Press.

Smoke, R. (1996), *Perceptions of Security,*Manchester, Manchester University Press.

Umland, A. (1997), "The Post-Soviet Russian Extreme-Right", *Problems of Post-Communism*, Vol. 44, No. 4, July-August 1997, pp. 53-61.

8 Misleading Perceptions on Minority Rights in Greece

DIMITRI CHRISTOPOULOS

An Ambivalent Historical Heritage Towards Minorities

The issue of minority discourse in contemporary Greek politics seems to oscillate between two poles: disapproval of cultural diversity within the country and a forced tolerance towards minority rights. There are reasons for both. Public opinion, a considerable portion of the Greek academia, the political leadership and the Orthodox Church believe that the recent history of the Balkans plus Greece's fragile contemporary geopolitical position within the Balkan peninsula, are legitimate reasons to impose restrictions on minority behaviors. This denial of a minority's right to express its minority characteristics is believed to be in some ways imposed upon Greece by historical circumstances and geopolitical specificity of the so-called "powder-store of Europe", i.e. the Balkan peninsula, already well-burnt but still burning. The moral value of minority rights is either contested or regarded with (sometimes legitimate) suspicion. The threat of strategic minorities is even today omnipresent and overwhelmingly related to irredentist claims.

On the other hand, it is also argued today that things must change. Greece, a country with a high level of cultural and ethnic homogeneity, should not fear diversity among its citizens. Greece has been the only Balkan state that adopted the capitalistic mode of production after W.W.II. Since Greece is now a part of the liberal institutional context of Western Europe, it is believed that it could or should make some modifications on its dominant ideological pattern on Greek sovereignty, based on the identification of state, nation, language and religion.[1] According to this reformist strategy, Greek national identity must and can be more hospitable and generous towards minority identities[2] or show more tolerance for cultural diversity in general, since ethnic homogeneity has already more or

149

less been achieved. The few exceptions of non-Greek speaking populations are numerically insignificant and, in all cases, are radically decreasing. Most regional minority languages have gradually lost their communicative force.[3] This viewpoint also takes into consideration the fact that European unification has gradually become a factor in the political legitimization of minority demands. The institutional developments taking place within European organizations, notably the Council of Europe, the OSCE and to a lesser extent, the EU, have created an ideological framework in which minorities are no longer neglected. Today, Europe is "listening" to the minority voice as minorities are increasingly turning to Europe for help. The cost of hostile politics on behalf of the Greek state regarding minority rights is an insupportable weight for the country's (disputed by some) European profile.

However, both views, especially the first, neglect the fact that modern Greek political behaviors have not always been hostile towards minority issues.[4] Greek administrations have been far more liberal towards minorities during the century, and especially in periods, incomparably more unstable than the current one. Historical experience of the inter-war period provides sufficient evidence of a hyper-active and mobile official behavior towards minorities. The Greek administration did not hesitate to use the petitions system of the League of Nations and to expose the country to international control.[5] This system offered a very promising decision on the *Minority Schools in Albania*[6] to the Greek minority in Albania while the *Advisory Opinion* on the Greco-Bulgarian Convention of 1919 concerning immigration of respective minorities from both countries,[7] witnesses that the then administration accepted the internationalization of its minority issues, even the most sensitive ones.[8]

During this occasion, Greece, involuntarily of course, contributed at the most accurate conceptualization of minority rights that international law had ever achieved. In the case of *Minority Schools in Albania,* the Permanent Court of International Justice adopted an indirect approach to the question of minority definition and, by overlapping the then-on vicious circle of minority definition, proved to be more effective than a series of normative efforts aiming at the legal definition of minorities. The Court explained the purpose of the petitions system in a way, which cuts through all contemporary debates on minority rights or protection. The system intended to:

secure for certain elements incorporated in a State, the population of which differs from the in race, language or religion, the possibility of living peaceably alongside that population and co-operating amicably with it, while at the same time preserving the characteristics which distinguish them from the majority.[9]

The *Advisory Opinion* on the voluntary exchange of population between Greece and Bulgaria, offered an equally, if not more important, referential extract for international law:

The existence of communities is a question of fact; it is not a question of law. (...) From the point of view of the Convention, the question whether, according to local law, a community is or not recognized as a juridical person need not be considered.[10]

The above mentioned extract of the PCIJ is a slap for the post-W.W.II Greek official perception on minorities, which can be summarized in one simple sentence: *"in Greece there is one minority recognized by international treaty, the Muslims of Thrace, enjoying its rights and which makes up something more than the 1% of the population"*.

Times are Changing

On the 26th July 1999 the Greek Minister for Foreign Affairs, Mr. Yorgos Papandreou, referring to the Muslim minority of Western Thrace said: *"No one contests that there are many Muslims of Turkish origin. Of course, treaties refer to Muslims. From time to time, minority issues are related to territorial adjustments. If boundaries are not disputed, I really do not care whether one calls himself Turk, Muslim, Bulgarian, Pomak... On the contrary, if the term "Turkish minority" is used in order to create trouble, to change boarders, then of course this term creates a big problem."*[11] This statement and particularly its triumphal approval by the Turkish press[12] provoked a chain of very strong reactions from all sides of the Greek political spectrum and the press, most of these reactions being hostile to what we recently call in Greece, the *"right of individual self-determination"*. If we may summarize, the common ground of these reactions is that this statement *first,* changes the existing strategy of the country on the minority issue. *Secondly,* it provides the ground for irredentist arguments coming both from Turkey and FYR of Macedonia on behalf of the respective minorities in Greece. *Thirdly,* it can and will be used in order to protest and limit the country's national sovereignty on issues related to human and minority rights. *Last but not least,* it is dictated by the State Department in order to facilitate American involvement in the Greek-Turkish dialogue and actually reflects US views on the dispute.

This debate caused the intervention of Mr. Max van Der Stoel, High Commissioner on National Minorities of the OSCE. In his public statement of August 23, the HCNM offers his generous approval of the Papandreou statements, while trying to clarify aspects on the contemporary view of minority rights.[13] It is worth noting that this letter is the only official statement of the HCNM on Greece. According to the Minority Groups Research Centre,[14] "the various normative commitments adopted at the European and world level were implemented in spite of attempts made by Greece and some other states to restrict them as much as possible". Greece has traditionally been negative on the development of minority rights and has been at the forefront of the "conservative camp" of states, which have been against such developments. In several instances Greece has reacted on the spur-of-the-moment, reminiscent of the past (e.g. issues whose emphasis is on bilateral relations, reciprocity, rejection of a right to self-definition, non-interference in internal affairs and so on).[15] Since it is a common secret among all international bodies that the minority issue is among the most problematic of the country's behavior, the international organizations dealing with minorities have adopted a very delicate approach.

In this short study we will stand for the view that the term *"individual right to self-determination"*, is - according to recognized human rights standards - an obvious individual freedom, related to freedom of expression, as recognized by Article 14 of the Greek Constitution and Article 10 of the European Convention for Human Rights.[16] Furthermore, we shall attempt to lay down some basic principles on human rights and minorities in Greece, in order to contribute to a clarification of these concepts which have often been abused or misused and which ultimately have led to false conceptions.

The basic idea expressed here is the following: the choice of a (Greek) citizen to define his ethnic or national belonging according to his personal preference is *prima facie* an act carrying no legal importance. Such an act can be criticized as being based in false historical arguments. It can be considered as being a sign of a certain ethnic affiliation. It can finally be politically neglected as a traditionalist approach to identity – incompatible with modern liberal view of the self - or even morally rejected as a reactionary behavior. But, in all cases, it cannot be legally banned. What recently in Greece is defined as "the individual right to self-determination" or self-definition, is but a simple version of the individual freedom right to the development of personality. It is a right.

This right has been specifically referred to by individuals belonging to minorities in the notorious Copenhagen Concluding Document of the CSCE of 1989, then the cornerstone of contemporary European conception of minority protection, according to which *"belonging to a national minority is a matter of a person's individual choice and no disadvantage may arise from the exercise of this choice"* (article 32).

Minority Discourse in Greece

Let us, initially, attempt a definition of the term *minority discourse.* In Greek, the word for discourse is *logos,* a word carrying a double meaning. It can denote *reason* or *cause.* In this particular context, it conveys what in English is called the minority cause or issue. It can also, however, mean *speech* or *voice* i.e. the linguistic articulation necessary to establish communication with another individual or group. Here, in the minority context, it conveys the following meaning: the type of verbal expression a group chooses to use to express its needs or claims. It is obvious that the first definition of 'logos', meaning minority cause or question, refers to the *content* while the second, refers to the *form* of expression the minority voice takes.

This fluidity of meaning makes it difficult, if not impossible, to attempt any kind of classification of minority discourse. We are not adverse to minority typology, *in abstracto,* for it is a helpful tool in the field of political science and statistical research. Indeed, it offers specific data by locating phenomena or behaviors, such as linguistic or religious, which can then be used to make general deductions. However, care must be taken because the process of classifying phenomena (linguistic, religious, cultural, ethnic awareness or belonging) refers to minorities collectively and can only be estimated approximately. It does not account for individual divergence or exceptions.

For instance, the phrase "*Greeks are Christian Orthodox*" seems to be at first glance correct since a majority of Greeks are Christian Orthodox. However, it is misleading[17] since there are also Greek atheists, Catholics, Protestants etc. and Greek Muslims, a minority that has been classified and recognized by law as a religious minority by the Lausanne Treaty. These kinds of generalizations are at the core of the minority problem, are the essence of the minority cause. If we continue this train of reasoning further, the statement "*the Western Thrace minority is Muslim*" is incorrect, as well, since within the boundaries of the minority group one can also find atheists.[18]

The minority of Western Thrace has been recognized as a religious minority and is classified as such by the Greek administration.[19] This classification, however, gives birth to another claim, an inevitable claim which is a determinative factor in minority group politics; its claim to be recognized as an ethnic minority or its claim to acquire a national identity.[20] This claim acquires a concrete foundation because of the Lausanne Treaty, which endorses the legality of such classification techniques. Had the Greek government recognized Western Thrace's minority as an ethnic one or, for that matter, had it taken a neutral position on minority expression, such as that of ethnic or national consciousness as Minister Papandreou supported (cf. *infra*), the claim that was put forth, which today is considered the basic element of Western Thrace's minority discourse, would not be an issue at all.

The Two Paths of the Minority Cause

Although a minority cause refers to collective group behavior, it does not exclude the possibility of individual divergence from the group.[21] There are two roads of divergence.

Assimilation

The centrifugal forces at work in contemporary capitalistic societies, where market forces often attempt to dictate a unique cultural behavior pattern as the only sustainable one, often render the status of belonging to a minority unbearable, even if that particular group is not legally or politically persecuted.[22] The changes taking place within contemporary Europe, not only within the EU as a whole, but also within each separate state, changes such as the accumulation of capital, the urbanization of large portions of rural populations, the creation of a united market and current, the effort to achieve cultural unity within the context of the development of a European and universal economy, have brought about the gradual integration of large numbers of minority linguistic communities, including the ones in Greece.

Many of the characteristics, which differentiate minority groups from the majority, have already been assimilated or are still undergoing assimilation. In Greece, this process of integration has already been achieved by a big part of non-Greek speaking populations, with the exception of Western Thrace's minority and a portion of Slav-speaking Macedonians situated in the western and central part of the district of Macedonia, which, however, can be regionally considered as a numerous population.

In regards exclusively to the cultural aspect of language usage, some minority languages have begun to eclipse, as they are only spoken by a limited senior population. Such examples are the Arvanite (an Albanian dialect[23]) and to a lesser degree the Vlach language (a neolatin language[24]), both of which have fallen into decline. Especially for the Arvanite language, it appears that this decline is irrevocable and that in a generation or two the language will disappear, with some limited local exceptions.[25] The Vlach and to a lesser extent the Macedo-bulgare are no doubt under a process of marginalization. Efforts have been made to revitalize the latter through a radical political activism of a number of ethnic Macedonians. This language is, since 1945, the official one of the Socialist Republic of Macedonia and since 1991, the official language of the independent Republic. This is how the second path of the minority cause, the revival of the regional identity, makes itself visible to the public eye.

Divergence Towards the Minority: Revival of the Regional Identity

Today, in Europe we are witnessing the resurgence or ethnicisation of certain regional identities. The individual who seeks to re-establish contact with his cultural heritage, sees the group as a point of reference from which he can acquire a sense of belonging and is therefore drawn toward the group. Here, we see a rekindling of local customs and culture (folklore, songs). It is through these activities that the individual learns of his heritage. Regional identity offers a safe, visible and hospitable community environment.

The co-existence of these two tendencies within a group is possible, as we have seen with the examples cited above. This seems to be the case with the considerable portion of the Slav-speaking Macedonians located in Western and Central Macedonia. A significant part of the group's population follows the first path, i.e. the steady but gradual alienation from its cultural regional identity, while another part shows a growing desire to retain, protect and promote its heritage. Often enough the second path leads to a gradual change of view of its own past and to a political radicalization, often hostile to the Greek administration. The case of *Sidiropoulos against Greece* (1998),[26] a case well known in the European case law of human rights, is the most recent juridical specimen of this ongoing latent conflict between ethnic Macedonian activists and the Greek administration.

Recognition and Protection

Institutionally speaking, in order for a minority voice to be heard, there must first be a claim. A claim for minority *recognition* must be put forth. This status must be acknowledged by and bound to the legal framework of the state. Once the minority's existence is established in the public forum, it must then put forth a claim for *protection*. Actually, the claim for protection and recognition can be unified. This claim for protection of the minority's right to existence presupposes that it considers itself at a social disadvantage. Otherwise, general human rights standards applying for everyone would be enough.

It is usually the weak that ask for protection. Therefore, the group recognizes its own weakness because it feels directly threatened by the process of assimilation. When a minority group lays claim to the need for protection, in actuality, it recognizes the threat posed on its survival by assimilative forces. So, the road to forming a minority cause entails two stages: a claim for recognition *and* protection.

Let's examine the second stage first. From the moment the minority puts forth a claim for protection, we can say that the group has already formed its voice. The fact that the minority of Western Thrace has repeatedly requested better educational conditions constitutes a verbalization of the minority cause.[27] The form of expression used by a group to convey the message is of no matter, here. It can go through conventional channels, such as the filing of petitions, memoranda, resolutions etc., or it can take a more radical form of expression. In 1994, radical Muslim representatives burnt new schoolbooks issued by the Greek Ministry of Education, which were designated for minority use.[28]

Let us now examine the first stage, that of gaining recognition status. Here complications arise. We can distinguish *two cases*. First, the minority's explicitly expressed desire to be institutionally recognized. We can speak of three different procedures a minority can follow to legitimize its existence. First, a constitution can legitimize a minority. A number of European Constitutions have either directly recognized the multi-ethnic character of their countries or passed laws which guarantee the right to territorial or political autonomy, or, in a more general sense, consolidated that right by acknowledging the use of the minority's native language. Any consideration that the Greek Constitution might eventually in the foreseeable future include clauses relative to minorities is wishful thinking, a false historical and teleological perspective for reasons already given and analyzed. Mere mention of it would be counter-productive.

A minority can also be recognized by the signing of international, multilateral or bilateral agreements, which mutually bind the contracting parties to protect the minorities within their territories. The minority of Western Thrace falls into this category. Lastly, a third route is to gain indirect recognition, via national law, which regulates internal policy. An example of this would be the implementation of a minority educational program.

The fact that a group puts forth a claim to be granted a minority status through the above mentioned channels definitely constitutes a minority cause, which varies here according to the content, the type of expression used and the recipient of the claim. It stands to reason that the state would be the prime recipient of such a claim, since it complies with the fundamental principles a sovereign state follows. It is the state, which, in the final analysis, grants rights; therefore, it is to the state that minority claims are referred to. However, the state is not, nor has ever been the sole or even the prime recipient of these claims. Rarely do minorities solve their differences *directly* with the state. In most cases it has been through the intervention of international institutions that solutions have been found. And today we see this intervention to a greater extent than in previous times. International law, since its genesis, has dealt with minority protection.[29] Europe has played an increasingly important role in this direction since 1989. It has set up regional organizations and channels for human rights protection and security. The Council of Europe and the Organization for Security and Co-operation in Europe are such institutions. The process of unification that Europe is undergoing and the urgent need for solution have changed the fundamental parameters of the minority question. Once it was a cause for national strife and destabilization, now it is the key to long-term peace, stability, security and co-operation in Europe. Once it was the cause for discrimination, now it has become a human rights issue. And finally, it was once a reason to crusade for cultural unity. Now it has become a reason to protect and preserve the continent's cultural heritage.

Minorities in Greece, such as the Western Thrace Muslims (Turks, Pomaks and Roma), the Slav-speaking Macedonians – including (the ones considering themselves as) ethnic Macedonians - and other religious minorities have appealed to the above mentioned European institutions in their efforts to legitimize their claim for ethnic or religious identity. The fact that a number of individuals seeking justice have appealed to the European Court for Human Rights and have been partially vindicated, indicates that minority cause in Greece is obviously not being respected, or at least that is what these minorities believe. The physical presence and active participation of Thrace's Muslim and Slav Macedonian minorities in conferences held by the *Human Dimension* of the OSCE, is but another indication that minority questions seek, through European intervention, a perspective for their solution.

Minority Cause: Locked Between the Claim to Difference and the Request for Indifference

Is divergence *toward* a group an expression of minority cause in all cases? The delicate question for states that ensues here is the following: can we have divergence toward a group, revitalization of a regional identity without necessarily fulfilling the requirements of the existence of a minority? Our answer on this question is a positive one. Indeed, one can not speak of a minority cause when individuals simply seek to *express* aspects or characteristics of their culture. The existence of minority languages does not necessarily presuppose the existence of linguistic minorities. There are people who although speak a minority language, ask nothing more than to speak it freely. But does speaking your native language freely constitute a special minority right?[30] Of course not. We can say that, prior to and independent of the formal steps that a group takes to acquire a minority status through the channels we cited above, (ex. the implementation of educational programs in the minority's native tongue or the formal teaching of that language), there exists a completely different form of claiming.

It is not the right to show that one is *different* from the majority, but the request towards the state to remain *indifferent vis-à-vis* the regional identity. "*Let us speak our mother tongue in peace, let us protect it, let us set up associations for its promotion etc.*" That is all and it is enough. This is the case, we believe, for most of the speakers of minority languages in Greece. We are referring to the overwhelming majority of Vlachs, the Arvanites, as well as a large portion of Slav-speaking Macedonians, with the exception of that nationally not very significant but locally considerable portion we made mention of.

In the above example, we see that the centripetal movement toward the group does not form a minority cause. However, at first glance it appears that the form of expression used does refer to (and/or externalize) the group's behavioral patterns since it indicates its preference to use its native language freely. This action, however, does not constitute a specific minority right, since freedom of expression is one of the inalienable rights *every* individual in a rule of law regime has. It is evident that from the moment freedom of expression is guaranteed each individual is free to choose in which language this expression will be.

In short, we believe that the minority cause in Greece, from a human rights perspective, oscillates between *difference* and *indifference*. We must emphasize that this view does not aim to confine the broader social theory disciplines dealing with the minority issue, within the limits which we deem necessary to legally define the term, i.e. the claim for recognition and protection Social sciences, such as sociology, linguistics, ethnology, anthropology, political geography etc., evidently do not need to define the basic elements of their interpretations of minority cause though a legal prism. Besides, it is the point of view from which, we researchers aim to prove a theory, which creates, in the final analysis, scientific query.[31]

In law, therefore, minority cause can not exist unless a claim has been put forth. But really, what kind of social bond is necessary to unite two individuals which the only thing they have in common is a common descent? A common heritage is insufficient, even if it is the starting point from which a group is made. The group's claim is the important legal point from the moment jurisprudence is called upon to lay down the legal foundations for the peaceful co-existence between communities or to institute laws which protect human rights. Not a single minority can be protected if it does not first ask for protection. Law is not called upon to "discover" cultural communities; that is the goal of other sciences, such as anthropology. It is called upon to establish a set of rules or conditions, which will bring about the peaceful and just co-existence of a country's many different cultural communities. Follows a policy of *laissez faire*. But in order to do so, there must be a starting point. This point is not cultural diversity *in abstracto,* but the group's claim to it. If this condition is not met, the minority remains invisible in the public sphere. On a discursive level, the claim expresses the minority will only through its spokespersons attempting to *represent* the group. *Representation is a presupposition of the claim.*[32] Talking on behalf of the group requires the existence of an authority within the group and a sign of submission of the represented to the persons assuming that representation. The fundamental problem of this process is the impossible articulation between *representation* and *representativity.*[33] As we have said, within the group there are internal minorities. But the center of the group's legal order which assumes the representation states, what itself considers to be important enough and therefore able to be claimed. This paradox of the modern concept of representation does not concern only minorities but every represented group (syndicates, political parties etc.).[34]

What finally constitutes a minority for legal theory is its claim, while for other social sciences (ethnology, sociology, anthropology, geography, etc.) this criterion functions only subsidiarily. It is from this claim that the *moral* and *legal minority rights* are derived and, it is from the claim the necessity of *protection* is derived.

As already stated above, minority cause in Greece oscillates between the claim to be accepted as a different entity and the demand to the State to remain indifferent to the manifestation of the particularity. Legal order cannot but remain indifferent to the second phase of this dialectic vacillation. As we have said, the individual who speaks his native language or any language for that matter, or freely expresses his ethnic preference cannot be considered to be exercising a minority right. Nor can the freedom to express a sense of belonging, or what is termed in Greece as "the right of individual self-determination," be considered a right belonging solely to an individual belonging to a minority.

Greek legal order must adopt a stance of total indifference in regards to those Greek citizens who do not want to be considered Greek but prefer to be called Turks or Macedonians. The juridical debate that went on in the European Human Rights Commission in the *Sadik v. Greece* (1995) case essentially introduces an ethical question as to the individual's right to freedom of expression (article 10). The Commission *"has declared admissible the applicant's complaint that his conviction of having disrupted public peace, by distributing printed material referring to the Muslim population of Western Thrace as "Turks" violated his rights (...). As his conviction involved his writings, the Commission considered that the main issue arose under Article 10 of the convention"* (§33). It further asserted that *"in order to avoid rifts between the Christian and Muslim population of Western Thrace and to maintain their peaceful co-existence, moderation in political discussion may be desirable. However, it cannot find that, in the circumstances of this case, and in the absence of clear elements of incitement to violence, the imposition of a prison sentence for the use in public, namely in an election campaign, of the "Turk" in respect of the Muslim minority in that area can reasonably be regarded as a "necessary" measure in a democratic society"* (53§).[35] In other terms, since every individual has the right to freely say whether he belongs to or does not belong to a minority, he equally has the right to determine the nature of his belonging to the group. Greek law and order ought to remain indifferent in situations such as these and immediately cease penalizing the minority discourse. Whether Greece will at some future point grant minority recognition and pass laws for its protection is indeed another issue.

It is often difficult to distinguish between the claim to be different from the demand that the State should remain indifferent. Requiring *specific* minority rights is an issue of crucial political importance for the minority of Western Thrace. These claims focus on the improvement in minority education, reinforcement of religious freedom, administrative and civil law issues. The most characteristic example which balances between the two opposite poles (difference and indifference) thus making it difficult to distinguish, is that of the Slav-speaking Macedonians. It is impossible to make general deductions. We shall attempt however, to give a schematic representation of the phenomenon by using a typology, even with its inevitable faults. In this case we can discern three homocentric circles. Beginning with the outer circle, we find a group of people having as the only binding element the language spoken by their (grand) parents. The absence of minority cause here is evident and can be easily distinguished. As we continue toward the center of the circle, we enter a second level of cultural unity, which is more cohesive than the first one, since apart from the common heritage, they also share and use the same language. But again, this does not constitute minority cause. It is in this circle that the claim to indifference surfaces. The group's preference to use its mother tongue does not lay claim for it to be officially recognized. This fact shows that its stance is one of indifference towards any minority cause. This stance is founded on the human right to freedom of expression. The third and smallest circle is the minority's core. It is here that the right to an ethnic or national self-definition surfaces. It is here that the minority wants to establish its right to an ethnic Macedonian identity.[36] One could support the view that this too, lies well within the definition of freedom of expression, but equally calls for adoption of certain specific minority rights.

It should be noted that during the 90s - and especially due to the Greek position against the use of the name "Macedonia" by its north ex-Yugoslav neighbor - a new tendency of radicalization of Macedonian national consciousness emerged, as a collective reaction against the official Greek policy of denial of ethnic Macedonian identity. Most outstanding is the fact that such an attitude appeared equally within the ranks of a population that does not even speak the Macedo-bulgare. As it has correctly been said the Greek State "may be nurturing the very nightmare it wishes to dispel".[37]

The fact that the Greek state refuses to grant its citizens the right of belonging to a minority, if they choose to do so, has resulted in magnifying the problem and radicalizing group behaviors. The phrase *"I am Macedonian"* lies in the sphere of indifference and does not (or at least should not) affect a liberal legal order. Just as easily one can say one is Macedonian, Swedish or African in a rule of law regime without this meaning that claim for recognition has been laid forth. The above phrase *"I am Macedonian"* becomes an expression of minority discourse because the content of the phrase has been interpreted by Greek courts as an illegal action. The European Court for Human Rights in July 1998 (*Sidiropoulos against Greece*) condemned the Greek State for not having recognized a civil association created by ethnic Macedonians, just because the association's statute aimed at the protection and promotion of its cultural heritage. Van der Stoel's remarks about freedom of association were not for nothing.[38] In this case, Greece violated a simple human right to association and not any special minority right.[39] The fact that some individuals choose to deal with their culture so as to preserve it does not lie within the sphere of a minority right, but of a human right. On the contrary, the sentence *"I'm Macedonian, therefore, I want the right to be educated in my mother tongue"* can undoubtedly be considered a minority cause element because, in this case the individuals claim specific minority rights.

Human Rights and Minorities in Greece

High-ranking Greek officials and the overwhelming majority of scholars and intellectuals have acknowledged the rudimentary character of minority protection in Greece.[40] Greek citizenship policy - the principal aim of which is to protect national homogeneity - even after the abolition of notorious article 19 of the Greek Code of Citizen-ship[41] is in absolute need of reform,[42] for not only is it under heavy human rights criticism[43] but it has also been proven ineffective as far as its goals and results are concerned.

The inclusive character of the Greek national identity, traditional Orthodox Church and State ties, the reproduction of local decision-making structures on clientelist behavioral patterns, a fragile geopolitical environment and irredentist claims from neighboring countries provoking legitimate fears have lead to misleading perceptions of minority - as human- rights in modern Greece. However, in a rule of law regime, human rights and minority cause converge to the advantage of both the state and the minorities. When these two divert, then we have a reason for conflict.

The history of human rights is a history of continuous demands and claims. These demands become rights from the moment the situation is deemed dangerous and unsafe for the surrounding community. It is then that the community decides to legitimize the claim. That is the way that minority discourse is legalized. This seems to be the strategy Europe is following regarding the minority question and it appears that Greece, too, is now beginning to ponder the issue. A different approach to what we have already critically presented is equally possible and necessary. It is towards this fertile goal that we have tried to contribute with this brief essay.

Notes

[1] The Greek specificity here is only the last element of this ideal chain of four singular elements: religion. The first three, i.e. nation, state, language, were already the norm in France, from where a good number of Greek intellectuals imported the revolutionary ideology of Nation-State. In order to understand the Enlightenment's impact on Ottoman Balkan society, we must consider the relationship between class position and ethnicity. In the pre-1820s Ottoman Balkans, most of the urban strata, mercantile groups and religious and secular elites were either ethnic Greeks or acculturated into the Greek *ethnie* (...) After 1750, the influence of the Western Enlightenment led to secularization, liberalism and an undermining of the religious world view of the Eastern Church. With the French revolution, this trend intensified. Greek-Orthodox intellectuals reconceptualised the Orthodox *Rum millet*. They argued for a new, secular "Hellenic" national identity". V.Roudometof, "From *Rum Millet* to Greek Nation: Enlightenment, Secularization, and National Identity in Ottoman Balkan Society, 1453-1821", *Journal of Modern Greek Studies,* Volume 16,1998, p. 11. "Historical descent, language, culture and religion were triumphant in circumscribing the parameters of the reconstructed Greek ethnonational identity. Those who did not meet all these criteria were not considered authentic Greeks even if they were Greek citizens and even if their ancestors had lived in Greece for centuries; religious minorities, as well as ethnic minorities, were marginalised. The political regimes of the Metaxas dictatorship (1936-40), the post World War II semi-democracy culminating in the Papapodoulos-Ioannides military rule (1967-74) whose slogan was "Greece of Christian (Orthodox) Greeks", all espoused an exclusive ethnic identity in which religion was *sine qua non.*" A.Pollis, "Greece; a Problematic Secular State", *Legal issues of religious diversity in Greece,* D. Christopoulos (ed.) Kritiki publishers, Athens, 1999, (in Greek) pp. 165-197. Cf. also, "Greek National Identity: Religious Minorities, Rights and European Norms", *Journal of Modern Greek Studies,* Vol. 10:2, 1992, pp. 171-195.

[2] As the Greek historian T.Veremis writes: "The great changes in Europe impose a definitive abandon from the narrow-minded state conception of the cold war. Time is to return as nation to the generous views of Constantinos Paparigopoulos for a more hospitable identity, which has been the gnomon of the Greek civilization through out history." *Identities in Macedonia,* V. Gounaris, I.Michailides, G. Angelopoulos (ed.) Papazisi Pub. Athens, 1997 (in Greek), p. 8.

[3] It is has been asserted, however, that a country like Greece, having plenty of reasons to regard its national language as already a minority language within the context of the European Union, has equally plenty of reasons to advocate rights of minority languages. Cf. K. Tsitselikis, *The International and European Status of Linguistic Rights of Minorities and the Greek Legal Order,* Ed. Ant. Sakkoulas, Athens-Komotini 1996, p. 336 (in Greek).

[4] As the constitutionalist N. Alivizatos writes: "Orthodox religion and Greek language have been the fundamental pillars of its modern identity and any approach to current Greek realities which would not take seriously into account these factors will no doubt lead to false

interpretations and constructions. What ought to be stressed however is that in addition – or perhaps in spite of the above – modern Greek society and especially her elites have never really systematically opposed openness." "The Constitutional Treatment of Religious Minorities in Greece." *Mélanges en l'honneur de Nicolas Valtikos - Droit et justice,* Paris Pedone, 1999, p. 641.

[5] It is significant of the level of the current academic debate on minorities that the only comprehensive study of the repercussions of the minority protection system of the League of Nations in Greece (of L.Divani, *Greece and Minorities,* Nefeli Pub. Athens) was only published in 1995.

[6] Permanent Court of International Justice *Series A/B*, No 64, 1923.

[7] Permanent Court of International Justice *Series B*, No 17, 1930.

[8] The Greek administration went, as far as to issue – under intractable political circumstances, it is true - a schoolbook for the country's Slav speaking population: the Abecedar. Cf. I. Mihailides, "Minority Rights and Educational Problems in Greek Interwar Macedonia: the Case of the Primer Abecedar", *Journal of Modern Greek Studies,* Vol. 114:2, 1996, pp. 329-343.

[9] *Minority Schools in Albania,* PCIJ, op.cit. p. 67. While the use of the term "race" obviously witnesses the date of the decision and evidently cannot serve as reference today, it is worth observing the absolute conceptual equilibrium between rights and sovereignty, provided in this paragraph.

[10] *Op. cit.* p. 2 and p. 23.

[11] Magazine *KLIK,* 26 July 1999.

[12] First page in the *Hourriet* of the 30 July: "Bravo Yiorgo."

[13] Van Der Stoel's letter reads as follows: "In the last weeks a number of requests have reached me to give my opinion on the ongoing discussion in Greece regarding the question of national minorities. In the light I should like to make the following comments.

In June 1990, the then Government of Greece, led by Mr. Constantine Mitsotakis, together with the governments of other states participating in the OSCE, agreed to the Document of the Copenhagen meeting of the Conference on the Human Dimension of the OSCE. The Copenhagen Document commits governments' i.a. to provide persons belonging to national minorities the right freely to express, preserve and develop (individually as well as in community with other members of their group) their ethnic, cultural, linguistic and religious identity and to maintain and develop their culture in all its aspects, to profess and practice their religion, and to establish and maintain organizations or associations.

The discussion in Greece during the last few weeks on the subject of national minorities gives me the impression that there is a certain confusion about the commitments contained in the Copenhagen Document. Some comments give the impression that the recognition in the Copenhagen Document of the right of persons belonging to national minorities freely to express preserve and develop their ethnic, cultural, linguistic and religious identity is tantamount to recognizing the right of self-determination of persons belonging to national minorities. In reality, however, these are two completely different concepts. The right of self-determination relates to the status of territory. In this relation paragraph 38 of the Copenhagen Document makes it clear that none of the commitments mentioned in the Copenhagen Document may be interpreted as implying any right to engage in any activity or any action in contravention of the principle of territorial integrity of States. This means for instance that a State with a population which has predominantly the same ethnicity as that of an ethnic minority of another State will never be able to refer to the commitments of the Copenhagen Document as a justification for efforts to secede. In other words: the right of persons belonging to national minorities to express, preserve and develop their identity is to be exercised within the existing boundaries of the State.

Paragraph 35 of the Copenhagen Document does refer to the formula of territorial autonomy "*as one of the possible means to create conditions for promotion of the identity of persons belonging to national minorities.*" However, territorial autonomy is mentioned as an *option*, not as a right or an obligation.

A second misunderstanding is that in order to acquire or enjoy the rights mentioned in the Copenhagen Document a minority would have to be formally recognized by the State. The Copenhagen Document makes it clear that this is not necessary. Paragraph 31 states i.e. "*persons belonging to national minorities have the right to exercise fully and effectively their human rights and fundamental freedoms without any discrimination and in full equality before the law.*" The same principles of non discrimination and equality before the law" apply pursuant to Article 14 of the European Convention on Human Rights. However, when an association of persons belonging to a national minority wants to acquire legal personality for purposes of enjoying one of their enumerated rights, Greek law obliges them to be registered. But the requirements for registration cannot be different from those for associations not composed of persons belonging to national minorities. To require otherwise would constitute a violation of the principle of non-discrimination. Nor can registration be refused because of the mere fact that it is an association of persons belonging to a national minority; this would be a violation of Article 11 of the ECHR and Article 12 of the Greek Constitution regarding the freedom of association. On the other hand, Article 105 of the Greek Civil Code opens a possibility to dissolve any association with aims different from those laid down in its memorandum of association or if its object prove to be contrary to the law. Finally, there seems to be confusion about the relationship between the Treaty of Lausanne of 1923 and the Copenhagen Document. The Treaty of Lausanne (Article 45) deals with the religious rights of the "Muslim minority" in Greece. But that does not mean that the Copenhagen Document has no relevance for persons belonging to the Muslim minority in Greece. Within the wider religious group, there are smaller groups with an ethnic or linguistic identity of their own, such as Turks, Roma and Pomaks to which the provisions of the Copenhagen Document do apply."

[14] The Minority Groups Research Centre is a non-profit making association formed in 1996. Its members, young scientists and established academics who are experts on the topic of minorities, aim at the interdisciplinary study of the minority phenomenon in Greece and elsewhere. From its creation in 1996, the MGRC has organized scientific conferences, colloquies, published monographs, participated in governmental and non-governmental think-tanks, as well as organized study visits or field research in Greece, Albania, FYR of Macedonia and Bulgaria.

[15] *Delphi, 1-3 November 1996: Two day scientific meeting on the topic Greece-Europe-Minorities - Summary of minutes and formulation of outcomes*, D.Christopoulos, K. Tsitselikis, (ed.) Athens, 1997, pp. 41-42.

[16] Which reads as follows: "*1. Every one has the right to freedom of expression. This right shall include freedom to hold opinions and to receive and impart information and ideas without interference by public authority and regardless of frontiers. This article shall not prevent States from requiring the licensing of broadcasting, television or cinema*

enterprises. 2. The exercise of these freedoms, since it carries with it duties and responsibilities, may be subjected to such formalities, conditions, restrictions or penalties as are prescribed by law and necessary in a democratic society, in the interests of national security, territorial integrity or public safety, for the prevention of disorder or crime, for the protection of health or morals, for the protection of the reputation or rights of others, for preventing the disclosure of information received by confidence, or for maintaining the authority and the impartiality of the judiciary."

[17] According to the French philosopher of science, Gaston Bachelard, the first view is *always* wrong. Cf.his monumental work: *La formation de l'esprit scientifique*, Paris, Librairie Philosophique Vrin, 1993.

[18] Actually the whole legal problematic on minorities derives from the very existence of *internal* minorities. It depends where we define the boundaries of the institutional framework within which majorities and minorities coexist. This can be the Nation-State, but this can also be a minority group itself. "Without respect for internal minorities, a liberal society risks becoming a mosaic of tyrannies; colorful perhaps but hardly free. The task of making respect for minority rights is thus one that falls not just to the majority but also to the minority groups themselves". L. Green: "Internal Minorities and their Rights", *Group Rights*, J. Baker (ed.), University of Toronto Press, 1994, p. 111.

[19] Ottoman control over the area of Thrace finished with the Balkan Wars. Mass population exchange took place, after Ataturk's victory over the Greek forces in 1922. The rights of the Muslim minority in Western Thrace have been guaranteed under Section III of the Treaty of Lausanne signed on 24 July 1923 by Greece and Turkey besides other countries. The Lausanne Treaty provided for an exchange of the Muslim-Turk and Greek-Orthodox population then living in Greece and Turkey respectively. Muslims of Western Thrace and Christians of Istanbul were exempted from this compulsory exchange. The rights of the Muslim community of Western Thrace continue to be guaranteed by article 45 of the Lausanne Treaty. It has to be noted that the Lausanne treaty is one of the few normative undertakings concerning minorities that remained valid after the end of the W.W.II. Cf. *Study of the Legal Validity of the Undertakings concerning Minorities*, UN Doc. E/CN.4/367, 1950.

[20] As correctly asserted by H. Pulton: "Self-identification as *Muslim* by Balkan Muslim communities themselves takes on a meaning markedly different from that intended when the label is applied by their foes and those who see them as sectarian survivals form the Ottoman age who pose an intractable problem for the successor states." *Muslim Identity and the Balkan State*, H.Poulton, S.Taji-Farouki (ed.), Hurst and Company London, 1997, p. 4.

[21] W. Kymlicka writes: "We need to distinguish two kinds of claim that an ethnic or national group can make. The first involves the claim of the group against its own members; the second involves the claim of a group against the larger society. Both kinds of claims can be seen as protecting the stability of national or ethnic communities, but they respond to different sources of instability. The first kind is intended to protect the group from the destabilizing impact of *internal dissent* (e.g. the decision of individual members not to follow tradition practices or customs) whereas the second is intended to protect the group from the impact of external decisions (e.g. economic or political decision of the larger society). To distinguish these two kinds of claims, I will call the first 'internal' restrictions and second 'external protections'." *Multicultural citizenship*, Oxford, Oxford University Press, 1995, p. 35.

[22] "The minimal requirement for full citizenship, for effective moral membership of a modern community is literacy. This is the minimum; a certain level of technological competence is probably also required. Only a person possessing these can really claim and exercise his rights, can attain a level of affluence and style of life compatible with current notions of human dignity, and so forth. (...) But: an educational system in some medium, some language. (...) Now consider the possible forms of the impact of modernity on such a society: increase in the proportion and in the importance of literacy, consequent on the transformation of economic life; greater mobility of various kinds; the emergence of an industrial proletariat; and above all the fact that *one* of the languages ... has become *the* language of the modern organizations, of the new industrial, governmental and education machines. The local structures are being eroded." This is how someone like E. Gellner analyses the formation of national states in Europe through linguistic assimilative procedures. ('Nationalism', in *Thought and Change,* Weidenfeld and Nicholson, London, 1964, p. 158 and p. 163).

[23] "Arvanite is spoken in small isolated communities widely separated from each other in present-day central and southern Greece. Its not clear how large the present number of Arvanite speakers is. (...) The language is only used on an informal basis." This is what the *European Bureau for Lesser-Used Languages,* gives as a brief data for the Arvanite. *Mini Guide to Lesser-Used Languages of the EC,* The European Bureau of Lesser-Used Languages, Dublin, 1998, p. 52.

[24] According to the same data (*ibid.*), "Vlach speakers are found scattered across Thessaly, Pindus and Ipiros (the mountainous regions of the Hellenic peninsula). (...) There are no reliable estimates of the number of speakers of the language. (...) The language is confined to family and colloquial use." p.53.

[25] According to one of the few Greek linguists that have studied bilinguism in Greece, E.Sella, both languages, the Vlach and the Arvanite, belong to the group of lesser used languages of a limited life expectancy, (E.Sela, Bilinguism and lesser used languages in Greece, in D.Christopoulos & K.Tsitselikis, *The Minority Phenomenon in Greece – A Contribution of the Social Sciences,* Kritiki, Athens, 1997, in Greek, pp. 349-413. English literature provides a monumental reference on the Arvanite language of L. Tsitsipis: *Arvanitica (Albanian) and Greek in contact: A linguistic anthropology of linguistic praxis and language shift,* Oxford University Press, 1997. On the Vlachs history, the reference is T. Winnifrith's *The Vlachs – History of a Balkan People,* St Martins Press, New York, 1987. According to publications of two young researchers on minority languages in Greece, L.Baltsiotes and L.Empirikos, the cases of the two languages differ. While the use of the Arvanite language does not appear to concern younger generations at all (with some limited exceptions), the Vlach language is still a communicational tool in numerous bilingual communities, enjoying a higher status of appreciation among the Vlachs. (Cf.articles in review *Synchrona Themata,* vol. 66-67, in Greek). It is worth noting, however, that both linguistic communities – for different reasons each - are extremely sensible at any vis-à-vis attempts to name them "minorities", even linguistic ones.

[26] Cf *infra* note 39.

[27] In 1997 the Greek Ministry of Education launched an ambitious project aiming at the reform of the minority education in Western Thrace. The program *Education of Muslim Children* has an initial duration of three years and it appears that it is going to be extended.

[28] E. Hobsbawn in his *Nations and Nationalism since 1780,* (Cambridge 1990) quotes an old George Simmel observation, according to which: " Groups, and especially minorities, which live in conflict... often reject approaches or tolerance from the other side. The closed nature of their opposition, without which they cannot fight on, would be blurred...Within certain groups, it may even be a piece of political wisdom to see to it that there be some enemies in order for the unity of the members to be effective and for the group to remain conscious of this unity as its vital interest." (p.175). No doubt the Greek State, with some of its policies, offered a fertile ground for such behaviors to develop within the minority of Western Thrace.

[29] The treaties of Westfalia (1648), milestones on the road to the European State system, abolished the principle *cuius regio eius religio,* which had given princes the right to determine and change the official religion of their dominions.

[30] "...the rights, obligations and their modalities become actual only upon certain conditions of fact being fulfilled. Clearly, the general permission to be educated or to express opinions freely is valid even if a lot of persons do not have the means to educate themselves (or their children) or do not feel the inclination to express any opinion whatsoever. (...) '*Rights-conditions*', then, denote those societal (factual) conditions, which are necessary for the use of rights-norms in the given social context. (...) Rights-conditions exist in a certain society and in respect to a given right, if the individual having the right is in the position to decide to make use of the right or not to claim it. Thus, the egalitarian version of equality does not demand, and still less would justify, a 'factual' egality among members of community ; rather, it requires that the community make available the use of rights (their 'claiming') to ever member of community. (...) *Minorities are groups of persons who do not possess the rights-conditions.* Their claim to differential treatment is, as it were, a subsidiary right; minority rights are not contrary to equality as far as they are not claiming something different in kind. " A. Bragyova, "Are There Any Minority Rights?" *Archiv für Rechts und Sozialphilosophie,* vol. 80, 1994 -Heft 4, p.505.

[31] As the French linguistic F. de Schaussure observes: "c'est le point de vue qui crée le sujet." *Cours de linguistique générale,* Paris, Payot , 1968, p. 23.

[32] O. Braud, " '*Repräsentation*' et '*Stellvertretung*': sur une distinction de C. Schmitt" *in Droits,* N° 6, *La représentation,* PUF, 1987.

[33] O. Braud, "Théories de la représentation, Introduction", *in La représentation, F.* D'Arcy (dir.) Paris, Ed. Economica, 1984, p. 34.

[34] S. Rials, "Ouverture: Représentation de la représentation", *in Droits, op. cit.,* and p. 3.

[35] European Commission of Human Rights, Application No.18877/1991 *Sadik Ahmet against Greece,* Report of the Commission (adopted on 4 April 1995).

[36] An interesting -though sometimes simplistic in its methodology and its conclusion-presentation of the situation of the Slav-speaking Macedonians in Greece is the one included in the Minority Rights Group International report *The Southern Balkans* (The Slavomacedonian minority in Greece: a case study in Balkan nationalism) by MRG Greece.

[37] L.Danforth, "Claims to Macedonian identity: the Macedonian question and the breakup of Yugoslavia", *Anthropology Today,* Vol.9, No 4, 1993, p.8.

[38] Cf. the last paragraphs of the letter of the HCNM, *supra* note 13.

[39] On 18 April 1990 the applicants, who claim to be of "Macedonian" ethnic origin and to have a "Macedonian national consciousness", decided together with forty-nine other people to form a non-profit-making association called "Home of Macedonian Civilisation."

According to clause 2 of its memorandum of association, the association's objects were "(a) the cultural, intellectual and artistic development of its members and of the inhabitants of Florina in general and the fostering of a spirit of co-operation, solidarity and love between them; (b) cultural decentralisation and the preservation of intellectual and artistic endeavours and traditions and of the civilisation's monuments and, more generally, the promotion and development of [their] folk culture; and (c) the protection of the region's natural and cultural environment". The Greek Courts, based on a mere suspicion as to the true intentions of the association's founders and the activities it might have engaged in once it had begun to function, prohibited the registration of the association.

The Court of Strasbourg in its decision, took into account the fact that Greek law does not lay down a system of preventive review for setting up non-profit-making associations. It also reminded that Article 12 of the Greek Constitution provides that the forming of associations cannot be made subject to prior authorisation and that Article 81 of the Civil Code allows the courts merely to review lawfulness and not to review desirability. The Court did not rule out that, once founded, the association might, under cover of the aims mentioned in its memorandum of association, have engaged in activities incompatible with those aims. Such a possibility, which the national courts have seen as a certainty, could hardly have been belied by any practical action as, having never existed, the association did not have time to take any action. If the possibility had become a reality, the authorities would not have been powerless: under Article 105 of the Civil Code, the Court of First Instance could order that the association should be dissolved if it subsequently pursued an aim different from the one laid down in its memorandum of association or if its functioning proved to be contrary to law, morality or public order. In the light of the foregoing, the Court concluded that the refusal to register the applicants' association was disproportionate to the objectives pursued. That being so, the Court figured a violation of Article 11 of the ECHR and Greece added and its unfortunately rich record in front of the European Court of Human Rights one more condemnation. (*Case Sidiropoulos against Greece*, Decision, Strasbourg 10 July 1998).

[40] Cf C. Rozakis, "The International protection of minorities in Greece", *in Europe in Change - Greece in a Changing Europe*, K. Featherstone and K. Yfantis (ed.) Manchester University Press, 1996, pp. 95-116.

[41] The recently (1998) abolished Article 19 of the Greek Citizenship Code allowed for the withdrawal of Greek citizenship from persons who were not of Greek origin and who had left the country without intention of returning.

[42] Cf. the comprehensive study of S. Stavros, "Citizenship and the protection of minorities," *in Europe in Change - Greece in a Changing Europe*, K. Featherstone and K. Yfantis, op.cit. p. 123.

[43] It is worth noting that the *Annual Report of the Greek Ombudsman (1998)* includes a long list of cases involving the Greek legislation of citizenship, pp. 31-36. In 1999, the Ombudsman's office has equally elaborated a special report on the reform of the relevant legislation.

References

Alivizatos, N. (1999), "The Constitutional Treatment of Religious Minorities in Greece",

Mélanges en l'honneur de Nicolas Valtikos - Droit et justice, Paris Pedone, pp. 629-642.

Baker, J. (ed) (1994), *Group Rights,* University of Toronto Press.

Bragyova, A. (1994), "Are There Any Minority Rights?" *Archiv für Rechts und Sozialphilosophie,* vol. 80, 1994 -Heft 4, pp.505-525.

Braud, O. (1984), "Théories de la représentation, Introduction", *La représentation,* D'Arcy F. (ed.) Paris, Ed. Economica.

Christopoulos, D. (ed) (1999), *Legal issues of religious diversity in Greece,* Kritiki, Athens, (in Greek).

Danforth, L. (1993), "Claims to Macedonian identity: the Macedonian question and the breakup of Yugoslavia", *Anthropology Today,* Vol.9, No 4.

Droits (1987), N° 6, *La représentation,* PUF, 1987.

European Bureau of Lesser-Used Languages (1998), *Mini guide to Lesser-Used Languages of the EC,* Breathnach D. (ed), Dublin.

Gellner, E. (1964), "Nationalism", *Thought and Change,* Weidenfeld and Nicholson, London.

Gounaris, V., Michailides, I., Angelopoulos, G. (ed) (1997), *Identities in Macedonia,* Papazisi Pub., Athens, 1997 (in Greek).

Hobsbawn, E. (1990), *Nations and Nationalism since 1780,* Cambridge, Cambridge University Press.

Kymlicka, W. (1995), *Multicultural citizenship,* Oxford, Oxford University Press.

Michailides, I. (1999), "Minority Rights and Educational Problems in Greek Interwar Macedonia: the Case of the Primer Abecedar", *Journal of Modern Greek Studies,* Vol. 114:2, 1996, pp. 329-343.

Minority Groups Research Centre (1997), Delphi, 1-3 November 1996: Two day scientific meeting on the topic Greece-Europe-Minorities - Summary of minutes and formulation of outcomes, D.Christopoulos, K. Tsitselikis (ed.), Athens.

Minority Rights Group International, MRG Greece (1997), *The Southern Balkans* The Slavomacedonian minority in Greece: a case study in Balkan nationalism.

Office of the Greek Ombudsman (1998), *Annual report.*

Permanent Court of International Justice (1923), *Series A/B,* No 64.

Permanent Court of International Justice (1930), *Series B,* No 17.

Pollis, A. (1992), "Greek National Identity: Religious Minorities, Rights and European Norms", *Journal of Modern Greek Studies,* Vol. 10:2, pp. 171-195.

Poulton, H., Taji-Farouki, S. (ed) (1997), *Muslim Identity and the Balkan State,* Hurst and Company London.

Roudometof, V. (1998), "From *Rum Millet* to Greek Nation: Enlightenment, Secularization, and National Identity in Ottoman Balkan Society, 1453-1821", *Journal of Modern Greek Studies,* Volume 16, pp. 11-47.

Rozakis, C. (1996), "The International protection of minorities in Greece", *Europe in Change - Greece in a Changing Europe,* K. Featherstone and K. Yfantis (ed.), Manchester University Press, pp. 95-116.

Schaussure, de F. (1968), *Cours de linguistique générale,* Paris, Payot.

Sela, E. (1997), "Bilinguism and lesser used languages in Greece", D.Christopoulos and K.Tsitselikis (ed.), *The Minority Phenomenon in Greece – A Contribution of the Social Sciences,* Kritiki, Athens (in Greek), pp. 349-413.

Stavros, S. (1996), "Citizenship and the protection of minorities," *Europe in Change – Greece in a Changing Europe,* K. Featherstone and K. Yfantis (ed.), pp. 117-129.

Tsitselikis, K. (1996), The International and European Status of Linguistic Rights of Minorities and the Greek Legal Order, Ed.Ant. Sakkoulas, Athens-Komotini (in Greek).

Tsitsipis, L. (1997), Arvanitica (Albanian) and Greek in contact: A linguistic anthropology of linguistic praxis and language shift, Oxford, Oxford University Press.

United Nations (1950), Study of the Legal Validity of the Undertakings concerning Minorities, UN Doc. E/CN.4/367.

Winnifrith, T. (1987), *The Vlachs – History of a Balkan People*, New York, St Martins Press.

9 Citizenship in Contested States Post 2000: The Northern Ireland Peace Agreement and its Global Implications

JOHN DOYLE

The Northern Ireland Peace Agreement signed in Belfast in 1998,[1] and still in a process of development, is one of a number of peace agreements emerging from apparently intractable conflicts, since the end of the cold war. This article focuses on a relatively unexamined aspect of the Agreement - the international relevance of its innovative provisions on equality of citizenship and internationalised governance and the means by which it links the equality issues of citizenship to constitutional questions. The Belfast Agreement both implicitly and explicitly deals with the problematic issue of citizenship in a state, which is highly contested at the constitutional level. Its development of an equality agenda and dynamic cross-border institutions of governance in a situation where ultimate sovereignty and allegiance remains contested is a departure from current international norms. The peace process around the Agreement also reflects a significantly increased international involvement in the Northern Ireland conflict. External support and mediation was essential in brokering an Agreement and will inevitably be important in sustaining the new forms of citizenship, which are promised in its provisions. Both in its processes and in the framework for citizenship and governance suggested by the Agreement, Northern Ireland can provide a useful example to the increasing number of nationalist conflicts in the post cold war world.

The Northern Ireland peace process and the Agreement of 1998 offer a number of challenges to the international literature on citizenship, which has to date not engaged with the issues and problems thrown up when the nature and existence of a state are contested. This is reflected in the theoretical assumptions in the literature about the nature of citizenship that have underpinned political analysis of the Northern Ireland conflict and its potential solutions. The dominant analysis assumes that most nationalists living in Northern Ireland (those seeking a united Ireland) would prioritise justice and equality over constitutional issues, and secondly that unionists (those defending the Union with Britain) prioritise that Union over the maintenance of discriminatory measures[2] and would therefore support internal reform if the constitutional threat from nationalists was removed. These assumptions are based on the idea that the existing state will gain legitimacy in nationalists' eyes and envisages that the conflict will end when nationalists are offered and accept full citizenship of the British State. The conflict resolution strategies resulting from this approach sharply divided sovereignty and equality and have sought a trade-off between the two. This strategy failed for a number of reasons. Firstly, it is not clear that nationalists are in fact willing to abandon nationalism for guarantees of 'internal' equality and justice within Northern Ireland. Neither is there any evidence that unionists see such a trade off as practicable or in their interests. Rather, as discussed below, Ulster unionists fear that concessions on issues of equality for nationalists, because it would mean a reconfiguring of the public sphere, would strengthen Irish nationalism and weaken the Union with Britain and the political position of unionists. Thus exclusion of nationalists from the public sphere and full citizenship continues to be an important element of modern Ulster unionism.

In summary the 1998 agreement provides a balanced package of measures designed to end years of political stalemate and create a dynamic for change. This dynamic element has been crucial in persuading the Irish Republican Army (IRA) to end its 25-year armed campaign but it is also the very element, which causes most difficulty to supporters of the status quo. The Agreement asserts that there will be no change in the constitutional status of Northern Ireland without the support of a majority of its people (over 40% of whom at the moment vote for nationalist parties). The Irish Government agreed to recommend a change in the Irish constitution to reflect this position. In return for this guarantee on 'sovereignty' the parties agreed to set up a power-sharing consociational executive made up of nationalists and unionists. A legislative assembly would be established but could only take decisions by 'cross-community' consensus. A new all-Ireland Ministerial Council was to be established modelled on the EU Council of Ministers, with two representatives from Northern Ireland and two from the Irish Government, which must meet frequently and where Ministers are duty bound to try and reach agreement. This council would oversee cross-border 'implementation bodies' with decision-making powers in at least six areas to be agreed. The Agreement also commits the British Government to far reaching reforms in the equality arena including criminal law reform, security measures, employment equality and Irish language rights. The issue of policing was too controversial to be resolved and was passed to an independent international commission, which reported in September 1999. It was agreed that all political prisoners would be released by May 2000 and that all parties would use their influence to secure the disarming of paramilitary organisations by May 2000.

The Northern Ireland peace process has made progress because it abandoned previous dogma which saw equality as a concession to be granted once the constitutional challenge to Northern Ireland from nationalists was ended. The 1998 Agreement has sought to fundamentally change the nature of citizenship, by dividing issues of citizenship rights, institutions of governance and the ethos of the state from the question of formal sovereignty. The debate on the equality agenda has therefore become part of the definition of citizenship rather than a material 'carrot' to entice people away from the allegedly symbolic arena of nationalism. If the Northern Ireland Agreement succeeds it will have done so without requiring nationalists or unionists to abandon their political goals or their political and ethnic identities, but will have shifted the contest over the future of the state onto a peaceful and democratic footing.

Citizenship in a Contested State

Within Northern Ireland the major source of opposition to the Agreement has come from the unionist population.[3] Their disagreements with the peace process are not confined to the central constitutional issues but also embrace the reform provisions around the equality agenda. This absolute rejection of the extension of citizenship rights, which would be, seen as uncontroversial in most democratic states, to the nationalist population, is incomprehensible in the context of the mainstream academic literature on citizenship and highlights its inadequacy in contested states. What is crucial in Northern Ireland, but masked by the existing literature on citizenship, is that the unionist parties - because the state is contested - link absolutely equality issues in employment, cultural rights and policing, to the primary constitutional question. This is why so many unionists opposed the Agreement and why pro-agreement unionists are having so much difficulty accepting the actual implementation of the accord in practice. Given the small size and marginality of dissident nationalist and republican movements, who oppose the peace process, it is the mainstream unionist opposition, which offers the greatest barrier to the successful implementation of the Agreement, and therefore an understanding of their perspective is essential to political progress.

It is unionism's opposition to provisions on equal citizenship that needs to be understood and dealt with, without giving in to their rejection of reform, if progress is to be made and it is the means by which this can be achieved that is of most international significance.

Unionists' rejection of the 'equality agenda' put forward by nationalists on the grounds that it threatens the Union, is not simply paranoia, or a cultural predisposition to reduce all matters to history or sovereignty (e.g. Crozier, 1989, p.20). In a sense, unionist elites are right. The Northern Ireland State is contested on all fronts. The refusal of nationalists to support the Royal Ulster Constabulary (RUC),[4] their desire to include nationalist symbols in the public sphere, opposition to Orange marches[5] and the desire for stronger fair employment legislation are not just individual stand alone issues of justice. They are for nationalists part of a broader political programme. Sinn Féin President Gerry Adams MP was quite explicit in arguing that if unionism rests on power and privilege, as he believed it did, then the mobilisation of a nationalist consensus with sufficient international support to make progress on an 'equality agenda' would weaken unionism (Adams, 1995, p.231). Sinn Féin recognised that such a consensus could not be mobilised at this time to press for a British withdrawal, but that it could be built around 'equality' issues and North-South links and it would be difficult for the British government to resist the pressure for reform.

Ulster unionists have long argued that a 'guarantee' on the final handover of sovereignty from Britain to Ireland is irrelevant if unionists cannot prevent changes in the actual ethos and governance of the state.[6] Reform measures are opposed not only on their own merits but because they represent a shift in the political resources available to each community. They are part of the 'war of position' over the future of Northern Ireland, part of the hegemonic battle, which precedes the struggle for ultimate political power.[7] Each of the key areas of the equality agenda in Northern Ireland, would be described in the international literature as citizen-rights within a state, yet in spite of this, reforms in these areas are seen by unionists as having the potential to undermine the state. If the nature of citizenship in Northern Ireland is changed, mainstream unionists believe that nationalists will use their increased economic, political and cultural resources to challenge the constitutional position.[8] Mainstream unionists, for example, believe that RUC reform will weaken the capacity of the state to defend itself, as nationalist recruits, nationalist influenced controlling bodies and a force with a non-unionist ethos would not be committed to the defence of the Union.[9] Even symbolic changes to the RUC's name or use of emblems are rejected.[10] Ken

Maginnis MP, security spokesperson for the mainstream and pro-agreement Ulster Unionist Party (UUP) attacked proposals to replace the symbols and Royal prefix of the RUC, claiming that this would produce a 'neutered RUC, bereft of identity and effectiveness from a lack of self confidence'. Likewise, he rejected the need to replace the oath of allegiance to the English Queen because taking the oath shows 'loyalty to the state, the constitution … towards those subjects who seek the maintenance of their freedom, civil rights and security and protection against crime and subversion'.[11] Those refusing to swear allegiance to the Queen are, in Maginnis' view, not suitable police officers.

Fair employment legislation is seen by the major unionist parties to weaken the link between loyalty and material rewards, reduce nationalist emigration and shift the population balance. It increases the economic resources and ultimately the political resources available to nationalism, through its impact in key institutions such as the civil service.[12] Mainstream unionist parties also reject the need to include nationalist cultural symbols, such as Irish language signs in the public sphere, or reduce the use of exclusively British or unionist symbols, because such action in their view reduces the 'Britishness' of Northern Ireland.[13]

In mainstream unionists' view, nationalists have no right to reform in these areas under the mantle of 'equal citizenship'. Since nationalists refuse to support the British State, they have no right to claim equal recognition and support from the state. Indeed offering such 'equality' of citizenship is opposed by unionists because in their view it recognises and even increases the contested nature of the state.[14]

The debate on equality and citizenship in Northern Ireland is not adequately addressed by the contemporary literature on ethnicity, minority rights or even citizen duties. These issues are given a specific resonance when changes in the nature of citizenship are not simply about the distribution of rights and resources within the state but are part of a conflict over the existence of the state itself. The three dominant models of citizenship in the current international literature - republican, multicultural and ethnic - are so heavily premised on being constituted within an uncontested nation-state that they lose their strength in a situation such as Northern Ireland and can even reinforce the tendency for exclusion in unionist ideology.

Assimilationist views of citizenship have little to offer an analysis of Northern Ireland. Nationalists clearly do not seek inclusion as undifferentiated members of a British political community. In any case unionists reject such approaches, seeing the full inclusion of nationalists as a threat the state. Even though multi-cultural models of citizenship allow for ethnic and cultural differences to be given expression in the public sphere, they too are premised on an acceptance of the constitutional nature and boundaries of the state.

Multiculturalism is seen as a pluralist expression of citizenship *within* a clearly defined state (Baldwin-Edwards and Schain, 1994). As presently constituted it still assumes that an excluded group is seeking entry in the context of uncontested state. Moderate unionists are closer to a multi-cultural position, generally arguing that giving nationalists a greater sense of ownership would reduce nationalist 'alienation' and ultimately stabilise the state. This more moderate view is, as represented by the Alliances Party's electoral support a minority and diminishing perspective within unionism, receiving 6% and 2%, respectively in the 1998 Northern Ireland Assembly and 1999 European Union elections. However, even for Alliance the rights on offer are those with fewest political implications. Advocates of a multicultural citizenship assume the long-term continuation of British sovereignty and there is no acceptance by them of nationalists' right to use overtly nationalistic symbols in the public sphere, such as the Irish national flag and even official Irish language signs.[15] Furthermore nationalists refusal to support the RUC was seen, even by moderate unionists as an absolute breach of their duty as citizens, with negative implications for the rights they could expect.[16]

The ethnic model of citizenship, classically represented by the German system of citizenship through bloodline rather than residence at birth/naturalisation (Brubaker, 1992) - has some similarities to mainstream unionists' closed view of citizenship. Its focus on 'belonging' and its incapacity to fully integrate 'new' entrants reflect elements of the unionist perspective. The classic ethnic model of citizenship does not, however, capture the totality of unionists' exclusionary views. Certainly in broad terms nationalists could be said to be excluded as an ethnic group, but fundamentally it is their political allegiance rather than their ethnic inheritance which is at issue. Neither is there any widespread use of racist-supremacist language by mainstream unionist elites. Nationalists are more often stereotyped as cleverer and more politically sophisticated and not less so.

Theoretically at least, unionists can include the mythical quiet Catholic who is not a nationalist. It is nationalists' political aspirations, which are used to exclude them. Catholics who support the union can be allowed within the citizen band even if there are few in reality. Perhaps more significantly, Protestants who 'go native' who take an anti-unionist political position are excluded despite their 'ethnic' inheritance.[17] The nature of exclusion is driven by the political threat to the Union rather than by the dangers of cultural mixing highlighted by Barker

(1981) and McVeigh (1998) as characterising 'new racism'. Ethnic exclusion is traditionally characterised by a fear that allowing 'outsiders' to enter the body politic will change the nature of society, simply because they are 'different'. In classic ethnic exclusion it is their presence and their difference which is highlighted and not their political aspirations. In Northern Ireland, it is nationalists' political opinions, the perceived threat from the Republic of Ireland, unionists' image of the British government as an unreliable ally, and their siege mentality, which drives exclusionary politics within unionism and not a fear of ethnic dilution.

The importance of the contested nature of the Northern Ireland State in unionist conceptions of citizenship, therefore, leads to a political strategy based on resistance to reform and defence of the status quo. This heightens unionists' siege mentality and acts as a disincentive to political reform including moves towards equal citizenship. There are also however pressure for change in citizen relations in Northern Ireland. The increasing internationalisation of the Northern Ireland conflict, while adding somewhat to unionists' sense of siege mentality also creates, at times, irresistible pressures for change. The split within unionism in response to the peace process and the Northern Ireland Peace Agreement might be seen as evidence of an emerging different perspective on citizenship within unionism, or the Agreement itself could be viewed as a trade off between inclusiveness for nationalists and constitutional guarantees for unionists. However, such interpretations would be a misreading of unionism's reaction to the peace process. The split on the Agreement and the decision by pro-agreement unionists to support the deal is best understood as primarily a tactical divide in response to the changing political environment in which unionism operates. There is little to suggest that pro-Agreement unionists have fundamentally altered their view of citizenship, but they have a stronger pragmatic sense of what is possible. There was also a fear that the British and Irish governments might have implemented even more far reaching reforms over unionists' heads if they had withdrawn from talks.[18] The different tactical responses by unionists have created very sharp and bitter divisions but have not, at least yet, led to any ideological realignment.

The International Environment

Unionist perceptions of citizenship and the security of the state during the past 30 years produced a political position which opposed almost all attempts at reform, despite strong pressure from the nationalist community. The Irish government and nationalists in Northern Ireland did not have the political strength to force trenchant unionism in a different direction or to persuade the British government to implement reforms over their heads. Until the ending of the Cold War there was also minimal international pressure for a resolution of the Northern Ireland conflict. The USSR saw little advantage in intervening and the USA was unwilling to challenge its most important NATO ally - Britain. Northern Ireland was seen as an internal British affair and Irish governments were politely informed, even in crisis situations, that the US administration would not intervene (Cronin, 1987, p.192; Keogh, 1994, p. 194; O'Grady, 1996, pp. 2-7). Other international initiatives were equally low key, with the UN Security Council never likely to get involved as Britain held a permanent seat and a veto, and the EEC/EC also took a minimalist view on its role (Ruane and Todd: 280).[19]

The ending of the Cold War however opened up much greater possibilities. It weakened or at least lessened the absolute priority accorded to strategic security and military alliances in US (and indeed British) foreign policy. This gave Bill Clinton, the first US President elected after the Cold War, the flexibility to pursue foreign policy goals, which might strain relations with Britain. Relieved of the overwhelming weight of Cold War concerns, Clinton could ignore the advice of the US State Department, the FBI and the CIA in granting Gerry Adams a visa to enter the USA[20] and in intervening more forcefully in the developing Irish peace process. This is not to ignore the domestic pressure on Clinton, a product of his party's need to win back Irish Americans who were part of the Reagan-Democrat bloc and also under pressure from a much more professional and influential Irish American lobby - itself partly a response to the changing strategy of Sinn Féin in Ireland (O'Dowd, 1993, p.20). However, the domestic pressures and the urgings of Irish governments could have been ignored if global strategic interests were at stake. The fact that the US administration and President Clinton personally have been so heavily involved in the negotiation process undeniably increased the pressure on political actors, including unionists, to reach agreement.

Other international factors were also significant at this time. Political conflicts and 'struggles' which the Sinn Féin leadership had drawn inspiration from or sought to compare themselves with, in South Africa, Palestine and Central America were moving towards peace negotiations and settlements (Cox, 1997, pp. 676-82; Cox, 1998, pp.75-7; Munck, 1998).[21] At an ideological level, and in the case of South Africa at the level of extensive personal contacts,[22] the emergence of international peace processes had a significant impact on republican thinking. Furthermore, in a post-Cold War world there was always a possibility that the British establishment, relieved of its Cold War fears, would be less antagonistic to new political arrangements for the island of Ireland, if a new dynamic could be created to put Northern Ireland on the international agenda. As republicans believed that a new military dynamic was unlikely, given the stalemate between the IRA and the British Army, pressure mounted for a new 'unarmed strategy' within the republican movement itself.

Prior to the end of the Cold War, unionists by virtue of their siege mentality had made limited use of international contacts. Such parallels as were drawn tended to be with what were perceived as similar communities under siege such as Israel, Turkish Cypriots and apartheid South Africa or other 'abandoned' British settlers such as the white community in Rhodesia/Zimbabwe (Clayton, 1996, pp.40-6).[23] As white rule became not only discredited but increasingly unstable it was clear that drawing such parallels did the unionist cause more harm than good. Furthermore as the Israeli government opened talks with the PLO, and the white South African government with the ANC, so pressure mounted on unionists, and the British government, to engage with Sinn Féin and seek progress in Northern Ireland.

These changes increased the pressure on unionism to engage with the mainstream international community and in particular with Washington. Unionists could not credibly argue it was a purely internal 'British' matter when the British government was increasingly involving the Irish government in the search for a settlement (Ruane and Todd, 1996, p. 289) and this added to the pressure to relate to the international community more seriously. Post cease-fire unionism has had a greater level of serious contact with the US administration than any previous generation of unionist leaders and it has not all been negative and defensive. There is now a section of the UUP which believes it can engage with the USA - traditionally seen as unsupportive - and make progress (Ruane and Todd, 1996, p. 321). Such engagement is however a two way process. As unionist leaders deepen their contact with senior US policy makers, so too are they open to pressure from the US to shift their own position in response to US efforts at mediation. In many ways this is a follow on from the UUP's self image as an insider group in Westminster politics and their preference for insider deals. The emphasis placed by the UUP on their good contacts leaves them open to reverse pressure. The influence of the White House and US talks chairperson George Mitchell during the negotiations is well documented (e.g. Mitchell, 1999) and the personal intervention of President Clinton in making phone calls to the leading negotiators including David Trimble on the eve of the Northern Ireland

Peace Agreement being reached is further evidence of the pressure for a settlement from the US administration.

Domestic Pressures for Change

In addition to these international influences unionist political elites had also to respond to the strategic changes within Irish nationalism and republicanism, itself strongly related to the changing international relations environment. The strategic shifts in thinking within the IRA and Sinn Féin and the response to those changes by more moderate nationalists was crucial to the building of a new political environment. It is important therefore to establish the fundamental basis of these strategic developments to contextualise the response of unionist political elites. While unionism has held a relatively undifferentiated view of Irish nationalism, it has benefited from the sharp divisions within nationalist elites on the use of political violence. The first signs of 'new thinking' and the creation of a new political environment came in the late 1980s. Sinn Féin acknowledged publicly that the republican movement was not strong enough, on its own, to achieve a united Ireland and that therefore a 'broad front' of nationalist parties and organisations or a 'nationalist consensus' was required to achieve that goal (Bew and Patterson, 1990, p. 213).[24] There followed a shift in attitudes to constitutional nationalism.[25] Though still rivals in elections and for leadership, the moderate nationalist SDLP and the Irish government (especially Fianna Fáil and to some extent the Irish Labour Party) were now seen as potential political allies rather than as simple collaborators with British rule. In a new policy document *Towards a Lasting Peace* (1992) Sinn Féin placed the Irish government, and the need for a nationalist consensus, at the heart of its political strategy - marking a reversal of previous perspectives.

The narrative of the peace process has been provided elsewhere, but it is clear that the process released a new political momentum. The IRA cease-fire and the dynamic of the peace process quite suddenly placed Ulster unionism in a position where standing still was not an option. The actions of the Irish government, constitutional nationalism, the US administration and to some extent the European Union, in seeking to reinforce the cease-fires and the peace process created a dynamic for political progress. While the reliance of the Conservative British government led by John Major on UUP support at Westminster relieved some of the pressure on unionism, this rebounded on unionists when Labour came to power in Britain in May 1997. Determined not to follow the Conservative's reluctant engagement with the peace process, and imbued with a generalised commitment to constitutional reform, the new Labour government, with its large Westminster majority added to the pressure on unionists to involve themselves actively in the process and that process was inevitably going to include reform of citizenship and developments in the equality agenda.

Ulster Unionism was faced with an Irish nationalist consensus that was growing and becoming increasingly politically united. In addition, the leaders of Irish nationalism, including northern nationalists, had formed an effective alliance with a US administration and a reasonable working relationship with the British Labour government which seemed likely to be in power for a considerable time. Northern nationalists now made up over 40% of the voting population, moderate unionism as represented by Alliance could mobilise between 2 and 5%; the centrist Northern Ireland Women's Coalition (NIWC) 1% and the loyalist paramilitaries 3%. Mainstream unionism, for the first time since Partition, was faced with the possibility that it could become an electoral minority within Northern Ireland.[26] Nationalists were still a long way from securing a majority for a united Ireland, but if nationalists were united they could clearly secure majority support in Northern Ireland in a referendum for far-reaching political change. The UUP leadership was quite explicit about this threat during the negotiations. Antony Alcock argued that if the UUP walked out it was likely that a section of mainstream unionists would vote in a referendum to accept a peace deal, which had been negotiated in their absence.[27] The bottom line for the UUP leadership was that however unhappy they were with key elements of the deal, any likely alternative was going to be much worse from a unionist perspective.

The rejection of the deal by Ian Paisley's Democratic Unionist Party (DUP) and UUP dissidents was not surprising as they had been on the record over many years as opposing compromises and reform well short of what was in the Northern Ireland Peace agreement. From Sunningdale to the present they have followed a relatively consistent position. All mainstream unionist elites have traditionally insisted that there is little point having a veto on the 'final handover' of sovereignty if they cannot prevent political decisions which change the character of the state and/or which move them towards a united Ireland. All the major unionist parties, including those who ultimately supported the agreement, as recently as 1997 articulated this position.[28] It is the adherence of the unionists who oppose the agreement to traditional unionist positions that presents difficulties for Ulster unionist leader David Trimble. He must convince unionists that either the commitments on sovereignty are more absolute now than they have been previously, a difficult task, or persuade unionists that they have little choice but to go down this route - a more accurate but politically difficult message to sell.

The Northern Ireland Peace Agreement has only required mainstream unionist elites to abandon the ideological basis of their previous constitutional position in a very limited way, but they still signed an agreement which signalled major shifts in the position of the nationalist community and this was the problem for unionists. The opponents of the deal might offer the clearest continuity with the traditional and exclusionary model of citizenship favoured by unionism, but even those unionists supporting the deal have not, as yet, been required to break with it decisively and this has created huge difficulties since 1998 in the implementation of the deal. This is not to suggest that change in the unionist position is impossible, indeed if the Agreement is implemented in full change will be almost inevitable. However, the key elements of the mainstream unionist approach to the talks - the strong exclusionary view of citizenship, the resistance to accept internal reforms as a *quid pro quo* for constitutional guarantees and a lack of trust in British intentions - which have acted as a restraint on political reform are still visible in the public statements of mainstream unionists who support the agreement.[29] It is also clear that the state is still contested and 'unsettled'. It is stretching credibility to suggest that Sinn Féin or indeed even the Irish State have ended their political ambitions for a united Ireland. David Trimble focused on the 'consent principle' and the changes to the Irish constitution to argue that the state is now more secure than previously and that therefore the Northern Ireland Peace Agreement could be supported. Paul Bew also argued this point.[30] However the attitude of pro-Agreement unionist elites since the Agreement is not indicative of a group who believe their political future has been secured, rather the reluctance to engage with this process was outweighed by the considerable external pressures to enter talks and support the deal. The talks leading to the Agreement were successful not because of a change in internal attitudes to match the previous conflict resolution strategies, but rather due to the new international environment, related changes in Sinn Féin and because the designers of the Agreement moved beyond absolute sovereignty to create new visions of citizenship and governance.

A New Vision of Citizenship?

The centrality of the contested state to politics in Northern Ireland is by no means unique. The period since the end of the Cold War has seen an increase in the level of secessionist challenges to existing states. Initially the focus of this debate was limited to the former Soviet Union and Eastern Europe and it was assumed that the impact would be limited to that geographical region or to former communist states. However, in Central Africa, the Middle East, East Timor, Eritrea/Ethiopia, Sudan, Quebec, Scotland and Spain, to give just some contemporary examples, there are now significant and continuing challenges to state boundaries. It is also now clear that change in the territory of the former Soviet Union and in Eastern Europe was not a once off event but will have a continuing impact in the Russian border regions, the Caucuses and the Balkans at least. Indeed, the sharp link between citizenship and national identity in contested states was starkly highlighted by the actions of the Serbian police in Kosovo during the 1999 conflict, in stripping fleeing Kosovars of their official badges of citizenship - passports, identity cards, birth certificates and even car registration plates.[31] While not all of these states share the historic experience of Northern Ireland - not all contested states enclose settler societies - secession and boundary change is no longer a marginal issue for international relations and academic debates need to reflect this changed environment. Specifically, the debate on citizenship needs to be able to move beyond its assumption of uncontested and settled nation states.

Political conflict in contested states is almost by definition based on challenges to, and defence of, the political status quo. As with unionism, in a situation where a dominant community has based their entire political programme around the defence of the status quo there is often no incentive for them to move or compromise on ideas of equal citizenship. External intervention is necessary to provide an incentive to move towards political negotiations and compromise. The nature of international intervention in regional conflicts is, however, changing since the end of the Cold War. Released from the grip of superpower confrontation, international and regional organisations have the potential to provide a more flexible response to regional conflicts. The major international organisations and the dominant states within them, however, still act on the assumption that state borders are best left unchanged in most circumstances, though there are some shifts in this position in situations such as East Timor. The Rambouillet plan for Kosovo, was also a departure of sorts in that it sought to guarantee by external intervention, levels of autonomy, which in fact would have fundamentally changed the nature of citizenship and sovereignty in Kosovo. This was reinforced in the proposals by the French and German governments in early 1999 for EU or UN protectorate status for Kosovo, within the Yugoslav federation.

There is, however, no consistent basis for intervention by either international organisations or indeed by individual states, and *realpolitik* has left the Kurds, for example, outside such new dialogue for the moment at least. The main international organisations such as the UN, or individual powers such as the USA, can in conflict situations, decide to uphold the status quo or insist on a search for a negotiated solution. It is in the situation of engagement that new models of citizenship become a normative requirement, if solutions that combine justice with political stability are to be achieved. As, interference in the 'internal affairs' of sovereign states is now out of the realm of superpower conflict, intervention is less likely to involve covert operations and aid to irregular forces and instead it is more likely to be based on formal and open public debates and interventions by the UN, NATO and the USA. The shift from covert or arms length operations to open interventions requires new procedures and agreements on the nature of, and the basis for, such decisions. It also indicates a shift from interventions designed to secure a victory for one side to a process where mediation, peace negotiations and future external guarantees of citizenship rights are of greater relevance. In the post-Cold War situation, there is a need for new models of citizenship and new modes of externally guaranteeing political agreements which may be based on a state remaining contested but where the form of the contest is peaceful rather than violent, in the hope that in an externally guaranteed 'safe' situation, a stable political solution can emerge over time. The resort to military action against Iraq and Yugoslavia does not necessarily invalidate this argument. These attacks were designed to bomb political leaders into political submission or bring them to the negotiation table but the 'enemy state' was intended to survive the military strikes and thus ultimately negotiations were, and are, required to finalise the details of the new situation.

In spite of the development of new pressures for intervention in regional conflicts there has been no equivalent debate on the new forms of citizenship and governance, which will be needed to broker settlements in contested states. A new discourse on citizenship is required, that can explain developments in citizenship in contested states and that can create new models of citizenship capable of guaranteeing subordinate national or ethnic groups their citizenship rights outside the context of a 'settled' nation-state. This is not simply a matter of allowing dual citizenship or making citizenship and allegiance a private choice. Rather it requires changes in the public relationship between citizenship and state allegiance. The dominant perspectives on citizenship are analytically inadequate when transported outside of their Anglo-American and continental western European origins. The nature of citizenship in much of the world cannot be adequately analysed without situating citizen-relations in the context of the contested state - the context often having its roots in colonialism. The existing literature does not explain the basis of the perspective on citizenship held by Ulster unionists. Attempts, which have been made to reduce all such conflicts to being, in effect, extreme versions of German ethnic-nationalism, are not plausible. Citizenship in Israel, for example, is about more than alternative identities (though it includes an ethnic dimension): it is also grounded in Israel's security dilemma, the wider Middle East conflict and the impact of settler colonial ideologies.

Citizenship is not a unitary value - the product of a simple modernisation process. The model set out by British sociologist T. H. Marshall (1963) of slowly evolving citizenship rights from civil to political to social is not (and was never intended by Marshall to be) an analytical paradigm for all societies. Rather, citizenship is part of the arena of political conflict and models of citizenship are part of the outcome of such conflicts. Just as the national-democratic revolutions of the nineteenth century advanced demands for parliamentary democracy and political citizenship (at least for men), and the class conflicts of the nineteenth and twentieth century developed social rights in industrial democracies, so too do political conflicts over colonialism and over the boundaries and nature of the state mould the form of citizenship in contested states. This relationship of politics to citizenship is recognised to a significant degree in debates on class and gender but it needs to be extended to include political conflicts over ethnic and national allegiances.

A new discourse on citizenship in contested states, in addition to offering a much more convincing explanation of the nature of citizenship, and the perspectives held by political actors in such states, can also play a role in developing new visions of citizenship. A new model of citizenship is clearly required in Northern Ireland and in other similar societies. This vision of citizenship needs to assert that members of such national or ethnic communities have a right to full citizenship, while retaining their own identity and political aspirations, and that they have these rights regardless of their unwillingness to give allegiance to the dominant state. These rights need to be clearly expressed in both individual and groups terms and need to be grounded in a commitment to see a new vision of equal citizenship reflected in concrete public policies, designed to promote actual equality of treatment between the communities.

Even with a commitment to guarantee traditional rights of citizenship outside the context of an agreed state, some of the issues of contention in Northern Ireland would remain unresolved. For example, disputes over Orange marches and unionists' insistence on a monopoly of British symbolism in the public space would not be resolved by reference to traditional debates on citizenship rights. Disputes on the use of 'political' symbols are a common feature of conflict in contested states, but are rarely discussed in the literature on citizenship (e.g. Ghanem, 1998; Ben-Rafel, 1998; Rouhana, 1997; Memmi, 1990). An additional element is, therefore, also required if a new model of citizenship is to have a significant egalitarian impact. Rights of citizenship needs to be extended to include a specific right to hold allegiance to a nationalist identity other than the previously dominant one and to have that reflected in the culture of the public sphere.

A new model of citizenship designed to operate in contested states therefore requires two distinct elements. Firstly a *new form* of citizenship which is guaranteed outside the framework of an uncontested state and secondly an *extension* of citizenship to cover new types of rights - specifically, in the case of Northern Ireland, focused on nationalists' right to have their group identity reflected in the ethos, culture and practice of the state.

This requirement for new forms of citizenship will clearly often conflict with the *realpolitik* of individual political disputes. There is at present no global structure of governance capable of providing any consistent guidelines for intervention. Yet, as in the case of Northern Ireland, citizenship in contested states is only likely to be transformed with a significant international intervention. Indeed almost by definition, a model of equal citizenship in a contested state will rely much more on transnational governance than citizenship in a 'settled' state. Contemporary forms of transnational governance are too fragmented, based on power inequalities, inconsistent and dominated by US/Western *realpolitik* rather than ideas of supranational law, to provide this external dimension on anything other than an ad-hoc basis. Current international governance simply does not possess the necessary human rights and citizenship protections found in democratic states and which are needed to implement equal citizenship in contested states.

Given the absence of suitable supranational institutions or legal mechanism, for the present at least, the only short-term potential for external mediation and mechanisms to guarantee citizenship in contested states is in the real political benefits such an approach can bring to key political players involved in the conflict, the protagonists, neighbouring states and interested international or regional powers. If a new more equal model of citizenship can provide lasting and stable political settlements, it may play a useful role, even in a world dominated by *realpolitik*. While this provides a less democratic and less consistent approach than a global or regional human rights and citizenship framework it is the motivation most likely to operate in practice.

In Northern Ireland a combination of *realpolitik*, the historic and geographic framework, and the post-Cold War environment produced a type of external intervention which proved acceptable to the political actors and yet provided the necessary dynamic to push the peace process forward. The role of the Irish and British governments operating as both political actors in their own right and also as external guarantors, combined with US mediation, proved successful in reaching an agreement in Northern Ireland. There was also a history of external pressure by NGOs on fair employment and policing, in particular. It is also clear that there are limits to this level of international intervention. There are already signs that the two governments would like to move on to other priorities of their own and leave the implementation of the deal to the parties in Northern Ireland. Continuing high level US interest is not guaranteed beyond the Clinton Presidency. However, without external pressure the Northern Ireland Peace Agreement would not have been signed and without continuing external involvement it will not survive. External intervention, in Northern Ireland cannot be seen as a once off mediation role at a conference or in negotiations, it will need to continue for some time.

It is beyond the scope of this chapter to set out the parameters for such external intervention or specific elements for peace agreements on a global scale, but the Northern Ireland case does provide some indications of the important elements. Irish government involvement in the early 1990s offered the IRA and Sinn Féin an alternative strategy to armed struggle, in putting together a nationalist consensus to pressurise the British government towards a position of reform. US involvement was seen to strengthen this alliance.

Continuing Irish government involvement as set out in the Agreement, the North-South Ministerial Council and its cross-border and all-Ireland implementation bodies, also offer long-term constitutional links recognising the identity of nationalists in Northern Ireland and providing an institutional framework for North-South co-operation which is dynamic rather than static and which can develop over time. The British government, as the sovereign power, also held out the threat that if no deal was reached then they could proceed with an imposed programme of reform including fair employment, cultural rights, a new police force, prisoner releases if the cease-fires held, and even a North-South council made up of nominated rather than elected persons. US involvement produced individual decisions such as the visa for Sinn Féin leader, Gerry Adams, which helped produce the IRA cease-fire, a mediation role during the talks and some external guarantee that the agreement would be implemented. Crucially, however, the Northern Ireland Peace Agreement contains institutions of transnational governance in the North-South Ministerial Council and the inter-governmental conference (and to some extent in the British-Irish Council), which creates a structured basis for continued external involvement.

The mediation role of 'external' players is however just one dimension of the Northern Ireland Peace Agreement's international significance. More importantly perhaps, is its role in exploring new solutions to conflicts. The provisions on equal citizenship are a central part of the Agreement, seen by Republicans as offering a dynamic for future change which allowed them to accept a deal which re-affirms partition in the short to medium term. These equality provisions are not restricted to internal reform as a substitute for constitutional change, but rather are linked to new ideas of citizenship and sovereignty, which recognise nationalists' identity and political goals. Unionist opposition to equality measures are also placed, for the first time, in their proper context - as part of their broader political position, rather than a negotiating ploy, hiding a more accommodating bottom line. Unionists fear reform on issues of equality because they believe that a new constitutional framework, which recognises and guarantees nationalists' rights to equal citizenship, will weaken their own political position and ultimately weaken the link with Britain. Citizenship in contested states is thus part of the constitutional framework, not something separate from it and the recognition of this fundamental point is central to the emergence of the Northern Ireland peace process.

Notes

[1] Full text of Agreement is available at www.irlgov.ie.

[2] The key issues of controversy in the equality arena between nationalists and unionists in Northern Ireland are policing and emergency laws, employment equality and cultural and language rights.

[3] More than 99% of nationalists in Northern Ireland and 95% of the population of the Republic of Ireland, voted for the deal in the May 1998 referendums. Only some 51% of unionists voted Yes.

[4] The RUC is the sole police force in Northern Ireland, but its officers are drawn almost exclusively (over 92%) from the unionist community. It is also avowedly unionist in its symbols and oath of office.

[5] The Orange Order is a unionist and anti-Catholic organisation which organises over 2,500 public marches each year, some of which go through residential areas which are almost entirely nationalist. This causes huge resentment among the nationalist community.

[6] e.g. David Trimble (UUP leader) NI Forum, 12 Sept. 1997, vol. 42, p.3.

Anthony Alcock (UUP) NI Forum, 6 June 1997, vol. 33, p. 38.

Bob McCartney, NI Forum, 6 June 1997, vol. 33, p.4.

UUP *Response to Frameworks for the Future*, 1995 [on www.uup.org, 20 May 1997].

[7] Phrase 'war of position' from Antonio Gramsci (1971).

[8] Peter King (UUP), *Ulster Review*, no. 23, Autumn 1997.

[9] Peter Weir (UUP), NI Forum, 23 Jan. 1998, vol. 58, p.44.

[10] e.g. Ken Maginnis, House of Commons, 15 Dec. 1997, vol. 303, col. 61-9.

David Trimble in same debate at col. 96.

Extensive debate in NI Forum 23 Jan. 1998, vol. 58.

[11] Ken Maginnis, House of Commons, 15 Dec. 1997, cols. 63 and 69.

[12] e.g. John Taylor, House of Commons, NI Committee, 16 May 1991, col. 14.

Orange Standard, July 1993.

Response by UUP to Review of fair employment legislation, 4 Jan. 1996 [www.uup.org, 29 Nov. 1996].

[13] e.g. Jeffrey Donaldson, NI Forum, 20 June 1997, vol. 35, p.12.

Ken Maginnis, *Irish Independent*, 21 Aug. 1986.

[14] Editorial, *Belfast Telegraph*, 19 Jan. 1995.

Similar views from David Trimble, *Newsletter*, 22 Dec. 1994.

[15] See *Irish News*, 19 Aug. 1997.

[16] e.g. *Alliance News*, Jan. 1987. Northern Ireland Forum, vol. 24, p. 7, 17 Jan. 1997.

[17] See for example unionist reaction to Protestants in the Women's Coalition, in the business organisations or in the churches when they challenge mainstream unionist positions.

e.g. Jack McKee (DUP), NI Forum, 7 Feb. 1997, vol. 27, p. 46.

John Hunter (UUP), NI Forum, 24 Oct. 1997, vol. 48, p.10.

David Campbell (UUP), NI Forum, 13 June 1997, vol. 34, pp. 37-8.

[18] e.g. Anthony Alcock, NI Forum, 3 Oct. 1997, vol. 45, p.10.

Reinforced even after the agreement during various difficulties in its implementation e.g. David Ervine (PUP), *Irish Times*, 21 Jan. 1999.

[19] Also statement by Jacques Delors, *Irish Times*, 4 Nov. 1992.

[20] Niall O'Dowd, cited in Coogan (1995, p. 373).

[21] Also see *An Phoblacht*, 11 Nov. 1993.

[22] e.g. *Irish Times*, 20 Apr. 1998; 30 Apr. 1998.

[23] See also: *Combat*, Aug. 1974; Sept. 1974;

Jim Kilfedder, House of Commons, 6 Mar. 1978, vol., 945, col. 1003;
David Trimble, House of Commons, 30 Oct. 1996, col. 633.

[24] Private Documents from the republican leadership from this period were later published by the *Sunday Tribune*, 23 Apr. 1995, which substantiate this analysis.

[25] This is clearly reflected in the editorial style of *An Phoblacht* (the republican weekly newspaper). The pejorative term 'Free State' was no longer used to describe the Republic and its government but more neutral terms like 'the South' or the '26 Counties' and the 'Dublin administration'.

[26] See article by Brendan O'Leary 'Unionists will lose electoral dominance', *Irish* Times, 2 July 1997.

[27]NI Forum, 3 Oct. 1997, vol. 45, p.10.

[28] For example UUP response to the framework documents [www.uup.org, 20 May 1997] and Antony Alcock, NI Forum, 7 Feb. 1997, vol. 27, p.21.

[29] e.g. David Trimble, *Irish Times*, 23 June 1999.

[30] *Irish Times*, 15 May 1998.

[31] *Irish Times*, 9 April 1999.

References

Adams, G. (1995), Free *Ireland: Towards a Lasting Peace,* Brandon, Dingle, Co. Kerry.

Baldwin-Edwards, M. and M. Schain, eds. (1994), *The Politics of Immigration in Western Europe*, Frank Cass, London.

Barker, M. (1981), *The New Racism,* Junction, London.

Ben-Rafael, E. (1998), 'Arab Citizenship in Israel', *Ethnic and Racial Studies*, vol. 21:3, pp. 579-85.

Bew, P. and H. Patterson, 'Scenarios for Progress in Northern Ireland', in J. McGarry and B. O'Leary (eds.), *The Future of Northern Ireland*, Oxford University Press, Oxford, pp. 206-19.

Brubaker, R. (1992), *Citizenship and Nationhood in France and Germany*, Harvard University Press, Cambridge, Mass.

Pamela Clayton, *Enemies and Passing Friends: settler ideologies in twentieth century Ulster*, Pluto Press, London.

Coogan, T.P. (1995), *The Troubles: Ireland's Ordeal 1966-1995 and the Search for Peace*, Hutchinson, London.

Cox, M. (1997), 'Bringing in the International: the IRA cease-fire and the end of the Cold War', *International Affairs*, vol. 73:4, pp. 671-93.

Cox, M. (1998), 'Northern Ireland: the war that came in from the cold', *Irish Studies in International Affairs*, vol. 9, pp. 73-84.

Cronin, S. (1987), *Washington's Irish Policy 1916 - 1986: Independence, Partition, Neutrality*, Anvil Books, Dublin.

Crozier, M. (1989), *Cultural Traditions in Ireland*, Institute of Irish Studies, Queens University Belfast.

Dixon, P. (1996), 'The politics of antagonism: explaining McGarry and O'Leary', *Irish Political Studies*, vol. 11, pp. 130-41.

Ghanem, A. (1998), 'State and minority in Israel: the case of the ethnic state and the predicament of its minority', *Ethnic and Racial Studies*, vol. 21:3, pp. 428-44.

Gramsci, A. (1971), Selections *from the Prison Notebooks.* Q. Hoare and G. Nowell Smith (eds.), Lawrence and Wishart, London.

Keogh, D. (1994), *Twentieth Century Ireland*, Gill and Macmillan, Dublin.

Marshall, T. H. (1963), *Sociology at the Crossroads and other essays*, Heinemann, London.

Memmi, A. (1990), *The Colonizer and the Colonized*, Earthscan, London.

Mitchell, G. (1999), *Making Peace: the inside story of the making of the Good Friday Agreement*, Heinemann, London.

Munck, R. (1998), 'Irish Republicanism: A New Beginning?', in J. Anderson and J. Goodman (eds.), *Dis/Agreeing Ireland: Contexts, Obstacles, Hopes*, Pluto Press, London, pp. 176-92.

McVeigh, R. (1998), 'Is Sectarianism Racism? Theorising the Racism/ Sectarianism Interface', in D. Miller (eds.), *Rethinking Northern Ireland: Culture, Ideology and Colonialism*, Longman, London, pp. 179-98.

O'Dowd, N. (1993), 'The Greening of the White House: Clinton's Irish Agenda', *Irish America Magazine*, Jan./Feb. pp. 20-24.

O'Grady, J. (1996), An Irish Policy Born in the USA', *Foreign Affairs*, vol. 75:2, pp. 2-7.

Rouhana, N. (1997), *Palestinian Citizens in an Ethnic Jewish State: Identities in Conflict,* Yale University Press, New Haven.

Ruane, J. and J. Todd (1996), The dynamics of conflict in Northern Ireland, power, conflict and emancipation, Cambridge University Press, Cambridge.

Part III
Communications and Economies

10 Banking Regulation and Reform: Implications for the New Millennium

NAYANTARA HENSEL

As the new millennium begins, the worldwide banking sector is in the process of a revolution which will result in larger, more regionally integrated banks that offer a variety of financial products and have a substantial presence in international markets and online markets. During the process of consolidation and technological expansion, banks face the challenges presented by globalization and the consequent shift in the balance of power in the banking system. In the immediate future, banks must manage within the constraints presented by: (1) shifts in regional power due to local consolidation; (2) shifts in international power due to the wave of cross border mergers and consequent competition; (3) the need to expand into the online markets; (4) changes in financial regulatory policy, such as the repeal of the Glass Steagall Act in the US; (5) conflicts about national sovereignty in financial policy-making, especially in the EC; and (6) fluctuations in the domestic economy, especially in Asia. This paper examines the recent role that each of these challenges has played in the European, Asian, and American banking systems and discusses the possible future interactions of these forces as the international banking system evolves toward a new, stable equilibrium.

A number of mergers have occurred in Europe within countries, such as in France and Spain, and, increasingly, between countries, partially due to the launch of the euro in January, 1999. The introduction of a common currency has helped to facilitate this integration since it has resulted in some convergence of overnight rates in European interbank deposit markets ("Euro Signals"); now it is being furthered by plans to introduce a common euro clearing system, into which all of the national depositories would run. This would facilitate mergers because of the cost savings from eliminating dozens of connections to different clearing systems (*Financial Times,* May 4, 1999, "Banks to Start"), which would enable banks to do business more cheaply in other countries. Introduction of the euro also provides an impetus to European banking consolidation because a significant portion of bank revenues from the foreign exchange business will disappear. Other integration-facilitative forces include the increased competition due to technological innovation and the losses suffered by some banks in emerging markets countries. Nevertheless, cross-border mergers still face costly national regulatory obstacles.

Consolidation of banks within their national banking sector has been extensive, especially in Europe. Over the next several years, this struggle for survival will occur even more frequently as established banks fight to preserve their control of the domestic banking sector by blocking the mergers of rivals and destroying old relationships with banking partners. The situation will be worsened by the interlinkages between the European banks since many banks own shares of both their allies and their rivals, both in their country and internationally. The struggle of established, powerful banks to defend the status quo and resist a shift in the balance of power has recently been seen in the banking struggles occurring in Italy and in France.

In Italy, Mediobanca, a powerful Milan bank which has controlled the northern Italian banking industry for years, supported an alliance that, from its point of view, would be beneficial—the alliance between Banca di Roma and Banca Commerciale Italiana (BCI). In order to facilitate the Banca di Roma-BCI alliance, Mediobanca opposed a proposed merger between Banca di Roma and the Sao-Paolo-IMI Bank and then opposed the merger between BCI and UniCredito Italiano. This latter merger would have reduced Mediobanca's autonomy since each of the merging banks had an 8.8% share in Mediobanca. To derail the BCI-UniCredito Italiano merger, it severed its long-term relationship with the French bank Lazard Freres by ousting the senior partner of Lazard Freres from the board of the insurance company Assicurazioni Generali (in which Mediobanca was a large shareholder) because he supported the merger. This was a crucial move because Generali was one of BCI's largest shareholders, and Mediobanca did not want the BCI shareholders to approve the BCI-UniCredito merger. The replacement on the Generali board was chosen partially because he was likely to support the union of BCI and Banca Intesa, which Mediobanca now supported after its efforts at uniting BCI with Banca di Roma had failed. Nevertheless, by disrupting its relationship with Lazard, Mediobanca ran the risk of losing control of Generali if Lazard offered its stake in Generali for sale. Mediobanca's sacrifice of its relationship with Lazard to secure a favorable regional balance of power was also costly since it destroyed the joint access of Lazard and Mediobanca to each other's markets and clients. Since Mediobanca now supported the BCI-Banca Intesa merger, it began working to oust the BCI board members who supported the UniCredito merger and to secure a non-aggression pact from the Deutsche Bank (a large BCI shareholder), who supported the BCI union with UniCredito rather than Banca Intesa. Finally, when the BCI board turned down the proposal from UniCredito, Mediobanca won temporarily its battle for autonomy and continued control of the Italian banking sector ("Divorce"; "Banking Reform"; "Italy's Banks"; "Mediobanca Acts"; "Mediobanca Seeks"; "Generali"; "Italy's"; "BCI"; *Financial Times*, May 3, 1999).

This episode in the Italian banking sector shows the reaction of established banks to the trend toward regional consolidation and their willingness to sacrifice existing relationships on the altar of a favorable balance of power. Mediobanca and other established banks, by actively taking a role in disrupting mergers that would be unbeneficial from their point of view, ignore the fact that their fundamental problems and insecurities stem from the erosion of their influence through trends which they cannot change and that, as a result, these costly victories are only temporary. For example, globalization and liberalization have led to US investment banks taking the lead in Italian, and overall, European corporate deals, because of superior global distribution networks and technology. Examples of the growing US dominance in European deals include the role of DLJ and Lehman in Olivetti's raid on Telecom Italia, Goldman's role in the Daimler-Benz/Chrysler merger, and Goldman's role in BNP's attempt at a hostile takeover of SG/Paribas. Since 1990, the top 10 US investment banks have doubled their share in global business to 77%, while European retail banks have been exiting ("Top Ten"). Italian banks are partially trying to sustain their competitive advantage by merging. If Mediobanca continues its medieval, strong-arm tactics, but does not address the fundamental roots of its problems by improving its diversity of financial products, technology, or market penetration, it will become a victim of the millenial banking trends of global markets and cross-border mergers Indeed, with the increasing presence of foreign banks in domestic European banking sectors, Mediobanca may soon no longer be fighting Italian banks in Italy, but rather German or French banks in Italy, like Deutsche Bank and Paribas, which could buy up UniCredito or substantially increase their shares in it.

France, like Italy, is undergoing a shift in the balance of power in the domestic banking industry, as was most recently seen in the success of Banque Nacional de Paris (BNP)'s successful hostile bid for Banque Paribas. The new bank, BNP-Paribas, is twice as big as Societe Generale (SG), which had been the largest bank in France prior to BNP's hostile bid for both SG and Paribas. BNP's bid had disrupted the friendly merger between Societe General and Banque Paribas, proposed in February 1999. The SG-Paribas merger had the benefit that no jobs would be lost since Paribas, a wholesale bank, had few branches. Nevertheless, it was unclear whether there would be sufficient synergies, without job loss and elimination of duplicative branches. BNP, like Mediobanca in Italy, desired to maintain a strong position as the balance of power shifted and, therefore, offered to each of the two banks to buy them, on March 9, 1999, thus combining the three into the world's largest bank. This followed the failure of its February proposal to guarantee 30,000 of the jobs at the Credit Lyonnaise, in exchange for a dominant role in its privatization (*Financial Times*, March 15, 1999). After this initial plan had failed, BNP, like Mediobanca, had moved on to a new plan to maintain dominance—in this case, consolidation of the three banks into one. Analysts argued that BNP and SG, both commercial banks, could attain greater synergies through combining their branch networks than the SG-Paribas union would ("Paribas and SG"; *Financial Times*, February 18, 1999).

Although the financial markets reacted more favorably to BNP's bid than the SG-Paribas proposal, both SG and Paribas strenuously protested, and an advertising war ensued in the pages of the *Financial Times*, as each group tried to convince shareholders that its plan would add the most value. Both SG and Paribas circulated documents against the merger, while BNP circulated information in favor of it ("Paris Regulator") Paribas was half held by foreign investors, so it tried to suggest that the SG-Paribas merger would more beneficial to foreign investors than the BNP proposal, which focused on growing domestic retail banking. BNP tried to win the French business community, which held 60% of it (*Financial Times* May 7, 1999). To achieve greater transparency to shareholders and to strengthen their defense, SG and Paribas moved to quarterly statements on May 7 1999. As a result, on May 11, BNP announced that it would do the same for its shareholders (*Financial Times*, May 7, 1999, "BNP Publishes").

This French case not only paralleled the Italian case in the desire of domestic banks to protect themselves against unbeneficial mergers by rivals, but also in the sacrifice of old relationships in order to maintain the balance of power, as well as in the involvement of foreign banks. For example, as in the Italian case, dissenting bank board members were being asked to step down—the head of Axa was asked to step down from SG's board because he supported BNP's bid (*Financial Times*, May 26, 1999). Foreign banks became involved to support the domestic merger which would best favor their interests. For example, just as Deutsche Bank backed the UniCredito merger in Italy to facilitate its cross-border expansion, so the Banco Santander Central Hispanico (Spain's largest bank) supported the SG-Paribas merger over the BNP proposal ("Banco Santander").

Nevertheless, the French government implicitly supported the idea of a "national champion" bank since it would strengthen the domestic banking industry against foreign takeovers. Indeed, some interpreted the decision to offer foreign banks a position in the Credit Lyonnaise privatization as a means of minimizing international criticism of this "national champion" model.

The final decision of the French Credit Institutions Committee was announced at the end of August, 1999, as SG's trade unions demonstrated against BNP. BNP was allowed to combine with Paribas, in which it held 65% of the shares, but it did not secure sufficient control of SG, since it only had 31.8% of the voting rights. The denouement of the six month battle was ironic, since BNP had wanted to acquire SG more than Paribas, and had hoped to combine the three of them into a substantial retail banking giant in France. SG, although it was not able to combine with Paribas as it had originally hoped, was left free to explore cross-border alliances, including a possible one with its largest shareholder, Banco Santander Central Hispanico ("France Finance Minister"; "Lex Column—August 30, 1999").

Consolidation in the French domestic banking sector, with the growing involvement of foreign banks, will continue for the next several years. Indeed, in the first months of 2000, SG increased its share to 4% in the Credit Lyonnaise, which had recently been privatized. Since SG's future strategy has been in debate since the failure of the SG-Paribas plan, some analysts suggested that this might signal SG's intentions toward the Lyonnaise. When the Credit Lyonnaise was privatized, the Credit Agricole was given the dominant stake of 10% by the government, which was interpreted as signalling an eventual merger between the two. Because the Credit Agricole is a mutual, which does not have to pay dividends to shareholders, it is less likely to cut jobs to improve profitability if it ultimately merged with the Credit Lyonnnaise. A union by the Lyonnaise with another commercial bank, however, could lead to job loss from elimination of duplicative branches ("French Look"). Nevertheless, employees only have a 4% stake in the Lyonnaise, and are therefore less powerful than employees at SG had been in the BNP fight. Furthermore, the Agricole, because it is mutually owned, would have difficulty in fighting a listed bank, such as SG. The other core shareholders include: AGF (the French branch of the German insurance company Allianz) with 6%, Axa (the largest French insurance company) with 5.5%, Banco Bilbao Vizcaya (Spanish) with 3.75%, Commerzbank (Germany) with 4%, and Banca Intesa (Italy) with 2.75%. Since cooperation between the core group of shareholders did not materialize, as had been hoped, the group could fall apart. This is because, although they are prohibited from selling before

July, 2001, they are relieved of these rules if an outsider acquires a stake of more than 8% ("French Banks"; "Lyonnais"). Consequently, as of this writing, the Credit Lyonnaise is a viable vehicle for domestic or cross-border consolidation for SG or for another foreign bank. Already, ING, the Netherlands bank, made and then retracted a bid for the Credit Commerciale de France (CCF), which is one of France's ten largest banks. This deal, if it had succeeded, would have marked the first foreign takeover of a French bank ("French Banks";"ING").

In countries with a number of banks, a merger between two leading banks could trigger a chain reaction of mergers between other banks, eager to join in cost-cutting and market penetration to defend their turf against their merged rivals. This has been seen to some extent in France—SG is looking for a partner to offset BNP-Paribas— as well as in Italy. This phenomenon, which will be seen more frequently in domestic consolidation, has been evident in Portugal. In January, 2000, Banco Espirito Santo and Banco Portugues de Investimento announced their merger. A week later, Banco Comercial Portugues announced its absorption of Banco Portugues de Atlantico. Both parties then, as of this writing, announced their interest in Banco Pinto e Sotto Mayor ("Banco Comercial").

Some countries have been resisting entry into the domestic consolidation stage, due to regulatory policy concerns that, despite efficiency gains, a merger will increase concentration too much and lead to monopoly. For example, in Canada, the government prevented mergers of 4 of the 5 largest banks on the grounds that concentration might increase. These banks had wanted to merge to reduce expenses, increase their capital available for expanding outside Canada, and to share the cost of subsequent investment in technology. After the merger was denied, the banks which had wanted to merge—Bank of Montreal and Royal Bank of Canada—reported much lower earnings, while the only bank of the 5 which had not proposed a merger—Scotiabank—reported a gain ("Mixed Fortunes").

As competitive conditions evolve rapidly, especially with improvements in technology and mergers overseas, rules limiting concentration should be reconsidered and the industry structure reassessed. For example, the UK banking industry was traditionally highly concentrated with 4 banks controlling 80% of the market for providing finance to small businesses. A merger probably would not have received approval because it would have increased concentration in an already highly concentrated industry. Now, small businesses are less dependent on traditional bank borrowing, and the traditional big 4 are competing against S&L's and smaller banks. New entrants are gaining market share on the retail-side due to the evolution of new core-competencies in electronic banking, the internet, and technological change in back office processing, leading to scale economies (*Financial Times*, May 24, 1999). Introduction of entrants changes the market structure such that mergers which would have led to significant market power at one time would now primarily improve efficiency or reduce excess capacity in the market.

The next stage in the development of the European banking industry, following domestic consolidation, will be cross-border expansion. There have been only a few cross border mergers thus far—Merita-Nordbanken was formed in Sweden and Finland and Banco Santander Central Hispanico (Spain) recently bought four Portugese banks from the Champalimaud group. Different cultural attitudes have often been a problem, as was the case in ING's bid for CCF. Furthermore, although cross-border mergers provide banks with the opportunity to expand into their partners' territory, projected cost savings tend to be less than for domestic mergers ("An Uncertain Footing";"Bank Invaders").

Cross-border mergers will be further hindered by traditional nationalistic rivalries. For example, the Bank of Ireland (formed during the '60s wave of consolidation in the Irish banking industry from unions with National and Hibernia banks) wanted to join with the UK bank Alliance and Leicester (A&L). This created cross border issues since Bank of Ireland, the 3rd largest company in Ireland and its largest bank, would have reduced exposure to the Irish economy (falling from 70% to 30%) and it would have become increasingly exposed to the volatile UK mortgage market. The proposed structure where each shareholder kept their shares, with dividends and capital distributed according to fixed shares, helped to address the concerns of the Irish nationalists that a bank with 20-22% of the Irish domestic banking market would merge with a UK firm. The synergy in this case was less in cost savings, because the Irish banking industry consolidated in the '60s, and more in the cross- selling of Bank of Ireland's fund management and insurance products through A&L's UK retail channels. The Bank of Ireland would pool its UK mortgage holdings with those larger ones of A&L (*Financial Times*, May 25, 1999, May 26, 1999).

The Spanish bank, Banco Santander Central Hispanico (BSCH), is, and will continue to be, at the forefront of both cross-border integration, and online expansion (which will be discussed subsequently). BSCH was formed in 1999 through the merger between Banco Santander and Banco Central Hispanico. BSCH has followed the lucrative strategy of taking influential stakes in international banks, and thus influencing the course of intracountry banking consolidation. Indeed, as of this writing, it is supporting the bid of Royal Bank of Scotland, in which it holds a 9.6% stake, against Bank of Scotland's bid for National Westminster Bank, which doesn't want to join with either bank. In addition, with its 5% stake in SG, it is well placed to influence SG's further aspirations for alliances, and also has cross-equity agreements with San Paolo-IMI (Italy) and Commerzbank (Germany). BSCH has expanded its Latin American operations by acquiring Brazil's Meridional group, as well as banks in Chile, Peru, Venezuela, and Argentina ("BSCH"; "Spanish Banking War").

BSCH's strategy for expansion will be replicated by other banks over the next decade. After substantial domestic consolidation, banks will establish shareholdings in banks of other countries to influence the outcome of alliances within those countries. Then, as the bank establishes its relationship with the foreign bank, it will increase its shareholdings, and, ultimately, attempt a cross-border merger. The attempt could be hostile, as BNP's domestic attempt on Paribas and SG was, but it could be successful, depending on the degree to which banks in other countries with shareholdings in the merging banks want the cross-border merger to go through. As the bank triumphs in domestic consolidation and attempts its prelude to the cross-border merger, it could also increase its branch density in other countries.

As the banking industry enters the stage of cross-border mergers over the next decade, issues about the appropriate regulatory authority will increasingly surface. For example, in the case of Bank of Ireland and A&L (UK), would authority be in the UK or in the Central Bank of Ireland? One country is in the euro-zone and one isn't. Cross-border mergers have implications for banking concentration not only for particular countries, but for all of Europe.

Individual countries must move away from advocating rules in international and European banking reform which will further their own competitive advantage. The next few years will see conflicts, especially with Germany, involving this. This was seen at the recent negotiations for revising the 1988 Basle Accords, which requires banks to set aside 8% of their risk-weighted assets as a cushion. Germany argues that its commercial mortgages, because their default rate is so low, should have less capital set aside as a cushion than typical property loans. But setting aside less capital means that German banks can charge less for the loan than the banks in other countries and hence undercut them on price ("Fresh Drive";" US-German Animosity"; *Financial Times*, May 17, 1999).

The repeal of the Glass Steagall Act (1933) in the US will allow US banks to compete on an even footing with international banks in terms of diversity of products offered under one roof. This piece of legislation had separated investment banking from commercial banking activities in US banks after the 1929 crash because of the negative impact of alleged conflicts of interest on the banks' customers. The Bank Holding Company Act of 1956, which restricted the activities of banks in the insurance business, will also be modified. Restrictions on cross ownership of securities firms and insurance companies had already lessened prior to the repeal of the act, thus allowing the merger of Citibank with Traveler's Group to form the world's largest financial services company—Citigroup. Repeal of the legislation will allow the development of financial supermarkets, which would provide such items as checking accounts, mutual funds, and different types of insurance—car, life, home, etc.—under one roof. Opponents of the repeal of the act see it, however, as paving the way for megamergers, but not addressing any pressing problem. They argue that entrepreneurs and investors have easy access to each other anyway through the booming venture capital market, and that the emergence of online banking and investing will result in large financial entities being bypassed. Furthermore, the essential protection of Glass-Steagall had been in emphasizing the financial responsibilities of deposit banks to customers and limiting the effects of systemic risk by segmenting the banking industry ("A Requiem";"Congress").

Over the next decade, the US banking industry will witness a spate of mergers between banks and insurers and brokerage houses, providing integrated financial entities comparable to those in Europe. The US will be following the European trend of bancassurance—cross-selling of banking and insurance through the same channels, which will become especially important as banks gain greater control over baby boomer's retirement accounts. Consequently, mergers between large, regional banks, like the Fleet Boston Corporation, and life insurers, such as John Hancock, will be frequent ("Invasion").

The diversification in products allowed by the repeal of Glass Steagall will be helpful in strengthening the financial solidity of banks, such that they will no longer be dependent on one line of business. For example, fears about Goldman Sachs' IPO partially revolved around Goldman's heavy dependence on investment banking activity, which is highly volatile since the current wave of mergers may run out (*Forbes*, May 17, 1999). If it entered into deposit-taking and traditional commercial banking activities, this would provide a more stable source of revenue and cause less stock price fluctuation.

Whether large financial conglomerates will have a greater competitive advantage because they will provide one-stop shopping for a variety of customer segments is questionable. As of this writing, the success of the Citigroup merger is unclear, while the purchase of Montgomery Securities by NationsBank suffered difficulties. A recent consulting study notes that the average bank customer has only a checking account, a savings account, and maybe a credit card through the bank. Thus, existing attempts by banks at cross-selling have shown little results. Indeed, almost half of the customers at the sixth largest bank in the US, First Union Bank, have only one of the bank's products. Furthermore, consumers may care more about the quality of the product, than whether it is available through their local bank ("Empty Aisles"). The ease of investing online may take away business from superbanks offering financial products. Nevertheless, although some of the initial results on bank product diversity have not been impressive, it is important to note that they were not generated in an environment without Glass-Steagall. With the repeal of the act, more banks will have the legal authority to expand their product diversity over the next decade, and hence will have a greater opportunity move up the learning curve, in terms of targeting the right customer through the right channel with the right product.

In the US and Europe, the wave of the future will be online commercial banking and online investment banking, although online banking will never entirely replace branch banking. Over the next decade especially, however, the growth of Internet banks will provide a major challenge to existing, non-Internet banks. Investment in Internet operations to meet the competition of Internet banks, and in employee retraining to sell new financial products, initially eroded the profits of some of the established US banks, like the First Union Bank ("Profit Warning"). The Net enables banks to cut costs by gathering deposits and processing transactions more cheaply. Since they lack branches and tellers, Net costs are 1% of those at an actual branch, which results in Net banks offering higher deposit rates. Existing branch banks, like Wells Fargo, which are moving into the Net bank arena, could lose out to Net banks like NetBank, Telebanc Financial, and Security First Network Bank, if customers require continued Web and branch service and they have to bear both costs. Reputational concerns and fears of risky lending by Net banks, although unfounded so far, will slow the shift away from branch banks. The net gain in customers for online commercial banking for the fiscal year ending July 31, 1999 was 2% because almost as many customers joined online banking as left it. Poor customer service, an absence of branches where one could talk to tellers, and slow speed due to security measures were among the causes for this paltry gain ("Who's Afraid"; *Business Week*, May 10, 1999).

Online investment banks present a challenge to investment banks which aren't online. The largest initial public offering on the Net thus far has been Espernet, at $173 million, in October, 1999, while the World Bank, in January, 2000, made the first completely online fixed income offering with its $3 billion international bond. Online investment banks have lower costs, which they can pass onto clients, because they have fewer employees and can access a wider pool of capital. Moreover, their IPOs are less likely to be underpriced and hence to exhibit a spike on the first day of trading (the profits of this traditional spike would go to the initial holder, an institutional investor, rather than to the issuer). This is because online banks, such as OpenIPO.com, use an auction mechanism to get information about pricing from ordinary customers, rather than mainly relying on institutional investment firms' information, which is costly and is paid for via the first day spike ("OpenIPO"). Traditional investment banks are more geared toward an institutional clientele, while online investment banks allow access of a broader clientele to its offerings. Nevertheless, Internet investment banks are especially plagued with reputational concerns since the name-recognition of the investment bank affects the value of the securities it underwrites. Hence, the costs of advertising and research may increase the low overhead of online banks. Also, traditional investment banks have a variety of financial instruments which can meet other needs of the client, thus establishing a long-term relationship (*Business Week* , May 10, 1999; "Internet Threat").

European banks are expanding into the online business because it is a cheaper way than cross-border alliances or mergers to expand into new international markets and to undercut the domestic competition. Banco Bilbao Vizcaya Argentaria (BBVA), the second largest financial services group in Spain, launched on January 5, 2000 what they described as "the first 'Latin' internet bank," called Uno-e.com. This online bank is, as of this writing, in Spain and plans to expand shortly into Italy, Portugal, and France, as well as into Latin America. Bank of Scotland has already launched its internet home loan business in Ireland and the Netherlands, with great success ("Spanish Bank"; "BBVA"; "BoS"). Ultimately, over the course of the next 2 decades, American and European online banks may compete directly with each other in the same markets.

The online brokerage industry will also be a rapidly growing and competitive market in the next decade. As per trade commissions become smaller and smaller due to competition, firms, such as Merrill Lynch, Morgan Stanley Dean Witter, Prudential Securities, Salomon Smith Barney, and Charles Schwab, are moving toward charges based on flat fees, regardless of the number of trades made ("Wall Street's"). The next few years will see competition not only on price, but also on the quality of the package—access to and quality of research reports, charts, and analysts. The retirement of the Baby Boom generation will probably result in a greater demand for access to seasoned analysts and account executives, which could impede the ability of new, no-frills, low cost, do-it-yourself online brokerages to compete. Furthermore, more online brokerages will move toward fee-based income if Baby Boomers' retirement portfolios trade less than non-retirement portfolios.

Over the next several decades, US investment banks will take the lead over Asian investment banks because of their high-profile, extensive global financial network. Japanese banks have been exiting the investment banking market and, as of March, 1999, only one Japanese bank was in the top 20 global investment banks ("Top Ten"), although two Japanese banks ranked fifth and sixth in 1999 in terms of value of local M&A deals ("Japanese Banks"). Ample business for investment banks as financial advisors has been generated by the profusion of regional Japanese banks, which are in trouble because they are weighted down by bad loans from the 1980s. The dominant role of US firms in Asian restructuring highlights the increasingly prevalent perception of the financial system and its players as being global, not local, in scope. For example, the Tokyo Sawa Bank, which has a low capital adequacy ratio due to the bad loans, like many of the regional banks, called in the western investment bank Bear Stearns as its advisor. Goldman Sachs advised the LongTerm Credit Bank (*Financial Times*, May 27, 1999). The globalizing trend of greater international involvement in the Asian banking system has also already been seen in South Korea and Thailand. In South Korea, HSBC Holdings is buying Seoul Bank, and Thailand has sold 3 nationalized banks to foreigners with more experience ("Asian Financial Markets").

Foreign brokerage firms are also taking the lead over Japanese brokerage firms. This is because, as a result of deregulation of equity commissions in Japan, domestic brokerages suffered from price-cutting, but the foreign banks did not because they relied less on brokerage commissions, and more on M&A fees. Foreign banks account for 1/3 of all trades on the Tokyo Stock Exchange, with JP Morgan, Morgan Stanley, and Merrill as the leaders ("US Banks").

Over the next five years, Asian banks, like European banks, will undergo significant domestic consolidation. The forces underlying the Asian consolidation differ, however, from those underlying the European consolidation. Many of the mergers in Europe are the chain-reactions to one large merger, where the banks not involved in the large merger feel that they have to combine with other banks before their rivals do, so that they won't be left out in the cold as a small bank facing several large, monolithic entities. Asian consolidation, on the other hand, is more driven by the banks' need to survive and reduce costs in the wake of a number of exogenous, domestic crises. These domestic crises, in the medium-run, result in an absence of demand for loans as well as in a reduced confidence on the part of banks to lend. Hence, some of the methods used by banks to becoming internationally competitive—mergers and employee cuts—are common to Europe and Asia, but the underlying forces are different. Many of the Asian bank consolidations of tomorrow will be the result of Asian banks grappling today with the effects of the risky decisions that they made yesterday. For example, Japanese banks have been suffering from the number of bad loans that they made in the 1980s. Consequently, the next few years will probably see a lot of consolidation in the trust bank sector and the commercial bank sector because of the heavy losses posted by Japanese trust banks and commercial banks.

Although Japanese banks have often sought cost-cutting as their primary reform, their real problem is not excess employment, but rather a poor base of revenues because too many banks are chasing after the same business. More mergers will be needed to reduce capacity. Capacity-reducing mergers have also been seen in South Korea, which, like Japan, has been confronted with growing loan problems. Ten of the twenty-seven commercial banks have merged and one third of the employees have been cut. Thailand banks have also been faced with the need for increased lending opportunities, as well as the need to restructure debtor-creditor agreements ("Asian Financial Markets").

Indian banks confront challenges similar to those of Asian and European banks. Like Italian banks, Indian banks have faced substantial internal competition, as well as substantial international competition. Recently, like many of the Asian banks, Indian banks have been in the situation in which demand for lender funds has been low, although, unlike Asian banks, the supply of lender funds has been high. This situation has led Indian banks to move into new products, like credit cards. Interest rate deregulation has led to banks undercutting each other and narrowing profit margins. Deregulation has also stimulated internal competition between India's banks and the other financial institutions, and some believe that India will end up with a universal banking system. Finally, private sector banks and foreign banks are entering with new bank technologies. As in Europe and Asia, Indian banks will need to cut costs by eliminating the large branch network developed due to the nation-building desire to have branches in rural areas, and to cut the substantial overstaffing ("Indian Banking").

The Latin American banking system is similar to the Asian banking system in that it, unlike Europe, the US, and India, has been plagued with substantial economic turmoil. As in Asia, resolution of domestic turmoil precedes developments to achieve global competitiveness - efficiency-enhancing mergers, market penetration, technological competency, and introduction of new financial products. The confidence of the international financial community in the currency and in the country's financial institutions is a crucial factor in stimulating the cycle of prosperity and thus encouraging further bank expansion.

During the first several decades of the new millenium, the global financial community will see substantial adjustment in the competitive positions of international banks as they maneuver to achieve a new balance of power. The banks in each country are in different stages in their evolution toward a new, stable equilibrium. The lifting of the Glass-Steagall restrictions will place American banks at a similar stage of development with European banks, although American banks surpass European and Asian banks in their technological sophistication and online presence. The development of the Asian banks has been temporarily slowed by the Asian Crisis, but the resulting reconstruction of the banking sector has eliminated many structural weaknesses.

In conclusion, the international banking system faces tremendous challenges as it enters the new millennium, but also tremendous opportunities for rewards. Cross-border cooperation and efficiency-enhancing mergers, as well as introduction of new financial products and resolution of domestic crises, are vital prerequisites to weaving domestic banking systems into a globally integrated whole. National hegemony will be overshadowed by the desire for connectiveness, efficiency, and diversity in financial offerings. Hence, although re-positioning to achieve a new balance of power in the banking world will temporarily cause turmoil, the results will be well worth it.

References

"A Requiem for Glass Steagall," *Business Week*, November 15, 1999, p. 28 (cited as "A Requiem).

"An Uncertain Footing," *Financial Times*, January 10, 2000 (cited as "An Uncertain Footing").

"Asian Financial Markets," *Financial Times Survey*, April 30, 1999 (cited as "Asian Financial Markets").

"Banco Comercial to Mop Up BPA Minorities," *Financial Times*, January 26, 2000 (cited as Banco Comercial).

"Banco Santander May Help SG and Paribas Merge," *Financial Times*, May 28, 1999 (cited as "Banco Santander").

"Bank Invaders Scale the Pyrenees," *Business Week*. November 29, 1999, p. 62 (cited as "Bank Invaders").

"Banking Reform in Italy Hit by Merger Rejection," *Financial Times*, April 28, 1999 (cited as "Banking Reform").

"Banks to Start New Euro Clearing System," *Financial Times*, April 30, 1999 (cited as "Banks to Start").

"BBVA Launches First 'Latin' Online Bank," *Financial Times*, January 5, 2000 (cited as "BBVA").

"BNP Publishes First Quarterly Accounts," *Financial Times*, May 11, 1999 (cited as "BNP Publishes").

"BCI Board Turns Down UniCredito Merger Bid," *Financial Times Weekend*, May 15-16, 1999 (cited as "BCI").

"BSCH in $1bn Deal to Buy Brazilian Bank," *Financial Times*, January 20, 2000 (cited as "BSCH").

"BoS to Expand European Web Business," *Financial Times*, January 13, 2000 (cited as "BoS") *Business Week*, May 10, 1999.

"Congress and the White House Strike Banking Reform Deal," *Financial Times*, October 22, 1999 (cited as "Congress").

"Divorce, Italian-Style", *Business Week*, May 17, 1999, p, 53-56 (cited as "Divorce").

"Empty Aisles at the Financial Supermarket," *Business Week*, November 8, 1999, p. 40 (cited as "Empty Aisles").

"Euro Signals Burst of Activity," *Financial Times Supplement* (cited as "Euro Signals").

Financial Times, May 4, 1999.

Financial Times, March 15, 1999.

Financial Times, February 18, 1999.

Financial Times, May 7, 1999.

Financial Times, May 26, 1999.

Financial Times, May 24, 1999.

Financial Times, May 25, 1999.

Financial Times, May 26, 1999.

Financial Times, May 17 1999.

Financial Times, May 27,1999.

Forbes, May 17, 1999.

"France Finance Minister Indicates Approval for European Links," *Financial Times*, September 6, 1999 (cited as "France Finance Minister").

"French Banks May Face Pressure to Consolidate," *Financial Times*, January 10, 2000 (cited as "French Banks").

"French Look to Keep Banking in the Family," *Financial Times*, February 18, 1999 (cited as "French Look").

"Fresh Drive to Reform Bank Capital Rules," *Financial Times*, May 14, 1999 (cited as "Fresh Drive").

"Generali Chief Ousted in Industry Power Struggle," *Financial Times Weekend*, May 1-2, 1999 (cited as "Generali").

"Indian Banking and Finance," *Financial Times Survey*, April 28, 1999 (cited as "Indian Banking").

"ING Says It Does Not Plan to Bid for French Bank," *Financial Times*, May 10, 1999 (cited as "ING").

"Internet Threat to Traditional Firms," *Financial Times*, January 28, 2000 (cited as "Internet Threat").

"Invasion of the Superbanks?" *Business Week*, November 1, 1999, p. 175-176 (cited as "Invasion").

"Italy's Banks," *Financial Times*, May 6, 1999 (cited as "Italy's Banks").

"Italy's 'Noble' Dinosaur Struggles Against Extinction," *Financial Times*, May 4, 1999 (cited as "Italy's").

"Japanese Banks Take Local Lead in M&A Deals," *Financial Times*, January 21, 2000 (cited as "Japanese Banks").

"Lex Column," *Financial Times*, August 30, 1999 (cited as "Lex Column—August 30, 1999).

"Lyonnais Warns SG to Retreat," *Financial Times*, January 21, 2000 (cited as "Lyonnais").

"Mediobanca Acts to Oust BCI Chiefs," *Financial Times*, May 12, 1999 (cited as "Mediobanca Acts").

"Mediobanca Seeks German Pact," *Financial Times*, May 14, 1999 (cited as Mediobanca Seeks").

"Mixed Fortunes for Canadian Banks," *Financial Times*, May 27, 1999 (cited as "Mixed Fortunes").

"Paribas and SG Dissent May Emerge," *Financial Times*, April 6, 1999 (cited as "Paribas and SG").

"Paris Regulator Warns Banks on Takeover Tactics," *Financial Times*, March 18, 1999 (cited as "Paris Regulator").

"Profit Warning Hits First Union Shares," *Financial Times*, May 26, 1999 (cited as "Profit Warning").

"Spanish Bank Looks to Online Investment," *Financial Times*, January 26, 2000 (cited as "Spanish Bank").

"Spanish Banking War Moves On to Several Fronts," *Financial Times*, January 20, 2000, (cited as "Spanish Banking War").

"Top Ten Investment Banks Double Global Business," *Financial Times*, March 1, 1999, (cited as "Top Ten").

"US Banks Post Record Earnings in Tokyo," *Financial Times*, May 25, 1999 (cited as "US Banks").

"US-German Animosity Stalls Progress on Bank Capital Talks," *Financial Times*, May 13, 1999 (cited as "US-German").

"Who's Afraid of Online Banking?" *Business Week*, September 27, 1999, p. EB 14 (cited as Who's Afraid").

"W.R. Hambrecht + Co: OpenIPO," Harvard Business School Case N9-200-019 (cited as "Open IPO").

11 A Retrospective of the Asia Crisis: Origins and Outcomes

PHILIP J. BRYSON

The Intellectual Origins

In his classic work, *The General Theory of Employment, Interest, and Money*, Keynes established macroeconomics as a formal part of economic inquiry. In an incidental way, his treatise went beyond aggregative questions to address what today has come to be viewed as the question of corporate governance and national investments policies. In my view, doing this did not provide an unmixed contribution to contemporary global economic development. I attribute a part of the responsibility for the Asian crisis to this "defunct economist's" voice.[1]

Claims are now being made that the Asian crisis is nearly past. It seems appropriate, therefore, to look back at this troubled period from a different perspective. From the standpoint of the financial crisis, I agree that the crisis is abating. But this paper wishes to address some economic issues that remain troublesome and that might bode ill for Asia and for the global economy's future.

The Asian trauma has generally been seen rather strictly as an issue of international finance. That view will be reviewed very briefly below. At the same time, there has been rather general recognition that the finance crisis was not purely spontaneous. The underlying economic causes have been discussed, for example by Krugman, who is, interestingly, a contemporary advocate of aspects of Keynesian economics. He recently attributed the Asian crisis to "crony capitalism," defined as "dubious investments...cheerfully funded by local banks, as long as the borrower had the right government connections" (1998, p. 76).[2]

Keynes would have noticed that these "dubious investments" were not provided by shareholders and the stock market, but were funded as he had supposed would be through a less risky medium, through government auspices, sanctioned and promoted by specialists attached to a finance or planning ministry. He may have been given pause by the Krugman terms.

213

Such dubious investments and their causes are the concern of this paper. When the micro activities of Asian firms, conglomerates, and banks exploded in "self-reinforcing panic" and produced a massive capital flight from Asia, the world largely took notice only of the financial consequences of years of micro foundations. It is difficult to separate the macro and micro effects of the crisis, but ill-advised investments and poor planning practices had already set the stage for the international financial disaster.

Clearly, financial effects played an important separate role. At some point, an investments bubble began to distort expectations regarding investment returns and render judgments unrealistic. The fact that Japanese interest rates were extremely low for some who accessed capital from that country, meant that returns didn't have to be exceptionally promising to provide investment hopes where there should have been none.

In my view, Krugman correctly emphasizes that poor investments ultimately led to heavy debt portfolios in Asia. But he could have made the explanation of the Asian slump more complete[3] by associating John Maynard Keynes with the issues of corporate governance and central direction of national investment planning with the Asian case.

Keynes himself established an intellectual foundation for national investment planning, which produced the problematic climate from which the Asian crisis blossomed. It is difficult to say how much influence Chapter 12 of *The General Theory*, "The State of Long-term Expectation," had on postwar economic planning. But at the minimum, it certainly reflected the spirit of the times.

Personally acquainted with the uncertainties of investment prospects and their subsequent market performance, Keynes noted "the extreme precariousness of the basis of knowledge on which our estimates of prospective yield have to be made" (p. 149), i.e., the difficulty of mastering the uncertainty of the future. In his view, the speculative element in investments, especially strong in the United States, "finds its nemesis in the stock market" (p. 159). The uncertain future did not leave investors incapable of action, of course, since they were willing to act on the basis "of animal spirits--of a spontaneous urge to action rather than inaction, and not as the outcome of a weighted average of quantitative benefits multiplied by quantitative probabilities" (p. 161). Although Keynes believed it was really quite impossible for any investor to deal with the profound uncertainty of the future, he still expected people interested in the strictly short-term response to be outperformed by the enterprising investor with a more long-term orientation. For Keynes, the appropriate policy inference was that the state should take "an ever greater responsibility for directly organizing investment" (p. 164).

Planning Origins

In the postwar period, this sentiment ensured the adoption of economic planning by most of the important economies.[4] Policymakers remembered that in the years prior to the chaos of the war, the Soviet Union had achieved spectacular growth rates through the implementation of central economic planning. In that period, Soviet plan failure remained beyond perception because of the long years of shifting production capacities from peace to war and back again. Perhaps it was also important for the western nations that the exigencies of wartime defense planning had made it seem only reasonable and appropriate for the state to organize investment planning for postwar life as well.

Economic planning established the principles of national development policy as well for principal sectors as for the overall economy. Usually, production estimates complemented investment planning. Often a national plan was "considered synonymous with a program of investment projects,"[5] and was relatively innocuous as compared to the comprehensive and authoritarian planning of the Soviets. In a short period of time, it became apparent that little was being achieved by national planning agencies, and planning was quietly downsized into various forms of "structural policies."

One of the most famous planning efforts was directed through Japan's Ministry of International Trade and Industry, MITI. Potentially growing industries were targeted for competitiveness in the global market through the coordinated efforts of government and business leaders (Yamazaki, 1998, p. 156). Local banks, under the direction of the finance ministry, were to provide capital to targeted conglomerates and industries. This "guided capitalism" was perceived as the source of Japanese industrial power.

The United States faced neither the problem of reconstruction nor the perception of needed economic modernization in the postwar period. As others reconstructed their systems, ours simply continued to evolve, developing *inter alia* what is perceived today as a system of corporate governance. Ostensibly, this system merely has the purpose of assuring that investment projects provide shareholders with positive earnings. To some, even today, this is simply not the priority that can assure that the American economy can continue to be a key player in global competition. The system compels corporations to pay attention to short-term returns; since if a company doesn't roughly match the performance of firms of similar risk profiles, stockholders will walk, searching for the higher return they feel they have a right to expect. The market, therefore, requires continuous corporate preoccupation with the bottom line, a focus which sometimes appears hostile to long-term projects which might generate returns later but which are not currently profitable. The ostensible inability of American firms to look beyond the issue of short-term profitability is viewed from some quarters as anti-strategic. Such is the frequently heard concern of those who have no inclination to place any trust in markets.

In contrast to the American case, Japan's postwar development has been the product of a corporate governance system similar to that of Germany. Japan's early successes in steel, automobile and other world markets drove the general economic development. There has been a tendency to attribute Japan's early successes to industrial planning strategies more than to other proximate causes, *e.g.,* the adoption of high-quality manufacturing techniques and the receptivity of the American market to Japanese exports. Today, these other factors are usually considered more significant. In any case, as a result of rapid postwar development, Japan's industrial organization became a model for other Asian economies.

The huge export earnings stemming from Japan's initial trade successes combined with an immense pool of private savings. Later, as other Asian countries began to experience significant export earnings, a massive influx of Western capital also began to pour in. By the late eighties, the world became convinced that Japan was the economic superpower of the future and the United States was in serious decline. Michael Porter (1990) wrote that government is prominently discussed in treatments of international competitiveness. Many see it as a vital, if not the most important, influence on modern international competition. Government policy in Japan and Korea is particularly associated with the success these nations' firms have enjoyed.[6]

For Lester Thurow (1993), the most important question of international competitiveness for the 1990s was whether there would be any effective way to compete against Japan and Europe. He was certain there could be no positive answer without significant policy change. He advocated restructured antitrust laws to permit larger corporations to compete with the Japanese *keiretsu* and additional measures to orient the investments of American corporations to the long term. Although he refused to argue that German or Japanese governance systems were appropriate for the United States (p. 291), he was convinced that a national strategy or industrial policy was essential if we were to remain competitive in world markets.[7]

Korea and, to a lesser extent other Asian nations, had joined Japan in export-based development programs by the 1980s. State interventionist policies were perceived as the key to their success, including especially the use of trade barriers and subsidies to promote local industry. The common perception was that countries would be "stunted by failure to follow interventionist policies" (Amsden, 1989, p. 12). Ongoing governmental support for large business concerns was the *quid pro quo* for good performance, which was assessed in terms of production and operations management, not financial indicators. The Korean government mandated export performance for all large firms regardless of how politically connected they might be (p. 16).

Banks were to help the *chaebol* conglomerates accumulate capital rather than seek rents (p. 17) in pursuit of long-term returns. In the 1960s and 1970s, the Korean government was very much involved in entrepreneurship, since it was the national planning function to determine "what, when, and how much to produce in milestone investment decisions" (*ibid.*). Other Asian countries also adopted a basically Japanese model of corporate governance and industrial development style. Initial successes permitted capital accumulation, less from domestic savings (as in the Japanese case) than from export earnings and flows of direct foreign investment.

Genesis of Today's International Financial Environment

Globalization of investment processes has been one of the most important recent developments in the international arena. The generation of a huge, rather mobile pool of capital not previously experienced has made a rapid increase in industrial and economic capacity possible in investor-selected target countries. Henceforth it can be anticipated that Asian domestic saving, especially Japanese, will normally be very large and will represent another pool of capital available on the global scene. As the *World Economic and Social Survey* indicated a few years ago, a rising global investment level "means that world saving has risen to 'finance' it" (United Nations, 1995). The share of global expenditures invested rose rapidly with the recovery from recession in the early 1980s, but did not decline appreciably in the recession of the early 1990s. Hence, the total investment share was rising in the mid-nineties. By 1993, the net export earnings of Asia, especially of Japan, had come to represent another major component of the total funds available for Asian investment. As a result of cultural and political trade barriers, imports fell short of the level of exports. Thus, funds were available for other purposes and a considerable share of Asian investment flows came from Japan,[8] with other Asian countries also investing in the region to a lesser extent.

Other funds were available for global capital markets as well. In 1993 and 1994 the United States alone supplied $178 billion and $119 billion respectively (p. 46) in direct and portfolio investments to Asia and the rest of the world. Worldwide, foreign direct investment is by far the largest part of net financial flows to the developing economies. Of these global flows, nearly 75% are targeted to the ten largest recipients in Asia and Latin America (United Nations, 1998, p. 78). Gross direct investment inflows reached their pre-crisis peak in Asia at about $80 billion for 1997.[9]

The region's economic reversal was signaled by a precipitous decline in flows from the major Asian investors, especially from Japan and Korea, after the stock market and real estate bubbles of those countries burst. With the onset of the crisis in 22 countries in 1997, there was an outflow of approximately $92 billion in short-term borrowing, stock market net flows, and net outflows of funds from domestic residents (United Nations 1998, p. 76).

Outcomes: the Economic and Financial Crises

The reversal of investment funds represented the tip of the iceberg seen and understood by the world as the Asian crisis. Few seemed to notice in the first phase of Asian development as other Asian countries began successfully to follow the Japanese model, beginning with government policies which undervalued currencies to promote exports and selected industrial projects to promote industrial development. The world began to become conscious of the "Asian tigers" in the second phase of development as export successes produced net inflows complemented by flows of capital from the world investment community. As a boom started to develop, the resultant inflation was not permitted to depreciate national currencies of the region, since they were tied to the U.S. dollar. Nevertheless, the inflation experienced rendered these currencies overvalued. By this time a bubble economy was developing. Economic and investment activity became too brisk for the banks to monitor carefully the use of capital by client corporations and conglomerates. A plethora of capital had to be dealt with, but there were insufficient numbers of prospective investment projects.

Everything seemed to work against economic prudence in this period. Japanese rice subsidies, for example, inflated the value of land and helped promote the real estate bubble. Japanese interest rates were very low, which meant that nations accepting Japanese capital didn't need projects with high prospective returns. Funds could be repaid with very low yields, given the inexpensive capital available from Japan.

Bad debts began to accrue as loans and projects failed to yield positive returns. Speculative influences then suggested that banks and firms look for larger returns to shore up their positions. Unfortunately, prospects of larger returns are too often associated with higher risk projects, which ultimately exacerbate debt portfolios. Keeping the Finance Ministry away became a major concern of many such firms. All of this happened without much notice from the popular press. The finance problem resulted when, ultimately, long- and short-term investors began to be aware of the lack of returns.

At the first provocation, the process of capital flight began. As stocks were sold off and the proceeds were dumped on foreign currency markets in the repatriation process, stock market values plummeted and national currencies were devalued in devastating fashion. Import prices, both for productive materials essential for exports and for desperately needed consumption goods for the populace, soared. Severe recession began as consumption and production expenditures faltered.

In the first phase of the Asian "boom and bust" cycle, governments did not distinguish themselves with their selection of "winner" industries and the planning of investments. In the second phase, there were no controls in place to force managers to investment well. Market-type governance mechanisms would have required a yield for stockholders, German-type governance would have required effective banking regulation of corporate activity (and been less inclined to target national investments). The financial crisis was a function of capital flight, which in turn was the product of poor investments and the failure of national economies to provide effective corporate governance.

Outcomes: and Assessment of the Causes

By the early 1990s America's own propaganda about the economic power of Asia and the economic decline of the United States may have been an extra source of encouragement for the investment flows of capital into Asia. That is difficult to know with certainty; but that those investment funds were badly managed is much more certain.[10] Finance Ministries implemented the investment plans of government officials, directing funds through banks to the targeted industries and firms. The losses generated by so many of those firms were viewed as a strictly short-term phenomenon. The doctrine was that such industries would ultimately prove competitive in key global markets.

As debts continued to grow, Ministry of Finance officials had every right to be concerned. In Japan, bank personnel provided favors for the approbation or silence of Finance Ministry officials.

The inflow of funds was embarrassingly large. Managing it was more than a banker's delight, it was a serious problem. Banks always feel pressure to invest whatever funds are available, so the unprofitable loans to corporations and conglomerates continued. Ultimately, in such circumstances investors must become suspicious or simply grow impatient with very poor returns, and the process of capital flight is ready to begin. Banks, unable to pay off bad loans as they come due, find the corporations who are their borrowers likewise unable to repay.

The primary cause for the mismanagement of investment is just as Keynes described it. The future is uncertain and even the wisest investors cannot perceive the future directions of global industries. Yet this is the task that must be undertaken by the economic planner who is to select the industries targeted for development and global market dominance. Perhaps the task was not as difficult in early postwar Japan. Planners attempting to direct industrial development from ground zero, needing only to succeed in a few basic industries that will find resonance in the American market. But after the development of many basic industries and growing global competition, even from other export-driven Asian economies, the necessity of orchestrating the development of new technologies, processes and commodities is an exceptionally large challenge for the median government planner.

Part of the challenge for Asian planners was that the flow of funds requiring management became so large. The planner would logically rank prospective investment projects according to their marginal efficiency of capital (to use a Keynesian term) or their internal rates or return. He would then begin by funding projects with the highest returns and continue funding until the internal rate of return is equal to the interest rate affecting repayment. But what if the profitable investment projects proposed absorb only a fraction of the funds available for investment? In the Japanese case one could get the impression that planners were not unwilling to pour money into investments with zero or negative returns.

Another problem affecting Asian investments was that of asymmetric information. It can be very difficult for lenders when borrowers have better information as to the riskiness of their proposed projects and do not fully disclose negative information to the former. When interest rates are high, a rather large proportion of applicants for funds can be expected to seek loans, knowing that their high-risk projects could yield high returns.[11] At much lower interest rates, a smaller portion of loan applicants will present high-risk, high-return demands for loanable funds. If projects are funded without careful attention and research, the lender can mistakenly provide low-cost funds for high-risk projects. Which means the probability of default becomes very high.

When planners supply low-interest funds because supplies are not tightly constrained, the tendency can be expected to be as it was in Japan and Asia. The numbers of projects that promised abundant returns, funded first, will be too few to absorb the available funds. The normal banker will instinctively want to loan out all available funds and may grow somewhat insensitive to poorly documented, high-risk applications. The same people would demand better information in a more competitive environment.

The aggregate of these difficulties constitutes the whole of the Asian crisis. Aside from the finance issues, some analysts have viewed the Asian situation as fundamentally sound. The basic manufacturing capital stock, the talented labor force, the continuing managerial skills, etc. remain in place. Solve the financial problems, they tell us, and things can go on as before. But more is required. Corporate governance must provide more astute direction for the use of investment funds.

Huge investments in additional manufacturing capacity, in spite of excess global capacity, can be seen as a significant result of the Asian boom. In part, the crisis may simply be viewed as an early transition problem for Asia as some of its nations begin to move from a manufacturing/industrial to an information/service economy. Overcapacity suggests that a long-term adjustment out of manufacturing would be appropriate for the advanced economies in a position to lead out in this inevitable transformation.

Financially interested agencies and journalists began to pronounce the Asian Crisis past before it's underlying economic causes had been overcome. It is not clear whether investors will forget so quickly, but a restoration of currency values and stock market indices does not alone indicate that the corporate governance issues have been resolved.

Apparently, Asian governments are becoming less active in the choice of major industrial development projects, but even if governmental direction of economic development declines, what is to take its place? There is no apparent replacement for the industrial policy or planning initiatives of the past if there is no corporate governance system to protect shareholder interests, to supply a takeover threat to managers (provide assurance that alternative management teams are available) where decision making does not insure profitable investments, or to confront management teams with a board of directors or shareholders meetings to threaten their complacency or inertia.

The fundamental problem retains significance. In light of failed industrial policies and the lack of experience with a market-oriented governance system in Asia, are we ready to pronounce the Asian Crisis history?

Notes

[1] A popular quote by Keynes informs that policymakers are guided more often than they would recognize or desire, by the theories of some "defunct economist." "Madmen in authority" distill their frenzy "from some academic scribbler of a few years back," Keynes insisted (Breit and Ransom, p. v). In the case under investigation here, Keynes must bear the burden of some responsibility that, as yet, no one has laid at his feet.

[2] See his "Saving Asia: It's Time to Get Radical," *Fortune*, September 7, 1998, pp.75-80. The quotation here is from p. 76.

[3] Fox (1998) addresses the Japanese case, important because of its economic weight, but especially because it is the model of Asian corporate governance. Fox characterizes the Japanese development process as "squeezing out savings and investing them in Japanese industry. The Ministry of Finance "funneled cheap money to strategic industries," and, when industry couldn't absorb it all, in real estate and the stock market (p. 82). Fox speaks of "Japan, Inc." as bankrupt financially and ideologically, in part at least because Japanese companies have never been forced to pay "attention to return on equity and shareholder right" (p. 83). This is an important part of the explanation of the Asian flu.

[4]The economic plans of a score of nations is reviewed in a most helpful volume on the topic (Tinbergen, 1964).
[5]*Ibid.,* p. 46.
[6]See p. 126. At that time, even *Business Week* was advocating a national industrial policy. See "Industrial Policy: Call It What You will, The Nation Needs A Plan To Nurture Growth,"April 6, 1992, that Issue's lead story.
[7] See his p. 295. He also cited Robert Lawrence of the Brookings Institute contending that the U.S. must take the industrial targeting efforts of foreign countries more seriously and Paul Krugman insisting that our government should subsidize a few strategic sectors as an alternative to managed trade. See p. 297.
[8] See p. 46. As the dollar value of the yen depreciated during this period, Japanese investors became reluctant to purchase American securities. Avoiding the risk of dollar depreciation, Japanese investors in the 1990s increased investments in Asia with yen-denominated loans. Asia's central banks also shifted more of their massive foreign-exchange reserves into yen. See pp. 46, 47.
[9] Net Direct Investment inflows alone into Asia for the years from 1987 to 1997, as estimated by the Department of Economic and Social Affairs of the UN, ran as follows: 0.4 (billions of dollars, 1987), 3.3, 4.3, 4.3, 7.2, 11.9, 28.0, 33.4, 28.6, 30.9 and 30.1 (1997). (See United Nations, 1998, p. 158.)
[10] In the *World Economic and Social Survey 1998*, (United Nations, 1998, p. 41), the Department of Economic and Social Affairs of the UN described the crisis in Southeast Asia as follows:
"The downward spiral of currency depreciation and stock market decline started in mid-1997 undermined the viability of heavily indebted financial institutions and corporations, drying up liquidity and freezing investment and even production. Together with significantly higher interest rates throughout the region to shore up exchange rates, there began a flood of bankruptcies of heavily indebted but otherwise viable, corporations, which further weakened local financial institutions.
Because of contagion in financial markets, strong intra-regional trade and financial linkages and, in some cases, competition of exports in third markets, even the economies with much smaller imbalances, sustainable debt levels and relatively sound financial and corporate structures have been adversely impacted."
[11] Where interest rates are high, scarce pools of investment funds could be used for projects adversely selected. The high-return prospects seeking funding are associated with high risk or a high probability of default. Where high risks are present, lenders (bankers usually, or planners in the case of industrial policy practice) should ration credit and make sure they get the best information possible on the projects they fund (Acs and Gerlowski, 1996, pp.176-177).

References

Acs, Zoltan J. and Gerlowski, Daniel A. (1996), *Managerial Economics and Organization*, New Jersey.

Amsden, Alice H. (1989), *Asia's Next Giant: South Korea and Late industrialization*, New York, Oxford.

Breit, Roger L. and Ransom, William (1982), *The Academic Scribblers; American Economists in Collision*, 2nd edition, New York.

Fox, Justin (1998), 'Why Japan Won't Budge,' *Fortune*, September 7, pp. 82, 83.
'Industrial Policy: Call It What You Will, The Nation Needs A Plan To Nurture Growth' (1992), *Business Week*, April 6.

Keynes, John Maynard (1936), *The General Theory of Employment, Interest, and Money*, New York.

Krugman, Paul (1998), 'Saving Asia: It's Time to Get Radical,' *Fortune*, September 7, pp. 75-80.

Porter, Michael E. (1990), *The Competitive Advantage of Nations*, New York.

Thurow, Lester (1993), *Head to Head: The Coming Economic Battle Among Japan, Europe, and America*, New York.

Tinbergen, Jan (1964), *Central Planning*, New Haven, Yale.

World Economic and Social Survey 1995: Current Trends and Policies in the World Economy, New York, United Nations, 1995.

World Economic and Social Survey 1998: Trends and Policies in the World Economy, New York: United Nations, 1998.

Yamazaki, Masato (1998), 'Ministry of International Trade and Industry (MITI),' *Modern Japan: An Encyclopedia of History, Culture, and Nationalism*, New York.

12 European Enterprise Information Portals and Global Communications

RONALD R. SIMS, ERIC H. ERICKSON, III AND
JEFFREY P. ERICKSON

Introduction

The beginning of the new millennium continues to be a time for introspection—for countries, companies and individuals. Today, companies face a battery of challenges that include:

- Global competition
- Technological advances that occur in a nanosecond
- Profound changes in the workforce
- Pressures from conflicting special interests
- Confused, angry, disillusioned and cynical employees who have seen their ranks decimated
- An unforgiving marketplace, which places a premium on flexibility and adaptability
- A continuing effort to rationalize suppliers and customers
- The enormous burden of information management

Driven by these new realities, companies worldwide are on a quest for fresh approaches that will help them compete more effectively in the increasingly global marketplace. In many instances, fresh approaches will continue to come from technological advances that allow a company to better understand, manage and communicate information. For most companies, technological advancements related to the Internet are of prime importance as they strive to develop and maintain a competitive advantage.

This paper explores a number of issues confronting Europe's Internet business use. After briefly discussing a number of issues impacting the current European Internet scene, the discussion then focuses on some of the global changes that have occurred in Internet content, and the methods for communicating that content, from the Internet's inception to the present. The discussion will specifically address how the problems associated with manipulating various types of Internet content, as well as the opportunities presented in the introduction of new programming languages and hardware, will drive the future of Enterprise Information Portals (or Corporate Portals) in Europe.

Europe Today

Over the past decade, Europe has seen a tremendous amount of change. Political structures have shifted, market barriers and tariffs have been dissolved, and the Euro is firmly established as the new currency for the new millennium. For companies operating in this new economy, these changes have brought – and continue to bring – an urgent need to develop and use Internet content and services to their advantage. However, in order for this to take place European businesses must continue to make rapid advances in Internet adoption.

The benefits of a corporate Internet usage are well documented and understood. This is especially the case in the United States where several reports in recent years have noted that the European Internet penetration and usage still lags behind that of the United States by 1-4 years (MSDW, 1999). However, expectations hold that the European market will catch up, and in some Internet-related technologies surpass, the North American market within the next few years (Bowry, 1998; Harley, 1999).

Given the reality that Europe remains a region of separate nations and perspectives, of varied languages and culture, of different market focuses, and the disparity in Internet adoption on a country-by-country basis, catching up and closing the gap with the United States will be a daunting challenge. This challenge is even more difficult when one considers factors like the European Internet evolution in technology advancement. If the number of European adults using the Internet regularly doubles by the year 2000 and triples by 2003 as suggested by a recent Morgan Stanley Dean Witter report (MSDW, 1999), then European businesses must be prepared to implement new technology advances, particularly with respect to Internet infrastructure. The MSDW report suggests a few advantages which might help Europe to close the gap with the US: The current Internet growth cycle in Europe, learning from the US experience, leapfrogging US mistakes, and adopting the latest technology (MSDW, 1999).

Like technology advancements, the variety of cultures and languages in Europe is another important issue that must be confronted in efforts to close the gap with the United States. The variety of cultures and languages in the European region poses problems in and of themselves and are compounded when one considers the content and language of the Internet is still primarily English-based. For many individuals and corporations, non-host country Web sites can create barriers, especially when those sites use unfamiliar languages. Donald Hubbard, the executive director of Morgan Stanley's European technology team in London, notes "This is not like the United States, with its 50 similar states." Hubbard adds. "In Europe there are different backgrounds, different cultures, and different languages. A lot of hurdles need to be cleared" (Cukier, 1999). Additionally, as noted by Harley (1999), are the complexities that arise because of differences in national laws regarding Internet content.

Clearly, there are other issues that must be addressed as Europe continues it's Internet and Intranet adoption in the coming years. For instance, Cukier (1999) notes that there will be crucial differences between Europe's Net explosion and the one that hit the United States. In particular, is the fact that in Europe large offline companies are the prime drivers of the Net economy, while in the United States they tend to be "Johnny-come-latelies." Hubbard expects Europe's Internet industry to be "more measured" and to avoid the funding excess and hype that characterized the U.S. boom, in part because of the industrial players behind many of the new regional European startups.

Europe must also confront the use of Intranet technology. More specifically, there continues to be a disparity in the implementation, planning and usage of Intranets by companies and on a country-by-country basis. While some countries are more quickly closing the gap on the United States, others are lagging well behind. A suggested reason for this disparity is that the use of Intranet technology in Europe is somewhat askew. Harley (1999) suggests that because Europe is an emerging Internet access market, there are significant disparities among the nations of the region in terms of Internet sophistication and development. These differences are diminishing, particularly as acquisition minded competitors seek to capitalize on the enormous growth potential in the European market. Further, the European market is expected to remain buoyant as more companies follow through on their plans to deploy Intranets.

Christophe Agnus, the founder and editor of the French Magazine *Transfert,* which covers technology and society, suggest that another factor that may most restrain Europe's Internet boom is the lack of any tradition for investing in startups. Agnus says "Americans are willing to put a lot of money into the ground just to see if the tree will grow in, say, three years' time. In Europe, we're willing to put in some water, but just half a liter at a time." Several reasons for taking this approach are: Europeans are not big risk takers and often regard entrepreneurs with suspicion; the venture capital infrastructure is not yet highly developed; and debilitating taxes on stock options, as well as restrictive business laws which are not in place in the United States, serve to encumber the European high-tech sector (Cukier, 1999).

In spite of these drawbacks, recent advances in European mobile telephony (i.e., one in three Europeans will use be accessing the Internet through their mobile phone by 2004) (Middleton, 1999), the benefits Europe gets from the US experience, and adapting the latest technology, Europe is in a good position to meet Internet challenges, while also closing the gap with the United States.

The discussion now turns to a look at some of the changes that have occurred in Internet content and communication. It is our contention that these and other changes are important to understanding the Internet business landscape.

Internet Content and Communication in the Organization

Perhaps the best way to understand the Internet business landscape is to look at Internet content and communication by focusing on "where we were", "where we are" and "where we are going."

Where Were We?

In the late 1960s and early 1970s, the predecessor to the Internet, ARPANET, was successfully deployed as a network to allow scientists to share data and access remote computers. ARPANET became a high-speed messaging network as people used it to collaborate on research projects and discuss topics of various interests. The term "Internet" was first used in the early 1980s and email, originally designed as the messaging system of the Internet, quickly became its most popular application. Its content began as simple text and it was quickly adopted by commercial organizations. Email continues to be one of the most important methods of communications and widely used business "application" on the Internet.

What is the importance of email? Worldwide, billions of email messages are sent every year; its use has grown by 15 to 30% each year for the past 20 years. Everyone needs and uses it, whether for personal or business use, and it is the most ubiquitous Internet application in existence. Figure 1 notes that 94% of large and medium European companies use email; in contrast, the next closest application group in terms of current use is "Selling via Web" at 26%.

Figure 1: Use and Planned Use of Corporate Internet Applications by Large and Medium Enterprises

	1999	2000	% Change
Email	94%	97%	3%
Customer Service	25%	42%	68%
Fax	10%	24%	140%
Selling via Web	26%	38%	46%
Buying via Web*	19%	36%	89%
Voice	3%	16%	433%

(*business to business I-Commerce process e.g. web based EDI)

Source: IDC European Telecoms Manager Survey

653 companies with more than 100 employees

Clearly, email has been one of the most important media of global communications of the last few years and has served a myriad of uses in messaging.

As email proliferated it also became increasingly "misused"; "misused" because it was primarily designed as a simple text messaging solution. But as users began to adopt and explore email as a medium for communication they naturally pushed it beyond its original design specifications. The content communicated in emails, which started as simple text messages, began to change with the advent of 'attachments'. Email quickly became the delivery media for much more complex content (documents, applications, images, etc). A simple illustration of this can be found in any organization: how often do you see email used to coordinate/schedule events, vote on issues, share documents and images, perform opinion survey research, register for an event, etc? Used, as a simple messaging application for sending text-based content, email is incredibly efficient. But as an application for sharing and manipulating more complex content it is far less efficient than using an application specifically designed for such tasks.

Where Are We?

Today, organizations efficiently communicate shared content to a general audience by publishing pages on the Internet; these users "manipulate" said content in some way using Portals. In its most basic sense, a Portal is simply a "doorway" to finding the content you want on the Internet (the most well known example of a Portal is Yahoo!). The content in this case is text and pictures delivered to the desktop via the World Wide Web. In addition, many of today's Portals include applications designed to perform more complex manipulation of shared content. Adapting the Portal concept and taking it one step further, businesses are quickly developing their own internal Portals for use by their employees; these are called Enterprise Information Portals (EIPs) or Corporate Portals.

An EIP differs from a traditional file-management system in that it is more like a library visit. In a library, you can walk up and down the aisles looking for books, or leaf through a card catalog to find a description of a particular book and its exact location. Using an EIP, you can browse through a company site looking for the documents you want or use a "card catalog" to find a document's exact location. And because the EIP contains the actual document (and links to related external information) as well as directions on how to find it, it works fast.

Shilakes and Tylman (Brown, 1999) defined EIPs as "applications that enable companies to unlock internally and externally stored information, and provide users a single gateway to personalized information needed to make informed business decisions". An important advantage of EIP is that it can be tailored to present information based on the needs of a group of users or individual users. For example, the EIP at Advantage Sales and Marketing, a food wholesaler in Irvine, Calif., includes links to food industry publications as well as to different units of the company. The company plans to have links to the company's retail application in the future. "The content isn't just company data published to our Web server," CIO Kevin Paugh says (Quellete and Connolly, 1999). According to Fitzloff and Gardner (1999) as a concept borrowed from online applications, EIP is a data management strategy that provides a window into enterprise knowledge by bringing life to previously dormant data so it can be compared, analyzed, and shared by any user in the organization.

EIP's provide a personalized home base for a company's employees before they venture out into the wider Internet. In most cases, they combine information from the existing company Intranet and/or legacy data systems with selected links from the Internet. Many of them include access to corporate email, calendaring and custom workflow applications.

What is the importance of EIP? How do we know that the EIP sector is a key sector of current global communication? Although the Internet gained early popularity in educational institutions, it has been the commercialization of the medium, which has fueled its explosive growth over the last few years. And Merrill Lynch says the emerging category of EIP's hit $4.4 billion last year and will reach $14.8 billion by 2002 (Fitzloff and Gardner, 1999). Merrill Lynch claims EIP's will exceed the investment opportunities of the massive enterprise resource planning (ERP) market.

James Tobin, president and chief operating officer of Toronto-based Hummingbird Communications Ltd., suggests that EIPs hold the promise to be one of the "missing pieces" that will propel e-commerce into the "trillions" in the next decade (Brown, 1999). According to a report by the Delphi Group the number of U.S. businesses using EIPs is expected to climb to 80% by early 2001(this is up from 16% of businesses in 1999). Its Portal Report also found that 50% of the 300 Fortune 500 companies indicated they were already in the deployment phase of a corporate portal, with another 25% saying that they are following suit in the next two years (Brown, 1999). Intranet adoption is an important step in EIP adoption; Zona Research predicted that worldwide annual spending on Intranets would reach $13 billion by the end of 1999, up from $2 billion in 1998 (Brown, 1999). Other observers expect the global Intranet market to surpass that of the Internet by the end of 2000 (Bowry, 1998).

One early adopter says EIP has had a profound impact. "We can easily locate just the kinds of information we want, which leaves us without wasted time," says Jim Lind, president of Mercury Energy, in Dallas. According to experts, those who plunge into EIPs early earn a sizable competitive advantage, bolstered by lowered costs, increased sales, better deployment of resources, and internal productivity enhancements such as sharper performance analysis, market targeting, and forecasting (Fitzloff and Gardner, 1999). Clearly, EIPs offer users organized tours through the miles of data that companies are currently struggling to control, disseminate and manage. By putting the right information in the right hands EIPs improve decision-making and encourages collaboration throughout the organization.

Another important advantage of EIP technology is that it allows companies to access its resources across several platforms and deliver them to one simple point of entry, a particularly tricky business in a corporate climate where information is stored in a variety of ways across different platforms. EIP's offer several benefits. For example, they:

- provide an effective means of controlling and filtering information by delivering or pushing knowledge and information from pre-selected sources to each user
- present useful information from a variety of sources located both inside and outside an organization on one customizable user interface
- mine and distribute critical business information securely to those who need it
- add value to a company's existing intranet by combining corporate information with other external information, such as specialized subscription feeds, live news feeds and Web content
- allow individual users to establish their own personal preferences based on their current work assignments by selecting the most applicable sources of information, which can then be pre-sorted into industry categories
- allow the company to tie together suites of work-flow applications for all or selected employees to access
- present important shared company information – documents, images, phone lists, HR notices, sales resources – all centrally located
- ensure that best practices and policies are communicated corporate-wide
- give executives more control over what employees see allowing for highly effective reinforcement of company culture/procedures

While EIPs are still a relatively new concept, companies interested in adopting them will have little difficulty finding suppliers who are throwing portal software in the ring. Among them are a diverse group of companies to include several Internet start-up companies as well as some established software providers. Sequoia Software, for example, has roots in the healthcare field and in the organization of medical information, which position it well as an EIP player to watch (Robinson, 1999).

Despite the diversity of backgrounds of companies providing EIP solutions, the most solid solutions share the following common traits:

- an EIP tool should simplify the aggregation of information from multiple systems;
- the security and control access to this information; and

- the presentation of aggregate information to the user via HTML or XML (see below for further discussion of both these terms).

This latter trait eliminates the need for proprietary client application development.

Properly implemented EIPs can help companies cut costs and generate added revenues, which is a potent and attractive mix. Companies can realize the return on investment (ROI) for an EIP from increased productivity and, perhaps, reduced personnel costs. The former results from decreased search time and improved responses to queries. The latter accrues from empowering employees to quickly add and find documents on their own. It is possible for a company to reduce labor costs associated with system management, a saving that is easy to measure but hard to implement. Other savings can accrue from using the EIP as a knowledge base for providing self-service customer support and reducing the number of support calls. For example, there have been some estimates that a service call costs between $30 and $60; by contrast, if the user can repair the problem using data obtained from the EIP, the cost drops to almost zero (Millman, 1999). Additionally, by creating EIPs, companies can extend the benefits gleaned inside the company to the outside. Businesses can strengthen customer and supplier relations, and more effectively coordinate workflow, collaboration, and transactions with other companies. Access to information in today's rapidly changing business environment is a competitive advantage, and EIP provides opportunities for companies to address the seemingly insurmountable task of connecting user to the abundance of valuable information that resides in unconnected, unstructured systems throughout the organization.

What are the problems with EIPs? The fundamental problem with today's EIPs and associated applications is their limitations with respect to manipulating complex content, which is partially due to the structure of the language of the Web—known as the Hypertext Markup Language (HTML). Basically, HTML is a language that indicates to the browser the format for presenting information. To do this, HTML uses "tags" (what appears in <> brackets in the following are tags: < H1 >*some interesting heading*< /H1 > < BOLD >*some fascinating text*< /BOLD >). HTML is useful for displaying documents; however, HTML doesn't describe what the data represents. Therefore, if you want Web sites that take orders from customers accessing disparate systems, sort catalog records on-the-fly, or collect customer survey data for online processing, you will need another language for the Internet.

Frank Chen, group product manager for directory and security at Netscape Communications, suggests that another problem with EIPs is that their deployment appears to be small, and in many cases the content on them amounts to little more than the corporate telephone directory and newsletter. Chen says, "My experience is that such things as data mining are pretty far out. The things that keep people coming back to an EIP are scheduling, lists, and the password reset page. The current driver is data about people." Despite these concerns Chen believes that people will get to the data mining because the pieces are falling into place (Fitzloff and Gardner, 1999).

While Information Technology (IT) administrators say they like the EIP idea, they are worried about security and have a hard time weaning their end-users off the interfaces they have become accustomed to. In the end, the key for IT administrators is that information is handled responsibly. And, while many large corporations have already witnessed a number of benefits from EIPs, a number of users and analysts agree that the arrival of EIPs en masse may not be as soon as some software vendors assume – a least not until integral issues, such as security, get ironed out.

Members of the vendor community continue to react as if the EIP trend is inevitable and fast approaching. However, many established vendors, although enticed by the opportunity for EIPs, also worry about facing obsolescence, shakeouts, and changes in customer wants that a paradigm shift to EIPs could entail.

Where Are We Going?

More and more of today's business applications and data are not only being delivered via EIPs, but also maintained, supported, and upgraded—all for a low monthly price—from third-party Application Service Providers (ASPs). Most ASPs are better positioned to provide these services than their in-house counterparts because they are specialized in creating Web applications for the manipulation of highly complex content. In addition, many have developed multilevel partnerships to couple those applications with traditional services from a variety of external companies. What kinds of applications are in demand?:

- Calendars, email and to-do lists
- Workflow (with approval process)
- Supply-Chain Management
- Document sharing
- Expense reporting
- Procurement of parts and supplies

- Travel/Shipping arrangements
- Custom financial databases and competitive information gleaned from the Internet
- Corporate news

Clearly, companies will soon have the ability to give all employees access to every corporate service from a central location, regardless of whether they use a desktop in a satellite office, or a portable in a hotel room.

What other trends in terms of user access are important to keep in mind?

The increase in mobile workers Sales people, field support engineers, traveling consultants, telecommuters, satellite offices -- more and more people need centralized corporate services delivered to a computer anywhere in the world.

Technology advances Portable technology, including wireless, is fast becoming commonplace in the business world and this sector is seeing enormous investment flows.

The advent of portable "appliances" The concept of inexpensive, small, lightweight machines running programs from central servers is very popular with corporations.

Cost improvements In a few years, the cost effectiveness of providing employees a portable "appliance" and a suite of centralized services will be less than that of networked PC services.

What is considered a portable "appliance"? Definitions abound, but for the purposes of this paper, any inexpensive, small, lightweight machines capable of running a program will be referred to as an appliance. The most common appliances are Personal Digital Assistants (PDAs—such as 3Com's Palm Pilot), and mobile phones, including the new generation of European "smart phones" (mobile phones that can transmit data and graphics as well as voice).

What does all of this imply for the EIP? Companies hope to be able to provide their employees with "any service, anytime, anywhere" by giving them access to central servers running programs from within any computing device--from today's browsers to tomorrow's wireless appliances. In fact, according to an analyst with the Aberdeen Group: "We see wireless (communication) as a new frontier that could potentially threaten portals' dominance as information brokers." Why? Appliances, especially the wireless variety, allow for "information—anywhere, anytime". So, the challenge for all traditional Portals, including EIP's, will be to "downsize" their services into multiple software mini-applications that fit in appliances as well as in desktop browsers and still maintain all their features and functions. Some of the big general Portal companies like

Yahoo, Excite@Home, and MSN.com are already starting to do just that with their consumer Portals. Besides their standard content and e-mail, they are adding various "messenger" services in software applications that run in a small window on your desktop. You can access many of your favorite Portal services without even launching your browser; all you need is a connection to the Internet. This change will completely revolutionize the Portal world, which has up to now been confined to the inside of a browser window, and EIP's are sure to follow-suit.

What new software trends are important to keep in mind?:

XML A language, which will replace HTML in many scenarios, exists today and will be commonplace in commercial applications in the near future: Extensible Markup Language (XML). XML was completed in early 1998 by the World Wide Web Consortium and consists of simple rules to create a markup language specific to individual needs using a single small program to process the language. The tags in XML are metadata or data about data. Instead of describing how the data will be presented in a browser, they describe what the data *represents*. For example, consider a retailer who wants to order a product from a distributor. If the distributor uses XML to build a markup language for encoding product records, then your retailer's order would contain < order> < product_number > *12345* < / product_number > < price > *20,00* < /price > <currency> *Euro* < / currency> < /order >. Programming any appliance to recognize this standard medical notation and to add this order to a distributor database becomes quick and inexpensive.

Java Similarly, a language for creating, small, highly portable applications has been around for a few years. Java, which resembles C and C++, is a language created by Sun Microsystems for creating mini cross-platform applications or "applets". Applets run within the Java Virtual Machine which hides the underlying operating system from the application/appliance; this is the key to the ability to run on any platform. These applets download themselves and execute on demand each time you access a page that incorporates them, and then run from within any Java-enabled application or appliance.

WAP Wireless Application Protocol (WAP) provides a set of open standards that let mobile devices such as mobile phones, pagers and handheld computers browse content on the Web. Sites, however, must be reformatted to support a programming language called Wireless Markup Language, which supports text, and bitmap images (the communications protocol based on XML to format content for the screens of appliances giving users access to the Internet and Internet services).

In fact, 3Com has strengthened its commitment to Java by releasing its new virtual machine for the Palm Pilot, which uses far less memory than its predecessor. As a result, developers are able to build more complex applications based on Java for the device, in order to provide an ever-growing number of services. 3Com has also licensed a wireless Web browser as part of an effort to port its Palm Computing platform to a new generation of mobile phones. This browser's core is in the emerging Wireless Application Protocol (WAP). And Sun Microsystems Inc. has developed architecture for a new Java-based chip, called Microprocessor Architecture for Java Computing (MAJC), that it expects to be used to power devices in the emerging information appliances market.

So how might it work for an EIP to be "downsized" into several smaller software applications running in a device? A complex real-world situation would be one in which a company has a parts catalog consisting of parts data, documents and diagrams for a product line, all residing in multiple sources. In order to efficiently service this line, every field technician working at a client site would need to have all of the most current parts information in hand. Therefore, the first problem would be to join data from disparate sources into an immediately usable form. But the second problem would that the technicians working at a client site would need real-time connectivity to the original data sources, and so the parts information would need to be accessible while he is on-site, in real-time. To provide this service the parts data would need to move from a web server (which compiles the data from the various sources via XML), then to a WAP gateway, and finally to the WAP-enabled device. A system could be developed whereby each technician could access the parts data online from his mobile phone; while on-site he would then be able to sort, filter and pare the product records to just the relevant few in seconds, all from one simple application. He would be able to order required parts, and upload this order request from the same screens, automatically receiving an order confirmation online.

What is the importance of EIPs and online applications for appliances? Figure 1 shows that the percent changes in application usage other than email and voice are expected to increase from 1999 to 20000 from 46% to 140% (compare with email's increase of only 3%). The applications "Customer Service", "Selling via Web" and "Buying via Web" certainly represent Web programs-many designed to solve the misuses of email, and will almost assuredly incorporate XML, Java and WAP to avoid the problems associated with HTML. Additionally, according to International Data Corp., 7.4 million handheld computing devices were sold worldwide in 1998 and that number will increase to close to 11 million in 1999. And people use handheld computing devices in some capacity at 92% of corporations, according to a Forrester Research survey of 50 Fortune 1000 companies. In a report called "Western European Smart

Handheld Devices Review and Forecast, 1998-2003," IDC predicts that some 7.2 million such devices will be shipped in Western Europe in 2003 (that's just shy of the number sold *worldwide* in 1988).

The majority of these appliances will be what IDC calls smart phones, mobile phones that can transmit data and graphics as well as voice. In fact, the smart phone market is expected to take off much faster in Europe than in the U.S., due to the fact that the European mobile phone market is much more cohesive than its US counterpart due to the adoption of GSM (Global System for Mobile Communications). In addition, the introduction of mobile telephones using the new WAP, which formats Internet content for display on wireless devices, will help to drive demand.

Conclusion: Any Service, Anywhere, Anytime

The Internet has emerged as the globally accessible, interactive, and individually addressable communications and computing platform. This emergence will allow European businesses the opportunity to implement strategies that bring them closer to their value chain partners and to "recast their businesses" to reduce costs and improve profitability.

EIPs in particular continue to be one of the most effective ways of communicating globally (i.e., distributing, sharing and reusing corporate knowledge). As the European business market grows and companies strive to continue to realize the benefits of EIPs and more advanced technology, the challenge of finding useful and applicable information will continue to be a real problem. As we look to the future in Europe, it is important to recognize that EIPs have evolved from the early days of Intranets, when simple pages contained static information. Today's EIPs act as a middleware service, pulling real-time data from enterprise resource planning, mainframe and other operational systems, and presenting the information in a dashboard like manner within a browser window. It is also important to recognize that Intranets and EIPs can provide an effective means for controlling and filtering information.

To enable the most effective use of information, and alleviate the infoglut caused by the massive growth of content and users, many companies in the European market must introduce EIPs to sort, filter and push the appropriate internal and external information to a user's desktop. Additionally, portal developers and online application service providers must come to the conclusion that the future of the Internet, and indeed computing itself, lies beyond the desktop. New programming languages and hardware advances are enabling users a greater reach at a lower cost. For enterprises this means that future employees will have all of their corporate EIP services anytime and anywhere—including on their cellular phones, PDAs, television screens, as well as devices not yet created.

In the end, regardless of "where we were", "where we are" and "where we are going" the future looks bright for Europe, the largest single market in the world.

References

Bowry, K. (1998), 'Intranets: A European Perspective', *Technology &Business,* vol. 32, no. 3, pp. 12-14.

Brown, M. (1999), EIPs Could Propel e-commerce', *Computer Dealer News*, December 3, pp. 36-37.

Cukier, K.N. (1999), 'Europe Imports Internet Euphoria', *Red Herring*, December, pp. 2-3.

Fitzloff, E., and Gardner, D. (1999), 'Web Opens Enterprise Portals', *InfoWorld,* January 25, pp. 1, 34-38.

Harley, J. (1999), 'Closing the Gap', *America's Network,* April 15, pp. 26-30.

Middleton, G. (1999), One in Three Europeans to Use Mobile Internet by 2004. *Tornado-Insider.Com.*

Millman, H. (1999), 'Leveraging Web Portals', *InfoWorld,* January 4, pp. 43-45.

MSDW Report. (1999), *The European Internet Report*, June, Morgan Stanley Dean Witter.

Quellette, T. and Connolly, J.M. (1999), 'Opening Your Own Portal', *Computerworld* (August 9), 76-79.

Robinson, T. (1999), 'A Doorway Through the Data Dimension', *Data Management*, June 29.

13 The New Look of National Security in the Information Age

DANIEL S. PAPP AND DAVID S. ALBERTS

As we enter the Information Age, advanced information and communication technologies and the capabilities they provide are becoming an increasingly important factor in the national security equation of most major countries in the world, including the United States. Throughout the 1990s, these technologies, defined in this study as advanced semiconductors, increasingly capable computers, fiber optics, cellular technologies, better and more capable satellites, advanced networking, improved human-computer interaction, and digital technology including digital compression,[1] played larger and larger roles in enhancing military capabilities and in shaping the domestic and international components of the strategic environment within which national security is pursued. As we move further into the Information Age, the impact that advanced information and communication technologies will have on national security will become even more important.

The importance of advanced information and communication technologies for national security is not just about information and communication technologies and the capabilities that they provide. It is about how the technologies and their capabilities will alter military strategy, doctrine, tactics, and operations. It is about who will have new capabilities and about how ownership of new capabilities may change objectives. It is about how the technologies and the capabilities they provide are organized, and about the impact that the technologies, their capabilites, and their organization will have on national security decision-making. It is about how these technologies and their capabilities will change the strategic environment within which national security objectives are pursued.

These realities lead to the question that is the core subject of this essay: In the Information Age, what will be different --and the same-- about national security?

Precedents and Organization

A large number of works have already examined this relatively new question.[2] Some, like Alvin and Heidi Toffler's War and Anti-War: Survival at the Dawn of the Twenty-First Century, provide an overarching theory of Information Age warfare and conflict. Others, like John Arquilla's and David Ronfeldt's In Athena's Camp: Preparing for Conflict in the Information Age, divide conflict in the Information Age into categories on the basis of whether it occurs on the military or social side of the conflict spectrum, defining "cyberwar" as "a comprehensive information-oriented approach to battle that may be in the information age what blitzkrieg was to the industrial age" and "netwar" as "a comprehensive information-oriented approach to social conflict." Others, such as Winn Schwartau's Information Warfare, categorize conflict according to targets, identifying "Class 1: Personal Information Warfare" as "an attack against an individual's electronic privacy: his digital records, files, or other portions of a person's electronic essence;" "Class 2: Corporate Information Warfare" as "industrial espionage, ... economic espionage, ... the use of information, ... and "denial of service;" and "Class 3: Global Information Warfare" as "electronic warfare against industries, political spheres of influence, global economic forces, or even against entire countries." Some, such as Martin C. Libicki's What Is Information Warfare?, reject "information warfare" as a "separate technique of waging war", arguing that "there are several distinct forms of information warfare," all of which in one way or another involve "the protection, manipulation, degradation, and denial of information". All conclude that the Information Age is the dawn of a new era which will create a new strategic environment in which national security will be dominated by a revolution in military affairs, itself driven by advanced information and communication technologies.[3]

This essay adds to the dialogue by first exploring the meaning of national security. Confusion over the definition of national security sometimes leads to disputes over policy issues that could have been avoided. By defining national security, we at the outset provide a common point of departure.

Second, this essay explores some of the impacts that advanced information and communication technologies may be expected to have on human affairs. These impacts are fundamental to understanding what the strategic environment of the Information Age may look like and to understanding how national security affairs may change.

Third, this essay discusses impacts that advanced information and communication technologies may have on military capabilities and the strategic environment.

Finally, this essay presents one view of what the strategic environment of the Information Age may look like. This discussion is premised on the belief that present national security decisions will help shape the future strategic environment.

The Meaning of National Security

What, then, has national security meant in the years leading up to the Information Age? For all state actors in the international system, national security is a key objective, perhaps their primary raison d'etre. The term is difficult to define, but almost every state in its efforts to obtain national security in one way or another seeks to attain four distinct objectives for itself and its citizens: safety and protection from physical attack from foreign sources; economic prosperity and well-being for some or all of its citizens; protection of core national values; and the maintenance and improvement of the prevailing way of life.

Many factors affect a state's ability to attain its national security objectives. Some factors, like wealth, geography, military forces, transportation infrastructure, alliance systems, industrial potential, and educational levels, are for the most part tangible, objective, and easily measured. Others, like national strategy, organizational capabilities, scientific-technical knowledge, perceived threat, leadership capabilities, and national will and morale, are primarily intangible, subjective, and less easily measured.

What is more, the importance of given factors in a state's national security equation is not static. Rather, they often change over time. Some factors may decline in importance, and others may grow. This reality is particularly important as we move into the Information Age, where intangible and subjective elements of power such as knowledge are expected to grow in importance.

In addition, new factors sometimes emerge to occupy key positions or alter the importance of old factors. For example, the development first of aircraft carriers, then long-range jet bombers, and eventually ICBMs reduced the importance of geography in the U.S. national security equation. With the advent of these new technologies, each with longer reach and reduced delivery time in comparison to the technology that preceded it, geography no longer provided the degree of protection for the U.S. that it once did.

But geography's importance did not disappear. The resurgence of the debate in the 1990s over deploying a ballistic missile defense (BMD) to forestall the threat from states with newly acquired ballistic missile capabilities showed that geography remained a factor in the U.S. national security equation. Even in the late 1990s, geography provided security from potentially hostile states that did not have ballistic missiles. However, the debate over BMD illustrated that geography's importance was continuing to decline as more states acquired ballistic missiles and U.S. security concerns about those states increased.

Often, "national security" has been a synonym for "defense". In the past, this interchangeable usage presented few problems, just as before 1990, "state," "nation", and "nation-state" were often used as synonyms. However, as ethnic nationalism and the collapse of communism in the 1990s led to the dissolution of old states, the creation of new states, and the blurring of boundaries between civil war and international conflict, the specific meanings of these once-interchangeable terms acquired new importance. The same phenomenon may occur with "national security" and "defense" in the Information Age.

"Defense" and "defense policy" are concepts that have many meanings. Most refer to the protection of a state, its territories, and its peoples from physical assault by an external force. Issues involved in "defense" and "defense policy" generally include the recruitment, training, organizing, equipping, deployment, and use of military forces.[4] Most definitions of defense and defense policy center on military affairs and policy.

"National security" is a more comprehensive concept. One of the earliest references to national security appears in the National Security Act of 1947, which empowered the National Security Council to "advise the President with respect to the integration of domestic, foreign, and military policies relating to the national security so as to enable the military services and other departments and agencies of the Government to cooperate more effectively in matters involving the national security."[5]

But what exactly is national security, and how is it similar to and different from defense? Again, there is no single universally accepted definition. Despite lack of agreement, national security is more inclusive than defense or defense policy. As with defense and defense policy, national security includes the protection of a state, its territories, and its peoples by military forces from physical assault by external force, but it also encompasses the protection, not necessarily exclusively by military means, of other important state economic, political, social, cultural, and valuative interests, which if undermined, eroded, or lost could threaten the survival of the state.[6]

While national security focuses on military affairs, military policy, foreign affairs, and foreign policy, it often spills into economic, political, social and cultural, and valuative affairs. It often includes domestic components. In economic affairs, national security sometimes includes trade, international finance, monetary policy, economic sanctions, and resource dependency. In political affairs, it often includes diplomacy, diplomatic recognition, alliance formation, and alliance maintenance. In social and cultural affairs, national security may include language, ethnic, and immigration policies. In valuative affairs, it can encompass religion, human rights, and responses to ethnic cleansing.

By comparison, in domestic affairs and policy, national security often includes budgetary issues, the development of a domestic transportations infrastructure, the relationship between economic capabilities and performance and military potential, base closing questions, personnel policy, recruitment issues, congressional-executive relations, intelligence oversight, environmental impact statements, disaster relief, industrial preparedness, reserve and national guard questions, and other civil-military issues.

National security is thus a broad concept that has imprecise boundaries. Indeed, one of the primary recent debates in national security intellectual circles has been whether and where to place boundaries on the concept of national security. Some scholars argue that issues as diverse as declining domestic educational performance, organized crime, and international environmental concerns should be part of the national security equation, while others argue that inclusion of such a broad set of issues within a definition of national security renders the term for all practical purposes meaningless.[7] This debate has not been resolved. For our purposes, we shall use the following definition of national security:

> National security refers to the protection of a state, its territories, and its peoples from physical assault by an external force, as well as the protection of important state economic, political, military, social, cultural, and valuative interests from attacks emanating from foreign or domestic sources which may undermine, erode, or eliminate these interests, thereby threatening the survival of the state. Such protection may be pursued by military or non-military means.[8]

Impacts and Diffusion of Information and Communication Technologies

What impacts will Information Age technologies have on human affairs that will in turn impact military capabilities and the strategic environment? How widely have they been diffused in different societies at the beginning of the twenty-first century? Clearly, Information Age technologies will enhance humankind's ability to communicate, to utilize information, and to overcome obstacles presented to communication by distance, time, and location, but their generic impacts and degrees of diffusion differ widely.

The Impacts

Even so, a conceptual understanding of the generic impacts that these technologies may have can be developed. The impacts can be grouped into six areas.[9]

First, the speed at which information can be transmitted, managed, manipulated, and interpreted will increase significantly. Information flows within and between organizations and among organizations and international actors will also accelerate, although at differing rates depending upon a host of factors. Increased speed will matter more for some uses than for others. Some international actors will benefit more from more rapid information flows than will others. But in general, increased speed of information flow will increase the tempo of interactions within and between international actors.

Second, the capacity to transmit information will also increase significantly. Again, increased capacity will become available at different rates to different international actors. As with increased speed, greater information and communication capacity will benefit some organizations and international actors more than others will. Here, however, the point to stress is that for many international actors, the ability to transmit and interpret greater amounts of information will mean that decision makers will have a greatly enhanced picture of the world, themselves, and others upon which to base their decisions.

Third, Information Age technologies will enhance the flexibility of information flows. Those needing information will be able to reach out and get it from more sources. Those needing to communicate with someone will find it ever more easy to do so quickly and directly. Put differently, these technologies will decrease the location-dependence of information and communication transactions. This greater flexibility will be available to some more quickly than others and will matter more for some than for others.

Fourth, the new and emerging technologies will provide more individuals greater access to more people, organizations, and information than ever before. This, some observers have argued, will lead to the democratization of information and communication flows throughout the world, that is, a decreased ability of a few (e.g. governments, businesses, and the 'haves') to dominate information and communication channels.

Although this may be true, improved access will not occur --or in some cases, be permitted-- at the same speed throughout the world. Access will also be organized in different ways depending on the international actor. Some actors will also undoubtedly seek to impede, restrict, or otherwise control information flows. And again, all actors will not benefit equally. Thus, whether or not the optimistic scenario of the democratizing impact of information and communication technologies plays out remains to be seen.

Fifth, more types of messages --voice, data, and pictures-- will be sent with greater reliability and accuracy than ever before. Indeed, whereas, only little more than a century ago electronic communications were confined to sending electrical pulses that represented letters of the alphabet a few hundred miles along wire cables, it is today possible to send voice, data, and pictures from one side of the world to the other. To the extent that more complex messages such as pictures more accurately represent reality and are more quickly absorbed and understood than text messages, the expansion of message types from text to voice, data, and picture is an important factor in enhancing global connectivity.

Sixth, as Information Age technologies become more available, less expensive, easier to use, and more beneficial to achieve diverse objectives, heightened demand will result. Here, too, however, heightened demand for communications and information will occur unevenly throughout organizations, societies, and international actors.

None of these impacts mean that the importance of time, distance, or location on human affairs has died or will die. Indeed, as pointed out several times above, Information Age technologies will be absorbed, diffused, and operationalized by different international actors in different ways and at different speeds. This will lead to different types and rates of change in different international actors. Factors that will influence the way and rate in which advanced these technologies will be absorbed, diffused, and operationalized include but are not limited to: 1.) purchase and upkeep cost; 2.) age and utility of in-place technology; 3.) an actor's social and cultural receptivity to new technology; 4.) degree of insularity within an actor; 5.) level and reliability of an actor's human, technical and economic support infrastructures; 6.) level and strength of traditional values and outlooks within an actor; 7.) level of education within an actor; 8.) degree of technical sophistication of users and potential users of advanced information and communication technology within an actor; 9.) levels of concern over sovereignty on the part of states, and over control of decision-making processes on the part of the actors; and 10.) many political, social, and economic factors idiosyncratic to each actor and therefore impossible to detail.

Despite these constraints, Information Age technologies are lessening on a global basis the role that time, distance, and locations play in human interactions. It is also noteworthy --and fraught with implications for national security-- that these impacts are proceeding rapidly, globally, and unevenly. These three dimensions of diffusion, viewed together with the six impacts of new and emerging information and communication technologies discussed above, have immense implications for national security, both in the context of enhanced military capabilities and the context of a changed strategic environment. It is to these realities we turn now.

Military Capabilities, the Strategic Environment, and Advanced Information and Communication Technologies

How, then, will advanced information and communication technologies affect military capabilities and alter the strategic environment as it applies to national security affairs? Before we discuss these issues, however, some general observations are in order in both areas.

Impacts on Military Capabilities

The first point that must be made is that because of their relatively inexpensive cost and widespread availability, Information Age technologies that may be used to challenge or threaten the security of states and other international actors will be more widely available and easier to use than the primary major military technologies of Industrial Age conflict. Put simply, computer hardware and software and the ability to use it will be more widely available and more easily attainable than nuclear weapons, ICBMs, aircraft carrier battle groups, and main battle tanks. In the Information Age, given the lower costs and wider availability of technologies that could challenge national security, states will not be the only international actors potentially capable of threatening national security. Other international actors including multinational corporations, non-governmental organizations, terrorist and criminal groups, and even individuals, may develop such potential.

Even so, the impacts that advanced information and communication technologies will have on the military capabilities of international actors and their friends and enemies will be diverse and considerable. Similarly, the impacts that these technologies will have on an actor's military capabilities and on the military capabilities of its friends and enemies have extensive implications for military organization, strategy, and doctrine.[10]

At the same time, given the uneven but rapid and global nature of the diffusion of Information Age technologies, the military capabilities of all international actors will not be affected in the same way at the same time. In all probability, then, we are entering an era in which military capabilities of international actors will be even more varied --and sometimes unpredictable and surprising-- than they have been in the past.

In some areas, Information Age technologies will have a predictable impact on military capabilities. For example, they enhance an actor's ability to command, control, and communicate with its armed forces at the operational, tactical, and strategic levels. They help provide improved intelligence about the intentions, capabilities, and actions of enemies and potential enemies. They serve as force multipliers, especially with the inclusion of precision guided munitions and other "smart" and "brilliant" weapons into an actor's weapons inventory. And they contribute directly in a host of other indirect ways to the pursuit and attainment of an actor's national security objectives.

At the same time, even as Information Age technologies provide opportunities to enhance military capabilites, to the extent that data links and information flows can be degraded, denied, or altered, they have potential to increase vulnerabilities. For example, to the extent that military action depends on accurate knowledge of one's position provided by satellite-based global positioning systems, military action is vulnerable to interdiction of information flow between satellite and land, sea, or air receptor.

Similarly, secure data links and information flows are critical for aerial refueling. A potential enemy need not have the capability to shoot down bombers or fighters before or after they rendezvous with a tanker; he need only have the capability to alter electronically refueling coordinates that the bombers or fighters receive. Military vulnerability to data and information interdiction or alteration is not new, but as military forces move toward even greater reliance on data and information to enhance their capabilities in the Information Age, potential vulnerability to data and information degradation, denial, and alteration increases.

Organizationally, the capabilities afforded by Information Age technologies tend to be best used by networked organizations in which every decision node can communicate with every other decision node directly rather than by hierarchical organizations which require decision at every level before action is taken. This will present a challenge for traditional militaries --and other institutions-- which have historically been hierarchical as a result of requirements to command, control, and communicate with large organizations, implement large scale mobilization, and undertake large scale action. The organizational challenge for such bodies is that even in the Information Age they may best be able to accomplish certain appointed tasks if they retain a hierarchial organization, but they will in many cases be required to respond quickly as rapid information flows enable quick small scale action that may alter the strategic environment. Thus, the organizational challenges presented by capabilities afforded by Information Age technologies will revolve around how best to meld traditional hierarchical structures required for command, control, and communication with large scale organizations to initiate large scale mobilization and undertake large scale action, with new networked structures required for rapid information flow and quick, often small scale, action.

For military strategy and doctrine, the issues are much the same as for organization: how best can traditional strategy and doctrine, often based on command, control, and communication with large scale forces to initiate and undertake large scale mobilization and large scale action, be combined with the capabilities afforded by Information Age technologies that permit rapid information flow and often require quick, small scale action? This will be a considerable challenge for strategists and developers of doctrine.

Impacts on the Strategic Environment

Military capabilities, organization, strategy, and doctrine are important factors in an actor's security equation, but they should not overshadow the fact that Information Age technologies also help create and define the strategic environment in which international actors pursue their objectives. Under certain conditions, new and emerging information and communication technologies have potential to transform the strategic environment, much the way that the railroad and telegraph did during the 1860s and 1870s; the internal combustion engine, telephone, and radio did in the 1910s and 1920s; and nuclear weapons, television, and early computers did in the years immediately following World War II.

Domestically, information and communication technologies help create a state's --and other actor's-- domestic political, economic, and military capabilities. They also help define social, cultural, and valuative milieus. At the state level, these are important components of national security since every state, if it is to survive, must base a substantial portion of its national security policy upon its domestic capabilities and milieu.

Internationally, information and communication technologies extend the global knowledge and global reach of governments, businesses, militaries, and other international organizations and actors. They enable these actors to diseminate information (or disinformation). They aid and abet economic and cultural integration (or disintegration). They lend urgency to events half a world away. At the international level, information and communication technologies help establish the international system in which a state must pursue its national security objectives and the international norms which help influence, and in some cases determine, what is and is not acceptable international behavior. They may also provide new capabilities to some actors that under certain conditions substantially increase the importance of these actors in a given state's national security equation.

What will the emerging strategic environment of the Information Age be like? Analysts do not agree. Nor do they agree about the speed at which the environment will change. Nevertheless, national security analysts and planners must develop forces, organizations, doctrines, and strategies that can cope with this uncertain future. With this in mind, then, we in the final section of this chapter present one view of what the strategic environment of the Information Age may look like and four views of how it may evolve.

How the Strategic Environment May Evolve: Alternate Views

The Information Age, like the agricultural and industrial ages which preceded it, is a global phenomenon. Global communications are virtually instantaneous, computers and other Information Age technologies are found in even the most underdeveloped states, and almost every country has least one system connected to the Internet.

However, changes induced by Information Age technologies are taking place in different countries at different rates of speed, with different types of impacts, with different organizational characteristics, and with different depths of impacts. Different societies are acquiring different levels of capabilities as a result of advanced information and communication technologies, with some progressing more rapidly than others. As pointed out earlier, different societies absorb, diffuse, and operationalize Information Age technologies at different rates because of the purchase and upkeep costs of the technologies; the age and utility of in-place technology; a society's social and cultural receptivity to new technology; the degree of insularity of a society; the level and reliability of a society's human, technical, and economic support infrastructures; the strength of a society's traditional values and outlooks; the level of education within a society; the degree of technical sophistication of users and potential users of Information Age technology; the level of concern over sovereignty on the part of states, and over control of decision-making processes on the part of a society's leadership elites; and many other political, social, and economic factors idiosyncratic to each society and therefore impossible to detail.

What, then, will the emerging strategic environment look like? Here, we will present one view, that of Alvin and Heidi Toffler. Criticized by some as being too simplistic and by others as overlooking important historical facts, it is nevertheless a widely recognized view of what the strategic environment of the Information Age might look like.

The Toffler's View of the Strategic Environment of the Information Age

To the Tofflers, the world is moving toward a global socio-economic revolution that will lead to a global "trisected power structure." This new strategic environment will entail a trisected global power structure that will supersede the Industrial Age's bisected structure in which states that developed industrial "smokestack" economies enjoyed economic, social, and military superiority over more primitive agricultural societies.

In the Information Age, the Tofflers argue, states that use and benefit most from Information Age technologies will be at the apex of a three-tiered global power structure dominated by knowledge and knowledge-related "intangibles." They will be superior in capabilities to those states that depend on either an industrial or agricultural economy.[11] In an effort to gain advantages afforded by Information Age technological capabilities, some states may even attempt to bypass the industrial stage of development, moving directly from an agricultural to an information economy. But all three types of societies, with many countries not fitting clearly into one or another of the three dominant types, will coexist.

Countries at the apex of this trisected global power structure will be more dependent on the technologies of the Information Age than will be those that remain saddled with an industrial or agricultural economy. Because of this greater dependency, they as societies will be more vulnerable than industrial or agricultural societies to any alteration, disruption, or destruction of the technologies upon which they rely, much the same way as industrial societies are more vulnerable to disruption of energy and fuel supplies than are agricultural societies. Despite the enhanced economic and military capabilities that flow from the technologies of the Information Age, the security equation for post-industrial states will be complicated because of this vulnerability, as we will discuss later.

At the same time, as the trisected global power structure emerges, the capabilities provided by Information Age technologies are likely to further blur the boundaries between domestic and international affairs. In the emerging strategic environment, the combination of increased speed, capacity, and flexibility of information flow combined with greater access to, more types of, and heightened demand for information will make it increasingly difficult for states to control inward and outward information flows. Some states will try to control access to freely available information, as China has with access to Internet sites.[12] However, few will succeed unless they impose draconian social or technological solutions to their perceived problem. Such solutions might include capital punishment or long-term imprisonment for accessing unapproved information sites, restricting Internet access via licenses to only loyal subjects, or otherwise restricting access to advanced information and communication technologies. States that apply such solutions, while maintaining control of information flows, will suffer other social and economic losses, including limiting their ability to move from agricultural or industrial economies to an information economy.

Because of the capabilities that they provide, the technologies of the Information Age are also likely to increase the role that non-state actors play in the international system. Multinational corporations have long been major actors in the international scene, but they are likely to grow even more influential internationally as businesses become increasingly regionalized and globalized. Already, taking advantage of opportunities afforded by advanced information and communication technologies to increase the speed, capacity, and flexibility of information flows, many businesses have entered the international marketplace and increased profitability by moving their labor intensive back room operations to countries where labor costs are low. Similarly, nongovernmental organizations (NGOs) have proliferated, increasing in number from perhaps four thousand such organizations in the late1970s to perhaps as many as thirty thousand in the late 1990s. A significant but uncertain percentage of this growth is undoubtedly due to the ability that like-minded or like-interested people now have on a global base to share information and to communicate as a result of advanced information and communication technologies.

To the Tofflers, the emerging strategic environment will be more complex than today's. If the Tofflers are correct, more fissures of change and conflict will divide the global community than in the past. Inevitably, the technologies of the Information Age will continue to be absorbed, diffused, and operationalized at different speeds and with different results in different countries. States will remain the dominant international actor, but more types of actors, and more actors of each type, will gain importance. Given the potential provided by Information Age technologies for like-minded people to articulate and act on their viewpoints, and contrary to those who argue (or fear) that the Information Age will bring with it an era of global homogeniety, the strategic environment of the Information Age may well be more complex than any that preceded it during the twentieth century.

Speed and Extent of Change

How and when may this strategic environment arrive? There are at least four views about the speed with which the Information Age will usher in changes to the strategic environment, and about how extensive those changes may be.

A few voices urge caution about leaping to conclusions that an information and communication revolution and an Information Age is upon us. These analysts do not deny that change is taking place nor that advanced information and communication technologies provide humankind with capabilities beyond those previously available, but they are skeptical that much other than capabilities will change. This perspective is not widely shared, but it cannot be overlooked.

One skeptic is Frank Webster, who observes that there are immense difficulties in measuring what an Information Age means.[13] He warns that information by itself means nothing, and that one must take into consideration the meaning and quality of information, not just its quantity. Even with the proliferation of Information Age technologies, Webster wonders whether society will change profoundly enough to warrant calling the near term future an Information Age. While Webster fully admits that advanced information and communication technologies provide humankind with capabilities unimaginable a few years ago, his premise is that little in human interrelationships or organizations has changed or is likely to change fundamentally as a result of information and communication technologies.

What does this imply for national security affairs? If Webster's view is accurate, this means that new and emerging information and communication technologies will enhance military capabilities, but that the strategic environment will change little. Military systems, weapons platforms, and kill mechanisms may grow more capable, more lethal, more accurate, and obtain greater reach, but national security planners and strategists will be able to proceed with their planning as if little else other than capabilities have changed.

A second perspective sees strategic change taking place in an evolutionary rather than revolutionary way. Without denying that the cumulative impact of new and emerging information and communication technologies will be revolutionary, this school nonetheless sees change occurring in a paced and evolutionary manner. Advocates of this school of thought accept that future human and organizational relationships will be fundamentally divorced from past relationships, but that the changes that lead to this divorce will take place over time, permitting individuals and organizations to evolve.

For example, this perspective asserts that in business, a viable electronic commerce system requires a secure network linking buyers and sellers; a database replete with product information; easy-to-use buyer/seller interface software; reliable e-mail; and a mechanism for shipping, financing, and processing orders; and that it will take time to fully implement such a system. It accepts that electronic commerce will change the fundamental structure of how businesses distribute goods, products, and services, with three issues being of utmost importance: who will run electronic commerce networks, how will electronic commerce change the structure of distribution, and who will the winners and losers be. This perspective accepts that change will come in other areas of human endeavor as well.[14] But the key point is that even though change in the strategic environment may eventually be revolutionary, it will come in an evolutionary manner.

If this view is accurate, national security planners and strategists will be blessed with time to adapt their thought processes and planning procedures to the emerging strategic environment. A changed strategic environment will emerge, but it will emerge slowly. If this scenario --or the first-- eventuates, then military strategists and planners will be fortunate, for as Michael Howard commented in his 1986 Roskill Memorial Lecture, "psychological change always lags behind technological change." A slowly emerging changed strategic environment provides national security strategists and planners a margin of time during which they can grow accustomed to and assimilate the changes taking place.

This is not true in the last two scenarios. In the third scenario, analysts accept that humankind is in the midst of a revolution induced by Information Age technologies. They believe it will quickly produce profound change in the strategic environment.[15] They believe that the impacts that these technologies have will run the gamut of political, economic, military, social, cultural, and valuative spheres of human activity. Advocates of this school perceive a future of human and organizational relationships that will be fundamentally divorced from past relationships, and probably in the near future.

This school sees that as change proceeds and accelerates a premium will be placed on the ability of individuals and organizations to adjust and learn. Advocates of this perspective believe those who adjust and learn will prosper, but concede that those who do not will be in for difficult times. If this scenario is accurate, then security strategists and planners will need to develop strategies and tactics to achieve national security objectives in the absence of a full understanding of the emerging strategic environment in which they will be implemented. "Just-in-time" national security strategy may become not only the practice, but also the only viable option in a rapidly changing strategic environment.

Finally, some analysts believe Information Age technologies are driving the strategic environment toward rapid and even cataclysmic change that will require flexibility in thinking beyond the ability of most national security strategists. One such analyst is Michael Vlahos, who believes that change --what he terms "Big Change"-- may well be cataclysmic for established organizations and relationships.[16] To Vlahos, "Big Change" will have four components. First, new and emerging information and communication technologies are already driving a world economic revolution of "world-historical significance". Second, this economic revolution will "bring upheaval to world cultures as old ways of life are torn apart." Third, "new war will serve the needs of new meaning." And fourth, the U.S. will "not only still be fighting old war, but still be thinking old war".

What will the changes induced by Information Age technologies be like? When will they come? How will they arrive? There is little agreement, but only skeptics of the first school deny that Information Age technologies, the capabilities they provide, and the changes they will induce will alter the way people, their institutions, and their societies are organized, operate, and inter-relate. These changes will not come at once, nor at the same time in all locations. But there is little doubt they will come. The question is how the national security community will cope with this uncertain strategic environment.

National Security in the Information Age

What do the probable impacts of new and emerging information and communication technologies on human affairs, economic activity, military capabilities, and the strategic environment imply for national security in the Information Age? The implications are that the content of national security may well expand in three ways.

The Definition of "National Security" Will Expand

As we saw earlier, "national security" is already a relatively broadly based concept. In the Information Age, however, more types of issues than ever before may be widely perceived as national security issues. This observation flows from two facts.

First, as advanced information and communication technologies make the transfer of information easier, organizational boundaries, state borders, and other lines of demarcation within and between states and other sub-national, national, and international actors are become increasingly permeable and vague. Although national security has always included a domestic component, the increasing permeability and vagueness of the domestic-international dichotomy, combined with the probabilty of increased uncertainty of the source of many challenges and threats to security, it will be more difficult than ever to separate national security issues from law enforcement, policing, and related concerns. As a result, more and more issues may be defined as national security concerns.

Second, as Information Age technologies become pervasive and information societies grow increasingly dependent upon them, an information society's vulnerability to alteration, disruption, or destruction of those technologies grows. For example, in finance and banking, funds can be transferred electronically at a moment's notice from one location to another virtually anywhere in the world. This capability lessens the ability of states to control and monitor financial flows and business transactions across borders. Thus, states are less able than ever to maintain control of and knowledge about international finance and their own currencies. To the extent that control of finance and maintenance of monetary stability are national security concerns, this has potential to be a national security issue.

Whereas in the past information security was primarily a corporate or personal issue, the free flow of information of all types around the world via the Internet has potential to raise information security issues to the national security level. The transfer of funds, data, and other forms of information electronically across state boundaries, and even within states, opens opportunities for electronic theft, electronic blackmail, electronic corruption, electronic data alteration, and in the worst case, system disruption via electronic assault upon the economic, political, and social stability and well-being of a state. System disruption via electronic assault on stability and well being is clearly a national security concern, and under certain conditions, electronic theft, electronic blackmail, electronic corruption, and electronic data alteration could be as well. Thus, more issues than ever before could fall under the domain of national security in the Information Age.

An example may illustrate the point. If a single financial institution discovers that an unauthorized electronic transfer of funds, alteration of records, or system sabotage has taken place, the action likely emanated from an individual or small group for private purposes. Such an incident rarely has potential to become a national security concern. But if multiple financial institutions discover in a short time that multiple unauthorized electronic transfers of funds, alterations of banking records, or system sabotage have taken place from an unidentified source, then an electronic assault on the national financial system may be underway and national security may be involved.

To be sure, electronic security is a major concern for most public and private organizations and institutions. Many institutions and organizations have elaborate encryption systems in place to assure the security of sensitive data, with many banks and other institutions using 128 bit or even stronger security systems. But other institutions and organizations whose continued operations are just as vital to a modern society have much weaker encryption systems. Some have no security systems at all.

At what point, then, does a breach of security at a private or public institution or organization become a national security issue? Is any attempt at unauthorized entry into a Department of Defense (or Department of the Treasury) computer or electronic system a national security issue, or must the attempt be successful? How significant must the attempt be, and to what extent must vital Defense Department (or Treasury Department) operations or information be jeopardized before the incursion is a national security issue?

At some point, a threshold is crossed that elevates a given incident from a private concern, a local affair, a corporate matter, or a government issue to a national security concern. As the U.S. and other countries become increasingly dependent upon advanced information and communication technologies and the capabilites they provide, and as the boundaries and borders between international actors become increasingly permeable and vague, it is likely that more issues may be construed as national security concerns. The art, and the necessity, are determining when and where that threshold has been crossed.

More Diverse Sources of Challenges and Threats to National Security Will Emerge

In the Information Age, challenges and threats to national security may emanate from more diverse sources, including some sources, which in the past may not have been national security challenges or threats. As advanced information and communication technologies become less expensive and easier to use, they will be more widely adopted and increasingly employed. Their employment will no longer be limited to "leading edge" industries and organizations, nor will their employment be limited to select organizational functions and processes. More and more people, institutions, and organizations will have more and more access to information. Except for the most sensitive national and corporate data, this increased quantity of data will be accompanied by increased dissemination and access. At the same time, the locations at which information is located and from which information can be accessed will proliferate.

During the industrial era, it was a rare occurence for a single individual to present a true threat to a state's national security. Unfortunately, not all of the users of advanced information and communication technologies may be expected to have the best interests of a state in mind. Inevitably, attempts at electronic theft, blackmail, corruption, data alteration, and disruption of services will occur. Some will be successful. As discussed above, if they occur below a certain threshold, they will not constitute a national security issue. However, again as discussed, if any occur above a certain threshold, they may become a national security issue. Thus, given the nature of the capabilities afforded by Information Age technologies and the increased dependence of the U.S. and other societies on them, a highly capable person pursuing his own agenda could alter data, disrupt operations, or otherwise compromise information and communication systems critical to national security.

Similarly, other established types of international actors, especially multinational corporations (MNCs) and nongovernmental organizations (NGOs), could as a result of their technological prowess pursue objectives that challenge or threaten a state's national security. Again, as with individuals, this is not a new phenomenon resulting from the Information Age. But with the capabilities afforded by Information Age technologies, it is both more likely and more possible for MNCs and NGOs to challenge and threaten a state's ability to obtain its national security objectives.

This is not meant to imply that individuals, MNCs, or IGOs in the Information Age will suddenly become enemies of the state. Nor is it meant to imply that the Information Age will necessarily lead to a post-Westphalian international system in which states are increasingly threatened, increasingly weakened, and unable to protect themselves. Rather, it is to state that Information Age technologies will enable technically capable individuals, MNCs, and NGOs to challenge and in some cases threaten national security at a much higher level than in the past. For national security strategists and planners, then, the Information Age promises to bring with it a broader threat array than in the past.

Virtual Sources of Challenges and Threats to National Security Will Emerge

As if the emerging strategic environment is not complicated enough, virtual international actors may emerge to challenge national security, requiring new and innovative responses. Since the technologies of the Information Age will aid and abet individuals and organizations in scattered locations that have similar interests, outlooks, or objectives to communicate easily with one another, it is likely that the Information Age will witness formation of 'virtual' entities that stake claim to a role or an issue in domestic policy or international affairs. Some of these virtual entities will be ephemeral, coming into existence for short periods of time and concentrating on single issues.

Most probably will be ignored by established international actors. But some virtual entities who have strong views on specific issues and who have highly developed technological skills may become players in their own right on the international scene. It is not difficult to envision a technologically highly capable radical splinter group of an ethnic, religious, or environmental movement acquiring a virtual identity and demanding that a state or corporation undertakes an action or suffer consequences generated electronically from an unidentified site. Depending on the technical capabilities and credibility of the virtual radical group, such threats and demands could become national security issues. While it is difficult to foretell what impact virtual entities might have on national security, there is little doubt that such entities will come into existence, further complicating the complex national security decision-making environment of the Information Age.

Do these three factors --the multiplication of issues that may be widely perceived as legitimate national security issues, the proliferation of sources that challenge national security, and the emergence of new types of international actors that may challenge national security-- imply that the Information Age could bring with it the National Security State that was at one time so widely feared, so greatly decried, but which never quite materialized during the Cold War? Not necessarily, for as we will see in subsequent chapters, the technologies of the Information Age carry with them other implications as well.

In the Information Age, national security analysts, planners, and decision-makers will have their work cut out. They must be able to differentiate challenges and threats to national security from lower order dangers and threats, to identify where the threshold is between national security issues and other less pressing concerns. When a challenge or threat exists, they must be able to identify from where it emanates, what its intent is, the degree and type of danger that it poses, and how to respond to it most effectively. They must do this in a strategic environment that will be more complex. With the Information Age and its technologies, national security is indeed on the verge of a brave new world.

Notes

[1] For detailed discussions of these technologies, see David S. Alberts, Daniel S. Papp, and W. Thomas Kemp III, "The Technologies of the Information Revolution," in David S. Alberts and Daniel S. Papp (eds.), The Information Age: An Anthology on Its Impacts and Consequences (Washington: National Defense University Press, 1997), pp. 83-116.

[2] For example, see James Adams, The Next World War: Computers are the Weapons and the Front Line is Everywhere (New York: Simon & Schuster, 1998); John Arquilla and David Ronfeldt (eds.), In Athena's Camp: Preparing for Conflict in the Information Age (Santa Monica, CA: RAND, 1997); Martin C. Libicki, The Mesh and the Net: Speculations on Armed Conflict in a Time of Free Silicon (Washington, D.C.: National Defense University Press, 1995); Martin C. Libicki, What Is Information Warfare? (Washington, D.C.: National Defense University Press, 1996); Roger C. Molander, Andrew S. Riddile, and Peter A. Wilson, Strategic Information Warfare: A New Face of War (Santa Monica, CA: RAND, 1996); Winn Schwartau (ed.), Information Warfare (New York, NY: Thunder's Mouth Press, 1996); Stuart J.D. Schwartzstein (ed.), The Information Revolution and National Security: Dimensions and Directions (Washington, D.C.: Center for Strategic and International Studies, 1996); Alvin and Heidi Toffler, War and Anti-War: Survival at the Dawn of the Twenty-First Century (New York: Little, Brown, and Company, 1993); and William H. Webster, Arnaud de Borchgrave, et al., Cybercrime...Cyberterrorism... Cyberwarfare...Averting an Electronic Waterloo (Washington, D.C.: Center for Strategic and International Studies, 1998).

[3] For discussions about the revolution in military affairs, see Michael J. Mazarr, Jeffrey Shaffer, and Benjamin Ederington, The Military Technical Revolution (Washington, D.C.: Center for Strategic and International Studies, 1993); Williamson Murray, "Thinking About Revolutions in Military Affairs," Joint Forces Quarterly (Summer 1997); and Colin Gray, "The American Revolution in Military Affairs: An Interim Assessment," The Occasional, Number 28, (Strategic and Combat Studies Institute, September 1997). U.S. Naval Institute Proceedings (May 1995), pp. 35-39; and Lawrence Freedman, "The Revolution in Strategic Affairs", Adelphi Paper 318 (London: International Institute for Strategic Studies, 1998), p. 11.

[4] See Peter L. Hays, et al., "What Is American Defense Policy?" p. 9, in Peter L. Hays, et al. (eds.), American Defense Policy, Seventh Edition (Baltimore: The Johns Hopkins University Press, 1997).

[5] The National Security Act of 1947, July 26, 1947, in 50 U.S.C. 401.

[6] For lengthier discussions of defense and national security, see Peter L. Hays, et al., "What Is American Defense Policy?" pp. 8-16; Amos A. Jordan, et al., American National Security: Policy and Process, Fifth Edition (Baltimore: The Johns Hopkins University Press, 1999), especially pp.3-23; and Frederick H. Hartmann and Robert L. Wendzel, Defending America's Security, Second Edition (New York: Brassey's, 1990), especially pp. 3-25.

[7] This debate is encapsulated in International Security.

[8] This definition is an amalgamation of definitions contained in the works identified in footnote 6.

[9] For more detailed discussion of these six points, see Alberts, Papp, and Kemp, pp. 107-112.

[10] Detailed discussion of the military implications of the Information Age will be covered in the third volume of The Information Age Anthology.

[11] Alvin and Heidi Toffler, "Foreward: The New Intangibles," in Arquilla and Ronfeldt, pp. xiii-xxiv. See also Alvin and Heidi Toffler, War and Anti-War.

[12] See "A Trial Will Test China's Grip on the Internet," The New York Times, November 16, 1998.

[13] Frank Webster, "What Information Society?" The Information Society (Volume 10, Number 1), reprinted in Alberts and Papp, pp. 117-164.

[14] Robert L. Segal, "The Coming Electronic Commerce (R) evolution", Strategy and Leadership (November-December 1995) reprinted in Alberts and Papp, pp. 203-223.

[15] Thomas A. Stewart, "Welcome to the Revolution", Fortune (December 13, 1993), reprinted in Alberts and Papp, pp. 7-26.

[16] Michael Vlahos, "The War After Byte City", The Washington Quarterly (Spring 1997), pp. 41-72.

Part IV
The Individual at the Center

14 Legal Globalization and the New Human Rights Regime: Human Rights in a Post-Sovereign World

MARLENE WIND

Due to the centrality of sovereignty, modern international law has traditionally been regarded as a business between states rather than between people. Order and not justice has been at the center of attention. Since the end of the Cold War however, this convention has been under rapid transformation (Lyons and Mastanduno, 1995: 12ff). It seems now gradually to be replaced by an emerging consensus on minimal standards of international justice where the individual is (re)gaining its status as a subject of international law (Weller, 1999; Onuf, 1995; Linklater, 1999). Among some of the most obvious examples of this change within the past few years is the extradition case of the former Chilean leader General Pinochet which is expected to have substantial implications for the behavior of dictators worldwide.[1] Another example of the growing emphasis on the individual in international affairs, is the newly terminated Kosovo-war. Here human rights concerns overruled traditional occupations with national interests among the allied forces. One can discuss the overall success of the NATO operation but hardly the humanitarian motives behind it.[2] A third important indication of the increasing concern for human rights in world society is the Western power intervention in northern Iraq in 1991 in the aftermath of the Golf War. Following the Security Council Resolution 688 a military operation was launched in order to protect the Kurds from Iraqi armed forces after the Kurdish revolt against Saddam Hussein. The case is important because it was the first time this century that an intervention was interpreted 'a necessary act' in order to protect a minority from its own government (Brems Knudsen, 1999:170-188).[3] To many observers all the above examples reflect a general expansion of common values in world society.

Among the less flamboyant but no less important trends towards an increased consensus in international affairs, is the intensified communication among judges (Slaughter, 1997, 1994; Weiler, 1994). This phenomenon, which clearly is much harder to track down and 'prove' empirically, can be seen as part of an ongoing legal globalization process. It has thus become more and more difficult for national courts and judges to shield their national legal communities from debates and processes taking place in the international legal community. Legal globalization has thus in the past 15 –20 years resulted in the emergence of numerous common principles and standards, in particular in the human rights field.

Some scholars have talked about the above mentioned tendencies as examples of an emerging New World Order (Slaughter, 1997) or a new "Age of Rights" (Chinkin, 1999). Others speak of a renaissance of natural law due to the increased emphasis on universal human rights. It has in other words been argued with greater and greater frequency that neither sovereignty nor cultural differences can serve as an excuse for respecting basic humanistic principles (The Economist, December 1998. Special Issue on Human Rights).

This paper argues that due to these developments, sovereignty has come under increasing pressure. This is in particular the case after the end of the Cold War. It is hypothesized that both the Pinochet case and the 'humanitarian war' against Serbia to save civilian lives, represents a much deeper transformation that might put the individual at the center of attention in international society in the new millennium. The paper illustrates this[4] transformation by analyzing recent cases and by providing an overview over the development of the concept of sovereignty and human rights in different historical époques. The paper concludes by a critical examination of whether human rights at all can be generalized and promoted as a universal value across cultural differences.

Sovereignty under Pressure?

One of the things that makes a state sovereign is its right to rule over its own territory and people without the interference from any other state or agent (Kratochwil, 1995; Krasner, 1995:232). At least this is the conventional understanding. In the UN Charter it says that: "Nothing contained in the present Charter shall authorize the United Nations to intervene in matters which are essentially within the domestic jurisdiction of any state…"(Art. 2, 7). While this renders national sovereignty almost sacred, the UN Charter also speaks at lengths about reaffirming: "the faith in fundamental human rights, in the dignity and worth's of the human person...The purpose of the United Nations is to...promote(ing) and encourage (ing) respect for human rights and for fundamental freedoms for all without distinction as to race, sex, language, or religion...".[5] It is clear from this that there exist (and always has existed) an unresolved tension between these two considerations in international law. If one insists too eagerly on the rights of man, national sovereignty will be detained from any substantive meaning. If on the other hand, the principle of sovereignty and non-interference is overemphasized, universal human rights as expressed in the UN Charter will be little more than cheap rhetoric or wishful thinking.

Few would probably dispute that until recently, the principle of non-interference in other states affairs has been given higher priority than the protection of basic human rights. International law has in reality constituted the rules of the game for states while only national law has been able to guarantee individual rights. When domestic law has failed in this respect, international law has been left with very few tools to step in and help.

There seems nevertheless today to be growing international agreement on prosecuting those leaders responsible for atrocities against their own people. A significant breakthrough came with the war crimes tribunals in the 1990s[6] and the decision in Rome last year to create a permanent International War Crimes Tribunal. To this comes – as noted above - two cases or events which more than anything caught the attention of the broader public: the ongoing case against General Augusto Pinochet and NATO's recently terminated war against Milosevic. Together with the decision to establish a permanent court for war crimes, the two cases demonstrate that it has become harder to get away with gross human rights violations. Sovereignty is no longer sacred and the individual seems in the past years to have gained firmer ground in world society.

April 15, 1999 was a revolutionary day for international law. It was this day that the British Home Secretary Jack Straw announced that the extradition case against Chile's former dictator Augusto Pinochet could continue as planned. In saying so, Straw followed the verdict by the House of Lord's second ruling from March 1999, stating that Pinochet cannot be granted immunity for the crimes he committed during his function as a head of state.[7] As opposed to the first ruling, however, this second ruling was restricted both in time as well as in substance. It was now argued that Pinochet could only be charged for crimes committed after 1988 when Britain ratified the international Torture Convention. The limiting of the crimes for which Pinochet can be prosecuted does not question the broader implications of the case for international law however: No former or present dictator will in the future feel completely safe when seeking refuge in another country or when traveling abroad to receive medical treatment or to visit friends or family.

Prosecuting former state-officials for war crimes or crimes against humanity is however not as such anything new. The Nuremberg Tribunal after the end of the Second World War established this very clearly, as its Charter reads: "The official position of defendants, whether heads of state or responsible officials in Government Departments, shall not be considered as freeing them from responsibility or mitigating punishment". These principles have been recognized by the UN as international law and have been repeated in the Genocide convention[8] and in statutes establishing tribunals for the former Yugoslavia and Rwanda. The principles have also been employed in the cases against former Nazis who have been captured after having lived for years in exile in, for instance, Latin America.

Traditionally, immunity has, however, shielded many former Heads of State traveling abroad from prosecution. Diplomatic immunity has in fact been regarded as an inherent right of any state and its officials. It has in fact been part and parcel of the sovereignty principle itself. That this principle is in rapid transformation these years can be illustrated by the Pinochet case. The first Court, which treated the Pinochet case in Britain, used exactly this argument, as we are to see below. When Pinochet was arrested on October 16 last year, it was the third time after the end of his rule in 1990 that he was in Britain. He was arrested while receiving medical treatment and the request came from the Fifth Central Magistrate's Court of the National Court of Madrid. The charge was alleged murder of Spanish citizens in Chile between September 11 1973 and December 31 1983. On October 22 a second warrant was issued for torture, murder, detention of hostages and conspiracy. The prosecutor argued that under the authority of Pinochet a series of punishable actions were committed with the purpose of eliminating thousands of nationals and foreign citizens who were suspected to be opposing the right wing dictatorship and thus supporting the former democratically elected leader Salvador Allende.

Shortly after Pinochet's arrest several other countries followed the lead of the Spanish prosecutor and sought extradition on behalf of those of their own citizens who had also suffered during the Pinochet-regime. However, the British extradition case had first to go through the British legal system. The Court which first dealt with the case was as indicated earlier, the High Court. It followed a traditional reasoning arguing that even though Pinochet was not when he was arrested, a sitting Head of State, he could be granted immunity if one refer to the Vienna Convention on Diplomatic Relations. One could simply consider him a member of a diplomatic mission. The High Court also argued that the British State Immunity Act of 1978 did not contain exceptions, which would remove immunity from diplomatic actors who had committed crimes like torture and kidnapping. The Court then ended up granting the General immunity. Because the ruling had significant international implications however, the High Court opened for appeal and the case was handed over to the House of Lords. On November 25 1998 the House handed down its first ruling *denying* Pinochet sovereign immunity. The Lords argued (three to two) that immunity could not be given for the crimes committed, primarily because such violations could not be considered 'part of a head of states ordinary functions'. With the already mentioned reservations[9] and on March 24 1999 a majority of six judges to one came to the conclusion that the proceedings could continue. This opinion was reconfirmed at the House of Lords second ruling in March 1999.

Denying Pinochet immunity as the Lords did in both of their rulings, not only tells us that the principle of sovereignty is under transformation but equally that international norms for how much international society will tolerate when it comes to gross human rights violations has changed. As legal advisor to Human Rights Watch, Reed Brody has put it in commenting on the Pinochet case: "Tyrants can no longer terrorize their own populations, secure in the knowledge that at worst they'll face a tranquil exile. The Pinochet precedent has opened new horizons for justice".[10]

The above-described tendency was confirmed with the charges against Slobodan Milosevic in May 1999 issued by Chief prosecutor Louise Arbour at the international Court at The Hague.[11] Milosevic was in fact the first *sitting* head of state ever to receive an indictment for crimes against humanity and other war crimes.

But if the principle of diplomatic immunity is under transformation why has it then traditionally been the doxa of international law and relations? In the following section we will take a brief look at the manner in which the idea of human rights has changed during the past centuries.

A Renaissance of Natural Law?

Professor Amato several years ago wrote an article with the provocative title: "Is international Law Really Law?"(Amato, 1985). The article rearticulates the old but ongoing question of whether law needs a sovereign power to function as true and effective law. If a sovereign, as positivist lawyers would have it, is needed to issue and enforce laws, international law cannot be law as we normally understand it (Austin, 1832/1954). However, the entire idea that there is a fundamental difference between horizontally organized international law and hierarchically structured domestic law is in itself a modern invention. The natural law doctrines of Stoicism and religious humanism of antiquity had a different view of things and saw law as divine and universal and as such elevated above the particular interests of any given ruler (Ishay, 1997: xv). The individual was regarded as having divine universal rights and was thus considered to be a subject of the law on exactly the same terms as the Emperor, feudal lords or religious institutions. It was not until the emergence of the European state system in the late Middle Ages that the fundamental distinction between law inside and outside the state border began to take hold and this dramatically changed the status of the individual in world society. The founding fathers of international law such as Grotius, Gentili and Suárez were attentive to this dilemma and thus based their writings on secular as well as divine sources (Mernon, 1991). Rulers had to act in accordance with both established state practice and universal moral principles. The individual was however gradually squeezed out as a legitimate subject of the law and in the in the 18th and in particular the 19th century, the natural law elements of international law was replaced by positive law based on treaties and state practice (Kratochwil, 1995:23; Wind, 1998). This implied that for an international rule to function as valid law, it had to be explicitly consented to by the treaty making powers.

The invention of the principle of sovereignty after the end of the Thirty Years War in 1648 moreover implied that rulers were excluded from interfering in the domestic affairs of other legally recognized sovereigns. Religious strife could no longer be a legitimate reason for taking up arms. This turn had severe consequences for the individual however. The establishment of an orderly international system based on sovereignty and non-intervention simultaneously deprived the individual from the protection it had under the natural law doctrines (but see Wheeler, 1992:463-487; Brown, 1997: 469-482; Brems Knudsen, 1999; Finnemore, 1996).[12] Among the most hard-nosed positivists sovereignty thus came to imply that the head of state had exclusive rights over its own territory and people. Sovereignty in turn constituted the independent and ultimate power that recognizes no other law or morals above it Austin, 1832/1954; Kratochwil, 1997; Nardin, 1983). This does not exclude the existence of positive international law because positive international law is exactly what the sovereigns have consented to. No more and no less.

From the general acknowledgment of the sovereignty principle in international society followed then the just as commonly accepted idea that the sovereign alone is responsible for the well being of his own nationals. Until the Universal Declaration of Human Rights in 1948 and maybe even until today, this has been the doxa of international politics. One of the great advantages of the non-intervention principle has clearly been that Europe, over the past hundred years has managed to avoid being swallowed by one single power, which then dominated the continent. Despite the fact that the constant balancing and rivalry among the great powers often had serious consequences for smaller states, the principle of non-interference has most often been interpreted as a fundamental prerequisite for a diversified and prosperous European peninsula.

This diversity is, as we saw above, also celebrated in the UN Charter but exactly here we obviously face a paradox. The hailing of sovereignty as an almost sacred principle very often happened at the expense of ethnic minorities and other exposed groups with territorial borders. International law has simply not developed sufficient remedies to assist minorities assaulted by their own governments. The dissolution of Yugoslavia is a frightening example of this and the Kosovo crisis is also a good example of how powerless the international Community is when it comes to reacting against leaders responsible for the most gross human rights abuses within their own territorial borders.

If we follow international law strictly, the use of military power against another state can only be used on two occasions – in self defense and if international peace and security is threatened.[13] To this comes of course that any armed intervention to protect a civilian population should be backed by a Security Council Resolution. None of these requirements were met when NATO decided to intervene in Kosovo in the spring of 1999 to stop the Serbian atrocities against the Kosovo-Albanians. Due to opposition by Russia and China, the UN Security Council was unable to support the operation. Had it been for international law as we know it today in other words, Milosevic would probably long ago successfully have completed his ethnic cleansing mission in Kosovo. Intervening militarily in other states' affairs is thus a fundamental break with long acknowledged international law doctrines, in particular of course when this is without a UN Security Council Resolution. The question is nevertheless whether such a conservative interpretation of international law constitutes the spirit of tomorrow? James Rosenau is in no doubt. We have to accept that also international law doctrines may change and that new norms can transform the way we think about world affairs:

> ...Irrespective of the prevailing legal order, the odds are against international law's retaining its viability with respect to the prerogatives of statehood...the dictates of the law provide no more than an intermittent pause in political relationships. The present pause has lasted some hundred years, but that is not to say that it is beyond being undermined. All the

indicators point to the contrary. They all suggest that the legal status of sovereign rights is bound to be subverted by the transformative dynamics currently at work in world politics

(Rosenau, 1995: 221).

Legal Globalization and the Victory of Liberalism?

Why is it then that the Western powers could not let the atrocities in Kosovo happen when they have been doing exactly this in so many other international crises where leaders have assaulted their own people or perhaps even committed genocide? We clearly have to look at some deeper transformative trends in international society to find an answer to this question.

Even though observers might agree that things have changed the past 10 years, it would obviously be overly optimistic to assume that all those states who until recently have shown very bad human rights records, suddenly should have changed their mind and started to take these more seriously. Still, despite the continuous flow of rapports about abuse, torture and other degrading treatment, several indications show a changing mentality both when it comes to human rights but equally when it comes to letting international norms play a more decisive role in domestic affairs. As James Rosenau makes this general observation:

...this appears to be exactly what has occurred in this turbulent post-cold war era. Calls for supervised elections, for international peacekeeping forces, and for IMF involvement seem to have acquired increasing degrees of legitimacy. Put differently, it is no accident that supervised elections, UN peacekeeping efforts, and IMF-induced adjustments tend to occur in rapid-fire succession. Each such event is part of an aggregative international process that undermines traditional interstate norms and sets precedents for future interventions

(Rosenau, 1995: 218).

It thus seems that after the end of the Cold War and the defeat of Communism, common values have increasingly come to dominate over particularistic ideas and norms – also when we look at the Third World (Barnett, 1995). Examples of this go from the European Unions pressure on the Central and Eastern European applicant states to meet the standards of the European Human Rights Convention when it comes to the protection of their own ethnic minorities, to the lessening economic support for Third World dictators. Demands for democratic reforms are these years more often than not linked to donations when Western ministries and agencies line up projects in the Third World (Barnett, 1995). Even though human rights violations certainly has not been eliminated and reports of offences even has increased in number, it is equally obvious that there also has been a dramatically raising interest, in particular among NGO's, to inform about these atrocities. Where critical studies of human rights violations in the 1960s and 1970s by many nations were considered unacceptable interference in domestic affairs, such investigations has now been accepted as 'standard practice'. This in particular as more and more states actually ratify the most basic international human rights conventions (Lyons and Mastanduno, 1995: 10). As the British Magazine 'The Economist' put it in its special Human Rights Survey in December 1998:

> For any western politician visiting China, raising the question of human rights with Chinese leaders has become a necessary ritual, rather like the obligatory state banquet or visit to the Beijing opera.
>
> (The Economist, December 5th 1998).

It was as noted earlier also human rights concerns that made otherwise reluctant Western governments get involved in risky humanitarian interventions in Somalia, Rwanda, Iraq, Bosnia and Kosovo. These interventions have certainly not all been successful but here again we need to recall that what matters when analyzing normative change is not primarily the success-rate but rather how the individual interventions were motivated. To the extent that humanitarian concerns superseded great power or national interests one can talk about a strengthened position of the individual and of solidarist sentiments in international society. Studies of the past 10 years humanitarian interventions actually demonstrate that humanitarian concerns have dominated over power political interests (Brems Knudsen, 1995: 21). Francis Fukuyama would no doubt interpret this as yet another sign that liberal values have prevailed after the fall of Communism (Fukuyama, 1993). More reflectivist scholars in international relations would probably be more modest and simply say that what this tells us is that norms *do* matter in international affairs and that these can change and gain increasing weight over time (Finnemore, 1996: 153-186; Risse-Kappen, 1995: 491-517).

The increased focus on human rights in recent years is however not the only example of the strengthening of international norms in international relations. We see the same tendency in our own part of the world where the past 45 years of integration in Europe has resulted in the development of a unique international legal system. In the EU legal order, which over the years has transformed Community law from traditional international treaty-law to resemble more and more that of constitutional law, the individual plays a very central role as well. Even though the European Community officially (still) is based on an international treaty, the European Court of Justice already in 1962 and 1963[14] in two of its most crucial rulings, announced that not only member states but also individual citizens can be legitimate subjects of Community law (Wind, 1998). This radical interpretation has made it possible for individual citizens to take their own governments to court if for instance a certain Community regulation has not been implemented or is implemented incorrectly in the national legal order (Rasmussen, 1986; Burley and Mattli, 1993). When the national governments slowly realized that their own citizens in fact could prosecute them for breaking Community law, they obviously protested loudly (Stein, 1981). The member states saw themselves as the only true subjects of Community law, which they insisted on regarding as traditional international law (Schilling, 1996; Weiler and Haltern, 1996). The ECJ did not change its mind however and instead insisted that legal certainty, predictability and fair competition for the individual European citizen in the internal market was far more important than favoring often projectionist national governments. At the same time, even though the governments were highly frustrated about this development they could not agree on how to change the treaties to curb the ECJ's power (de Witte, 1996). Since the ECJ even encouraged citizens and business-enterprises to use their national courts and the EU system to monitor efficient Community law implementation in their respective member states, individuals have in fact been among the prime motors of integration in Europe (Burley and Mattli, 1993; Weiler, 1994, 1997; Wind, 1998). When looking at the European integration process in this manner, it seems that some greater forces are at play. This is not just a unique European phenomena but should rather be interpreted as a sign of some broader global development where national and international courts more and more often cooperate and where individual citizens are gaining ground as legitimate subjects of a globalizing legal system.

A New World Order?

After the end of the Golf War the American President George Bush proclaimed the arrival of a 'New World Order'. The end of the Cold War had, as Bush argued, opened the possibility for the development of a unique security Community among nations across the former East-West divide. In the American journal Foreign Affairs recently, Harvard Professor and international lawyer Anne-Marie Slaughter corrects this vision arguing that the '*Real* New World Order' is not to be found in the security field but in the legal field (Slaughter, 1997). Slaughter's point is that courts and judges within the past 10-15 years have intensified their cross-border communication and even started to duplicate each other's verdicts (Slaughter, 1994; 1997). This phenomena was obvious in the Pinochet-ruling where the judges referred to resembling court cases in other countries to make their point, apart of course, from national and international law. These observations are not meant to imply that national courts have not always kept an eye on dispute resolution in other legal systems when drawing up their own judgements. However, the nation building process in Europe in the 18th and 19th century, turned courts and judges into keen cultivators of their own national distinctiveness. Judges were thus eager to differentiate themselves both from their Roman law heritage and from international law and the law of other nations (Kelly, 1992: 302; Wind, 1998: 186ff). Domestic law and constitution should appear unique and by drawing on national sources alone (or copying other states' judgements in secret) courts and judges could contribute to creating the myth of the nation as founded on a distinct organic essence (Kelly, 1992). The fact that judges and courts in different countries in recent years have started to duplicate and publicly refer to each other's rulings thus constitutes a new and important feature in world affairs. If this tendency of 'juridical cross-fertilization' as Joseph Weiler has called it, continues, we might just experience the emergence of more and more common standards in fields as diverse as human rights, business and constitutional law.

This tendency is perhaps most out-spoken in the European Community where the whole structure and function of Community law is based on the willingness of national courts to copy each other and the ECJ produced case law.

It is normally said that international law does not have a doctrine of precedent and that one case is not "binding upon subsequent cases"(Armstrong, 1999: 533). This is however not a correct interpretation when looking at the EU where previous juridical decisions have enormous importance for the outcome of subsequent legal cases. In case of doubt as how to interpret a Community regulation a national court will always either look to former decisions or practices by other European courts or simply put a question to the ECJ. It is however important to notice that this all is based on the willingness of the national courts themselves to play the game. The authority and legitimacy of the legal regime in Europe is in other words based on the outstanding and in many ways highly peculiar loyalty of the national courts towards a supranational legal system.[15] I am grateful for comments to this chapter by the participants at the CISS/ISA Conference in Paris August 9-10 1999. I am particularly indebted to Peter Viggo Jakobsen and Elin Skaar for substantial and very helpful criticisms of earlier drafts of this paper. One of the puzzling things about the European integration process, which no scholar has been able to explain satisfactory until today, is in fact why lower national courts over the past 45 years have been more willing to obey an international court like the ECJ, than their own higher courts and governments (Weiler, 1994; Slaughter, Sweet, Weiler, 1997; Wind and Weiler, forthcoming).

If we go from the regional to the global level similar tendencies can be found. What is most evident here is the post-cold war rise in number of constitutional courts. Juridical review is thus no longer a purely North American or – as in recent years - Western European phenomena. Since the Second World War countries as diverse as Japan, Turkey, India, South Africa and several Western European as well as Latin American countries have introduced constitutional review in some form. The same goes for several former communist states like Poland, Hungary, Russia, the Czech Republic and others. In all these countries constitutional courts have been given the power to overrule parliamentary legislation as well as administrative regulations if they were perceived to have contradicted basic constitutional norms (Shapiro and Stone, 1994: 397). One can only interpret this as an experienced need to check the executive and legislative branches of government and thereby to reemphasize the classical division of power between the executive, legislative and the juridical domains. It thus also represents a broader global trend towards a juridicalization of politics (Shapiro, 1994; Vallinder, 1994). If this indeed is the case one may of course have to raise the question of whether the incentive to solve political disputes juridically will contribute to an intensified protection of basic rights worldwide.

The remaining issue is now how the enhanced role for the individual in international law and the increasing international surveillance of human rights violations we have experienced in recent years, may come to influence the principle of sovereignty in the longer run. To this comes perhaps a just as important and until now discarded question, namely whether it at all is possible and reasonable to generalize about human rights and Western democratic values when many countries still have culturally founded reservations about such ideas? Do we at all have a right to insist on the superiority of these values and even enforce them militarily as in Kosovo?

'The Human Rights Culture'

In an article on the UN's new role in world affairs, the American scholar Michael Barnett explains how the UN Security Council in recent years has begun to regard civil wars as just as serious threats to international peace and security as traditional wars (Barnett, 1995: 79-97). Where the state border formerly represented the limit to how far international society could go when it came to involvement in wars and conflicts in the developing world, the new UN policy makes it legitimate to attempt to influence the warring parties and eventually to intervene militarily if no other option is available. Barnett describes this as a radical transformation as a change from a 'juridical' to an 'empirical' concept of sovereignty. There is moreover today a much greater tendency to try to influence internal democratic reform processes when international agencies are aiding in reconstructions after wars and natural disasters. It would however be a mistake to argue that everyone approves of these changes. What the skeptics fear is very simply that national self-determination will be undermined when international agencies and judges start speaking 'of the common good' and of how other cultures and societies should organize themselves. Parts of the critiques go even further and question whether human rights at all can be regarded as universal values elevated above cultural and other differences. Some have even argued that the Western emphasis on human rights represents 'cultural imperialism' (Huntington, 1996). Samuel Huntington holds that in many non-western cultures such as Asian, Islamic, Hindu, Buddhist etc., society and religion is much more important than individual rights. Huntington warns that it may backfire if the West attempts to push its own values too far in parts of the worlds where they simply do not 'fit':

> Western concepts differ fundamentally from those prevalent in other civilizations. Western ideas of individualism, liberalism, constitutionalism, human rights, equality, liberty, the rule of law, democracy, free markets, the separation of church and state, often have little resonance in Islamic, Confucian, Japanese, Hindu, Buddhist or Orthodox cultures.
>
> (Huntington, 1993:40).

The American philosopher Richard Rorty has partly followed up on this point by emphasizing that human rights should not be regarded as universal in the natural law sense of the term, but rather as part of a Western 'human rights culture' (Rorty, 1993). This does not make them less legitimate or less important to fight for, but they should not, Rorty says, be presented and hailed as if they were divine and entirely independent of any historical and cultural context. A third scholar Michael Walzer, has suggested that even though one cannot establish 'a thick moral code' of rights which is applicable universally, it should still be possible to establish 'a thin one' containing minimal prohibitions against genocide, torture and ethnic cleansing (Walzer, 1994; Rengger, 1999). Considering that the majority of the world's nations in fact have signed the Universal Declaration of Human Rights, this is perhaps what one might hope for. However, the fact that a right is generally accepted obviously does not make it universal in a philosophical sense. But as the British Scholar Chris Brown has noted:

> ...it may not be possible to produce a philosophically watertight defense of rights, but most people are not philosophers, and it is on the strength of the popular support for universal human rights that the idea will flourish or die in the next century

> (Brown, 1998: 481).

Notes

[1] I am grateful for comments to this chapter by the participants at the CISS/ISA Conference in Paris, August 9-10, 1999. I am particularly indebted to Peter Viggo Jakobsen and Elin Skaar for substantial and very helpful criticisms of earlier drafts of this paper.

[2] Extradition represents a formal request by a state to hand over a person to the jurisdiction of another state to prosecute that person for a criminal offence. Both international and domestic law is codifying the more formal procedures and the offence committed should be punishable with imprisonment of at least 12 months. Augusto Pinochet replaced the democratically elected President Allende of Chile by a coup d'etat on 11 September 1973. On June 26 he announced himself as head of State, a post that he maintained until March 11 1990. In resigning the Pinochet-rule awarded itself immunity for acts carried out during their 17-year rule and Augusto Pinochet was granted the title of Senator for life.

[3] This is not entirely true of course. Some observers have suggested that NATO needed the war to prove its potential as more than just a defense alliance after the Cold War. See for instance Robert McCalla 1996; Stephen Walt 1997.

[4] The Kurds escaped into the mountains in Northern Iraq where those who had not been massacred by Saddam's forces suffered from starvation and cold.

[5] UNCharter Preamble and Chapter 1, Art. 1 (3). See also http://www.un.org/aboutun/charter

[6] These were set up after the civil war in Rwanda and as a consequence of the bloody wars that led to the break up of Yugoslavia.

[7] It was moreover held that only the charges of torture brought by the Spanish prosecutor met the criteria of an extradition crime under UK law. Several critics have found this latest more restrictive ruling hypercritical, arguing that Britain has signed tons of international conventions forbidding torture, murder and degrading treatment and needed not rely on any particular convention to extradite Pinochet. International law would under all circumstances have required the British government either to extradite or prosecute him, the critiques argued. One could perhaps have interpreted the State Immunity Act pragmatically as the two dissenters in the first Lords panel did, but this would counter the line otherwise struck out by the British government. Britain thus adheres to several treaties and international customary laws that mandate a very restrictive reading of the Immunity act. These include the Genocide Convention and the statues establishing the various international Tribunals, including the new International Criminal Court decided last summer in Rome.

[8] See also United Nations Convention on the Prevention and Punishment of the Crime of Genocide (1951) Art. IV.

[9] The first ruling by the House of Lords was declared void due to one of the judges, Lord Hoffmann's, close relations to Amnesty International. Amnesty was itself highly active in the attempt to get Pinochet extradited. A new panel then had to reconsider the case.

[10] Reed Brody on February 1999: http//:www.hrw.org/hrw/press/1999/feb/pin0204.htm

[11] Milosevic's arrest warrant was issued on May 27th 1999.

[12] Several studies have however demonstrated that humanitarian intervention – of some kind at least – has been a relatively common feature in world affairs for centuries. We are here speaking of for instance Christian powers intervening to protect Christian minorities who have been victims of assault in non-Christian cultures or societies. See Finnemore 1996; Brems Knudsen 1999.

[13] Chapter 7 in the UN Charter opens the possibility for the use of force if there is a threat to international peace and security.

[14] Normally referred to as Van Gend and Costa. Case 26/62, Van Gend en Loos v. Nederlandse Administratie der Belastingen, 1963 ECR: 12. Case 6/64, Costa v. ENEL. 15 July 1964. ECR: 585.

[15] In particular the lower courts. The High Courts in the member states have been much more reluctant to go along and accept the supremacy of Community law over national law. See Schilling 1996; Slaughter, Sweet and Weiler 1997; Weiler and Wind forthcoming.

References

Amato, A. (1985), 'Is International Law Really 'Law'?', *Northwestern University Law Review*, vol. 79: 1293-314.

Armstrong, D. (1999), 'Law, Justice and the Idea of a World Society', *International Affairs*, vol. 75/3:547-563.

Austin, J. (1832/1954), *The Province of Jurisprudence Determined*, London: Weidenfield & Nicolson.

Barnett, M. (1995), 'The New United Nations Politics of Peace: From Juridical Sovereignty to Empirical Sovereignty', *Global Governance*, (1): 79-97.

Brems Knudsen, T. (1995),' Sovereignty under Pressure: Humanitarian Intervention in the Post-Cold War Order', Paper presented at the Annual Conference of International Studies Association, Chicago, February. 1995. Revised version.

Brems Knudsen, T. (1996), 'Humanitarian Intervention Revisited: Post-Cold War Responses to Classical Problems', *International Peacekeeping*, vol. ¾: 146-165.

Brems Knudsen, T. (1999), *Humanitarian Intervention and International Society: Contemporary Manifestations of an Explosive Doctrine*, PhD-thesis, University of Aarhus 1999.

Brown, C. (1998), 'Human Rights', in J. Baylis and S.Smith (eds.), *The Globalization of World Politics*, Oxford: Oxford University Press, pp. 469-482.

Burley, A.M. and W. Mattli (1993), 'Europe Before the Court: A Political Theory of Legal Integration', *International Organization*, vol. 47/1: 41-76.

Chinkin, C. (1999), LSE Magazine 1999, London: LSE.

de Witte, B. (1996), 'International Agreement or European Constitution?' in J.A. Winter, D. Curtin, A.E. Kellermann and B. de Witte (eds), *Reforming the Treaty on European Union*, Asser Institute: Kluwer Law International.

Finnemore, M. (1996), 'Constructing Norms for Humanitarian Intervention', in P.
    Katzenstein (eds), *The Culture of National Security: Norms and Identity in World
    Politics*, New York: Columbia University Press: 153-186.
Fukuyama, F. (1989), 'The End of History', *The National Interest*, 16: 5-18.
Fukuyama, F. (1992), *The End of History and the Last Man*, London: Hamish Hamilton.
Haltern, U. and J. Weiler, (1996), 'The Autonomy of the Community Legal Order – Through
    the Looking Glass', *Harvard International Law Journal*, vol. 37/2: 411-448.
Huntington, S. (1993), 'The Clash of Civilizations?' *Foreign Affairs*, Summer 1993, pp. 22-
    49.
Ishay, M. (1997), *The Human Rights Reader: Major Political essays, Speeches, and
    Documents from the Bible to the Present*, New York: Routledge.
Kelly, J.M. (1992), *A Short History of Western Legal Theory*, Oxford: Clarendon Press.
Krasner, S. (1995), 'Sovereignty and Intervention', in Lyons, G.M. and M. Mastanduno
    (eds), *Beyond Westphalia: State Sovereignty and International Intervention*,
    Baltimore and London: The Johns Hopkins University Press.
Kratochwil, F. (1995), 'Sovereignty as Dominum: Is there a Right of Humanitarian
    Intervention?' in Lyons, G.M. and M. Mastanduno (eds), *Beyond Westphalia:State
    Sovereignty and International Intervention*, Baltimore and London: The Johns
    Hopkins University Press.
Kratochwil, F. (1997), 'Sovereignty and All That', Paper given at a talk on IR Theory
    Towards a Paradigm Shift? Institute of Political Science, University of Aarhus, March
    5th 1997.
Linklater, A. (1999), 'The Evolving Spheres of International Justice', *International Affairs*,
    vol. 75/3: 473-483.
Lyons, G.M. and M. Mastanduno (1995), 'Introduction: International Intervention, State
    Sovereignty, and the Future of International Society', in Lyons, G.M.
    and M. Mastanduno (eds), *Beyond Westphalia: State Sovereignty and International
    Intervention*, Baltimore and London: The Johns Hopkins University Press.
McCalla, R. (1996), 'NATO's Persistence after the Cold war', *International Organization*,
    50/3: 445-475.
Mernon, T. (1991), 'Common Rights of Mankind in Gentili, Grotius and Suarez', *American
    Journal of International Law*, vol. 85 pp.110-116.
Onuf, N. (1995), 'Intervention for the Common Good', in Lyons, G.M. and M. Mastanduno
    (eds), *Beyond Westphalia: State Sovereignty and International Intervention*, Baltimore
    and London: The Johns Hopkins University Press.
Rengger, N. (1999), 'Justice in the World Economy: Global or International, or Both?',
    International Affairs, vol. 75/3: 469-473.
Risse-Kappen, T. (1995),'Democratic Peace- Warlike Democracies? A Social Constructivist
    Interpretation of the Liberal Argument', *European Journal of International Relations*,
    vol. 1 (4), pp. 491-517.
Rorty, R. (1993), 'Human Rights, Rationality, and Sentimentality', in S. Shute and S.
    Hurley (eds), On Human Rights: The Oxford Amnesty Lectures, Basic Books: 111-
    135.
Rosenau, J. (1995), 'Sovereignty in a Turbulent World', in Lyons, G.M. and M. Mastanduno
    (eds), *Beyond Westphalia: State Sovereignty and International Intervention*, Baltimore
    and London: The Johns Hopkins University Press.
Schilling, T. (1996), 'The Autonomy of the Community Legal Order: An Analysis of
    Possible Foundations', *Harvard International Law Journal*, vol. 37/2: 389-409.
Shapiro, M. and A. Stone (1994), 'The New Constitutional Politics of Europe', *Comparative
    Political Studies*, vol. 26/4: 397-40.

Slaughter, A.M. (1994), 'A Typology of Transjuridical Communication', *University Of Richmond Law Review*, vol. 29 (1): 99-137.

Slaughter, A.M. (1997), 'The Real New World Order', *Foreign Affairs*, vol. 76 (5): 183-197.

Slaughter, A.M., A.S. Sweet and J. Weiler, (1997), 'The European Courts and National Courts: Doctrine and Jurisprudence, Oxford: Hart Publishing.

Vallinder, T. (1994), 'The Juridicalization of Politics – A Worldwide Phenomenon', *International Political Science Review*, vol. 15 (2): 91-99.

Walt, S. (1997), 'Why Alliances Endure or Collapse', *Survival*, vol. 39/1: 156-179.

Walzer, M. (1994), *Thick and Thin: Moral Argument at Home and Abroad*. Notre Dame: University of Notre Dame Press.

Weiler, J. (1994), 'A Quiet Revolution: The European Court of Justice and its Interlocutors, *Comparative Political Studies*, vol. 26 (4): 510-534.

Weiler, J. and M. Wind (eds) (2000), *When High Court's Clash Rethinking Constitutionalism in the European Union*, Cambridge: Cambridge University Press, forthcoming.

Weller, M. (1999), 'On the Hazards of Foreign Travel for Dictators and other International Criminals', *International Affairs*, vol. 75/3:599-619.

Wheeler, N.J. (1992), 'Pluralist or Solidarist Conceptions of International Society: Bull and Vincent   on Humanitarian Intervention', *Millennium: Journal of International Studies*, vol. 21/3:463-487.

Wheeler, N.J. (1998), 'Humanitarian Intervention and World Politics', in J. Baylis and S. Smith (eds), *The Globalization of World Politics*, Oxford: Oxford University Press, pp. 391-408.

Wind, M. (1998), *IR. Theory Meets European Union Law: Constitutional Battles, Sovereign Choices and Institutional Contingencies in the Legacy of the European Integration Process*. Ph.D.-thesis, European University Institute, Florence. Forthcoming London Macmillan 2000.

Wind, M. (1998), "A Survey of Human-Rights Law", in *The Economist*, Dec. 5th – 11th.

15 Children's Rights as Human Rights: A Case Study of India

REKHA DATTA

"I believe we should claim certain Rights for children and labour for their universal recognition." (Jebb, 1923).[1]

Millions of children in the developed as well as the developing world are forced to work in factories and mines and deprived of their childhood experiences and basic school education. Many of these child workers are bonded for life, are tortured by their employers, and often have to work as long as twelve to fourteen hours a day. Does such treatment of children constitute a violation of human rights? If they do, how do states and international agencies address the issue of children's rights violations? Focusing on India where child labor is a deeply entrenched social and economic problem, this study will examine the following issues:

- Does child labor constitute a violation of human rights?
- What is unique about child labor in India form the human rights perspective?
- How has the government of India addressed the issue of children's rights violations and child labor?
- Does Legislation Work? A Look at some industries using child labor.
- The role of International Agencies and NGOs in addressing child labor.
- Analysis and Assessment. The Limits of Legislation and relevance of an integrated approach.

Does Child Labor Constitute a Violation of Human Rights?

A child's right to adequate schooling and the need to address child labor have been recognized in Europe since the 19th century. This, compounded by the suffering of the children in the First World War prompted the League of Nations to initiate an international agreement to protect the rights of the child. After the Second World War, this awareness increased. (Young, 1996). Subsequently, attempts toward establishing some international standard to uphold the rights of children began in 1959 when the UN General Assembly adopted the Declaration of the Rights of the Child. Even though this declaration upheld the interests of the child, because it was not a treaty, its principles, however commendable, were not binding.

In 1979, also declared the year of the Child, the UN Commission on Human Rights set up a working group to examine the question of a Convention on the Rights of the Child. On November 20, 1989, the General Assembly adopted the Declaration. The following year, the Convention of the Rights of the Child (CRC) entered into force as international law after the necessary 20 states ratified it. To date, all member states, with the exception of the United States (signed only, has not ratified it) and Somalia (neither signed nor ratified it) have ratified the CRC.

The CRC has revolutionized the way states look at children. It is the first comprehensive document that includes children's rights in civil, political, economic, social and cultural areas. According to Article 27 of the 1989 United Nations CRC, signatory states recognize the right of every child to a standard of living adequate for the child's physical, mental, spiritual, moral and social development.

While this article does not specifically refer to child labor, it lays the foundation for establishing fair standards and conditions under which children can work. Subsequent articles, however, emphasize the nature of acceptable children's employment and working conditions. For example, Article 32 of the CRC provides that:

1. States Parties recognize the right of the child to be protected from economic exploitation and from performing any work that is likely to be hazardous or to interfere with the child's education, or to the child's health or physical, mental, spiritual, moral or social development.
2. States Parties shall take legislative, administrative, social and educational measures to ensure the implementation of the present article. To this end, and having regard to the relevant provisions of other international instruments, States Parties shall in particular:
- Provide for a minimum age or minimum ages for admission to employment;

- Provide for appropriate regulation of the hours and conditions of employment;
- Provide for appropriate penalties or other sanctions to ensure the effective enforcement of the present article.

Recognizing that the core of the problem behind child labor, the CRC also talks about the right to education for children. Article 28 states:

1. States Parties recognize the right of the child to education, and with a view to achieving this right progressively and on the basis of equal opportunity, they shall, in particular:

- make primary education compulsory and available free to all;
- encourage the development of different forms of secondary education, make them available and accessible to every child, and take appropriate measures such as the introduction of free education and offering financial assistance in case of need;
- make higher education accessible to all on the basis of capacity by every appropriate means;
- make educational and vocational information and guidance available and accessible to all children;
- take measures to encourage regular attendance at schools and the reduction of dropout rates.[2]

Although these provisions are quite broad and general, they provide for the foundations of the recognition of children's rights in the area of work and schooling. When these provisions are considered together with the instruments provided by the International Labor Organization, the directives and standards of hiring children become clearer.

For instance, Article 1 of the ILO Convention No.138 of 1973 concerning minimum age for admission to employment encourages states to ensure "the effective abolition of child labor and to raise progressively the minimum age for admission to employment or work to a level consistent with the fullest physical and mental development of young persons." (ILO, 1973). This convention also sets a minimum age for employment to be not less than the age of compulsory schooling, and in any case, not less than 15 years. According to the CRC, children below the age of 18 are not to be employed, in hazardous work.

Based on the Declaration of the Rights of the Child, and ILO Convention 138, which are discussed above, there emerges three areas that together could be construed to constitute a violation of human rights. First, the age and wage structures need to be examined. At what age can children be employed in factories and other industries and do they get **fair wages** and adequate working conditions? Secondly, are they subject to serious **health hazards** which impair their healthy living even in their adulthood? And finally, are they deprived of a **basic school education?**

Therefore, it is our contention that states that have signed the CRC are under obligation of that convention to eradicate child labor. The ensuing will examine whether the government of India has responded to the stipulations under the CRC to eliminate child labor based on the criteria listed above.

What is Unique About Child Labor in India From the Human Rights Perspective?

Apprenticeship has played a key role in many societies. The argument is that children learn valuable work skills through apprenticeship. This perspective, though overlooks the dangerous implications of using children as apprentices. "Learning by doing is a sound educational principle, but its economic and moral implications must not be ignored; unless procedures are carefully monitored, the free child labor creates adult unemployment, keeps adult wage levels under restraint, and encourages employers to increase the work load without having to worry about the cost of overtime" (Sawyer, 1988, p.139).

This economic argument aside, the phenomenon of child labor in India is not restricted to apprenticeship alone. While the economic argument is valid in that children seek employment as added sources of income for their families, it is the nature of their relationship with their employers that violates human rights very directly. This relationship is based on "bonded" or "mortagaged" labor. Children are used as slaves of their employers. Usually families and parents who are unable to post assets as security against loans from individual money lenders in rural areas pledge the labor of their children as security. Unable to pay up the loans in time or as guarantee they send their children to work for them. The "service" that was originally pledged often increase with time and it is not unusual for children to remain bonded for life. This increase of service time may result due to arbitrary decision of the employers if the children have been slow or slacked in their work. The employers decide to cut their pay and increase their service time as they see fit. There is no monitoring institution or system in place. It is purely based on arbitrary decisions of the moneylenders. The parents who "loan" their children to this system have no say in the matter other than not borrowing the money at all, which is often not an option because of dire financial necessity.

Bonded labor is widely used in a variety of industries and in the agriculture sector. According to a 1996 study by Human Rights Watch, despite the Bonded Labor (Abolition) Act of 1976 and other international laws prohibiting bonded labor, between 10 and 15 million children in India work as bonded labor. The children work in agriculture and cottage industries and small manufacturing. The manufacturing areas include hand-made cigarette (*beedi*) industry, silver manufacturing industry, diamond cutting, carpet weaving and in the manufacture of footwear. (*The small hands of slavery: bonded child labor in India*, 1996, Human Rights Watch/Asia.)

Another study related the story of "mortgaged child labor"(Mehta, 1996). At a meeting of the National Union of Working Women (NUWW) in Tamilnadu in South India, women *beedi* workers said that they are paid very low wages for rolling *beedis*. Usually they make about Rs. 4 (10 cents) a day after working for 10 to 12 hours. When they were asked how they manage on such low wages, their response was prompt and spontaneous, "We mortgage children." To explain how this works, one woman said, "I have mortgaged my seven-year-old girl and eight-year-old boy to a Sheth [local moneylender or businessman] three years ago for a loan of Rs.200 (Rs.100 for each child) [$50.00]. Two years later, my husband was mortgaged to the same Sheth for a loan of Rs.200. My two children and their father roll 4,000 *beedis* a day. They work all the time for the master. Their total wage should be at least Rs. 20 a day. However, the Seth pays them each Rs. 2.50 per day, out of which he deducts half the money every day. My husband also gets the same wage as the children. The Seth does not give them any food. They come home to eat. They work for him all the time … ." This story was corroborated by several other women who described the gruesome reality of the practice. They said, "All of us are forced to mortgage our children. What else can we do? When we mortgage other items to the Seth, we lose control over those items, like our utensils and jewellery. We don't have these any more. We have only children. When we mortgage them, we lose control over them, as we lose control over other items" (Cited in Mehta, 1996, pp.2-3. [ ] added.).

This and similar situations expressed by other women at that meeting underscored the fact that bonded labor or "mortgaged labor" is nothing but slavery. An elderly woman was very clear about this. "I took a loan of Rs.500[About $10.00] for the funeral of my husband some four years ago. He was a driver. He was killed in a road accident. In exchange I gave my 10-year-old boy, 17-year-old boy and 10-year-old girl. Since then they have been rolling beedies for the Sheth. They roll 4,000 beedies a day. Their daily wage should be at least Rs.20 a day. However, the three children together have been getting Rs. 12 a day... Our grand-children are also mortgaged. We are like bonded labour. We are slaves. We just give birth to children and then leave them to work for the moneylenders. We can ask no questions. We have to follow them, like slaves. Husband, children, grand-children all work in this way. All are slaves."(Quoted in Mehta, 1996, pp.3-4).

These children are also beaten severely and whipped by the moneylenders. When the children do not want to go to work out of fear, their families force them to go to work as they are afraid that the moneylenders will extract more from them or they may not get any more loans if they need it. It is clear that this is symptomatic of the absence of a larger network of credit or lending institutions. The children are 'pledged' orally by the parents and the moneylenders. There is no documentation of the loans that the people take, and when they ask for their children after the loans are paid up, the moneylenders demand the original principal of these poor families. Since the families do not have this kind of money, their children are held in a state of constant and vicious cycle making them bonded labor, sometimes for life! (Mehta, 1996, p.4).

Bonded child labor is also present in other industries. Among them it is prevalent in the carpet industry throughout South Asia, India included. While the process works very much like the *beedi* industry, the use of bonded labor in the carpet industry has risen alarmingly since the 1970s. It is interesting to note that it was in the 1970s that the Shah of Iran banned the use of children in the carpet industries in Iran. The demands for Oriental and Persian rugs is so great worldwide that the carpet manufacturers naturally focused on areas that were yet to ban using child labor in manufacturing carpets. South Asian countries proved to be a haven of manufacturers who tried to keep costs down by using child labor (*Economist*, 1996, p. 43).

How Has the Government of India Addressed the Issue of Children's Rights Violations and Child Labor?

While accurate data on child labor is difficult to obtain, between 13.6 million to 100 million children work in farms and factories in India. (Boyden and Myers, 1995, p.4). Several dimensions of child labor are pertinent in the case of India. They include bonded labor, where the families, unable to pay their debts and often pledge their children's labor in lieu of payment. As in the case of the *beedi* industry, these children become slaves of the moneylenders.[3] Other children are employed in farms and industries such as the carpet industry, brass industry, fireworks factories, etc. All these dimensions make the study of child labor in India relevant.

The Indian government has introduced a number of initiatives to combat and eliminate child labor. Governmental efforts fall into the two broad categories of legislation against the use of child labor and promotion of free compulsory primary education. The argument is that it is not enough to prevent the use of child labor. In a poor country like India where families are unable to send their children to school for economic reasons, it is imperative that the government provides for free and compulsory education. As we shall see in the ensuing, there are several laws that seek to eliminate child labor, but the government has yet to implement free and compulsory education throughout India.

The legacy of the British colonial rule is evident in the series of laws passed against the use of child labor in factories and industries. The 1881 Indian Factories Act, passed under the British Raj set the minimum age for employment at 7 years. Ten years later, the act was amended and the age was raised to 9 years. By 1922, the Act was amended to correspond to the ILO convention No.5 and it raised the minimum age to 15 years. The 1929 Whitley Commission report documented the use of child labor in various industries and plantations, initiating various endeavors by these industries and tea plantations to reduce the use of child labor (Sekar, 1997). Many critics argue that the context of these laws, which were generated by the British authorities, did not take into consideration the cultural and economic complexities in India, implying the need for indigenous laws (Boyden and Myers, 1995).

After India's political independence form Britain in 1947, the government passed several laws addressing child labor. The Minimum Wages Act was passed in 1948. According to this Act, children below the age of 14 could not work for more than 4 ½ hours a day with no provision for overtime. In 1949, the Constitution of India Act was adopted by the Constituent Assembly. It prohibited employment of children below fourteen years of age in factories, mines and hazardous employment. This was spelled out as a fundamental right. Hence, from the beginning of the free union, the state was cognizant of the need to respect and establish the basic freedoms of children (*Towards Eliminating Child Labour- A Report*: 1996, p.73). The 1952 Mines Act stipulated that children below the age of 15 years could not work in mines. Subsequently, the 1954 Factories Act required that children under the age of 17 years could not be employed between 10 p.m. and 7 a.m.

Guided by ILO Conventions, the Indian government abolished night work by children in 1950. In 1955, employment of children under 14 was prohibited, both in private and public industrial undertaking (*Towards Eliminating Child Labour - A Report*: 1996, p.74).

In reviewing the successive legislation and committees that the government has set up since 1947 to review the situation of child labor in the report mentioned above, there appears to be some contradictory conclusions that the committees have reported. For instance, the 1969 Report of the National Labour Commission recommended combination of work with education and flexible employment hours which would not inhibit education (p.74). While this may be a realistic assessment in a country where a lot of children work for financial reasons, it can have damaging consequences. Since compulsory education is only a directive of the constitution, the state can easily put it on the back burner. In the absence of compulsory education and the presence of extreme poverty, the flexibility to go to work and school usually will be meaningless, most children would opt to work as much as possible, for economic reasons.

This has been corroborated by many findings. Despite the passage of these and related laws, several committees set up by the National Commission of Labor between 1966 and 1986 observed that largely due to economic necessity children continued to be employed, ignoring previous laws and state directives. One such committee, the Gurupadaswamy Committee, recommended in 1979 that the state adopt a comprehensive, uniform law addressing issues of minimum age and wage, implementation of laws, etc. Based on these and other recommendations of similar committees, a voluntary agency, Concerned for Working Children (CWC) drafted a bill called the Child Labor (Employment) Regulation, Training, and Development Bill in 1985. The next year, this draft bill was passed in both houses of Parliament as the Child Labor (Prohibition and Regulation) Act of 1986. This law was comprehensive and prevented children below the age of 14 years from working in various factories and industries such as carpet weaving, cement manufacturing, cloth printing, manufacturing of matches, explosives, and fireworks, and other hazardous occupations.

India signed and ratified the CRC in 1992. To date, there are several laws in place in India which seek to prohibit the use of child labor. Yet, reports initiated by governmental agencies and non-government organizations alike present a grim picture citing the extent and nature of the use of child labor in several industries. In addition, as our discussion in the ensuing will show, there are practical difficulties associated with the implementation of child labor laws.

Does Legislation Work? A Look at Some Industries Using Child Labor

The Carpet Industry

In 1993, the Child Labor Cell of the National Labor Institute conducted a study to analyze the situation of the child workers in the carpet weaving industry in the state of Jammu and Kashmir. This study focused mainly on hiring practices of girl children in the carpet industry. One of the aims of the study was to highlight the exploitation that occurred in clear violation of the CRC and all standards of human rights (*Child Workers in the Carpet Weaving Industry in Jammu and Kashmir, 1993*, Child Labor Cell, National Labor Institute).

This study concludes that the carpet industry is a labor-intensive industry and entrepreneurs try to cut cost by hiring children. During the training period, which usually lasts for the first six months to a year, the children are not paid any wages. The rationale that the employers use is that the children are learning valuable skills, which would benefit them in the future. This report also concluded that in the two states of Jammu and Kashmir, the majority of the children worked for less than 4 hours or between 4 and 6 hours a day (*Child Workers in the Carpet Weaving Industry in Jammu and Kashmir*, 1993, Child Labor Cell, National Labor, p.6).

Apart from the fact that the children working in the carpet industry are paid very low wages without any recourse for the child workers, perhaps a worse form of human rights violation occurs in the area of health hazards. The children work for long hours in inadequately lit and poorly ventilated sites. They suffer from weakness of eyesight and breathing problems. The report concludes that "A continuous strain of work, conspicuous diseases and poor nutritional diet on account of general poverty, result in poor health and force carpet weavers to retire early from work -- during their middle ages itself-- and push their children to work at an early age to compensate for the loss of income caused by the elders' own retirement." (*Child Workers in the Carpet Weaving Industry in Jammu and Kashmir, 1993*, National Labor Institute, p.6). Thus the cycle of poverty continues and the basic human rights of childhood-- schooling and play, are denied to them.

The Beedi Industry

The working conditions that prevail in the *beedi* industry resemble what the Royal Commission of Labour had described in 1931. According to that description, "Many of these places are small airless boxes, often without windows, where workers are crowded so thickly on the ground that there is barely room to squeeze between them; others are dark semi-basements with damp mud floors...workers sit or squat on the floor throughout the working day"(quoted in "Child Pledging in Beedi Industry in North Arcot District" (1987) National Labor Institute, p.4). When children are subject to extended periods of time under these conditions, they develop emotional and physiological problems. In addition, the owners often beat the children, injuring them (Mehta, 1996, p.4).

The 1938 Child Labour (Abolition) Act had declared *beedi*-making to constitute hazardous employment. However, the law declares *beedi*-making in factories to be hazardous. The work that is done through middlemen and in "cottage industry" setting, usually in small rooms—do not strictly fall under the purview of the law. Thereby the stipulations of this legislation are easily violated without even jeopardizing the productivity (Child Pledging, 1987, p.7). Even if there is evidence of violation of the law, there is widespread corruption and secrecy that prevent the local authorities from reporting such instances. As a result, even though child pledging has been banned, practical resistance to implement the provisions of legislation has prevented the situation from alleviating ("Child Pledging in Beedi Industry in North Arcot District," (1987) National Labor Institute, p.8). With this and moving *beedi*-making to the unorganized sector, child labor in this industry will be even harder to eradicate.

The Fireworks Industry

The fireworks industry in Sivakasi in the southern state of Tamil Nadu also employs large numbers of children, sometimes very young. More than a decade ago, it was estimated that 45,000 children between the ages of 3 ½ and 15 were employed in the match industry. Children as young as 3 ½ years were picked up in buses very early in the morning and sent to work in match factories. There have been several reports of accidents and cases of children being roasted alive. Poverty is a major cause for the large concentration of child labor in such areas. There is also a complex mix of economic and social constraints that contribute to the perpetuation of the problem. The fireworks industry is owned by the Nader caste, which capitalizes the fact that the region is barren and drought prone. They prevent the spread of agriculture in the area so the people are forced to depend on the fireworks industry as a means of livelihood. Thus whereas child labor is common in farmlands where children help out in the farms, children in this region have no other alternatives other than working in the fireworks factories (Whitehead, 1986, p.19).

Working in a match industry is "hazardous." One researcher found that "Children were engaged in mixing, steaming chemicals in the boiler room; stamping frames of match splinters in trays of wet phosphorous and drying them on hot sheets of metal in a huge furnace; filling frames with sticks; placing and storing the frames in racks; filling match boxes; labeling match boxes; packing boxes into packages of dozens. Each stage of the process has its inherent hazards and nervous strain... Children mixing chemicals in the boiler room get lungfulls of toxic fumes, suffer high degrees of intense heat and run the risk of being badly injured in fire accidents" (Iyengar, 1983, pp.28-29).

A 1993 research conducted by the Child Labor Cell of the National Labor Institute in Noida, India systematically documented the human rights violations that occur in this area. (Sekar, 1993).This report is very striking as it was based on data collected by interviewing 115 girl child workers and their parents. In addition, 15 factory owners, 3 medical practitioners, 10 advocates, 9 village leaders, 12 teachers, and several government officials were also interviewed. As a result the study incorporated a thorough cross section of the people involved in the practice of using child labor in the match industry in the Sivakasi region.

The average income of girls in a match factory is about Rs. 38 per week (this is equivalent to less than a dollar). The age structure is piece rated-- i.e. the girls get a particular rate after doing a specific job. For instance, after filling 52 sticks in 52 scales of one frame, they get .55 p. (less than a penny).

When asked how they were treated at the factories, an overwhelming 86% of the girls reported harsh behavior, and only 3% said their employers were kind to them. 11% reported that employers were indifferent toward them. The report concluded that since the children were away from parental and other forms of protection, such treatment and working environment "is certain to adversely affect the psychological and emotional development of the children" (Sekar, 1993, p.20).

The Brassware Industry

Moradabad, north of New Delhi, is the home for the famous brasswares such as flower vases, ornate wall decorations, and other housewares. For many decades, the brassware industry was a cottage industry. As such it was family based and rarely sought hired help. With time, however, there developed an inernational market for the goods produced along with demand for items that required more sophisticated technology, such as tea services, planters etc.

In January 1992, a State Level Workshop on Situation of Working Children in Uttar Pradesh was held in Agra in Uttar Pradesh. This workshop was sponsored by the Ministry of Labour, Government of India, Department of Labour, Government of Uttar Pradesh, UNICEF, and the Child Labor Cell of the National Labor Institute. The summary report of the workshop describes how this growth necessitated the introduction of technology to increase production. At the initial phase, children were not hired in the larger factories. Children were not tall or strong enough to handle the machinery. Moreover, child labor was banned under the Factories Act and employers did not want to take the risk of being caught and prosecuted. These same factory owners, however, "would sub-contract the jobs of moulding, polishing, electroplating to workshops in which child labor was freely used and abused without attracting legal liability for doing so" ("Child Labour in the Brassware Industry," Unpublished Report, 1992, pp.1-5).

This summary also reports that out of 25,000 workers who polish the semi-finished goods, 12,000 are children. Children work with chemicals, acid, and emery powder to polish the wares. One fourth of those engaged in electroplating are children. They work with wires and substances such as ammonium chloride on a daily basis. 7,000 of 10,000 workers who do the welding are children. While the adults wear protective glasses, the children do not. In addition children inhale metal dust and often suffer from chest ailments, sometimes fatal (pp.10-11).

In evaluating the implications of legislation that could address the problem of using child labor in the brassware industry, the Report argues that clearly what is happening here would violate the Child Labour (Prohibition and Regulation) Act of 1986 which states that children are prohibited from working in hazardous jobs provided they are not working as part of family labor. In the brassware industry, the children are not hired in big factories. Thus they are not appear to be part of the factories, they often work in the sub-agents, along with adults and may appear to be family labor. Hence, employers can argue that the 1986 Act does not apply to them (p.9).

Clearly then this demonstrates the need to have effective instruments that implement legislation. That is the purpose of the National Policy on Child Labour and National Child Labor Project (NCLP) of 1987. While the brassware industry is covered by this project, it is hardly effective. ("Child Labour in the Brassware Industry," 1992, Unpublished Report, pp.11-13; *Towards Elimination of Child Labour-* A Report, Background Papers, 1996, pp.66-77). When analyzing why it is not effective, it is not difficult to identify the loopholes of the project. For one, only 500 children are covered under this project. The numbers that we can derive from the summary report is well over 20,000 in Moradabad. Moreover, there has to be increased awareness among the people of the region that child labour is not an alternative. The economic benefits of hiring children at cheaper rates than adults would also have to be addressed.

The Pottery Industry

The use of child labor in the pottery industry resembles the work that child potters would do in the nineteenth-century England. It usually consists of child laborers carrying empty moulds to workers and then bringing the filled moulds to the sun to dry. According to one estimate in the town in the state of Uttar Pradesh a child worker makes "about one thousand trips, runs five kilometers a day with a ten-kilogram load." There were innumerable instances when children as young as 8 or 9 carried weights up to twenty kilograms, their bodies bent and frames trembling with the effort. (National Labor Institute, 1992, p.9). In addition to this, there is the hazard factor.

Child labor in the pottery industry is a fairly new phenomenon. Mass production demands necessitate the use of cheap labor. Likewise, the children who work fit the traditional profile of economic and social backward class. Unlike the profile which matches the traditional description, the argument that was used in the past child laborer acquires skills that they can use in later life hardly applies to the pottery industry. None of the work they do teaches them any skill, which they can use later (National Labor Institute, 1992, p.11).

The Lock Industry

The use of child labor in the lock industry is not widely known. A 1992 study conducted by the Child Labor Cell of the National Labor Institute in India found that 7 to 10,000 children are employed in the lock industry located in the town of Aligarh in the northern state of Uttar Pradesh (Burra, 1992).

This study found that out of 6936 workers, 2475 were children below the age of 14. Thus, 35.68 % of the workforce in the sample were children.

They work long hours and are primarily engaged in electroplating, polishing pieces on buffing machines, spray painting and working on hand presses. "The hand-presses become particularly dangerous because children are made to work very long hours, anything from 12-14 hours a day. Carelessness or lapse of concentration caused by exhaustion are the main causes of accidents and often children lose the tips of their fingers on the machines" (Burra, 1992, p.7). Polishing is also a very hazardous job. In the process, the child worker inhales emery powder and metal dust. In these units, children as young as 8 and 9 years work into the night. Finally, electroplating, in which 70% of the workers are children below the age of 14, involves work with chemicals such as potassium cyanide, trisodium phosphate, sodium silicate, hydrochloric acid, sulfuric acid, sodium hydroxide etc. Children use these solutions with bare hands for long hours (Burra, 1992, p.8). All of this pose severe health hazards such as lung cancer, tuberculosis, bronchitis, asthma etc.

The wage structure varies but the disparity in the wages of an adult and a child for the same work is clear. For example, in the polishing unit, for a 12-15 hours of work, an adult earns Rs.25 but a child earns Rs.15. Children do not receive any wages during the period of their apprenticeship days. Then they earn about Rs.50 a month for working 12-14 hours a day. With several years' experience this rises to about Rs.150 a month, but with no medical or other benefits (Burra, 1992, p.10).

The Role of International Agencies and NGOs in Addressing Child Labor

Interfacing with the government's Department of Women and Children UNICEF has has been involved in a variety of activities concerning the elimination of child labor. It has maintained regular working contacts with the Ministries/Departments of Education, Health, Rural Development, Urban Development, Welfare, and Information and Broadcasting. In 1983, it began working with the Ministry of Labor on the issue of child labor.

UNICEF has developed a multifaceted research and training program for the elimination of child labor. Its assistance has helped to establish the child labor cell within the National Labor Institute. The child labor cell has conducted valuable studies of child labor violations in various industries across several states. It has documented occurrence and incidence of child labor, thus facilitating action by the government and NGOs in the eradication of child labor. As this chapter has shown, especially in areas such as bonded labor and mortgaged labor, lack of documentation prevents families and children who are held hostage from seeking redress. Alongside, UNCIEF has provided financial and technical assistance for the training of factory and labor inspectors, government officials, and NGOs, for the organization of meetings and workshops, and for studies on street children in various cities and child labor in various occupations.

We have discussed the condition of children working in the fireworks industry in Sivakasi in Tamilnadu in South India. UNICEF joined the state government's **Child Labor Action Support Scheme (CLASS)** in North Arcot district, aimed at eliminating child labor in the *beedi* rolling industry, It provided technical inputs and funds for sensitization, education, and training, It also supported the district administration in developing an elimination strategy (Chanda and Datta, forthcoming).

As an integrated model, the UNICEF-Rugmark-SAACS coalition is an excellent enterprise to prevent the use of child labor in the carpet industry. Rugmark Foundation is a joint international initiative which began in 1992. It involves the UNICEF, the Indo-German Exporter Promotion Program, carpet manufacturers, and NGO'such as the South Asian Coalition on Child Servitude(SAACS). Rugmark has become a very effective mechanism to monitor, control, certify and label carpets that are made without using child labor. This was initiated because of efforts of NGOs such as South Asian Coalition on Child Servitude (SAACS) and threats from industrialized countries of sanctions on imports of goods made with child labor. Thus, UNICEF along with Rugmark, has helped to develop an inspection system to ensure that Indian carpets are child-labor-free. UNICEF is a board member of the Rugmark Foundation which supervises this system and it also manages the rehabilitation funds collected under this scheme (Kruijtbosch, 1995).

Other instruments that have been effective include the ILO established International Programme for Elimination of Child Labour in 1990. This is a partnership between ILO, Germany and Belgium. India was one of the first to join. IPEC seeks to abolish child labor in the long run. It also seeks to enhance the ILO constituents' capacity as well as that of NGOs to design, implement, and evaluate programs for the elimination of child labor. It also focuses on creating social awareness, which would create an environment in which there will be widespread effort to eliminate child labor (Towards Eliminating Child Labor: Report- Background Papers, 1996, p.70).

IPEC provides an effective integrated model of international and national cooperation. At the international level, representatives of the ILO, the donor nations, and participating countries form the Programme Steering Committee. At the national level, there is the National Steering Committee headed by the Labour Secretary. In addition, there is a National Programme

Coordinator who coordinates the work of the agencies receiving the assistance and the Ministry of Labour and the ILO. At the level in which action is taken it is very flexible. NGOs decide on local needs of strategies and actions that will best suit them. With close scrutiny from the National Labour Ministry and the ILO, the NGOs are under supervision too. Since 1992, 89 projects have so far been approved and are under different stages of implementation. Since 1995, the government of India has been making large allotments, thus eliminating the need for outside donations for these projects. These projects are engaged in a variety of activities seeking to eliminate child labor. Some are developing models for collecting statistics on child labor. Others are identifying the safety hazards of employment of children in industries. Above all, these organizations are seeking to intervene where child labor is occurring as well as sensitizing the local people as well as employers that child labor is not inevitable (*Towards Eliminating Child Labour*: Report, Background Papers, 1996, p.70 & 78).

Analysis and Assessment: Limits of Legislation and the Need for an Integrated Approach

This discussion has so far established that the Indian government has made several efforts toward achieving the three goals of minimum age/wage; eliminating hazardous conditions of children's work; and compulsory education. Yet, as the analysis of the reports from the carpet, fireworks, pottery, *beedi,* brassware, and lock industries presented here show, these principles are systematically violated in these and other industries. This raises the question of enforcing legislation. It seems that the government has not been able to implement and enforce the legislation adequately.

Quite obviously, the question that arises is why has the government not been effective and how the problem can be addressed. I argue that the problem arises because the issue of child labor is rooted in confusing rhetoric. While it is almost universally agreed upon that child labor is a social evil, responding to child labor is a very challenging task. Part of the problem is the puzzling nature of the phenomenon itself, especially in developing countries. Some analysts have rightly pointed out that the prevailing thinking is that children work for economic reasons (Grootaert and Kanbur, 1995, pp.187-203). Most poor families find it almost imperative that their children work. They do not have the economic capability to feed, clothe, and educate them. Moreover, they also find that they are dependent on their children's income. From such a standpoint, abolishing child labor may not be the answer. The answer to successfully combating child labor lies in deeper concerns and ramifications in the society and the economy, both domestic and international.

Most analysts and governments alike consider child labor an economic necessity in poor countries, thus ignoring the basic civil and social rights of children who are subjected to inhuman treatment and deprived of education, long established as a basic right for children in Europe and by the CRC. The UNICEF position in this regard is helpful in providing a clear perspective and focus to the issue. It argues " that child labour in reality violates many of the Articles of the CRC, both those related to civil and political rights and those related to economic, social, and cultural rights" (Young, 1996, p.3). According to this view, this indivisibility of rights is the core of the issue. Child laborers are denied these basic rights on a daily basis. This position thus prompts one "to seriously challenge the view that child labor is the inevitable result of poverty, illiteracy and parental need to use the child's labour for family survival. This mindset is not only inaccurate, it also generates paralysis and a feeling that little can be done to eliminate child labour" (Young, 1996, p.3).

Therefore, an integrated approach is needed to address the issue. This chapter has discussed the integrated model that the government, the ILO/UNICEF, and NGOs are implementing to some success. Essential in this approach is the need to complement compulsory primary education and legislation (Weiner, 1991). Especially in a poor country like India where a majority of the population is struggling to remain above the poverty line and where a large portion of the workforce is engaged in agriculture, engaging children in family farms and businesses seem the only feasible alternative to many. Instead of going to school, millions of children go to factories and farms every morning.

To be sure, making education compulsory has been suggested as a solution to ending child labor. People who use and benefit (economically) from using child labour will want to continue doing that. The government needs to be more forthright about about eliminating child labor (Weiner, 1996, pp.9-16). There are several recommendations made by researchers and analysts who have studied the impact of education in eradicating child labor. Among them are suggestions that the entire primary education system needs to be overhauled. As it currently stands, compulsory education is a Directive Principle of the Indian constitution, hence it is not enforceable in a court of law. While the government's efforts have addressed the issue, the efforts toward making education compulsory has still not been quite successful. People with vested interested have quite naturally resisted the pressures to make education compulsory. The Government has been reluctant in this area and has also used it as a rationale not to implement it because of the economic argument. That is, poor families may need to put their children work in order to survive economically (Charnaraj, 1996). This rationale, however, is faulty and will keep India's child laborers in the vicious circle of poverty, need to work, illiteracy, and more poverty.

It is therefore obvious that government initiative alone is neither adequate nor effective. Hence, to supplement them, international pressures, public awareness, and non-governmental organizations are attempting to ensure that employers and the public become aware of the cruel practice of using child labor to cut costs. There are many non-governmental organizations in India and abroad that collaborate to address the problem. Rugmark is one such NGO and its success notwithstanding, more cooperation between such organizations across nations is needed. According to a recent issue of the organization's Newsletter, "...Child labour is not usually found now on the looms registered with us but on others. We can do very little about these children on the other looms. Rugmark inspectors have no power or authority to ask the loom owners to open their doors for inspection. It is an all voluntary exercise by which consumers, importers, exporters, loom-owners and weavers join hands with Rugmark to eliminate child labour from the carpet industry. Each motivates the other down the line to cooperate with Rugmark. Therefore there is need for greater effort from NGOs in the developed countries to make consumers, including the importers, aware of their roles in the task of restoring childhood to child carpet weavers" (Sondhi, 1998, p.2).

The government has to standardize and stabilize wage structures. Such standardization will dissuade employers from hiring children. If wages are flexible, employers will tend to hire children at lower wages, thereby keeping the profit margin higher. If minimum wages are firmly determined and practiced, employers will tend to hire adults who can deliver more with the same wages. This analysis has shown that what is needed is a fundamental shift in the industrial and small business hiring process. There has be more institutionalized effort at all levels to maintain records and documents so that when agencies are inspecting sites, they have evidence and records which they can use to challenge and address any violation of legislation. This calls for more awareness of the legislation and the need for elimination of child labour, and perhaps the efforts such as NCLP and IPEC will address these more thoroughly.

Some analysts argue that structural adjustment programs have also had an impact on child labor. In the changing environment of globalization of the market, many developing countries are finding it almost imperative to engage in structural adjustment programs to compete as well as to qualify for various kinds of financial assistance from international lending agencies such as the World Bank and the IMF. As the recent protests in Seattle at the December 1999 meeting of the World Trade Organization have demonstrated, despite the economic benefits of globalization, we need to address the social costs. The case of the brassware industry has shown that in the quest toward generating more productivity, children are often employed. Costs are thereby kept down, and the returns are profitable. Structural adjustment programs can require governments to reallocate funds from social welfare and child labour elimination from such expenditures. Hence they benefit which can have a negative effect on efforts to curb child labor (Swaminathan and Ramachandran, 1993).

In addition to the above, making education compulsory will address the problem of keeping children in schools. But women can play an important role in making the decision to send children to school. If there is a choice between sending male or female children to school, male children inevitably get preference. Female literacy can go a long way in ensuring reproductive decision-making in which women can have say in deciding on the number of children the family is to have and who to send to school. Studies on women and literacy have shown that literacy is related to population control. For example, the state of Kerala in India has the highest literacy rate (90%). It also has the highest female literacy rate (65%). It has also completed the "demographic transition" to replacement level birth rate.(Weiner, 1991). The state has the lowest school dropout rate and high female enrolment rate (49% of total school enrolment in 1991). Although systematic research is needed to establish the link between school attendance and elimination of child labor, and there is evidence that children in Kerala still work in home-based production, "the achievement of universal education in Kerala seems at least to have prevented the worse forms of child labour found elsewhere in India" (Boyden and Myers, 1995, pp.9-10).

How did this happen? Kerala is a very good example of the relationship of gender to child labor. As we have seen, even though not the sole cause, poverty remains an important determinant of child labor. Over-population or the inability of families to feed their children is a related cause. In this situation, traditional notions of the need to educate male children as opposed to female children become a factor in reinstating child workers in schools. The vicious circle that India is in is simple to understand but difficult to confront. Given the traditional preference for the male child, they always get a priority when it comes to education. Unless women are educated and obtain a decisive role in family planning, families will continue to have children who they cannot feed or educate and hence send to work at tender ages to make ends meet. Hence, it is crucial to educate women so they can make these decisions. As research has shown, educating women is the foundation of family planning and population control. It is a crucial variable in eradicating child labor as well (Young, 1996, p.4).

In conclusion, this analysis has shown that international agencies, conventions, and national laws have established that children's rights are human rights. In particular, use of child labor does violate their rights to basic education, right to childhood recreation, and health. However, the challenge is to prevent the use of child labor in hazardous industries and in bonded slavery effectively. Like other premises of human rights, the implementation remains a problem. An integrated approach involving international law, state laws, NGO activism, public opinion, and instrument of international labor standards together might address the issue more effectively.

Notes

[1] Eglantyne Jebb, founder of Save the Children Fund, wrote this in 1923. Details about this can be obtained form the Internet site *http://www.savechildren.or.jp/alliance/crc-hist.htm*

[2] The text of the articles form the CRC are available in the following web site: *http://www.freethechildren.org/uncrcdoc.htm* pp.1-9.

[3] For a fuller description of the forms of child labor prevalent in India, see Rupa Chanda and Rekha Datta, Policies and Strategies of International Organizations in Combating Child labor in India: A Win-Win Analysis, in Stuart Nagel (ed.) (forthcoming) *Handbook of Global Economic Policy*, New York: Marcel Dekker.

References

Boyden Jo and William Myers (1995) "Exploring Alternative Approaches to Combating Child Labor: Case Studies from Developing Countries," *Innocenti Occasional Papers*, International Child Development Center, UNICEF, Florence, Italy, p.4.

Burra Neera (1992) *Child Labor in the Lock Industry of Aligarh*, Summary of Report prepared for UNICEF, published by the Child Labor Cell of the National Labor Institute, Noida, India.

Chanda, Rupa and Rekha Datta, 'Policies and Strategies of International Organizations in Combating Child labor in India: A Win-Win Analysis', in Stuart Nagel Ed. (Forthcoming) *Handbook of Global Economic Policy* , Marcel Dekker, New York.

Child Labour in the Brassware Industry: A Summary (1992) Unpublished; Charnaraj, K. (1996)"Chalking in Change", in *Humanscope*, July. Document available in the National Labour Institute, Noida, India.

Child Labour in the Brassware Industry: A Summary (1992) Unpublished; National Labor Institute, Noida, India.

Child Workers in the Carpet Weaving Industry in Jammu and Kashmir, 1993, Child Labor Cell, National Labor Institute, Noida, India. *The Economist*, September 21, 1996.

Grootaert, Christiaan and Ravi Kanbur, 'Child Labour: An Economic Perspective', *International Labour Review*, Vol.134, No.2, 1995, pp.187-203.

Human Rights Watch/Asia-Human Rights Watch Children's Rights Project (1996) *The small hands of slavery: bonded child labor in India,* New York: Human Rights Watch.

International Labour Rights Education Fund, 'Rugmark Label Gathers Support amidst Carpet Industry Violence', in *Workers' Rights News*, August 1995.

Iyengar, V.L.(1983) '"Pyre of Childhood:" Child Workers in the Match Factories of Sivakasi,' in K.D. Gangrade and J.A. Gathia ed. *Women and Child Workers in the Unorganized Sector*, Concept: New Delhi.

Jebb, Eglantyne (1923) *http://www.savechildren.or.jp/alliance/crc-hist.*

Kruijtbosch ,Martine (1995)*Rugmark: A Brief Resume of Concept to Reality for Visual Guarantee of Carptes Made Without Child Labor* New Delhi: SAACS.

Mehta, Prayag "Mortgaged Child Labour of Vellore: Women Beedi Workers' Tale of Woe," (1996) Unpublished article. Documentation Center, National Labor Institute, Noida, India.

National Labor Institute, *Working Children of the Pottery Industry of Khurja, U.P.* (1992) Child Labor Cell, National Labor Institute, Noida: India, p.9.

Sawyer, Roger (1988) *Children Enslaved*, New York: Routledge Press.

Sekar, Helen R. (1997) *Child Labour Legislation in India*, V.V. Giri National Labor Institute, Noida, India.

Sekar, Helen R. (1993) *No Light in their Lives: Girl Child Labor in the Match Industry in Sivakasi*, Research Report, Child Labor Cell, National Labor Institute, Noida, India.

Sondhi, Maj. Gen.(Retd). 1998 "Letter from Executive Director," *Rugmark Foundation, Special Newsletter*, Rugmark Foundation, India.

Swaminathan, M. and V.K. Ramachandran, (1993) 'Structural Adjustment Programs and Child Welfare', *Indira Gandhi Institute of Development Research*, August.

Towards Elimination of Child Labour (1996) National Labour Institue, Noida, India.

Weiner, Myron (1996) 'Child Labour in India, Putting Compulsory Primary Education on the Political Agenda', *Economic and Political Weekly*, Nov 9-16.

Weiner, Myron (1991) *The State and the Child in India*, Oxford University Press, New York.

Whitehead, Christine (1986) 'The Economics of Children at Work', *New Statesman*, 12 December, p.19.

Young, Richard H. (1996) 'Child Rights and Child Labour: Obligations Under the Convention on the Rights of the Child,' Paper Presented at the AIOE- FICCI-ILO Workshop in *Combating Child Labour: An Integrated Approach*, New Delhi, India, August, p.3.

16 From Poverty in Mexico to Poverty in the United States

ELAINE LEVINE

My paper will analyze how a large percentage of the Mexican origin Latino population in the US has made a transition from being poor in Mexico to being poor in the United States. Since 1994 it is the Latino population, and not Afro-Americans, as was previously the case, that has the highest poverty rate in the US. Mexicans and Puerto Ricans tend to be the most disadvantaged, but all of the groups that make up the Latino population showed some increase in their poverty rates during the first half of the 1990s. We will explain how the ongoing economic crisis in Mexico interacts with the changing conditions prevailing in the US labor market – in response to foreign competition and globalization– to channel a vast majority of the newly arriving Mexicans into low paying jobs that are generally rejected by most sectors of the US born population. The Mexican origin Latino population, confronts a highly segmented labor market, and a school system characterized by enormous inequalities between rich school districts and poor ones, as well as de facto segregation resulting from "white flight" to the suburbs and exurbs. Changes implemented in 1996 have eliminated access, by persons entering the US after 1997, to what was already a highly inadequate system of public assistance programs. Thus – given the combined effect of all of these adverse circumstances– it is even more difficult, for recent Mexican immigrants and their children to experience any significant upward socioeconomic mobility, than it was for other groups who arrived in the US prior to 1980.

Apparently globalization has made the world a smaller and more interconnected place. Many of the barriers Imposed by time and space have been overcome. Worldwide communications have become practically instantaneous. Goods and services can be delivered to almost point on the globe. People move from city to city, country to country, or continent to continent more frequently and rapidly than ever before. However this enhanced interconnectedness has strengthened old inequalities and even produced new ones. As Saskia Sassen points out, "the overall result of the transformation of the economic structure is a tendency toward increased economic polarization," which manifests itself in the structures of social reproduction, the organization of the labor process, and the spatial organization of the economy (Sassen, 1998, p. 159). The ways in which the US labor market is currently absorbing Mexican and other Latino workers clearly exemplify these manifestations of increasing inequalities within the framework of existing economic and social structures.

In spite of two very long periods of sustained economic growth since 1980, the socioeconomic situation of Latinos in the United States has declined with respect to the rest of the population. Their poverty rate has grown significantly and they constitute an increasing percentage of those in poverty. Most Latino men and women have much lower incomes than non-Hispanic whites and lower than Afro-Americans as well. While socioeconomic indicators for Afro-Americans have slowly improved over the last two decades those for Latinos have declined in relative terms. Furthermore each one of the national origin groups within the Latino population experienced a rising poverty rate during the first half of the nineties.

The simplest explanation for this decline is the large influx of Latino immigrants, especially Mexicans, since 1980. No doubt Latino's socioeconomic indicators reflect the recent arrival of growing numbers of poor and poorly educated immigrants. However the increased inequality in the overall distribution of income and a poverty rate persistently above the historical minimum attained in 1973, would seem to suggest that there are other factors contributing to the relative socioeconomic decline that Latinos have experienced recently.

The objective of this paper is to explore how far behind Latinos have fallen and to analyze the underlying causes of their situation. In spite of its significance, the immigration process by itself cannot sufficiently explain the highly adverse economic circumstances that so many Latinos experience in the US. Globalization and corporate restructuring have transformed the labor market to such an extent that less skilled workers have very little opportunity for improving their earnings. Well paying jobs that don't require high levels of education are extremely scarce. It is much harder now to achieve upward economic mobility than it was just a few decades ago.

Latinos increasingly find themselves relegated to the lowest paying and most undesirable occupations. The proliferation of low wage jobs and the growing stratification and segmentation of the labor market limit their access to better positions. Low educational attainment further restricts their occupational mobility. The cost of higher education in the US makes it inaccessible for most low-income families, thus creating a vicious circle that often limits socioeconomic advancement for second and third generations.

With the changes adopted in 1996, public assistance programs have become even more restrictive than before. Thus marginalized groups have little chance of improving their situation, which tends to perpetuate itself in spite of favorable macroeconomic performance. The socioeconomic status of the Latino population, especially those of Mexican origin, has declined with respect to the rest of the population. This is the result of two simultaneous and interacting tendencies, 1) adverse conditions in their countries of origin that have increased the migratory flow and 2) the consolidation, in the US, of more rigid and less permeable institutional structures in the labor market, the school systems and even government assistance programs.

There are currently about 29 million persons classified as "Hispanics" in the US, approximately 11% of the total population. It is often pointed out that this is the most rapidly growing minority and that by 2005 Latinos will outnumber African Americans. The experiences of the many different groups that make up the Latino population are colored as much by their time of arrival and place of residence as by their country of origin and their social class. However the enormous influx of Mexicans, along with people from many other parts of Latin America, in recent decades has added a special significance to the process. As Susanne Oboler points out "those born after 1970 represent the first generation born and raised in this country who have been specifically designated by mainstream institutions as Hispanics" (Oboler, 1995, p. xix). They live in an era when differences are more openly recognized but that does not necessarily mean that there is greater acceptance of and tolerance for these differences by all sectors of the national society.

In spite of the marked economic, political, social and cultural differences that exist among those classified as Hispanics, their designation as such is something they have in common. After living in the US for several years people, who didn't speak a word of English when they arrived, have probably acquired certain habits and customs that make them strangers in their native land. Second generations or those who arrived at an early age usually acquire a cultural identity that cannot be clearly defined as belonging to one place or the other. The same thing happened before with other groups of immigrants; but no other migratory wave ever extended itself over such a long period of time, constantly replenishing all kinds of ties with the native country.

While geographic distances diminish in importance social and economic ones become more difficult to span. Social mobility in the US has become more difficult because of increased polarization in the labor market and hence of wage and salary scales. Furthermore racism is an ever present reality even though many of its overt manifestations are prohibited by law. Even though acts of racial discrimination may be difficult to prove, their effects are clearly evident. The subtle demarcation of neighborhoods, de facto segregation in the schools, and labor market segmentation limit the socioeconomic perspectives of increasing numbers of Latinos. If current trends continue Latinos will not only consolidate their status as the largest minority group in the country but also the poorest.

Poverty Rates, Unemployment Rates and Income Levels for Latinos

The economic expansion of the eighties was not as favorable for Latinos as for other sectors of the population and the recession of the early nineties seems to have affected them more. Only Latinos, and particularly those of Mexican origin, registered an increase in their poverty rate between 1980 – the last year of the Carter administration – and 1989 – the last year of the expansion that started at the end of 1982. From the outset, the recession that began in mid 1990 had strong adverse effects for Latinos. Their poverty rates rose more than those of others. From 1994 until 1998, they have had higher rates than Afro-Americans, which is historically unprecedented.

The substantial increase in immigration is one of the most frequently cited causes of the Latino populations' relative socioeconomic decline. However the economic success of Asian immigrants –whose rate of increase is even higher– contrasts sharply with the Latino experience. Thus immigration alone cannot fully explain this situation, even though the newly arrived generally tend to be disadvantaged for a time.

Fifty four percent of the growth registered for the Latino population between 1980 and 1989 is due to immigration, as well as 49% of the increase between 1991 and 1996 (U.S. Department of Commerce, Bureau of the Census, 1997, p. 14, 53). However while about 36% of the current Latino population is foreign born, immigrants constitute only around 8% of the total US population. According to census data one third of the Mexicans living in the US are foreign born. Seventy two percent of the Cubans are immigrants as well as 54% of other Latinos. By 1990, only 26.2% of all foreign born Latinos had become American citizens (U.S. Department of Commerce, Bureau of the Census, 1993a, p. 1-10).

In terms of median family income there is a considerable gap between Latinos and the rest of the population and it is even larger in the case of immigrants. The differences among Latino subgroups are also significant. Cuban families have the highest median, followed by other Latinos.

Mexicans are in third place and the median for Puerto Ricans is the lowest. Even though per capita income is higher for Puerto Ricans and they tend to earn more than Mexicans, family incomes tend to be higher for Mexicans because there are generally more workers per family and fewer female headed households (U.S. Department of Commerce, Bureau of the Census, 1993a, p. 1-10 and 119-123).

The most exploited and impoverished Latinos are no doubt those who have entered the US illegally. According to official estimates there were approximately five million illegal aliens in the country in 1996. About 54% of them, 2.7 million are Mexican and at least another 830 thousand (17.6%) come from other Latin American countries. Thus more than 70% of all illegals are Latinos. The remaining 30% or so come from a wide variety of countries, some as prosperous as Canada or as far away as China. Official calculations are that two hundred to three hundred thousand undocumented aliens enter the country each year (U.S. Department of Commerce, Bureau of the Census, 1993a, p. 12, and Lee, 1996, p. 18).

In spite of the difficulties undocumented aliens face and the possible repercussions for other Latinos, Puerto Ricans –the only ones not affected by this problem– have the highest poverty rate. Since 1980 their rate has been even greater than Afro-Americans'. Between 1980 and 1989, when poverty increased so sharply for Mexicans, from 22.9 to 28.4%, Puerto Ricans showed a slight improvement. However as a result of the 1990 recession their rate surpassed previous levels and was still close to 38% in 1995 (Bean and Tienda, 1987, p. 371; and U.S. Department of Commerce, Bureau of the Census, 1991, p. 10-11; 1993b, p. 16-17; 1998a, cps94/sumtab2-txt, 1998b,cps96/sumtab2-txt).

The first half of the nineties brought higher poverty rates to all groups within the Latino population even the Cubans. Between 1980 and 1989, their poverty rate grew from 12.7 to 15.2%, and then increased much more reaching 21.8% in 1995. After a big jump in poverty among Mexicans in the previous decade, the increase for them, from 28.4% in 1989 to 31.2% in 1995, was less pronounced. Since the categories "Central and South Americans" and "other Hispanics" are made up of people from many different countries, it is difficult to draw conclusions from this data, nevertheless it is significant that in both cases poverty rates increased by more than five percentage points between 1989 and 1995 (Bean and Tienda, 1987, p. 371; and U.S. Department of Commerce, Bureau of the Census, 1991, p. 10-11; 1993b, p. 16-17; 1998a, cps94/sumtab2-txt; 1998b,cps96/sumtab2-txt).

Even though the percentage of those living below the poverty line grew for the whole population during this period, the increase stems mainly from the deterioration experienced by Latinos. Their numbers, among those living in poverty, have risen consistently since 1973. The increase was slow at first, from 10.3% in 1973 to 11.9% in 1980. Over the next decade it rose to 17.9% in 1990, and reached 23.8% in 1996. Meanwhile the proportion of non-Hispanic whites declined from 55.9% of those in poverty in 1980 to 45.1% in 1996. The relative weight of Afro-Americans also dropped slightly over this period from 29.3% to 26.5%.

It should be pointed out that the number of persons living below the poverty line rose from 29.3 million in 1980 to 36.5 million in 1996. The number of poor Afro-Americans grew, with some fluctuations, from 8.6 million in 1980 to 10.9 million in 1993 and then dropped to 9.7 million in 1996. For non-Hispanic whites the number increased from 16.4 million in 1980 to 19.5 million in 1983. Then it declined until the end of the eighties. It had risen again to 18.9 million in 1993, and thereafter fell to 16.5 million in 1996. For Latinos, however, growth in the number of persons living in poverty has been almost uninterrupted, rising from 3.5 million in 1980 to 8.7 million in 1996 (U.S. Department of Commerce, Bureau of the Census, 1998c, hstpov14.txt).

As is to be expected there is a certain degree of correspondence between the incidence of poverty and unemployment rates. Generally the unemployment rate for Afro-Americans is about twice as high as it is for whites and the rate for Latinos falls somewhere in between. This order still holds even after 1994, when the rate of poverty for Latinos became the highest, but Latino women did have a slightly higher unemployment rate than Afro-American women in 1996. Puerto Ricans have the highest unemployment rates among Latinos, followed by Mexicans and then Cubans, whose rate is nonetheless somewhat higher than that of non Hispanic whites. Historically unemployment tends to be slightly lower for Puerto Ricans than Afro-Americans, however it was higher in 1994 and 1995 and Puerto Rican and Mexican women had higher rates in 1995 and 1996 (U.S. Department of Commerce, Bureau of the Census, 1996, p. 380; U.S. Department of Commerce, Bureau of the Census, 1997, pp. 398, 402; and U.S. Council of Economic Advisers, 1998, p. 331).

There tends to be an inverse relationship between poverty and labor force participation rates. As a whole the labor force participation is rising but male participation has declined somewhat since 1970, when it was 79.7%, to 74.9% in 1996. Female participation, in contrast, has increased from 43.3% in 1970 to 59.3% in 1996. These same patterns of change hold for Afro-Americans and Latinos, but in the latter case are less pronounced. In general participation in the economically active population (EAP) is higher for whites, followed by Latinos and then Afro-Americans. Mexican origin Latinos have the highest rate, followed by Cubans, and then Puerto

Ricans (U.S. Department of Commerce, Bureau of the Census, 1997, pp. 397, 398).

Of the three most numerous groups of Latinos, Mexicans currently have the lowest incomes. Throughout the nineties, for all men and women with earnings, as well as for those who work year round full time, their median income has been consistently lower than either Puerto Ricans' or Cubans'. The differences usually range from four to six thousand dollars annually. Between these two latter groups, the difference in median earnings is not nearly so great (U.S. Department of Commerce, Bureau of the Census, 1991, p. 8-9; 1993, pp. 16-17; 1998a, cps94/sumtab2-txt; 1998b, cps96/sumtab2-txt).

In spite of individual earnings levels, however, median family and household incomes are consistently higher for Cubans, and even for Mexicans, than for Puerto Ricans. Even though Puerto Rican men and women individually usually have higher earnings than Mexican male and female workers, and sometimes even higher than Cubans, the great number of female headed families (41.5% in 1996, compared with 18.8% and 21.3%, respectively for Cuban and Mexican families) means that median family income is very low. In addition there are more Puerto Rican families with no one employed and fewer with two or more workers per family (U.S. Department of Commerce, Bureau of the Census, 1991, p. 12-15; 1993b, p.19, 21; 1998a, sumtab-3.txt, sumtab-4.txt; 1998b, sumtab-3.txt, sumtab-4.txt; and 1993a, p.119-123).

For the total population, and whites, blacks and Hispanics as groups, real per capita incomes rose between 1980 and 1996. There are some fluctuations, during this period, which correspond more or less to changes in the overall rate of economic growth. However the gap between whites and the rest of the population does widen. Per capita incomes for Latinos and Afro-Americans are very similar up to 1987. From that point on there is a small but growing difference. While Afro-Americans' per capita income moves slowly upwards, it declines continuously for Latinos until 1995. By 1996 Latinos were the only group whose per capita income remained below the previous peak, registered at the end of the eighties (U.S. Department of Commerce, Bureau of the Census, 1998d, po1.html, po1a.html, po1b.html, po1d.html).

Over this same time span, median earnings for males fifteen and over showed a downward tendency, whereas females' earnings have been on the rise since 1970. Nevertheless there is still a considerable gap between male and female income levels. The net effect of these simultaneous changes, along with changes in the composition of the EAP and modifications in family structure, is that real median family and household incomes increased only slightly, between 1980 and 1996, in spite of the strong growth in GDP. Latinos suffered not only relative but also absolute declines. The differences in median family and household incomes between Latinos and Afro-Americans diminished steadily as they dropped in real terms for the former and increased slightly for the latter (U.S. Department of Commerce, Bureau of the Census, 1998d, ho5.html, fo7.html, fo7a.html, fo7b.html, fo7d.html).

From 1994 to 1996 the median of family income was in fact lower for Latinos than Afro-Americans. The marked decline in Latino men's earnings and the stagnation in women's has changed the position of their families with respect to Afro-American ones, even though among the latter there are more female headed families (47%, which is even higher than for Puerto Ricans) and often fewer workers per family. Quite evidently the economic expansion of the eighties was less beneficial for Latinos, and the recession at the beginning of the nineties more detrimental, than for the rest of the US population.

Between 1980 and 1996 the US economy experienced two important recessions and two exceptionally long periods of continuous economic growth. During this time personal consumption increased 57%, in real terms while, GDP and disposable personal Income grew 50%. Since these growth rates were accompanied by increased inequality in the Income distribution, real median family and household incomes rose only slightly; For the Latino population the results of the period were negative in both cases. The net increase in median income for all households was only 5.1%. The median rose by 3.4% for white households and 14.4% for Afro-American ones, while for Latinos it dropped by 4.3%. In the case of families, the overall median rose by 5.5%. For white families it grew 7.2%, and 9.6% for Afro-Americans, but the median income of Latino families dropped 6.7% (U.S. Department of Commerce, Bureau of the Census, 1998d, ho5.html, fo7.html, fo7a.html, fo7b.html, fo7d.html; and U.S. Council of Economic Advisers, 1998, p. 282, 317).

The Latino Population's Employment Status

Between 1970 and 1990 the Latino population in the US more than doubled in size, growing from 9.1 to 22.4 million. About half of the increase registered since 1980, when there were 14.6 million Latinos, was the result of immigration (U.S. Department of Commerce, Bureau of the Census, 1993c, p. 2, 15). One of the most important motivations for these people to leave their homelands and migrate to the US is the expectation of finding employment. Latino men have a higher labor force participation rate than both non-Hispanic whites and Afro-Americans. Even though the participation rate is somewhat lower among Latino women than for the other groups mentioned it has increased significantly in recent years.

Given that Latinos have high immigration rates, high birth rates and high labor force participation rates, as well as a lower average age, than other groups within the population, their weight within the work force will increase significantly over the next several years. Many workers in the US have confronted increasingly adverse labor market conditions in recent decades. Latino workers, because of their generally low educational attainment and limited command of English, as well as the discrimination they frequently suffer, have been particularly affected by these adverse conditions, in a labor market that is continuously becoming more segmented and stratified.

The changes coincided with a relative decline in US hegemony and increased competition among industrialized countries. The almost instantaneous mobility of monetary capital demands that countries and firms be increasingly more competitive and more efficient. This in turn requires greater flexibility and constant innovation of production processes combined with lower costs. Changes in the international economic panorama along with changes in the internal economy have significantly reshaped working conditions in the US.

What is so striking in the case of Latinos, however, is that their relative socioeconomic status has deteriorated so much in the past two decades. Latino workers –the fastest growing group of workers with low wages and high unemployment rates– confront the possibility of suffering long term set backs due to changes in employment and wage structures. Gregory DeFreitas, after an extensive study of Latino participation in the US labor force, concluded that this group would be the most vulnerable to increasing changes in the wage structure that mainly affect less qualified workers (DeFreitas, 1991, p. 5).

A significant sector of the Afro-American population has improved its socioeconomic status thanks to, among other things, higher educational attainment. Considerable numbers of Latino workers, particularly those of Mexican origin, are not well prepared for the new labor market conditions. Thus they find themselves being relegated to the least desirable and lowest paying positions.

In addition to some factors that distinguish Latinos from the rest of the US population, there are also enormous differences among the various groups identified as Latinos. In general the Cubans have incomes and educational levels close to those of non-Hispanic whites. The situation of most Mexicans and Puerto Ricans is far less favorable. Their educational levels and incomes tend to be considerably lower. Mexicans have the highest school drop out rates and on the average their earnings are lower than Afro-Americans'.

Latinos have a relatively low participation in the upper end of the occupational structure and are more likely than others to have low paying jobs. Those of Mexican origin seem to be the most disadvantaged. Only 11.4% of all Mexican workers held managerial or professional posts, compared to 29.8% of whites and 20.0% of Afro-Americans. The rate for all Latinos was 14.2% due to the preponderance of Mexicans, since Puerto Ricans and Cubans show significantly higher rates (19.0% and 21.7%, respectively). The percentage of Mexican workers in technical, sales or administrative support posts (21.2%) is also lower than for other groups (whites 29.8%, Afro-Americans 28.6%, Puerto Ricans 32.1% and Cubans 32.7%). Mexicans do have the highest participation (13.1% in 1996) in precision production, crafts and repairs, which are often well paid posts. However the difference is not very large (11.1% for whites, 9.4% Puerto Ricans, and 12.7% Cubans) except with respect to Afro-Americans, and some of these jobs have the disadvantage of being irregular (U.S. Department of Labor, Bureau of Labor Statistics, 1997, p. 171-8).

On the other hand, the percentage of Mexicans employed as operators, fabricators and laborers (24.7% in 1996) is somewhat higher than for Afro-Americans (20.6%), much higher than for either Puerto Ricans (18.6%) or Cubans (17.4%), and double that of whites (13.6%). Afro-Americans have the highest participation in service jobs (21.8% in 1996) –where median earnings are almost as low as in agricultural occupations– followed by Puerto Ricans (19.8%) and Mexicans (18.9%). Cubans and whites have much lower participation rates in these types of jobs (14.6 and 12.5%, respectively). In the case of protective services however, which are generally well paying jobs, Afro-Americans or Puerto Ricans are three or four times more likely to fill these posts than Mexicans (U.S. Department of Labor, Bureau of Labor Statistics, 1997, p. 171-8). Some localities have implemented policies of hiring minority group members with the hope that they might be more effective in controlling the problems that arise in their own neighborhoods. Participation in agriculture tends to be low in general, yet the rate for Mexicans (8.0% in 1996) is much higher than that of any other group (whites 3.1%, Afro-Americans 1.0%, Cubans and Puerto Ricans 1.2%) (U.S. Department of Labor, Bureau of Labor Statistics, 1997, p. 171-8).

An analysis of relative participation by Latinos in the various occupational categories and sub categories reveals that in 1996 they had what I have called concentration –that is they represented a higher percentage of those employed in a particular category than in the labor force as a whole, which was 9.2%– in 126 of the occupational categories and sub categories contained in the Labor Department's detailed occupational categories tables. They exhibited what I have called a high degree of concentration –a percentage between two and three times greater than their overall participation (above 18.4%)– in 31 of these 126 categories, and a very high concentration –over three times greater– in nine categories or sub categories (U.S. Department of Labor, Bureau of Labor Statistics, 1997, p. 171-8).

None of the categories or sub categories with a high or very high concentration of Latinos fall within the general classifications: I.Managerial or professional specialties, or II.Technical, sales and administrative support. The highest concentrations of Latinos, 25% or more of those employed, are found among agricultural workers, graders of non agricultural goods, domestic service, sewing and pressing machine operators in textile and textile goods industries, wrapping and filling machine operators, butchers, or gardeners. Other categories with high concentrations of Latinos, 18% or more, are distributed among various categories within the general classifications III.Services, IV.Precision production, crafts and repairs, and V.Operators, fabricators and laborers (U.S. Department of Labor, Bureau of Labor Statistics, 1997, p. 171-8). Several of these occupations have high health or safety risks –operating cutting or slicing machines for example, or spray painting or fiber filling processes, where harmful effects may build up slowly over a long period of time– or may be associated with an inferior social status, as in the case of cleaning services or domestic service.

Only 16 of the 126 categories with some degree of concentration of Latino workers, provided median weekly earnings above the general median of $490 in 1996. Of the forty categories with a high or very high concentration of Latinos only two, tile setters and concrete and terrazzo finishers, paid weekly wages close to the general median. Median earnings in the rest of the categories where 18% or more of the workers are Latinos are significantly below the overall median (U.S. Department of Labor, Bureau of Labor Statistics, 1997, p. 171-8, 206-210).

Even though there is a high degree of correspondence between low wages and the concentration of Latino workers, the relationship is not a linear one. Latino workers are much more concentrated in some categories of each general classification than others. These differences may be due in part to certain characteristics of the groups that make up the Latino population as well as to socioeconomic and educational differences within each group. Furthermore this behavior is consistent with the "discontinuities" that, according to Michael J. Piore characterize labor market segmentation.[1] Data for female workers lends further support to the hypothesis of a highly segmented labor market.

Although farm occupations employ only a small percentage of all Latino workers, barely 6% of the total, this category deserves special mention because of the high concentration of Latinos, mainly Mexicans. In 1996, 37% of all agricultural workers were Latinos, and they constituted 68% of the graders and sorters of agricultural goods (U.S. Department of Labor, Bureau of Labor Statistics, 1997, p. 171-8). The greatest concentration is found in California where approximately 90% of all agricultural workers are Latinos, here again predominantly Mexican, and almost all of them are foreign born.[2]

Over the last fifteen or twenty years Mexican workers have become the most exploited and impoverished group in the US. Their current socioeconomic situation is the result of a series of changes in the US labor market that coincided with the continuous decline of real wages in Mexico –because of the recurrent economic crises the country has suffered since the late seventies. Each new wave of crisis in Mexico produces new waves of people crossing the border. In addition to the five hundred thousand legal immigrants from Mexico admitted each year, estimations are that anywhere from several hundred thousand to a million or more cross the border illegally. Almost all of them are driven by hunger and poverty and drawn by the hope of finding work and earning in dollars.

Even though a minimum wage job In the US doesn't provide enough income to maintain a family of three above the poverty line, it is at least nine times more than the minimum wage in Mexico. Almost 80% of the labor force in Mexico earn up to only a third of the US minimum. Only slightly more than half of the EAP in Mexico is employed in the formal sector of the economy.

Obviously, if so many Mexicans leave their homeland it is not just because they suffer from hunger and low wages, but also because there is work to be found on the other side of the border. Mexican immigrants fill many jobs that Americans, both Afro-Americans and whites, systematically reject. Not only are Mexican workers often unable to resist the adverse working conditions imposed upon them –given the terrible deterioration of wages and the extreme precariousness of employment in their own country– the majority of them are most willing to accept what they perceive as a significant improvement afforded by jobs in the US, even though they are systematically channeled into the lowest paying, least desirable occupations.

Starting on the very lowest rungs of the pay scale has always been the fate of poor immigrants with few skills. Wages that do not exceed the poverty line in the US amount to several times as much as most Latinos earned in their homelands. Thus the working and salary conditions they confront in the US seem more favorable to them than those they left behind. Furthermore there is always the expectation that the next generation will do better.

Low Educational Attainment Poses a Serious Problem for Latinos

In previous periods and for other groups of immigrants, education played a fundamental role as a means of assimilation and socioeconomic mobility. For a great number of Latino immigrants today, however, it has not fulfilled that role. On one hand, this is the case because in many ways the labor market is much more segmented and stratified than before. On the other hand, Latino children have suffered the effects of the multiple forms of de facto segregation that persist in American schools.

Even though they have made enormous progress since the 1960s, racial and ethnic minorities in the US are still behind in term of educational attainment. In 1972, 81.7% of all whites between 18 and 24 years old had graduated from high school. The figure was 82.6% in 1994. The increase was very small because the percentage was already quite high in 1972, especially in comparison with other groups. At that time only 66.7% of the Afro-Americans between 18 and 24 had finished high school. By 1994 the completion rate for Afro-Americans was 77%. For the Latino population, in the same age range, the high school completion rate was 51.9% in 1972, and only 56.6% in 1994. In all cases the completion rates were slightly higher for females at both points in time (U.S. Department of Commerce, Bureau of the Census, 1996b, p. A-29 to A-36).

In spite of the increasing correlation between years of schooling and income levels, and the ever more limited economic perspectives for those without higher education –much less for those without a high school diploma– school drop out rates remain critically high for Latinos. Between 1972 and 1994 the high school drop out rate for the white population from 18 to 24 years old decreased from 15.2 to 12.7%. The Afro-American population showed marked improvement over this period, from 26.2% in 1972 to 15.5% in 1994. Although the decline for Latinos was significant, from 40.4% to 34.7%, their high school drop out rate in 1994 was twice as high as that of Afro-Americans, and almost three times greater than the rate for whites (U.S. Department of Commerce, Bureau of the Census, 1996b, p. A-29 to A-36).

Unfortunately the possibilities of entering college are practically nonexistent for those who never finished high school. Whereas improvement in the high school completion rate was rather small for the white population –only 2.5% because it was high to begin with– there was an important increase between 1972 and 1994 in the percentage of those from 18 to 24 enrolled in college, from 26.4 to 35.3%. If the comparison is limited to only those who graduate from high school the growth is slightly higher, from 32.3 to 42.7%. For Afro-Americans and Latinos the increases range from 5.4 to 8.5%, thus widening the gap with respect to whites in both cases. In 1994, 27.3% of Afro-Americans aged 18 to 24 were enrolled in college, as were 18.8% of the Latino youths.

For those Latinos who did graduate from high school, college enrollment improved greatly from 25.8% in 1972 to 37.1% in 1992. Thus the disadvantage of 2.3% with respect to Afro-Americans became a 3.3% advantage. However their enrollment dropped by 4 percentage points between 1992 and 1994. Furthermore, Latinos still have very high high school drop out rates; this limits the possibilities of improving their educational attainment and leaves them far behind the rest of the US population (U.S. Department of Commerce, Bureau of the Census, 1996b, p. A-29 to A-36).

Mexicans are even further behind than most Latinos. By March 1996, only 46.9% of the Mexican origin Latinos 25 and older had at least finished high school, compared with 60.4% of the Puerto Ricans, 63.8% of the Cubans, 61.3% of Central and South Americans, and 66.4% of other Latinos. The figure for the entire non-Latino population was 82.5%. At the same time only 5.3% of all Mexicans over 25 had a Bachelor's degree or more, compared to 10.8% of the Puerto Ricans, 19.2% of the Cubans, 12.6% of Central and South Americans, and 12.6% of other Latinos. At that point, 23.7% of the non-Latino population had a Bachelor's degree or more (U.S. Department of Commerce, Bureau of the Census, 1998b, sumtab-1.txt).

Furthermore, approximately 40% (1994 figure) of the Latinos enrolled in college attend community colleges or junior colleges, which do not grant a Bachelor's degree. In addition to that, the proportion of Latinos who are full time students is slightly lower than for either whites or Afro-Americans. In fact, Latinos have the lowest enrollment levels at both ends of the educational cycle; they generally start school later and leave school at an earlier age than the rest of the population.

Currently about 42% of those graduating from high school enroll in college, but those who drop out of high school don't even have the option to pursue higher education. Since dropping out of high school is highly correlated, over the long run, with unsteady employment and economic insecurity, Sara S. McLanahan and Larry Bumpass maintain that high school completion is the most important transition point for explaining socioeconomic differences among cohorts and for understanding the intergenerational transmission of poverty (McLanahan and Bumpass, 1988, p. 196).

The fact is that poor children live in poor neighborhoods and go to poor schools, where even the barest essentials necessary to provide an appropriate setting for learning to take place are lacking, as Jonathan Kozol so eloquently illustrates in his book *Savage Inequalities* (1991). It is in fact hard to believe that the differences described by Kozol exist; but what he describes explains quite well why performance is so poor among children who attend some of the schools he visited. The formula for financing public education, which depends largely on revenues from local property taxes within each school district, extends the economic hardships poor children face at home into their schools as well. Within most public school systems in the US rich children and poor children do not usually attend the same schools because they don't live in the same neighborhoods.

In other terms, most white children do not go to the same schools as most Afro-American or Latino children. Out of the approximately 20.5 million children between 7 and 13 years old, enrolled in school, only 22% of the white children attending in 1994 went to schools located in central cities, compared with 54% of the Afro-American and Latino children (U.S. Department of Commerce, Bureau of the Census, 1996b, p. 4-7). These overall figures barely suggest the situation in some city schools where 90 to 100% of the students belong to a racial or ethnic minority.[3]

Jorge Chapa and Richard R. Valencia point out that segregation has increased rapidly for Latino students in recent years, to the point where they now have the terrible distinction of being the most segregated group in American schools (Chapa and Valencia, 1993).[4] Perez and De La Rosa Salazar cite the findings of a National School Board Association study indicating that 80% of the Latino students in the south and northeast attend schools where the majority of the students are members of a minority group, just as 71% in the west and 52% in the Midwest. They maintain that in large cities Latinos are even more likely than Afro-Americans to attend schools that are virtually segregated (Perez and De La Rosa Salazar, 1993, p. 206).

If current labor market trends continue, practically the only people with good perspectives for maintaining or improving their economic status will be those with college degrees. For the Latino population the economic and academic obstacles to attaining higher education persist for several generations. Numerous studies have shown that the differences in educational attainment for Mexican-Americans and the rest of the population have remained more or less constant even for third generations (Perez and De La Rosa Salazar, 1993, p. 220).

Several decades ago, almost any progress in terms of years of schooling was accompanied by some improvement in earnings. Immigrants who increased their educational level frequently found good jobs in manufacturing and earned enough to maintain their families, even without a college degree (Rothstein, 1993, p. 193). Given the conditions prevailing in the US labor market today, this is no longer possible for the majority of the young people who, for one reason or another, do not have access to higher education. The employment perspectives and the income levels of those with only a high school education have diminished considerably in recent decades. Richard Rothstein maintains that the earnings of young Latinos with one to three years of college have also declined. The economic benefits of higher education, he insists, are only clearly evident for those who obtain their degree (Rothstein, 1993, p. 192-3).

This author believes that many young Latinos have difficulty in perceiving the benefits of education when the immediate goal –graduating from high school– shows declining rewards. Referring to young Mexicans, he states that educational attainment is unlikely to show dramatic improvement "until these students and their families can believe that realistic goals –high school and junior college completion– will be rewarded in the market place" (Rothstein, 1993, p. 193). This kind of scenario is unlikely, given the current labor market trends. According to Rothstein, by the end of the century 7.3 million college graduates will be employed in jobs that do not require a college education (Rothstein, 1993, p. 194). Thus it is hard to believe that many Latinos in the US will have good perspectives for achieving higher levels of education and consequently obtaining better jobs, any time in the near future.

Latino Participation in Public Assistance Programs

Given the obstacles that so many people face to obtaining regular, well paying jobs, it might be assumed that a country as rich as the United States would have a broad, coherent system of public assistance programs to assure a certain minimum level of well being for everyone. However that is not the case. The existing programs are not at all sufficient to assist the growing numbers of those who are becoming increasingly marginalized.

Undeniably the need to resort to government public assistance programs is more prevalent for Afro-Americas and Latinos than for non-Hispanic whites. Twenty four percent of Afro-Americans and 18.9% of Latinos participated in at least one means tested government program throughout 1991 and 1992, whereas the participation rate for whites was only 5.8% (U.S. Department of Commerce, Bureau of the Census, 1995, p. 2).[5] In absolute terms, however, the majority, or 57.9% of those receiving some benefit over this period, are white; 36.2% are Afro-American and

20.9% Latinos (U.S. Department of Commerce, Bureau of the Census, 1995, p. 5).

Considering the composition of the total population –in 1992, 83.5% were white, 12.4% Afro-American and 9.5% were Latinos– the preceding figures seem to be out of proportion. However when the point of departure is the population with incomes below the poverty line (which is in fact the basis of eligibility for these programs) the disproportion largely disappears. In 1992, 66.5% of the people classified as poor were white, and 49.6% were non Hispanic white; 28.8% were Afro-American, 18.0% Latinos, and 4.7% belonged to other ethnic or racial groups (U.S. Department of Commerce, Bureau of the Census, 1993d , p. xi).

If we take into account the poverty rate for each group, the correspondence with rates of program participation is even greater. The overall poverty rate was 14.8% in 1992 and 13.4% of the population participated in at least one means tested program. For whites the poverty rate was 11.9% and the rate of program participation was 10.3%. The percentages for Afro-Americans were 33.4% and 33.0% respectively, and among Latinos 29.6% were considered poor and 26.9% participated in at least one of these programs (U.S. Department of Commerce, Bureau of the Census, 1995b, p. 480; 1995a, p. 3).

Nevertheless in the case of direct monetary aid for individuals or families with very limited means –AFDC (Aid for Families with Dependent Children)[6] or General Assistance from state and local governments– participation rates are low compared to poverty rates. The participation rates for these programs in 1992 were 4.7% overall, 3.0% for whites, 14.8% for Afro-Americans and 10.2% for Latinos. In all cases the corresponding poverty rates for the same year –which were 14.8, 11.9, 33.4 and 29.6%, respectively– were twice as high (U.S. Department of Commerce, Bureau of the Census, 1995b, p. 480; 1995a, p.3).

Even though the majority of the people who receive welfare are white (53.8% in 1992), dependency is proportionally higher for Afro-Americans and Latinos. One cannot overlook the fact that there are relatively more Afro-American and Latino women raising their children alone and that more of these female headed households are poor. The poverty rate for female headed Latino families was 48.8%, and it was 49.8% for Afro-American families of this type, compared with 28.1% for female headed white families (U.S. Department of Commerce, Bureau of the Census, 1993d, p.1).

The social security system in the United States was not designed to resolve poverty and marginalization. The great depression of the 1930s obliged the federal government to take measures to counteract severe market fluctuations and assure a minimal income for those too old or physically unable to work, but nothing more. OASDHI, Old Age, Survivors, Disability and Health Insurance, the federal programs commonly referred to as "social security", and "medicare" have played a very important role in reducing poverty among the elderly. However most of what is spent under these two programs provides benefits for people with medium or even high incomes. Less than one third of what is designated as federal government social spending is destined specifically for people with low incomes.

The social programs implemented in the sixties, and the rhetoric they generated, created great expectations that were entirely out of proportion with the funding allocated to these programs. In spite of this limitation and with the help of favorable macroeconomic conditions the poverty rate was reduced to its historical minimum in 1973. The rise in poverty after that point in time provoked so much debate over welfare that finally in 1996 the responsibility for designing and administering public assistance programs was turned over to the state governments. Even though the last two economic expansions have been quite favorable in terms of economic growth, the poverty rate is currently higher than it was in 1973. In other words economic growth in and of itself has not been an adequate policy measure for reducing poverty. This will not be accomplished without the political will to do so and a change in the prevailing conception of the causes of poverty.

As long as this does not take place, the poor in general will be stigmatized, and those who receive any sort of public assistance even more so. Over half of the people receiving public assistance are white; however, the proportion of Afro-Americans and Latinos is high with respect to their weight in the overall population. If the number of persons in poverty is the reference point this is not the case. Nonetheless the conventional wisdom in the US is that poverty, marginalization, and even inequalities, are basically individual problems rather than social ones. Furthermore these kinds of ideas are more easily sustained when elements of otherness exist, as in the case of Afro-Americans or Latinos.

Conclusion

In the United States the period from 1980 to 1996 was characterized by high levels of macroeconomic growth. However, this favorable performance was accompanied by increasing inequality in the income distribution and relatively high poverty rates. Furthermore it seems evident, as Lawrence Mishel and Jared Bernstein point out in their report *The State of Working America: 1992-93*, "that the system of taxes and transfers designed to mitigate these market failures was less effective than in the past" in reducing poverty (Mishel and Berstein, 1992, p. 314). Latinos were the group most affected, as evidenced by a significant decline in real median incomes and a marked increase in their poverty rate. Thus recently they have been increasingly obliged to resort to public assistance, as the meager government funding for this purpose becomes less effective in alleviating the plight of the poor.

Over the past two decades millions of new low paying jobs have been created, that don't provide enough to keep an American family out of poverty. At the same time, an income that is below the poverty threshold in the US exceeds by far the earnings of most families in a country like Mexico. Therefore there is an inexhaustible supply of people from all over the world who are most willing to move to the US and fill those jobs. Since 1980, the recurrent economic crises in various Latin American countries, particularly Mexico, have provoked increased flows of immigrants to the US.

Latino immigrants usually accept wages and working conditions that are unacceptable to most Americans, and have a reputation for being hard workers. The living and working conditions often seem much better to them than the ones they left behind even though they occupy the lowest rungs of the socioeconomic ladder. However, they pay a high price, in non-material terms, for what they perceive as an improvement in material conditions. Daily life in Latino neighborhoods, and poor neighborhoods in general, is charged with violence and tensions that reflect, in a very special way, the contradictions and inequalities that characterize American society today.

What we are interested in underlining here is the fact that the economic growth experienced in the eighties and nineties has been accompanied by greater inequalities. Furthermore, this growing economic polarization has had a very strong impact on the Latino population. Their socioeconomic status has declined with respect to that of other groups. This situation takes on a new dimension given the fact that Latinos will soon be the largest minority group in the US, and that by the middle of the next century they will constitute about one fourth of the total population. Therefore it would seem that the most important challenges facing the US in the next few decades will be posed by the internal social and economic transformations –in particular the increasing inequalities currently being generated– more than by challenges from external rivals, even though these two spheres are becoming more and more intertwined.

Notes

[1] See Suzanne Berger and Michael J. Piore, *Dualism and Discontinuity in Industrial Societies*, Cambridge University Press, Cambridge, 1980.

[2] See Juan Vicente Palrem "Farm Worker Enumeration Report", second part, preliminary version, 1991, p. 5; and Wayne A. Cornelius, "The Structural Embededness of Demand for Mexican Immigrant Labor: New Evidence from California" in Marcelo M. Suarez-Orozco, editor, *Crossings: Mexican Immigration in Interdisciplinary Perspectives*, Harvard University Press, Cambridge, Massachusetts, 1998, p. 115-144.

[3] See *Hispanic Education a Statistical Portrait 1990*, National Council of La Raza, Washington, D.C., 1990, p. 20.

[4] They in turn cite Donato, R., Menchaca, M., and Valencia, R.R. (1991) "Segregation, desegregation and integration of Chicano students: Problems and prospects" in R.R. Valencia, ed. *Chicano school failure and success: Research and Policy agendas for the 1990s*, The Stanford series on Education and Public Policy, p. 27-63, Basingstoke, England: Falmer Press; and Orfield, G. (1992), *Status of school segregation: The next generation*, Washington. D.C.: The National School Board Association.

[5] The programs considered here are Aid to Families with Dependent Children AFDC, General Assistance, Supplemental Security Income SSI, Medicaid, food stamps, rental assistance and subsidized housing.

[6] This program, Aid to Families with Dependent Children, was eliminated in 1996 and substitutes by a new program TANF, Temporary Assistance for Needy families, which is generally has more restrictions.

References

Bean, Frank D. and Marta Tienda (1987), *The Hispanic Population of the United States*, Russell Sage Foundation, New York.

DeFreitas, Gregory (1991), *Inequality at Work: Hispanics in the U.S. Labor Force*, Oxford University Press, New York.

Kozol, Jonathan (1991), *Savage Inequalities*, Crown Publishers, New York.

Lee, Kathleen (1996), *Illegal Immigration*, Lucent Books, San Diego.

McLanahan, Sara S. and Larry Bumpass (1988), "Comment: A Note on the Effect of Family Structure on School Enrollment" in Gary D. Sandefur and Marta Tienda, Eds. *Divided Opportunities, Minorities, Poverty and Social Policy*, Plenum Press, New York.

Mishel, Lawrence and Jared Bernstein (1992), *The State of Working America*, The Economic Policy Institute, Washington, D.C.

National Council of La Raza (1990), *Hispanic Education: A Statistical Portrait 1990*, Washington, D.C.

Oboler, Susanne (1995), *Ethnic Labels, Latino Lives, Identity and Politics of (Re)presentation in the United States*, University of Minnesota Press, Minneapolis.

Perez, Sonia M. and Denise De La Rosa Salazar (1993), "Economic, labor Force and Social Implications of Latino Educational and Population Trends" in *Hispanic Journal of Behavioral Sciences*, Vol. 15, no. 2, May, p. 206.

Rothstein, Richard (1993), "In Search of the American Dream: Obstacles to Latino Educational Achievement" in Abraham F. Lowenthal and Katrina Burgess, Eds. *The California Mexico Connection*, Stanford University Press, Stanford.

Sassen, Saskia (1998), *Globalization and its Discontents*, The New Press, New York.

U.S. Council of Economic Advisers (1998), *Economic Report of the President 1998*, United States Government Printing Office, Washington, D. C.

U.S. Department of Commerce, Bureau of the Census (1991), *The Hispanic Population of the United States: March 1990*, Current Population Reports, P20-449.

(1993a), *1990 Census of Population, Persons of Hispanic Origin in the United States*, United States Government Printing Office, Washington, D.C.

(1993b), *The Hispanic Population of the United States: March 1992*, Current Population Reports, P20-465RV.

(1993c), *Hispanic Americans Today*, Current Population Reports, P23-183.

(1993d), *Poverty in the United States: 1992*, Current Population Reports, Series P-60, no. 178.

(1995a), *Dynamics of Economic Well-Being: Program Participation, 1991 to 1993*, Current Population Reports, and P70-46.

(1995b), *Statistical Abstract of the United States 1995*, United States Government Printing Office, Washington, D. C.

(1996), *Statistical Abstract of the United States 1996*, United States Government Printing Office, Washington, D. C.

(1996b) *School Enrollment – Social and Economic Characteristics of Students: October 1994*, Current Population Reports, P-20-487.

(1997), *Statistical Abstract of the United States 1997*, United States Government Printing Office, Washington, D. C.

(1998a) Internet Release, *http://www.Census.gov/population/www/ socdemo/hispanic/cps94/ sumtab-2.txt*.

(1998b) Internet Release, *http://www. Census.gov/population/www/ socdemo/hispanic/cps96/ sumtab-2.txt*.

(1998c) *March Current Population Survey, http://www.census/ gov/ income/histpov/ hstpov14.txt*.

(1998d) *March Current Population Survey, Historical Income Tables, http://www.census.gov/hhes/income/histinc*.

U.S. Department of Labor, Bureau of Labor Statistics. (1997), *Employment and Earnings*, January.

List of Contributors

David S. Alberts is the Director of Research in the Office of the Assistant Secretary of Defense (C 31). He has also led organizations engaged in research and analysis of command and control system performance and related contributions to operational missions.

Philip J. Bryson is Associate Director, Kennedy Center for International Studies and Professor of Economics, Marriott School, and BYU. His writing has focused on centrally planned economies, especially the former GDR and the USSR. More recently he has researched the transition of the Czech and Slovak Republics and issues of international economics.

Erhan Büyükakinci is Assistant Professor of International Relations at Galatasaray University, Istanbul (Turkey). He has conducted research on the post-Communist problems and published articles on the foreign policy of the Central Asian countries and Russia.

Dimitri Christopoulos is Secretary General of the Greek League of Human Rights and a Senior Investigator to the Office of the Greek Ombudsman. His main research and publication focuses on diversity and human rights theory.

Rekha Datta is Assistant Professor of Political Science at Monmouth University. She has published widely on state-society relations and nuclear issues in South Asia. Her research interests currently focus on human rights and child labor in developing societies.

Linda L. Dolive is Professor of Political Science and coordinator of the International Studies Program at Northern Kentucky University. Her research focuses on comparative European politics. She is the author of a book on electoral politics in Germany and numerous other articles. Her current research interests center on political corruption.

John Doyle is Director of the Graduate Program in International Relations and lecturer in Government and International Relations at Dublin City University Business School (Ireland). His publications and research center on Northern Ireland politics and comparative nationalist and ethnic conflicts.

Eric H. Erickson, III has a decade of strategic information technology experience and was co-founder and President in charge of Business Development at BoundlessNetworks, a privately held Internet consultancy with offices in Europe and USA, before co-founding e-Tango.

Jeffrey P. Erickson brings seven years of Internet and information technology experience to e-Tango as Chief Technology Officer, responsible for managing the architecture, integration, and subsequent development of the company's solutions and online service offerings.

Nayantara Hensel is Assistant Director of Undergraduate Studies in Economics at Harvard University. Her research interests focus on international banking, corporate finance, and mergers and acquisitions.

Sai Felicia Krishna-Hensel is President and Program Chair of the Comparative Interdisciplinary Studies Section of the International Studies Association. She is coordinator of Interdisciplinary Global Studies Research at the Center for Business and Economic Development at Auburn University Montgomery. Her publications include an edited volume on global policy studies and numerous articles and contributed book chapters on urbanization in the third world. She is a Life Fellow of the Royal Geographical Society.

Liisa Laakso is a lecturer at the Department of Political Science, University of Helsinki, Finland and a president of the Finnish Peace Research Association. Her publications include several co-edited volumes on challenges to the nation-state in Africa.

Elaine Levine is a senior researcher at the Center for Research on North America (UNAM) in Mexico. She has written many articles on economic policy and income distribution in the US, and has contributed to several edited books. Her current research focuses on the declining socio-economic status of the Latino population.

Mehdi Mozaffari is Professor of Political Science at the University of Aarhus (Denmark). He is widely published on security policy of the Commonwealth of Independent States, violence, Shi'ite theory and evolution. His current research interests focus on globalization and civilization and international ethics.

Daniel S. Papp is Senior Vice-Chancellor for Academic Affairs for the University System of Georgia. He is the author or editor of nine books and has published over sixty articles concentrating on US and Soviet foreign and defense policies.

Guy Poitras is Professor of Political Science at Trinity University, San Antonio. He has published four books and monographs on international relations and Latin America as well as numerous articles and book chapters on Mexico and its relations with the United States.

James R. Scarritt is Professor of Political Science and Faculty Research Associate in the Institute of Behavioral Science at the University of Colorado at Boulder. He is the author of recent articles in the *British Journal of Political Science, International Interactions, Journal of Commonwealth and Comparative Politics* and *Nationalism and Ethnic Politics.*

Ronald R. Sims is the Floyd Dewey Gottwald Professor of Business Administration at the College of William and Mary. He is the author or co-author of fifteen books and more than seventy five articles on a variety of organizational, change and human resource management topics.

Marlene Wind is Assistant Professor of International Politics at the University of Copenhagen (Denmark). She has published substantially on international relations and European politics and legal integration.